History of Morgan's Cavalry

Basil W. Duke

History of Morgan's Cavalry

The present edition is a reproduction of previous publication of this classic work. Minor typographical errors may have been corrected without note, however, for an authentic reading experience the spelling, punctuation, and capitalization have been retained from the original text.

ISBN: 978-1-64799-184-5

TO THE WOMEN OF KENTUCKY,

FRIENDS AND RELATIVES

OF THE GALLANT MEN WHOSE HEROISM HAS BECOME PART OF THE HISTORIC HERITAGE OF THE STATE,

AND

To the Noble Women of the South,

WHOSE KINDNESS ALLEVIATED THE HARDSHIPS WHICH THESE MEN SO LONG ENDURED, AND FOR WHOSE SAKE THEY WERE PROUD TO SUFFER AND BLEED,

THIS BOOK IS RESPECTFULLY DEDICATED.

PREFACE

The writer presents to the reading public the narrative of an arduous and adventurous military career, which, commencing at a period but little subsequent to the outbreak of the late civil war, continued through the four eventful years.

He has endeavored to make the work a correct and graphic representation of the kind of warfare of which MORGAN was the author, and in which his men won so much celebrity. Strict accuracy has been attempted in the description of the military operations of which the book is a record, and it is hoped that the incidents related of personal daring and adventure will be read with some interest.

The author regrets that, for reasons easily understood, the book is far less complete than he desired to make it. The very activity of the service performed by MORGAN'S CAVALRY prevented the preservation of data which would be very valuable, and a full account of many important operations is therefore impossible. Limited space, also, forbids the mention of many brave deeds. If many gallant and deserving men were noticed as they deserve, the book could not be readily finished.

To the friends whose contributions assisted the work, the author returns his warmest thanks.

To Mr. MEADE WOODSON, to whom he is indebted for the maps which so perfectly illustrate his narrative, he is especially grateful.

He regrets, too, that many of his old comrades have altogether failed to render him aid, confidently expected, and which would have been very valuable. B.W.D.

CONTENTS

CHAPTER I

In undertaking to write the history of General Morgan's services, and of the command which he created, it is but fair that I shall acknowledge myself influenced, in a great measure, by the feelings of the friend and the follower; that I desire, if I can do so by relating facts, of most of which I am personally cognizant, to perpetuate his fame, and, at the same time, establish the true character of a body of men, who recruited and inured to war by him, served bravely and faithfully to the close of the great struggle. It may be that credence will be given with hesitation to the statements of one, who thus candidly confesses that personal regard for his chief, and *esprit-de-corps* mainly induce him to attempt the task I propose to myself. To all works of this nature, nevertheless, the same objection will apply, or the more serious one, that they owe their production to the inspiration of hatred, and those who have witnessed and participated in the events which they describe, must (under this rule), for that very reason, be denied belief.

General Morgan's career during the late war was so remarkable, that it is not surprising that the public, accustomed to the contradictory newspaper versions of his exploits, should be disposed to receive all accounts of it with some incredulity.

It was so rapid, so crowded with exciting incidents, appealed so strongly to the passions and elicited so constantly the comments of both sides, that contemporary accounts of his operations were filled with mistakes and exaggerations, and it is natural that some should be expected in any history of his campaigns, although written after the strife is all over.

Convinced, however, that, if properly understood, his reputation will be greater in history than with his contemporaries, and believing that the story of his military life will be a contribution not altogether valueless to that record which the Southern people, in justice to themselves and their dead, must yet publish, I can permit no minor consideration to deter me from furnishing correct, and, I deem, important information, which my relations, personal and official, with General Morgan enabled me to obtain. A correct representation of a certain series of events sometimes leads to a correct understanding of many more, and if the vail which prejudice and deliberate unscrupulous falsification have thrown over some features of the contest be lifted, a truer appreciation may perhaps be had of others of greater moment and interest. I may add that, as no one has been more bitterly assailed, not only while living but even after death, than General Morgan, so no man's memory should be more peculiarly the subject of vindication and protection to his friends.

But there are also other and cogent reasons why this tribute should be rendered him by some one, who, devoted to the interests of the living chieftain, is sensitive regarding the reputation he has left. The cruel ingratitude which embittered the last days of his life, has made his memory all the dearer to the many who were true and constant in their love and esteem for him, and they feel that he should be justly depicted. The fame which he desired will be accorded him; the reward for which he strove is his already, in the affection of the people by whom he hoped and deserved that the kindest recollections of him should be cherished and the warmest eulogies pronounced. In the glory won, in the tremendous and unequal struggle, in the pride with which they speak the names of the dead heroes whose martyrdom illustrated it, the Southern people possess treasures of which no conqueror can deprive them.

A man who, like General Morgan, uninfluenced by the public opinion of the State in which he resided, yet surrendered fortune, home and friends to assist the people of the South when embarked in the desperate and vital strife which their action had provoked, because sharing their blood and their convictions, he thought that they had an imperative claim upon his services; who pledged his all to their cause, and identified his name with every phase of the contest, until his death became an event of the last and most bitter—such a man can never be forgotten by them. It is impossible that the memory of his services can ever fade from their minds.

In the beautiful land for which he fought and died, the traditions which will indicate the spots where he struck her foes, will also preserve his name in undying affection and honor. The men of the generation which knew him can forget him only when they forget the fate from which he strove to save them; his name belongs to the history of the race, and it can not die.

A narrative of the operations of a command composed, in great part, of Kentuckians, must possess some interest for the people of their own State. So general and intense was the interest which Morgan excited among the young men of the State, that he obtained recruits from every county, numbers running every risk to join him, when no other leader could enlist a man. The whole State was represented in his command. Many Kentuckians who had enlisted in regiments from other States procured transfers to his command, and it frequently happened that men, the bulk of whose regiments were in prison, or who had become irregularly detached from them by some of the many accidents by which the volunteer, weary of monotony, is prompt to take advantage, would attach themselves to and serve temporarily with it. Probably every native citizen of Kentucky who will read these lines, will think of some relative or friend who at some time served with Morgan. Men of even the strictest "Union principles," whose loyalty has always been unimpeachable, and whose integrity (as disinterested and as well assured as their patriotism) forbids all suspicion that they were inclined to serve two masters, have had to furnish aid in this way to the rebellion. Frequently after these gentlemen had placed in the Federal army substitutes, white or black, for loyal sons of unmilitary temperaments, other sons, rebellious, and more enterprising, would elect to represent the family in some one of Morgan's regiments. It is not unlikely, then, that a record of these men, written by one who has had every opportunity of learning the true story of every important and interesting event which he did not witness, may be favorably received by the people of Kentucky. The class of readers who will be gratified by an account of such adventures as will be herein related, will readily forgive any lack of embellishment. My practical countrymen prefer the recital of substantial facts, and the description of scenes which their own experience enables them to appreciate, to all the fictions of which the Northern war literature has been so prolific.

The popular taste in Kentucky and the South does not require the fabulous and romantic; less educated and more primitive than that of the North, it rejects even the beautiful, if also incredible, and is more readily satisfied with plain statements, supported by evidence, or intrinsically probable, than with the most fascinating legend, although illustrated with sketches by special artists.

There rests, too, upon some one identified with this command, the obligation of denying and disproving the frequent and grave charges of crime and outrage which have been preferred against General Morgan and his soldiers. So persistently have these accusations been made, that at one time an avowal of "belonging to Morgan" was thought, even in Kentucky, tantamount to a confession of murder and highway robbery. To this day, doubtless, the same impression prevails in the North, and yet, when it is considered how it was produced, it is surprising that it should or could last so long.

The newspapers are of course responsible for it, as for every other opinion entertained at any time by the Northern public.

It will repay any one who will take the trouble to examine the files of these papers printed during the war, if he desires a curious entertainment. Among many willful misrepresentations of Morgan's as well as of other Confederate commands, many statements palpably false, and regarding events of which the writers could not possibly have obtained correct information, will be found under the most astounding captions, proclaiming the commission of "unheard of atrocities" and "guerrilla outrages," accounts of Morgan having impressed horses or taken forage and provisions from Union men, while highly facetious descriptions of house-burning, jewelry snatching, and a thorough sacking of premises are chronicled, without one word of condemnation, under the heading of "frolics of the boys in blue." In thus referring to the manner in which the Northern newspapers mentioned the respective combatants whose deeds their reporters pretended to record, I have no wish to provoke a renewal of the wordy war.

The Southern journals were undoubtedly sufficiently denunciatory, although they did not always seem to consider a bad deed sanctified because done by their friends. Nor have I any intention of denying that inexcusable excesses were committed at various times by men of Morgan's command. I freely admit that we had men in our ranks whose talents and achievements could have commanded respect even among the "Bummers." There were others, too, whose homes had been destroyed and property "confiscated," whose families had been made to "feel the war," who were incited by an unholy spirit of revenge to commit acts as well worth relation, as any of those for which the "weekly" of his native township has duly lauded the most industrious Federal raider, actuated by a legitimate desire of pleasure or gain. It will not be difficult to prove that such practices met with rebuke from General Morgan and his officers, and that they were not characteristic of his command. There are other impressions about Morgan and "Morgan's men" which I shall endeavor to correct, as, although by no means so serious as those just mentioned, they are not at all just to the reputation of either leader or followers. It is a prevalent opinion that his troops were totally undisciplined and unaccustomed to the instruction and restraint which form the soldier. They were, to be sure, far below the standard of regular troops in these respects, and doubtless they were inferior in many particulars of drill and organization to some carefully-trained bodies of cavalry, Confederate and Federal, which were less constantly and actively engaged in service on the front.

But these essential requisites to efficiency were by no means neglected or in a great degree lacking. The utmost care was exercised in the organization of every regiment to place the best men in office—General Morgan frequently interfering, for that purpose, in a manner warranted neither by the regulations nor the acts of congress. No opportunity was neglected to attain proficiency in the tactics which experience had induced us to adopt, and among officers and men there was a perfect appreciation of the necessity of strict subordination, prompt unquestioning obedience to superiors, and an active, vigilant discharge of all the duties which devolve upon the soldier in the vicinity or presence of the enemy.

I do not hesitate to say that "Morgan's Division," in its best days, would have lost nothing (in points of discipline and instruction) by comparison with any of the fine cavalry commands, which did constant service, of the Confederate army, and the testimony of more than one inspecting officer can be cited to that effect. More credit, too, has been given General Morgan for qualities and ability which constitute a good spy, or successful partisan to lead a handful of men, than for the very decided military talents which he possessed. He is most generally thought to have been in truth, the "Guerrilla Chief," which the Northern press entitled and strove to prove him. It will not be difficult to disabuse the minds of military men (or, indeed, intelligent men of any class) of this impression. It will be only necessary to review his campaigns and give the reasons which induced his movements, to furnish an authentic and thorough statement of facts, and, as far as practicable, an explanation of attendant circumstances, and it will be seen that he had in an eminent degree many of the highest and most necessary qualities of the General.

An even cursory study of Morgan's record will convince the military reader, that the character he bore with those who served with him was deserved.

That while circumspect and neglectful of no precaution to insure success or avert disaster, he was extremely bold in thought and action. That using every means to obtain extensive and accurate information (attempting no enterprise of importance without it), and careful in the consideration of every contingency, he was yet marvelously quick to combine and to revolve, and so rapid and sudden in execution, as frequently to confound both friends and enemies.

And above all, once convinced, he never hesitated to act; he would back his judgment against every hazard, and with every resource at his command.

Whatever merit be allowed or denied General Morgan, he is beyond all question entitled to the credit of having discovered uses for cavalry, or rather mounted infantry, to which that arm was never applied before. While other cavalry officers were adhering to the traditions of former wars, and the systems of the schools, however inapplicable to the demands of their day and the nature of the struggle, he originated and perfected, not only a system of tactics, a method of fighting and handling men in the presence of the enemy, but also a strategy as effective as it was novel.

Totally ignorant of the art of war as learned from the books and in the academies; an imitator in nothing; self taught in all that he knew and did, his success was not more marked than his genius.

The creator and organizer of his own little army—with a force which at no time reached four thousand—he *killed and wounded* nearly as many of the enemy, and captured more than fifteen thousand. The author of the far-reaching "raid," so different from the mere cavalry dash, he accomplished with his handful of men results which would otherwise have required armies and the costly preparations of regular and extensive campaigns.

I shall endeavor to show the intimate connection between his operations and those of the main army in each department where he served, and the strategic importance of even his apparently rashest and most purposeless raids, when considered with reference to their bearing upon the grand campaigns of the West. When the means at his disposal, the difficulties with which he had to contend, and the results he effected are well understood, it will be conceded that his reputation with the Southern soldiery was not undeserved, and that to rank with the best of the many active and excellent cavalry officers of the West, to have had, confessedly, no equal among them except in Forrest, argues him to have possessed no common ability. The design of this work may in part fail, because of the inability of one so little accustomed to the labors of authorship to present his subject in the manner that it deserves; but the theme is one sure to be interesting and impressive however treated, and materials may, in this way be preserved for abler pens and more extensive works.

The apparent egotism in the constant use of the first person will, I trust, be excused by the explanation that I write of matters and events known almost entirely from personal observation, reports of subordinate officers to myself, or personal knowledge of reports made directly to General Morgan, and that, serving for a considerable period as his second in command, it was necessarily my duty to see to the execution of his plans, and I enjoyed a large share of his confidence.

For the spirit in which it is written, I have only to say that I have striven to be candid and accurate; to that sort of impartiality which is acquired at the expense of a total divestiture of natural feeling, I can lay no claim.

A Southern man, once a Confederate soldier—always thoroughly Southern in sentiments and feeling, I can, of course, write only a Southern account of what I saw in the late war, and as such what is herein written must be received.

CHAPTER II

John Hunt Morgan was born at Huntsville, Alabama, on the first day of June, 1825. His father, Calvin C. Morgan, was a native of Virginia, and a distant relative of Daniel Morgan, the rebel general of revolutionary fame. In early manhood, Mr. Morgan followed the tide of emigration flowing from Virginia to the West, and commenced life as a merchant in Alabama. In 1823, he married the daughter of John W. Hunt, of Lexington, Kentucky, one of the wealthiest and most successful merchants of the State, and one whose influence did much to develope the prosperity of that portion of it in which he resided.

Mr. Morgan is described by all who knew him as a gentleman whom it was impossible to know and not to respect and esteem. His character was at once firm and attractive, but he possessed neither the robust constitution nor the adventurous and impetuous spirit which characterized other members of his family. He was quiet and studious in his habits, and although fond of the society of his friends, he shunned every species of excitement. When failing health, and, perhaps, a distaste for mercantile pursuits induced him to relinquish them, he removed with his family to Kentucky (his son John was then four years old), and purchased a farm near Lexington, upon which he lived until a few years before his death.

John H. Morgan was reared in Kentucky, and lived in Lexington from his eighteenth year until the fall of 1861, when he joined the Confederate army. There was nothing in his boyhood, of which any record has been preserved, to indicate the distinction he was to win, and neither friends nor enemies can deduce from anecdotes of his youthful life arguments of any value in support of the views which they respectively entertain of his character. In this respect, also, he displayed his singular originality of character, and he is about the only instance in modern times (if biographies are to be believed) of a distinguished man who had not, as a boy, some presentiment of his future, and did not conduct himself accordingly.

When nineteen he enlisted for the "Mexican War" and was elected First Lieutenant of Captain Beard's company, in Colonel Marshall's regiment of cavalry. He served in Mexico for eighteen months, but did not, he used to say, see much of "war" during that time. He was, however, at the battle of Buena Vista, in which fight Colonel Marshall's regiment was hotly engaged, and his company, which was ably led, suffered severely. Soon after his return home he married Miss Bruce, of Lexington, a sweet and lovely lady, who, almost from the day of her wedding, was a confirmed and patient invalid and sufferer. Immediately after his marriage, he entered energetically into business—was industrious, enterprising and prosperous, and at the breaking out of the war in 1861, he was conducting in Lexington two successful manufactories. Every speculation and business enterprise in which he engaged succeeded, and he had acquired a very handsome property. This he left, when he went South, to the mercy of his enemies, making no provision whatever for its protection, and apparently caring not at all what became of it. As he left some debts unsettled, his loyal creditors soon disposed of it with the aid of the catch-rebel attachment law.

When quite a young man he had two or three personal difficulties in Lexington, in one of which he was severely wounded. To those who recollect the tone of society in Kentucky at that day, it will be no matter of astonishment to learn that a young man of spirit became engaged in such affairs. His antagonists, however, became, subsequently, his warm friends. The stigmas upon General Morgan's social standing, so frequent in the Northern press, need not be noticed. Their falsity was always well known in Kentucky and the South.

The calumnies, so widely circulated regarding his private life, must be noticed, or the duty of the biographer would be neglected in an important particular. And yet, except to positively deny every thing which touched his integrity as a man and his honor as a gentleman, it would seem that there is nothing for his biographer to do in this respect. The wealth at the disposal of the Federal Government attracted into its service all the purchasable villainy of the press—North and South. It was not even necessary for the Government to bid for them—they volunteered to perform, gratis, in the hope of future reward. To undertake a refutation of every slander broached by this gang against a man, so constantly a theme for all tongues and pens, as was Morgan, would be an impossible, even if it were a necessary, task. It is enough to say that he was celebrated, and therefore he was belied. General Morgan was certainly no "saint"—his friends may claim that he had no right to that title and not the slightest pretension to it. While he respected true piety in other men, and, as those who knew him intimately will well remember, evinced on all occasions a profound and unaffected veneration for religion, he did not profess, nor did he regulate his life by religious convictions. Like the great majority of the men of his class—the gentlemen of the South—he lived freely, and the amusements he permitted himself would, doubtless, have shocked a New

Englander almost as much as the money he spent in obtaining them. Even had the manners of the people among whom he lived have made it politic to conceal carefully every departure from straight-laced morality, he, of all men, would have been the least likely to do so, for he scorned hypocrisy as he did every species of meanness. To sum up, General Morgan, with the virtues, had some of the faults of his Southern blood and country, and he sought so little to extenuate the latter himself, that it may be presumed that he cared not the least whether or no they were recorded.

While no censure can, of course, be directed against those who slandered him, as they did others, for hire—and it would be as absurd in this age and country, to gravely denounce the lie-coiners of the press, as to waste time in impeaching the false witnesses that figure before military commissions—nevertheless, as justice ought to be done to all, it should be remarked that among the *respectable* people who furtively gave currency to every story to his injury were some who owed their power to harm him to the generosity of his grandfather, who loved to assist all sorts of merit, but was particularly partial to manual skill.

The qualities in General Morgan, which would have attracted most attention in private life, were an exceeding gentleness of disposition and unbounded generosity. His kindness and goodness of heart were proverbial. His manner, even after he had become accustomed to command, was gentle and kind, and no doubt greatly contributed to acquire him the singular popularity which he enjoyed long before he had made his military reputation. The strong will and energy which he always displayed might not have elicited much notice, had not the circumstances in which the war placed him developed and given them scope for exercise. But his affection for the members of his family and his friends, the generosity which prompted him to consult their wishes at the expense of any sacrifice of his own, his sensitive regard for the feelings of others, even of those in whom he felt least interest, and his rare charity for the failings of the weak, made up a character which, even without an uncommon destiny, would have been illustrious.

His benevolence was so well known in Lexington, that to "go to Captain Morgan" was the first thought of every one who wished to inaugurate a charitable enterprise, and his business house was a rendezvous for all the distressed, and a sort of "intelligence office" for the poor seeking employment. His temper was cheerful and frequently gay; no man more relished pleasantry and mirth in the society of his friends, with whom his manner was free and even at times jovial; but he never himself indulged in personal jests nor familiarities, nor did he permit them from his most intimate associates; to attempt them with him gave him certain and lasting offense. There was never a more sanguine man; with him to live was to hope and to dare. Yet while rarely feeling despondency and never despair, he did not deceive himself with false or impossible expectations. He was quick to perceive the real and the practical, and while enterprising in the extreme he was not in the least visionary. His nerve, his powers of discrimination, the readiness with which he could surrender schemes found to be impracticable, if by chance he became involved in them, and his energy and close attention to his affairs, made him very successful in business, and undoubtedly the same qualities, intensified by the demand that war made upon them, contributed greatly to his military success.

But it can not be denied that not only the reputation which he won, but the talent which he displayed, astonished none more than his old friends. He would, I think, have been regarded as a remarkable man under any circumstances, by all who would have intimately known him, but he was born to be great in the career in which he was so successful. It is true that war fully developed many qualities which had been observed in him previously, and (surest sign of real capacity) he to the last continued to *grow* with every call that was made upon him. But he manifested an aptitude for the peculiar service in which he acquired so much distinction, an instinctive appreciation of the requisites for success, and a genius for command, which made themselves immediately recognized, but which no one had expected. Nature had certainly endowed him with some gifts which she very rarely bestows, and which give the soldier who has them vast advantages; a quickness of perception and of thought, amounting almost to intuition, an almost unerring sagacity in foreseeing the operations of an adversary and in calculating the effect of his own movements upon him, wonderful control over men, as individuals and in masses, and moral courage and energy almost preternatural.

He did not seem to reason like other men, at least no one could discover the logical process, if there was one, by which his conclusions were reached. His mind worked most accurately when it worked most rapidly, and sight or sound were scarcely so swift as were its operations in an emergency.

This peculiar faculty and habit of thought enabled him to plan with a rapidity almost inconceivable. Apparently his combinations were instantaneously commenced and perfected, and, if provided with the necessary information, he matured on enterprise almost as soon as he conceived it. His language and manner were often very expressive of this peculiar constitution of mind. In consultation with those whom he admitted to his confidence, he never cared to hear arguments, he would listen only to opinions. In stating his plans, he entered into no explanations, and his expressions of his views and declaration of his purposes sounded like predictions. At such times his speech would become hurried and vehement, and his manner excited but remarkably impressive.

He evidently felt the most thorough and intense conviction himself, and he seldom failed to convince his hearers. Advice volunteered, even by those he most liked and relied on, was never well received, and when he asked counsel of them he required that it should be concise and definite, and resented hesitation or evasion. Without being in the ordinary sense of the term an excellent judge of character, he possessed, in a greater degree than any of his military associates, the faculty of judging how various circumstances (especially the events and vicissitudes of war) would affect other men, and of anticipating in all contingencies their thoughts and action. He seemed, if I may use such expressions, capable of imagining himself exactly in the situations of other men, of identifying his own mind with theirs, and thinking what they thought. He could certainly, with more accuracy than any one, divine the plans and wishes of an enemy. This was universally remarked, and he exhibited it, not only in correctly surmising the intentions of his own immediate opponents, but also in the opinions which he gave regarding the movements of the grand armies. He sought all the information which could however remotely affect his interests and designs with untiring avidity, and the novel and ingenious expedients he sometimes resorted to in order to obtain it, would perhaps furnish materials for the most interesting chapter of his history. It was a common saying among his men, that "no lawyer can cross-examine like General Morgan," and indeed the skill with which he could elicit intelligence from the evasive or treacherous answers of men unwilling to aid, or seeking to deceive him, was only less astonishing than the confidence with which he would act upon information so acquired. In army phrase, he was a capital "judge of information," that is, he could almost infallibly detect the true from the false, and determine the precise value of all that he heard. His quickness and accuracy, in this respect, amounted almost to another sense; reports, which to others appeared meager and unsatisfactory, and circumstances devoid of meaning to all but himself, frequently afforded him a significant and lively understanding of the matters which he wished to know.

He had another faculty which is very essential to military success, indispensably necessary, at any rate, to a cavalry commander who acts independently and at such distances from any base or support as he almost constantly did. I believe the English term it, having "a good eye for a country." It is the faculty of rapidly acquiring a correct idea of the nature and peculiar features of any country in which military operations are to be conducted. He neglected nothing that a close study of maps and careful inquiry could furnish of this sort of knowledge, but after a brief investigation or experience, he generally had a better understanding of the subject than either map-makers or natives could give him.

However imperfect might be his acquaintance with a country, it was nearly impossible for a guide to deceive him. What he had once learned in this respect he never forgot. A road once traveled was always afterward familiar to him, with distances, localities and the adjacent country. Thus, always having in his mind a perfect idea of the region where he principally operated, he could move with as much facility and confidence (when there) without maps and guides as with them. His favorite strategy, in his important expeditions or "raids," was to place himself by long and swift marches—moving sometimes for days and nights without a halt except to feed the horses—in the very heart of the territory where were the objects of his enterprise. He relied upon this method to confuse if not to surprise his enemy, and prevent a concentration of his forces. He would then strike right and left. He rarely declined upon such expeditions to fight when advancing, for it was his theory that then, a concentration of superior forces against him was more difficult, and that the vigor of his enemy was to a certain extent paralyzed by the celerity of his own movements and the mystery which involved them. But after commencing his retreat, he would use every effort and stratagem to avoid battle, fearing that while fighting one enemy others might also overtake him, and believing that at such times the morale of his own troops was somewhat impaired. No leader could make more skillful use of detachments. He would throw them out to great distances, even when surrounded by superior and active forces, and yet in no instance was one of them (commanded by a competent officer and who obeyed instructions) overwhelmed or cut off. It very rarely happened that they failed to accomplish the purposes for which they were dispatched, or to rejoin the main body in time to assist in decisive action. He could widely separate and apparently scatter his forces, and yet maintain such a disposition of them as to have all well in hand. When pushing into the enemy's lines he would send these detachments in every direction, until it was impossible to conjecture his real intentions—causing, generally, the shifting of troops from point to point as each was threatened; until the one he wished to attack was weakened, when he would strike at it like lightning.

He was a better strategist than tactician. He excelled in the arts which enable a commander to make successful campaigns and gain advantages without much fighting, rather than in skillful maneuvering on the field.

He knew how to thoroughly confuse and deceive an enemy, and induce in him (as he desired) false confidence or undue caution; how to isolate and persuade or compel him to surrender without giving battle; and he could usually manage, although inferior to the aggregate of the hostile forces around him, to be stronger or as strong at the point and moment of encounter.

The tactics he preferred, when he chose to fight, were attempts at surprise and a concentration of his strength for headlong dashing attacks.

To this latter method there were some objections. These attacks were made with a vigor, and inspired in the men a reckless enthusiasm, which generally rendered them successful. But if the enemy was too strong, or holding defensible positions, was resolute and stubborn in resistance, and the first two or three rushes failed to drive him, the attack was apt to fail altogether, and the reaction was correspondent to the energy of the onset.

He did not display so much ability when operating immediately with the army, as when upon detached service. He would not hesitate to remain for days closely confronting the main forces of the enemy, keeping his videttes constantly in sight of his cantonments, observing his every movement, and attacking every detachment and foraging party which he could expect to defeat. But when a grand advance of the enemy was commenced he preferred making a timely and long retreat, followed by a dash in some quarter where he was not expected, rather than to stubbornly contest their progress.

He could actively and efficiently harass a retreating army, multiplying and continuing his assaults until he seemed ubiquitous; but he was not equally efficient in covering a retreat or retarding an advance in force. Upon one or two occasions, when the emergency was imminent, he performed this sort of service cheerfully and well, but he did not like it, nor was he eminently fitted for it. He had little of that peculiar skill with which Forrest would so wonderfully embarrass an enemy's advance, and contesting every inch of his march, and pressing upon him if he hesitated or receded, convert every mistake that he made into a disaster.

In attempting a delineation of General Morgan's character, mention ought not to be omitted of certain peculiarities, which to some extent, affected his military and official conduct.

Although by no means a capricious or inconsistent man, for he entertained profound convictions and adhered to opinions with a tenacity that often amounted to prejudice, he frequently acted very much like one.

Not even those who knew him best could calculate how unusual occurrences would affect him, or induce him to act.

It frequently happened that men for whose understandings and characters he had little respect, but who were much about his person, obtained a certain sort of influence with him, but they could keep it only by a complete acquiescence in his will when it became aroused. He sometimes permitted and even encouraged suggestions from all around him, listening to the most contradictory opinions with an air of thorough acquiescence in all. It was impossible, on such occasions, to determine whether this was done to flatter the speakers, to mislead as to his real intentions, or if he was in fact undecided.

He generally ended such moments of doubt by his most original and unexpected resolutions, which he would declare exactly as if they were suggestions just made by some one else, almost persuading the parties to whom they were attributed that they had really advanced them. In his judgment of the men with whom he had to deal, he showed a strange mixture of shrewdness and simplicity. He seldom failed to discern and to take advantage of the ruling characteristics of those who approached him, and he could subsidize the knowledge and talents of other men with rare skill. He especially excelled in judging men collectively. He knew exactly how to appeal to the feelings of his men, to excite their enthusiasm, and stimulate them to dare any danger and endure any fatigue and hardship. But he sometimes committed the gravest errors in his estimation of individual character. He more than once imposed implicit confidence in men whom no one else would have trusted, and suffered himself to be deceived by the shallowest imposters. He obtained credit for profound insight into character by his possession of another and very different quality. The unbounded influence he at once acquired over almost every one who approached him, enabled him to make men do the most uncharacteristic things, and created the impression that he discovered traits of character hidden from others.

General Morgan had more of those personal qualities which make a man's friends devoted to him, than any one I have ever known.

He was himself very warm and constant in the friendships which he formed. It seemed impossible for him to do enough for those to whom he was attached, or to ever give them up. His manner when he wished, prepossessed every one in his favor. He was generally more courteous and attentive to his inferiors than to his equals and superiors. This may have proceeded in a great measure from his jealousy of dictation and impatience of restraint, but was the result also of warm and generous feelings. His greatest faults, arose out of his kindness and easiness of disposition, which rendered it impossible for him to say or do unpleasant things, unless when under the influence of strong prejudice or resentment. This temperament made him a too lax disciplinarian, and caused him to be frequently imposed upon. He was exceedingly and unfeignedly modest. For a long time he sought, in every way, to avoid the applause and ovations which met him every where in the South, and he never learned to keep a bold countenance when receiving them.

It was distressing to see him called on (as was of course often the case) for a speech—nature certainly never intended that he should win either fame or bread by oratory.

When complimented for any achievement he always gave the credit of it to some favorite officer, or attributed it to the excellence of his troops. Nothing seemed to give him more sincere pleasure than to publicly acknowledge meritorious service in a subaltern officer or private, and he would do it in a manner that made it a life long remembrance with the recipient of the compliment.

When displeased, he rarely reprimanded, but expressed his displeasure by satirically complimenting the offender; frequently the only evidence of dissatisfaction which he would show was a peculiar smile, which was exceeding significant, and any thing but agreeable to the individual conscious of having offended him.

His personal appearance and carriage were striking and graceful. His features were eminently handsome and adapted to the most pleasing expressions. His eyes were small, of a grayish blue color, and their glances keen and thoughtful. His figure on foot or on horseback was superb.

He was exactly six feet in hight, and although not at all corpulent, weighed one hundred and eighty-five pounds.

His form was perfect and the rarest combination of strength, activity and grace. His constitution seemed impervious to the effects of privation and exposure, and it was scarcely possible to perceive that he suffered from fatigue or lack of sleep. After marching for days and nights without intermission, until the hardiest men in his division were exhausted, I have known him, as soon as a halt was called, and he could safely leave his command, ride fifty miles to see his wife. Although a most practical man in all of his ideas, he irresistibly reminded one of the heroes of romance. He seemed the *Fra-Moreale* come to life again, and, doubtless, was as much feared and as bitterly denounced as was that distinguished officer.

Men are not often born who can wield such an influence as he exerted, apparently without an effort—who can so win men's hearts and stir their blood. He will, at least, be remembered until the Western cavalrymen and their children have all died. The bold riders who live in the border-land, whose every acre he made historic, will leave many a story of his audacity and wily skill. They will name but one man as his equal, "The wizard of the saddle," the man of revolutionary force and fire, strong, sagacious, indomitable Forrest, and the two will go down in tradition together, twin-brothers in arms and in fame.

CHAPTER III

The position assumed by Kentucky, at the inception of the late struggle, and her conduct throughout, excited the surprise, and, in no small degree, incurred for her the dislike of both the contending sections.

But while both North and South, at some time, doubted her good faith and complained of her action, all such sentiments have been entirely forgotten by the latter, and have become intensified into bitter and undisguised animosity upon the part of a large share of the population of the former.

The reason is patent. It is the same which, during the war, influenced the Confederates to hope confidently for large assistance from Kentucky, if once enabled to obtain a foothold upon her territory, and caused the Federals, on the other hand, to regard even the loudest and most zealous professors of loyalty as Secessionists in disguise, or, at best, Unionists only to save their property. It is the instinctive feeling that the people of Kentucky, on account of kindred blood, common interests, and identity of ideas in all that relates to political rights and the objects of political institutions, may be supposed likely to sympathize and to act with the people of the South. But a variety of causes and influences combined to prevent Kentucky from taking a decided stand with either of the combatants, and produced the vacillation and inconsistency which so notably characterized her councils and paralyzed her efforts in either direction, and, alas, it may be added, so seriously affected her fair fame.

Her geographical situation, presenting a frontier accessible for several hundreds of miles to an assailant coming either from the North or South, caused her people great apprehension, especially as it was accounted an absolute certainty that her territory (if she took part with the South) would be made the battle-ground and subjected to the last horrors and desolation of war. The political education of the Kentuckians, also, disposed them to enter upon such a contest with extreme reluctance and hesitation.

Originally a portion of Virginia, settled chiefly by emigration from that State, her population partook of the characteristics and were imbued with the feelings which so strongly prevailed in the mother commonwealth.

From Virginia, the first generation of Kentucky statesmen derived those opinions which became the political creed of the Southern people, and were promulgated in the celebrated resolutions of '98, which gave shape and consistency to the doctrine of States' Rights, and popular expression to that construction of the relations of the several States to the General Government (under the Federal Constitution), so earnestly insisted upon by the master-minds of Virginia. The earlier population of Kentucky was peculiarly inclined to adopt and cherish such opinions, by the promptings of that nature which seems common to all men descended from the stock of the "Old Dominion," that craving for the largest individual independence, and disposition to assert and maintain in full *measure* every personal right, which has always made the people of the Southern and Western States so jealous of outside interference with their local affairs. It was natural that a people, animated by such a spirit, should push their preference for self-government even to extremes; that they should esteem their most valued franchises only safe when under their own entire custody and control; that they should prefer that their peculiar institutions should be submitted only to domestic regulation, and that the personal liberty, which they prized above all their possessions, should be restrained only by laws enacted by legislators chosen from among themselves, and executed by magistrates equally identified with themselves and appreciative of their instincts.

In short, they were strongly attached to their State Governments, and were not inclined to regard as beneficent, nor, even exactly legitimate, any interference with them, upon the part of the General Government, and desired to see the powers of the latter exercised only for the "common defense and general welfare."

Without presuming to declare them correct or erroneous, it may be safely asserted that such were the views which prevailed in Kentucky at a period a little subsequent to her settlement.

This decided and almost universal sentiment was first shaken, and the minds of the people began to undergo some change, about the time of, and doubtless in consequence of, the detection of the Burr conspiracy. Burr had been identified with the party which advocated the extreme State Rights doctrines, and his principal confederates were men of the same political complexion.

The utter uselessness of his scheme, even if successful, and the little prospect of any benefit accruing from it, unless to the leading adventurers, had disposed all the more sober minded to regard it with distrust. And when it became apparent that it had been concocted for the gratification of one man's ambition, the very people whom it had been part of the plan to flatter with hopes of the most brilliant advantages, immediately conceived for it the most intense aversion.

The odium into which Burr and his associates immediately fell, became, in some measure, attached to the political school to which they had belonged, and men's minds began to be unsettled upon the very political tenets, in the propriety and validity of which they had previously so implicitly believed. The able Federalist leaders in the State, pursued and improved the advantage thus offered them, and for the first time in the history of Kentucky, that party showed evidence of ability to cope with its rival. Doubtless, also, the effect of Mr. Madison's attempt to explain away the marrow and substance of the famous resolutions, which told so injuriously against the State Rights party every where, contributed, at a still later day, to weaken that party in Kentucky; but the vital change in the political faith of Kentucky, was wrought by Henry Clay. All previous interruptions to the opinions which she had acquired as her birthright from Virginia, were but partial, and would have been ephemeral, but the spell which the great magician cast over his people was like the glamour of mediæval enchantment. It bound them in helpless but delighted acquiescence in the will of the master. Their vision informed them, not of objects as they were, but as he willed that they should seem, and his patients received, at his pleasure and with equal confidence, the true or the unreal. In fact, the undoubted patriotism and spotless integrity of Mr. Clay, so aided the effect of his haughty will and superb genius, that his influence amounted to fascination. Although himself, in early life, an advocate of the principles of (what has been since styled) the Jeffersonian school of Democracy, he became gradually, but thoroughly, weaned from his first opinions, and a convert to the dogmas of the school of politics which he had once so ably combatted. The author of the American System, the advocate of the United States Bank, the champion of the New England manufacturing and commercial interests, with their appropriate and necessary train of protective tariffs, bounties and monopolies, could have little sympathy with the ideas that the several States could, and should, protect and develope their own interests without Federal assistance, that the General Government was the servant of all the States and not the guardian and dry nurse of a few—the doctrine, in short, of "State Sovereignty and Federal Agency." Mr. Clay fairly and emphatically announced his political faith in word and deed. He declared that he "owed a paramount allegiance to the whole Union: a subordinate one to his own State," and, throughout the best part of his long political life, he wrought faithfully for interests distinct from, if not adverse to, those of his own State and section. His influence, however, in his own State, has determined, perhaps forever, her destiny. If he did not educate the people of Kentucky (as has been so often charged) to "defer principle to expediency," he at least taught them to study the immediate policy rather than the ultimate effect of every measure that they were called to consider, and to seek the material prosperity of the hour at the expense, even, of future safety. He taught his generation to love the Union, not as an "agency" through which certain benefits were to be derived, but as an "end" which was to be adhered to, no matter what results flowed from it.

Mr. Clay sincerely believed that in the union of the States resided the surest guarantees of the safety, honor, and prosperity of each, and he contemplated with horror and aversion any thought of disunion. His own lofty and heroic nature could harbor no feeling which was not manly and brave, but, in striving to stimulate and fortify in his people the same love of union which he entertained himself, he taught many Kentuckians to so dread the evils of war, as to lose all fear of other and as great evils, and to be willing to purchase exemption from civil strife by facile and voluntary submission. After the death of Mr. Clay, Kentucky, no longer subjected to his personal influence, began to forget it.

In 1851, John C. Breckinridge had been elected to Congress from Mr. Clay's district, while the latter still lived, and beating one of his warmest friends and supporters. Under the leadership of Mr. Breckinridge, the Democratic party in Kentucky rallied and rapidly gained ground. During the "Know-nothing" excitement, the old Whigs, who had nearly all joined the Know-nothing or American party, seemed about to regain their ascendency, but that excitement ebbing as suddenly as it had arisen, left the Democracy in indisputable power. In 1856, Kentucky cast her Presidential vote for Buchanan and Breckinridge by nearly seven thousand majority. Mr. Breckinridge's influence had, by this time, become predominant in the State, and was felt in every election. The troubles in Kansas and the agitation in Congress had rendered the Democratic element in Kentucky more determined, and inclined them more strongly to take a Southern view of all the debated questions. The John Brown affair exasperated her people in common with that of every other slaveholding community, and led to the organization of the State-guard.

Created because of the strong belief that similar attempts would be repeated, and upon a larger scale, and that, quite likely, Kentucky would be selected as a field of operations, it is not surprising that the State-guard should have expected an enemy only from the North, whence, alone, would come the aggressions it was organized to resist, and that it should have conceived a feeling of antagonism for the Northern, and an instinctive sympathy for the Southern, people.

These sentiments were intensified by the language of the Northern press and pulpit, and the commendation and encouragement of such enterprises as the Harper's Ferry raid, which were to be heard throughout the North.

In the Presidential election of 1860, the Kentucky Democracy divided on Douglas and Breckinridge, thereby losing the State. After the election of Mr. Lincoln and the passage of ordinances of secession by several Southern States, when the most important question which the people of Kentucky had ever been required to determine, was presented for their consideration, their sentiments and wishes were so various and conflicting, as to render its decision by themselves impossible, and it was finally settled for them by the Federal Government.

The Breckinridge wing of the Democracy was decidedly Southern in feelings and opinions, and anxious to espouse the Southern cause.

The Douglas wing strongly sympathized with the South, but opposed secession and disunion.

The Bell-Everett party, composed chiefly of old Clay Whigs, was decidedly in favor of Union. Such was the attitude of parties, with occasional individual exceptions. The very young men of the State were generally intense Southern sympathizers, and were, with few exceptions, connected with the State-guard. Indeed, divided as were the people of Kentucky at that time, sympathy with the Southern people was prevalent among all classes of them, and the conviction seemed to be strong, even in the most determined opponents of secession, that an attack upon the Southern people was an attack upon themselves. Among the Union men it was common to hear such declarations as that "When it becomes a direct conflict between North and South, we will take part with the South," "The Northern troops shall not march over our soil to invade the South," "When it becomes apparent that the war is an abolition crusade, and waged for the destruction of slavery, Kentucky will arm against the Government," etc.; each man had some saving clause with his Unionism. It is no hazardous assertion that the Union party, in Kentucky, condemned the secession of the Southern States, more because it was undertaken without consultation with them, and because they regarded it as a blow at Kentucky's dignity and comfort, than because it endangered "the national life." Certainly not one of the leading politicians of that party would have dared, in the winter and spring of 1861, to have openly advocated coercion, no matter what were his secret views of its propriety.

Upon the 17th February, 1861, the Legislature met in extra session at the summons of Governor Magoffin. Seven Southern States had seceded, the Confederate Government had been inaugurated, and it was time for the people of Kentucky to understand what they were going to do. The Governor addressed a message to the Legislature advising the call of a State Convention. This the Legislature declined to do, but suggested the propriety of the assembling of a National Convention to revise and correct the Federal Constitution, and recommended the "Peace Conference," which was subsequently held at Washington. In certain resolutions passed by this Legislature, in reference to resolutions passed by the States of Maine, New York and Massachusetts, this language occurs: "The Governor of the State of Kentucky is hereby requested to inform the executives of said States, that it is the opinion of this General Assembly that whenever the authorities of these States shall send armed forces to the South for the purpose indicated in said resolutions, the people of Kentucky, uniting with their brethren of the South, will as one man, resist such invasion of the soil of the South, at all hazards and to the last extremity." Rather strong language for "Union" men and a "loyal" legislature to use. It would seem that Kentucky, at that time, supposed herself a "sovereign" State addressing other "sovereign" States, and that she entirely ignored the "Nation." Her Legislature paid as little attention to the "proper channel of communication" as a militia Captain would have done. The Union men who voted for the resolutions in which this language was embodied, would be justly liable to censure, if it were not positively certain that they were *insincere*; and that they *were* insincere is abundantly proven by their subsequent action, and the fact that many of them held commissions in the "armed forces" sent to invade the South. On the 11th of February the Legislature resolved, "That we protest against the use of force or coercion by the General Government against the seceded States, as unwise and inexpedient, and tending to the destruction of our common country."

At the Union State Convention, held at Louisville on the 8th of January, certain amendments to the Constitution of the United States were "recommended," and it was resolved, "that, if the disorganization of the present Union is not arrested, that the States agreeing to these amendments of the Federal Constitution shall form a *separate Confederacy*, with power to admit new States under our glorious Constitution thus *amended*;" it was resolved also that it was "expedient to call a convention of the border free and slave States," and that "we deplore the existence of a Union to be held together by the sword."

It almost takes a man's breath away to write such things about the most loyal men of the loyal State of Kentucky. For a Union Convention to have passed them, and Union men to have indorsed them, the resolutions whose substance has been just given, have rather a strange sound. They ring mightily like secession.

"If the disorganization of the present Union is not arrested," the Union men of Kentucky would also help it along. A modified phrase much in vogue with them, "separate State action" expressed their "conservative" plan of seceding. Unless the proper distinctions are drawn, however, the action of this class of politicians will always be misunderstood. They indignantly condemned the secession of South Carolina and Georgia. No language was strong enough to express their abhorrence and condemnation of the wickedness of those who would inaugurate "the disorganization of the present Union." But they did not, with ordinary consistency,

"Compound for sins they were inclined to
By damning those they had no mind to!"

They committed the same sin under another name, and advocated the "separate Confederacy" of "the border free and slave States," under our glorious Constitution thus amended.

"Orthodoxy," was their "doxy;" "Heterodoxy," was "another man's doxy." Every candid man, who remembers the political status of Kentucky at that period, will admit that the Union party propounded no definite and positive creed, and that its leaders frequently gave formal expression to views which strangely resembled the "damnable heresies of secession." Indeed, the neglect of the seceding States to "consult Kentucky," previously to having gone out, seemed to be, in the eyes of these gentlemen, not so much an aggravation of the crime of secession, as, in itself, a crime infinitely graver. There were many who would condemn secession, and in the same breath indicate the propriety of "co-operation." These subtle distinctions, satisfactory, doubtless, to the intellects which generated them, were not aptly received by common minds, and their promulgation induced, perhaps very unjustly, a very general belief that the Union party was actuated not more by a love of the Union, than by a salutary regard for personal security and comfort. It seemed that the crime was not in "breaking up the Union," but in going about it in the wrong way.

The people of Kentucky heard, it is true, from these leaders indignant and patriotic denunciations of "secession," and, yet, they could listen to suggestions amounting almost to advocacy, from the same lips, of "central confederacies" or "co-operations."

Is it surprising, then, that no very holy horror of disunion should have prevailed in Kentucky?

But any inclination to tax these gentlemen with inconsistency should be checked by the reflection that they were surrounded by peculiar circumstances. It appeared to be by no means certain, just then, that an attempt would be made to coerce the seceding States, or that the Southern Confederacy would not be established without a war. In that event, Kentucky would have glided naturally and certainly into it, and Kentucky politicians who had approved coercion, would have felt uncomfortable as Confederate citizens. The leaders of the Union party were men of fine ability, but they were not endowed with prescience, nor could they in the political chaos then ruling, instinctively detect the strong side. Let it be remembered that, just so soon as they discerned it, they enthusiastically embraced it and clave to it, with a few immaterial oscillations, through much tribulation. As was explained by one of the most distinguished among them (in the United States Senate), it was necessary to "educate the people of Kentucky to loyalty." It is true that in this educational process, which was decidedly novel and peculiar, many Kentuckians, not clearly seeing the object in view, were made rebels, and even Confederate soldiers, although not originally inclined that way.

But it is seldom that a perfectly new and original system works smoothly, and the "educators" made amends for all their errors by inflexible severity toward the rebels who staid at home, and by "expatriating" and confiscating the property of those who fled. A "States Rights Convention" was called to assemble at Frankfort on the 22nd of March, 1861, but adjourned, having accomplished nothing.

After the fall of Fort Sumpter and the issuing of the proclamation of April 15, 1861, Governor Magoffin responded to President Lincoln's call for troops from Kentucky in the following language:

"FRANKFORT, *April 16, 1861.*

"*Hon. Simon Cameron, Secretary of War*;

"Your dispatch is received. In answer, I say, emphatically, that Kentucky will furnish no troops for the wicked purpose of subduing her sister Southern States.

"B. MAGOFFIN, *Governor of Kentucky.*"

Governor Magoffin then a second time convened the Legislature in extra session, to consider means for putting the State in a position for defense. When the Legislature met, it resolved,

"That the act of the Governor in refusing to furnish troops or military force upon the call of the Executive authority of the United States, under existing circumstances, is approved." Yeas, eighty-nine; nays, four.

On the 18th of April a large Union meeting was held at Louisville, at which the most prominent and influential Union men of the State assisted. Resolutions were adopted,

"That as the Confederate States have, by overt acts, commenced war against the United States, *without consultation with Kentucky and their sister Southern States*, Kentucky reserves to herself the right to choose her own position; and that while her natural sympathies are with those who have a common interest in the protection of slavery, she still acknowledges her loyalty and fealty to the Government of the United States, which she will cheerfully render until that Government becomes aggressive, tyrannical, and regardless of our rights in slave property;" Resolved,

"That the National Government should be tried by its acts, and that the several States, *as its peers in their appropriate spheres*, will hold it to a rigid accountability, and require that its acts should be fraternal in their efforts to bring back the seceded States, and not sanguinary or coercive."

The Senate resolved, just before the adjournment of the Legislature, that "Kentucky will not sever her connection with the National Government, nor take up arms for either belligerent party; but arm herself for the preservation of peace within her borders."

This was the first authoritative declaration of the policy of "Neutrality," which, however, had been previously indicated at a Union meeting held at Louisville on the 10th of April, in the following resolutions:

"That as we oppose the call of the President for volunteers for the purpose of coercing the seceded States, so we oppose the raising of troops in this State to co-operate with the Southern Confederacy."

"That the present duty of Kentucky is to maintain her present independent position, taking sides, not with the Administration nor with the seceding States, but with the Union against them both, declaring her soil to be sacred from the hostile tread of either, and, if necessary, to make the declaration good with her strong right arm."

In other words, Kentucky would remain in the Union, but would refuse obedience to the Government of the United States, and would fight its armies if they came into her territory. Was it much less "criminal" and "heretical" to do this than to "take sides with the seceding States?"

What is the exact shade of difference between the guilt of a State which transfers its fealty from the Union to a Confederacy, and that of a State which declares her positive and absolute independence, entering into no new compacts, but setting at defiance the old one? Where was the boasted "loyalty" of the Union men of Kentucky when they indorsed the above given resolutions?

In May of that year, the *Louisville Journal*, the organ of the Union party of Kentucky, said, in reference to the response which it was proper for Kentucky to make to the President's call for troops: "In our judgment, the people of Kentucky have answered this question in advance, and the answer expressed in every conceivable form of popular expression, and finally, clinched by the glorious vote of Saturday, is; arm Kentucky efficiently, but rightfully, and fairly, with the clear declaration that the arming is not for offense against either the Government or the seceding States, but purely for defense against whatever power sets hostile foot upon the actual soil of the Commonwealth. In other words, the Legislature, according to the manifest will of the people, should declare the neutrality of Kentucky in this unnatural and accursed war of brothers, and equip the State for the successful maintenance of her position at all hazards?"

It is well known that loyalty means unqualified, unconditional, eternal devotion and adherence to the Union, with a prompt and decorous acquiescence in the will and action of the Administration. Although a definition of the term has been frequently asked, and many have affected not to understand it, it is positively settled that every man is a traitor who doubts that this definition is the correct one. It is impossible, then, to avoid the conviction that in the year 1861, there was really no loyalty in the State of Kentucky. A good deal was subsequently contracted for, and a superior article was furnished the Government a few months later.

Had their been during the winter and spring of 1861, a resolute and definite purpose upon the part of the Southern men of Kentucky, to take the State out of the Union; had those men adopted, organized and determined action, at any time previously to the adjournment of the Legislature, on the 24th of April, the Union party of Kentucky would have proven no material obstacle.

The difficulty which was felt to be insuperable by all who approved the secession of Kentucky, was her isolated position. Not only did the long hesitation of Virginia and Tennessee effectually abate the ardor and resolution of the Kentuckians who desired to unite their State to the Southern Confederacy, but while it lasted it was an insurmountable, physical barrier in the way of such an undertaking. With those States antagonistic to the Southern movement, it would have been madness for Kentucky to have attempted to join it. When at length, Virginia and Tennessee passed their ordinances of secession, Kentucky had become infatuated with the policy of "neutrality." With the leaders of the Union party, it had already been determined upon as part of their system for the "education" of the people. The Secessionists, who were without organization and leaders, regarded it as something infinitely better than unconditional obedience to the orders and coercive policy of the Federal Government; and the large class of the timid and irresolute of men, who are by nature "neutral" in times of trouble and danger, accepted it joyfully, as such men always accept a compromise which promises to relieve them of immediate responsibility and the necessity of hazardous decision. Disconnected from the views and intentions of those who consented to it, this "neutrality" will scarcely admit of serious discussion. Such a position is certainly little else than rebellion, and the principle or conditions which will justify it, will also justify secession. If a State has the legal and constitutional right to oppose the action, and to refuse compliance with the requisitions of the Federal Government, to disobey the laws of Congress, and set at defiance the proclamations of the Executive, to decide for herself her proper policy in periods of war and insurrection, and levy armed forces to prevent the occupation of her territory by the forces of the United States, then she can quit the Union when she pleases, and is competent to contract any alliance which accords, with her wishes. If, however, it be a revolutionary right which she may justly exercise in a certain condition of affairs, then the same condition of affairs will justify any other phase or manner of revolution.

The practical effects of such a position, had it been stubbornly maintained, would have been to involve Kentucky in more danger than she would have incurred by secession and admission into the Confederacy. A declaration of neutrality in such a contest was almost equivalent to a declaration of war against both sides; at any rate it was a proclamation of opposition to the Government, while it discarded the friendship of the South, and seemed at once to invite every assailant. The Government of the United States, which was arming to coerce seceded States, would certainly not permit its designs to be frustrated by this attitude of Kentucky, and it was not likely that the States, about to be attacked, would respect a neutrality, which they very well knew would be no hindrance to their adversary. But few men reason clearly in periods of great excitement, or, in situations of peril, look steadfastly and understandingly at the dangers which surround them. Nor, it may be added, do the few who possess the presence of mind to study and the faculty of appreciating the signs of such a political tempest, always honestly interpret them. As has been said, a large class eagerly welcomed the decision that Kentucky should remain neutral in the great struggle impending, as a relief, however temporary, from the harassing consideration of dangers at which they shuddered. Nine men out of ten, will shrink from making up their minds upon a difficult question, and yet will accept, with joy, a determination of it, however paltry and inconclusive, from any one who has the nerve to urge it. A great many Union men, who would have earnestly opposed a concurrence of Kentucky in the action of the seceding States, if for no other reason than that they regarded it as "a trick of the Democratic party," and yet as obstinately opposed the policy and action of the Government, thought they perceived in "neutrality" a solution of all the difficulties which embarrassed them. A few of the more sagacious and resolute of the leaders of the Union party, who were perhaps not incommoded with a devotion to their State, their section, or to the "flag," but who realized that they could get into power only by crushing the Democratic party, and knew that in the event of Kentucky's going South, the Democratic party would dominate in the State, these men saw in this policy of neutrality the means of holding Kentucky quiet, until the Government could prepare and pour into her midst an overwhelming force. They trusted, and as the sequel showed, with reason, that they would be able to demoralize their opponents after having once reduced them to inaction. The Kentuckians who wished that their State should become a member of the Confederacy, but who saw no immediate hope of it, consented to neutrality as the best arrangement that they could make under the circumstances. They knew that if the neutrality of Kentucky were respected—a vital portion of the Confederacy, a border of four or five hundred miles would be safe from attack and invasion—that the forces of the Confederacy could be concentrated for the defense of the other and threatened lines, and that individual Kentuckians could flock to the Southern army. They believed that in such a condition of affairs, more men would leave Kentucky to take part with the South than to enlist in the service of the Government.

Some time in the early part of the summer, General S.B. Buckner, commanding the Kentucky State-guard, had an interview with General Geo. B. McClellan, who commanded a department embracing territory contiguous to Kentucky—if, indeed, Kentucky was not included by the commission given him in his department. General Buckner obtained, as he supposed, a guarantee that the neutrality of Kentucky would be observed by the military authorities of the United States. He communicated the result of this interview to Governor Magoffin, and, immediately, it became a matter of *official* as well as popular belief that the neutrality of Kentucky was safe for all time to come.

The dream, however, was a short one, and very soon afterward the Federal Government commenced to recruit in Kentucky, to establish camps and organize armed forces in the State.

"Camp Dick Robinson," some twenty-six miles from Lexington, was the largest, first formed, and most noted of these establishments. For many weeks the Kentuckians were in a high state of excitement about "Camp Dick," as it was called. They used the name as if it were synonymous with the Federal army, and spoke of the rumors that "Camp Dick" was to be moved from point to point, as glibly as if the ground it occupied had possessed the properties of the flying carpet of the fairy tale.

The Legislature, notwithstanding its high-sounding resolutions about neutrality, stood this very quietly, although many citizens (Union men) endeavored to have these camps broken up and the troops removed. Others, again, professed to desire that the Federal troops should be removed, but clandestinely advised President Lincoln to rather increase than withdraw the forces, and offered their services to introduce into Kentucky guns for the armament of the loyal Home-guards. These men were of the class of "Educators." But the game required two to play it. On the 4th of September, in anticipation of a Federal movement upon that point, General Polk, of the Confederate army, occupied Columbus, in Kentucky.

In the midst of the excitement created by the information of the occupation of Columbus, Governor Magoffin sent in the following message:

"EX. DEP'T, FRANKFORT, *Sept. 9, 1861.*
"*Gentlemen of the Senate and House of Representatives*:

"I have received the following dispatches by telegraph from General Leonidas Polk, which I deem proper to lay before you,

"B. MAGOFFIN."

[If any answer were needed to the outcries of those who so strongly condemned his action, General Polk certainly furnished it. His first dispatch was a simple intimation to Governor Magoffin of his presence upon the soil of Kentucky, and of the authority by which he remained.]

"COLUMBUS, KENTUCKY, *Sept. 9, 1861.*
"*Governor B. Magoffin*:

A military necessity having required me to occupy this town, I have taken possession of it by the forces under my command. The circumstances leading to this act we reported promptly to the President of the Confederate States. His reply was, the necessity justified the action. A copy of my proclamation I have the honor to transmit you by mail.

"*Respectfully,*
"LEONIDAS POLK, *Major-General Commanding*."

In a letter of the same date, inclosing his proclamation, General Polk said, after explaining the cause of his delay in writing:

"It will be sufficient to inform you, which my short address here will do, that I had information, on which I could rely, that the Federal forces intended, and were preparing, to seize Columbus. I need not describe the danger resulting to West Tennessee from such success, nor say that I could not permit the loss of so important a position, while holding the command intrusted to me by my government. In evidence of the information I possessed, I will state that as the Confederate forces occupied this place, the Federal troops were formed, in formidable numbers, in position upon the opposite bank, with their cannon turned upon Columbus. The citizens of the town had fled with terror, and not a word of assurance of safety or protection had been addressed to them."

General Polk concluded with this language:

"I am prepared to say that I will agree to withdraw the Confederate troops from Kentucky, provided that she will agree that the troops of the Federal Government be withdrawn simultaneously; with a guarantee, which I will give reciprocally for the Confederate Government, that the Federals shall not be allowed to enter, or occupy any point of Kentucky in the future.

"I have the honor to be
"Your obedient servant, respectfully,
"LEONIDAS POLK, *Major-Gen, Com.*"

General Folk's proclamation was as follows:

"COLUMBUS, *Sept. 14, 1861.*

"The Federal Government having in defiance of the wishes of the people of Kentucky, disregarded their neutrality, by establishing camps and depots of arms, and by organizing military companies within their territory, and by constructing a military work, on the Missouri shore, immediately opposite, and commanding Columbus, evidently intended to cover the landing of troops for the seizure of the town, it has become a military necessity, worth the defense of the territory of the Confederate States, that the Confederate forces occupy Columbus in advance. The Major-General commanding has, therefore, not felt himself at liberty to risk the loss of so important a position, but has decided to occupy it. In pursuance of this decision, he has thrown a sufficient force into the town and ordered fortifying it. It is gratifying to know that the presence of his troops is acceptable to the people of Columbus, and on this occasion they assure them that every precaution will be taken to insure their quiet, the protection of their property, with their personal and corporate rights.

LEONIDAS POLK."

Dispatches, concerning the peculiar manner in which Kentucky observed her neutrality and permitted it to be observed by her Federal friends, began to pour in on the Governor about this time. He had already received, on the 7th, a dispatch from Lieutenant Governor Reynolds, of Missouri, on the subject. Governor Reynolds stated that, "The Mississippi river below the mouth of the Ohio, is the property of Kentucky and Missouri conjointly." He then alluded to the "presence of United States gunboats in the river at Columbus, Kentucky, to protect the forces engaged in fortifying the Missouri shore immediately opposite." "This," he went on to say, "appears to me to be a clear violation of the neutrality Kentucky proposes to observe in the present war." And then again on the 14th came a dispatch from Knoxville, Tennessee, as follows:

"*To his Excellency B. Magoffin*:

SIR: The safety of Tennessee requiring, I occupy the mountain passes at Cumberland, and the three long mountains in Kentucky. For weeks I have known that the Federal commander at Hoskin's Cross Roads was threatening the invasion of East Tennessee, and ruthlessly urging our own people to destroy their own road bridges. I postponed this precaution until the despotic Government at Washington, refusing to recognize the neutrality of Kentucky, has established formidable camps in the center and other parts of the State, with the view first to subjugate our gallant sister, then ourselves. Tennessee feels, and has ever felt, toward Kentucky as a twin sister; their people, are as our people in kindred, sympathy, valor, and patriotism; we have felt and still feel a religious respect for Kentucky's neutrality; we will respect it as along as our safety will permit. If the Federal forces will now withdraw from their menacing positions, the forces under my command shall be immediately withdrawn.

Very respectfully,

F.K. ZOLLICOFFER,

Brigadier General Commanding."

It would seem that each one of these communications put the case very clearly, and that, Kentucky having permitted her neutrality to be violated by the one side, after her emphatic and definite declaration that it was meant to be good against both, could consistently take no action, unless it should be such as Generals Polk and Zollicoffer suggested, viz: to provide for a simultaneous withdrawal of both Federal and Confederate forces. Certainly Kentucky meant that neither of the combatants should occupy her soil—as has been shown, her declarations upon that head were clear and vigorous. If she intended that troops of the United States should come into her territory, for any purpose whatever, while the Confederate forces should be excluded, it is unnecessary to say that she selected in "neutrality" a word, which very inaccurately and lamely expressed her meaning. The people of Kentucky had long since—two months at least, a long time in such a period, before this correspondence between their Governor and the Confederate Generals—ceased to do anything but blindly look to certain leaders, and blindly follow their dictation. The Southern men of the State, and their peculiar leaders, were sullen and inert; the mass of the people were bewildered, utterly incompetent to arrive at a decision, and were implicitly led by the Legislature to which all the politicians, who aspired to influence, now resorted. In view of the history of this neutrality, of the professions made, only a few weeks previously, by the same men who returned an answer from the Capital of Kentucky to the propositions of the Confederate authorities that Kentucky should act fairly, and not declare one policy and clandestinely pursue another—in view of the facts which are fastened in the record—what sort of men does that answer prove them to have been? This was the answer:

"*Resolved, By the General Assembly of the Commonwealth of Kentucky that his Excellency, Governor Magoffin, be, and he is hereby instructed to inform those concerned, that Kentucky expects the Confederate or Tennessee troops to be withdrawn from her soil unconditionally.*"

This, after a pledge to their own people, and a proclamation to both sections, of neutrality! After Federal troops, and Federal encampments had been for weeks upon the soil of Kentucky, and in response to action (which their own had invited) from men (to whom they had promised assistance in just such a contingency as was then upon them), when they resolved the previous January, that Governor Magoffin should inform the Governors of New York, Maine and Massachusetts, that when Northern troops should march to invade the South, "the people of Kentucky, uniting with their brethren of the South, will as one man resist such invasion of the soil of the South, at all hazards, and to the last extremity!" The Committee on Federal Relations, to which was referred the communications addressed to Governor Magoffin, exerted itself to outdo the resolutions given above, and reported resolutions of which the substance was, that as Kentucky had been invaded by the Confederate forces, and the commanders of said forces had "insolently prescribed the conditions upon which they will withdraw;" "that the invaders must be expelled, *inasmuch as there are now in Kentucky Federal troops assembled for the purpose of preserving the tranquillity of the State, and of defending and preserving the people of Kentucky in the peaceful enjoyment of their lives and property.*" A candid confession, truly, and one which it required nerve to make! Brave, honorable, consistent men—fit to be the guardians of a people's honor! Declare neutrality, and warn both combatants off the soil of their State! proclaim that Kentucky can and will take care of herself, and then coolly resolve, when the issue is made, "that as there are now Federal troops in Kentucky, for the purpose," etc., that the mask shall be thrown off, and deception no longer practiced. But the cup of shame was not yet full; this unblushing Legislature passed yet other resolutions, to publish to the world the duplicity and dissimulation which had characterized their entire conduct. After going on to set forth the why and wherefore Kentucky had assumed neutrality, it was resolved, "that when the General Government occupies our soil for its defense, in pursuance of a constitutional right, *it neither compromises our assumed neutrality*, nor gives the right to the Confederate forces to invade our State on the assumption that our neutrality has been violated, especially *when they first set foot upon our soil* upon the plea of military necessity."

"That when the General Government occupies our soil for its defense, it neither compromises our assumed neutrality," etc. Well! it is useless to attempt comment on this—"it is impossible to do the subject justice." We rebels never contended that the Government was bound to respect Kentucky's neutrality, if it had the right to coerce the seceded States. We denied the constitutional right and power of coercion—but if the Government had that power, we conceded that there was the same right and reason to employ it against Kentucky's neutrality as against South Carolina's secession. But for the neutrality-mongers to say this—were they generously striving to fool themselves also? And, then, in hearing, as they had been for weeks, of the morning and evening guns of "Camp Dick Robinson," to speak of the Confederates having "*first set foot upon our soil.*" Is it an unfair construction of such conduct, to suppose that the men guilty of it were, in part, time-servers, who had striven all the while to get upon the strong and safe side, and believed that they had succeeded, and, in part, politicians unscrupulous, if in plan consistent, who had deliberately deceived the people of Kentucky, and lulled them into a condition in which they would receive the handcuffs, to be slipped upon them, without resistance?

But now that the men of purpose saw that it was no longer necessary to conceal it, and the wavering had become satisfied which side it was safe and politic to adopt, there was no more dallying.

The Legislature prepared to finally crush the State-guard and "an act to enlarge the powers of the Military Board of this State," was passed. It was enacted, "That the Military Board created at the last session of the Legislature, are hereby authorized to order into the custody of said Board any State arms which may have been given out under the act creating said Board, or other law of the State, whenever said Board shall deem it expedient to do so; said Board shall have like power over the accouterments, camp equipage, equipments, and ammunition of the State." Willful failure or refusal "to return any of said property for forty-eight hours after the receipt of the order of the Board to that effect," was made a high misdemeanor, and punishable by fine of not less than one nor more than five thousand dollars, and imprisonment until the fine was paid, and the arms or other property restored. The removal, concealment, or disposal of any of the property, mentioned in the first section of the act, was made felony and punishable by not less than one nor more than two years in the penitentiary. A further resolution in the spirit of the same kind of neutrality was approved September 23rd, "That the Military Board be and they are hereby authorized to place any portion of the arms, accouterments, equipments, camp equipage, baggage trains, ammunition, and military stores of the State, not in use, under the control of the commander of the Federal forces in Kentucky," etc.

Having once gotten on the right track (as they were compelled to believe it, inasmuch as it was clearly the one which conducted to immediate profit and safety) these gentlemen thought they could not go too fast. "The people were educated to loyalty," now, and it was high time to commence the punishment of those who had shown an inaptness to receive the lessons, or a distaste for the method of instruction. The dignity of Kentucky had been sacrificed by the avarice and cowardice of her own sons, who sat in her councils—this is the way in which those legislative-panders sought to assert it again. They passed an act entitled "an act to prohibit and prevent rebellion by citizens of Kentucky and others in this State." By this act it was provided that any citizen of this State, who as a soldier or officer of the Confederate army, should, as part of an armed force, enter the State to make war upon it, should be punished by confinement in the penitentiary. "Making war upon the State," doubtless meant any attack made upon the "Federal soldiers assembled" (in the State) "for the purpose of preserving the tranquillity of the State." And it was farther enacted that, "any person who shall, within the limits of this State, persuade or induce any person to enlist or take service in the army of the so-called Confederate States, and the persons so persuaded or induced does enlist or take service in the same, shall be deemed guilty of a high misdemeanor and upon conviction, shall be fined in a sum not exceeding one thousand dollars, and imprisonment not exceeding six months." Whether, in passing this act, the Legislature of Kentucky was treating a question involving belligerent rights, is a matter for lawyers to pass upon; but that it was disgracing the State is patent. Such action might have been proper and competent—against both belligerents—had Kentucky adopted it as a measure necessary to the maintenance of her neutrality. It would have been, at least, dignified, had she earnestly and unequivocally declared, from the beginning, an adherence to the Government, and a resolution to support its policy.

But under all the circumstances, and after the repeated declarations of its authors that, to resist coercion, the very measures ought to be taken (for the punishment of which this act was now passed), it is difficult to stigmatize, with appropriate emphasis, such conduct.

The lapse of time has mitigated the hostility of the actual

combatants, but has only intensified the contempt, and deepened the distrust which the people of Kentucky feel for these men.

The sincere Union men of Kentucky, and the men who sincerely sympathized with the Southern movement and the Southern people, can mutually respect each other. The Kentucky soldiers, who fought against each other in the contending armies, can appreciate and admire the devotion to the chosen cause, the gallantry which each displayed. But for the men who showed so plainly by that they were attached to no cause and no principle, but were ready to sell and barter each and all, who manifested all through the struggle, that they were moved by the most groveling ambition, influenced by the meanest thirst for self-aggrandisement—for them there is no forgiveness.

All Kentucky has suffered from their duplicity, cowardice and heartless avarice of gold and power—now they have neither, and none regret it.

But, happily, the past political differences, and the animosity engendered by the long, bitter strife, are fast being forgotten by the Kentuckians who confronted each other under hostile banners. The sons of the same Mother Commonwealth (who in all sincerity gave their blood for her interests, safety and honor, as each believed they could be best conserved), are no longer antagonists—and, at no distant day, may find the respect they have felt for each other as foes, replaced by the cordial friendship and alliance, which the same blood and the same views should induce. May Kentucky have learned from her lesson in the past few years, and may she remember, that safety is never best consulted by giving heed to the suggestions of timidity, that the manliest and most consistent course, is also the most truly expedient, and that the interest and honor of a people go hand-in-hand, and are inseparable.

CHAPTER IV

When General Albert Sidney Johnson came to the command of the great Western Department, he found but a few thousand troops at his disposal to defend a territory of immense extent, and vulnerable at a hundred points.

At that time the Trans-Mississippi Confederate States were included in the same Department with the States of Tennessee, Alabama, and Mississippi. Missouri on the Western side of the Mississippi, and Kentucky on the Eastern—respectively the Northernmost of the Western and Middle Slaveholding States—were debatable ground, and were already occupied, the former by both, the latter by one of the contending forces.

General Johnson assumed command about the latter part of August, or first of September, 1861, and at once commenced his vast labor with a vigor and wisdom which were neither appreciated by his countrymen, nor were fruitful of happy results until after his glorious death. Missouri had become the theater of military operations some months previously. The people had partially responded to the proclamation of Governor Jackson, issued June 12, 1861, which called on them to resist the military authorities appointed in the State by President Lincoln.

Smarting under a sense of the aggressions and the insolence of these officials, believing that they were the victims of intolerable injustice and flagrant faithlessness, the Missouri rebels were eager to take the field, and irregular organizations, partisan, and "State-guard" were formed in various sections of the State. Several skirmishes, the most important of which were "Booneville" and "Carthage," occurred between these organizations and the Federal troops, before any troops regularly in the Confederate service were sent into the State. After winning the battle of "Carthage," and forcing Siegel to retreat until he affected a junction with Lyon, General Price was compelled, in his turn, to retreat before the then concentrated Federal army of Missouri.

On the 7th of August, Generals Price and McCullough, commanding respectively such portions of the Missouri State-guard as could be concentrated at that time, and the Confederate troops destined for service in the extreme West, making an aggregate, between them, of some six thousand effective men, established themselves in the vicinity of Springfield, a small town in Southwestern Missouri, confronting the Federal army which had pushed on to that point in pursuit of Price. On the 9th of August, the battle, called by the one side "Oak Hill," and by the other "Wilson's Creek," was fought. The Federal army made the attack, was repulsed and routed (with the exception of that portion of it commanded by Sturges, or protected by him in the retreat), and its commander, General Lyon, was killed. This victory laid open, and placed completely at the disposal of the Rebel commanders, the southwestern and middle portions of the State. Unhappily Generals Price and McCullough differed totally in opinion regarding the proper policy to be pursued after the battle, and the result of their disagreement was a separation of their forces. Price pushed forward into the interior of Missouri, where he believed that the fruits of the Victory just gained were to be gleaned. McCullough remained upon the Arkansas border. The campaign which General Price then made is well known. He captured Lexington, taking a large number of prisoners, and, what was much more valuable to him, a considerable quantity of military stores, many stand of small arms, and some artillery. He placed himself in a position to enable the scattered detachments of his State-guard to join him, and, encouraging the people, friendly to the South, by his bold advance into the heart of the State immediately after they had received the news of the victory he had helped to win, he obtained recruits and abundant supplies. He was subsequently compelled to retreat before a vastly superior force, but not until, taking into consideration the means at his disposal, he had accomplished wonders. Not only were his men perfectly raw, upon their first campaign, but no attempt was made to train or form them. Method, administration, discipline, drill, were utterly unknown in his camps; the officers knew only how to set a gallant example to their men; the men were rendered almost invincible by their native courage and the devotion they felt to their chief and their cause. Upon this campaign General Price exhibited, perhaps, more strikingly than ever afterward, his two great qualities as a commander—the faculty of acquiring the affection and implicit confidence of his men, and his own gallant and perfect reliance upon them. Without presuming to reflect upon General McCullough, who was a brave, honest, and zealous officer, it may be safely assumed that had Price, at this period, been backed by the force which McCullough commanded (much superior in equipment and organization to his own), he could have effected results which, in all probability, would have stamped a very different character upon the subsequent conduct of the war in the Trans-Mississippi States. The consequence of another such victory as that of "Oak Hill" gained in the heart of the State, as by their combined forces might very readily have been done, at the time when Price was forced to retreat, would have been of incalculable value to the Confederacy. But the fate, which throughout the contest, rendered Southern prowess unavailing, had already commenced to rule. At the date of the battle of "Oak Hill," General Hardee was advancing through Southeastern Missouri with about thirty-five hundred effective men.

His base was the little village of Pocahontas, situated, nearly upon the Missouri and Arkansas border, and at the head of navigation upon the Big Black river. Here General Hardee had collected all the Arkansas troops which were available for service upon that line, amounting to perhaps six or seven thousand men. Various causes contributed to reduce his effective total to about one half of that number. All of the troops were indifferently armed, some were entirely unarmed. The sickness always incidental to a first experience of camp life, in the infantry, had prostrated hundreds. Change of diet and of habits, and the monotony of the camp are sufficient of themselves, and rarely fail to induce diseases among raw troops, but a scourge broke out among the troops collected at Pocahontas which confounded all, at least of the non-medical observers. This was nothing more than measles, but in an intensely aggravated and very dangerous form. It was hard to believe that there was such a proportion of adult men who had escaped a malady generally thought one of the affections of childhood. It was so virulent, at the time and place of which I write, and in so many instances fatal, that many confidently believed it to be a different disease from the ordinary measles, although the Surgeons pronounced it the same. It was called "black measles," and was certainly a most malignant type of the disease. I have been since informed that it raged with equal fury and with the same characteristics among the volunteers just called into the field in many other localities. Its victims at Pocahontas were counted by the scores.

As the Big Black river is navigable for small craft at all seasons, General Hardee had no difficulty in supplying the troops stationed at Pocahontas, but after leaving that point he was compelled to depend for supplies upon wheel transportation, with which he was very indifferently provided, and upon the country, which was sterile and sparsely settled.

The only line of advance from Pocahontas which gave promise of important results, or which, indeed, was practicable, was by Greenville, distant some fifty-five or sixty miles from Pocahontas, and Frederickton, to Ironton, and thence along the Iron Mountain Railroad by the most practicable roads to St. Louis. The country between Pocahontas and Ironton is rugged and heavily wooded. It is penetrated by few roads, and, in 1861, by no means abounded in supplies. General Hardee advanced as far as Greenville, and threatened Ironton.

This latter place, the terminus of the Iron Mountain Railroad, is ninety-seven miles from St. Louis. It is a place of great natural strength, and was already, at the time that Hardee advanced toward it, partially fortified. General Hardee expected when he moved from Pocahontas to effect a junction with General Pillow at Frederickton, a small town to the east of north of Greenville, twenty miles from Ironton and on the line between that place and New Madrid. Pillow's force was six or eight thousand strong, and the best armed and accoutered of all the western Confederate commands.

General Pillow could very easily have reached Frederickton from New Madrid, as soon as Hardee could have gotten to the former place from Pocahontas, had there been a timely and definite understanding between them to that effect. And the united strength of the two Generals, with the addition of some two thousand of the State-guard, which were at hand under General Jeff. Thompson (as well armed and better organized than those which had already done such excellent service under Price), would have enabled them, most probably, to take Ironton. At any rate, by flanking and threatening to get between that place and St. Louis, they would certainly have compelled its evacuation, and then, either defeating the garrison in the open field, or driving it back in disorder and demoralization upon St. Louis, they would have become masters of the situation. They would have cut off and destroyed the defeated and routed army of Lyon, then in full flight for St. Louis.

General Price would have gladly embraced the opportunity of uniting with them—the whole State would have risen to join them. It is almost certain, when the number and condition of the Federal troops then in Missouri are taken into consideration, and the facts that but few troops were available from the neighboring States for the defense of St. Louis, and that the city was not fortified—it is almost positively certain, that St. Louis would have fallen into their hands, and that the entire State of Missouri, at least all South of the Missouri river, would have passed securely into their possession. At all events, General Hardee was extremely desirous of attempting just such a campaign.

It was deemed, however, more important, at that time, to occupy and fortify Columbus, in Kentucky, situated on the Mississippi river, some twenty-two miles below the mouth of the Ohio. This measure, it was thought, would protect the States lying along the Mississippi from invasion, by enabling the Confederates to hold the river, as it was by the river, only, that those States could be conveniently reached. General Pillow's forces were consequently ordered to that point. Finding that his plans were rendered impossible of execution, on account of the want of General Pillow's co-operation, Hardee returned to Pocahontas, and was shortly afterward transferred, with the greater portion of the troops under his command, to the eastern side of the river, and was ordered to Bowlinggreen as soon as that place was occupied. Up to the date of General Johnston's taking command, the chief difficulty in the way of action and decisive operations in the West (independently of the inferior number and miserable equipment of the troops) was the lack of uniformity and concert in the plans and operations of the various commanders. There was no one in supreme military control from whom the subordinate Generals could receive definite instructions, and orders which they felt obliged to obey. While an immense extent of country was included in one Department, and theoretically under one chief, yet practically every officer, no matter what was the strength or nature of his command, who happened not to be troubled with a senior immediately at his elbow, planned and acted for himself and with a perfect indifference to the operations of every one else. The President and Secretary of War were too distant to do any good, if such interference ever does any good, and a ruling mind was needed at the theater of events. It is true that General Polk, whose headquarters were at Memphis, was senior to the others, he being a Major-General, and all the rest but Brigadiers, and he was ostensibly in chief command and directed to a certain extent, the movements of all.

But, whether it was that, in a period when nothing was fairly organized, his authority was not clearly defined, or that he felt some hesitation in vigorously exercising it, it is certain that each of the Generals, who have been here mentioned, acted as if he knew himself to be, to all intents and purposes, in independent command.

This evil was completely remedied by the appointment to the chief command in the West of General Johnson, and the prompt and decided measures which he instituted. General Johnson's whole life had been one of the most thorough military training, and no officer of his years in the old army of the United States had seen more service; but more than that, he was a soldier by instinct, and Nature had intended him for military command.

He felt the full importance of careful preparation, and the establishment by order and system in every branch and department of the service. No martinet of the schools was ever more alive to the necessity of rigid method and exact discipline, for he knew that without their inauguration and strict observance, it would be impossible to even partially discharge the duties of his vast commission. But he also saw clearly the vital necessity of maintaining in tact the spirit which animated the men of his army, and which had summoned them into the field. He knew that to impair the ardor which had induced them to become soldiers was to destroy their morale; that to attempt to make them machines would result in making them worthless.

Although the troops at his disposal seriously needed instruction and more perfect organization, he did not waste precious moments in seeking to impart them then. He did not permit the high spirit of his gallant army to sink into lethargy, nor the interest which the people felt in the conduct of military affairs to abate by remaining inactive, and in a position which would reduce him, under all circumstances, to the defensive. A concentration of his forces any where upon the Tennessee border would not only have placed him at great strategic disadvantage, but would have been instantly accepted by the soldiery and the people as a signal of his intention to await the pleasure and movements of his adversary. Almost immediately after his arrival at Nashville, the troops which had collected at Camp Boone, the rendezvous of the Kentucky regiments, and the Tennessee troops which were available, were pushed into Kentucky. Kentucky's neutrality, for a time recognized provisionally, and so far as a discreet silence upon the subject amounted to recognition by the Federal Government, had already been exploded. The Government of the United States, having made the necessary preparations, was not disposed to abandon a line of invasion which led right to the vitals of the Confederacy, and promised a successful reduction of the rebellion in at least three of the seceded States, because of the partially rebellious attitude assumed by Kentucky.

Camp Dick Robinson had been organized and put into successful operation in July. General Anderson took command at Louisville on the 20th of September. The other portions of the state were occupied, and definite lines were established by the opposing forces, nearly about the same time. General Johnson advanced as far as Green river, making it his line of defense for his center, while his right rested on the Cumberland and the rugged ranges of its hills. His line might be said to extend from Columbus through Hopkinsville, Munfordsville and Somerset to the Virginia border somewhere in the vicinity of Pound Gap. The Federal forces were pushed down, almost simultaneously with General Johnson's advance to Green river, to Elizabethtown, and in a few days afterward to Nolin creek. Their line may be described as running almost directly from Paducah in the West, to Prestonburg in the East. This line gave them possession of the mouths of the Tennessee, Cumberland and Green rivers, of the Blue grass region, and of a greater share of the central and eastern portions of the State.

A single glance at the map will show the importance of Bowlinggreen as a strategic point. It will be seen that it is admirably adapted for a base of operations, offensive or defensive, in such a campaign as General Johnson was about to inaugurate at the time of its occupation. Situated upon the bank of the Barren river, it has that river and the Green river to protect it against attack from the front. The Barren river empties into the Green some twenty miles from and northwest of Bowlinggreen, and the Green flowing in a northwesterly direction, affords an admirable line of defense for many miles to the left. There are few fords and ferries of Green river after its junction with the Barren, and those which it has can be easily held. The danger of attack from the extreme left flank was guarded against, but as the result showed imperfectly, by Forts Henry and Donelson constructed respectively upon the Tennessee and Cumberland rivers. The one just upon, the other about ten miles from, the Kentucky and Tennessee border. As there was little danger to be apprehended in that direction, except from forces brought up those rivers and established in the rear of Bowlinggreen, these forts, whose strength was overrated, were thought to sufficiently protect that flank. The Cumberland river rising, in the mountains of Southeastern Kentucky, flows nearly due East and West and upon the same parallel of latitude on which Bowlinggreen is situated, until within sixty or seventy miles of that place, when it inclines to the Southwest. The Green river affords a line extending eastward, and defensible, beyond the point where the Cumberland begins to bend to the Southwest. At this point the two rivers are about thirty miles apart. The country throughout this section of the State is broken but accessible to the march of large bodies of troops. It is apparent, however, that an army, with Bowlinggreen for its base, unless immensely outnumbered, would have it in its power to take advantage of an opponent advancing upon Bowlinggreen by that route. Even if pressed in front, it could hold the river with detachments until with the bulk of its strength it struck the enemy coming from the East.

The line of march of the latter would render its communications, and concert of action with its friends, very difficult, and liable at any time to be entirely destroyed; while the General upon the defensive, if vigilant and active, could know the movements of both advancing columns, and attack either, with the mass of his army, when he pleased. Moreover, in the disposition of the Confederate forces, General Zollicoffer with some two or three thousand men, was stationed at Monticello, about ninety-five miles from Bowlinggreen, and a little to the south of east. Monticello is twenty-one miles from the Cumberland; all the neighboring fords were in Zollicoffer's possession, and his scouts explored the country for some distance beyond the river. It is plain that any hostile force moving upon Bowlinggreen by this eastern flank would have exposed itself to attack by Zollicoffer.

An army strong enough to hold all the approaches to Bowlinggreen might rest in perfect security regarding its communications. There is the railroad from Bowlinggreen to Clarksville, running through many important points, and affording communication with every thing upon that flank. Excellent roads run from Bowlinggreen to Monticello upon the south side of the Barren, affording secure communication with the right. Were both of these lines interrupted, there would remain means of certain and speedy communication with both flanks, in the railroad and turnpike running from Bowlinggreen to Nashville, the turnpike from Glasgow to Nashville, and the Cumberland river navigable to Fort Donelson on the one side and Burkesville on the other.

The country thus commanded is fertile, and almost exhaustless of supplies. The railroad from Bowlinggreen to Louisville, and the two turnpikes, respectively, from Bowlinggreen and from Glasgow to Louisville, and with which good roads running in every direction are connected, afford admirable facilities for offensive operations. These two turnpikes cross Green river within eight miles of each other, but an army, once on the north side of the river, and in possession of both roads, could march with perfect ease in any direction. It will scarcely be denied that if General Johnson had done nothing else to establish his high reputation as a strategist, his selection of this line would be enough to sustain it. In this advance into Kentucky, the Kentucky regiments under Buckner, about thirteen hundred strong in all, took the lead; the 2nd Kentucky infantry under Colonel Roger W. Hanson, to which were temporarily attached Byrne's battery of four pieces, and one company of Tennessee cavalry, was pushed on to Munfordsville on Green river. The rest of the Kentuckians and two or three thousand Tennesseeans (and some odds and ends) were stopped at Bowlinggreen.

All the cavalry which were available for that purpose, were sent to scout the country between the Cumberland and Green rivers, and subsequently Forrest's regiment was stationed at Hopkinsville, watching the country in that vicinity. Shortly after he was sent there, Forrest attacked and defeated at Sacramento, a little village not far from Hopkinsville, a regiment of Federal cavalry. This was the first cavalry fight in the west, and the Federals were completely routed.

Zollicoffer was sent to take position at Monticello, as has been described before, at or nearly about the same time of the advance to Bowlinggreen. Thus, it will be seen, that all the important points of the line were almost simultaneously occupied.

Columbus was occupied by General Polk, as has been stated, on the 4th, some days earlier.

It was generally believed that General Buckner, who, as has been already stated, led the van, would have had no difficulty in capturing Louisville had he pressed on. Very little doubt was entertained, then, of the adequacy of his command, small as it was, to have taken the place, and, I presume, no one doubts it now. An impression prevailed that General Buckner was strongly in favor of continuing his advance to Louisville, and that he urgently solicited permission to do so. But whether it was suggested or not, it found no favor with General Johnson. A plan to take and hold Louisville, without any provision for the occupation of other portions of Kentucky up to the Ohio river, would have been, to say the least, a very rash one, and at that time captures with a view only to temporary occupation were not in fashion. To hold the State, an army would have been required numerous enough to furnish strong garrisons for Paducah and Smithland, at the mouths of the Tennessee and Cumberland rivers, for the protection of the mouth of Green river for Carrollton, at the mouth of Kentucky river, for Louisville, Covington, and other points farther eastward. General Johnson could not have held

Kentucky two months after he had occupied her northern territory (if he had taken possession of it) with the forces which he had at his disposal. He would either have had to establish the garrisons, which have been indicated, and provide the supporting force, or he would have been compelled to adopt another plan, perhaps more advisable, viz: to have organized three separate corps, one for the western, one for the middle, and the third for the eastern portion of the State, each charged with the defense of a certain length of river line, and so disposed as to be readily concentrated, at short notice, at any point upon it.

To properly carry into effect either plan, many more troops would have been required than General Johnson had—it would have been folly to have attempted either with his handful of men.

Another line in advance of that of the Green river, might have been taken, which would have secured additional and very valuable territory. General Johnson might have established one half of his army at Muldraugh's Hill, thirty miles from Louisville, and upon the Louisville and Nashville railroad, and the other half in the country about Lexington and Frankfort, and have thus obtained possession of the greater part of central Kentucky, and the Blue-grass region. The country between the point indicated upon the Louisville and Nashville railroad, and Frankfort, and also in front of the line thus drawn, is extremely rugged and difficult of access The hills of Salt river, the Benson and Chaplin Hills, and those of the Kentucky, present a barrier not easily forced. Directly in front, too, of Frankfort and Lexington, at a distance of from twenty to forty miles stretches a belt of broken and defensible ground from the Kentucky to the main fork of the Licking river, and on to the eastward.

A thorough tearing-up of the Louisville and Nashville railroad, which would deprive the enemy of the use of the Bardstown and Lebanon junctions, and the destruction of the Lexington and Louisville, and Lexington and Covington railroads, would have rendered this line secure against any attack from the front, while the excellent roads traversing the region lying just south of it, would have made communication easy between the salient positions. But the left flank and the main line of retreat and of communication with Nashville, would have been constantly and dangerously exposed.

These were all matters for a military chief to study; but far above all mere strategic considerations, was the moral effect of these movements, and that, it is certain, had been profoundly pondered by General Johnson. The idea of an advance to the Ohio, of occupying the entire slaveholding territory east of the Mississippi, of subsidizing all of its resources, of arousing and recruiting from its whole population, was very fascinating then, and opens a wide field for speculation now. But then there was the reverse of the picture to be considered. The unsettled, bewildered condition of the Kentucky mind, has already been described. There were many who confidently predicted that the Kentuckians would flock to the Confederate standard as soon as it waved upon the banks of the Ohio, and innumerable bitter objurgations were launched against them, because so few resorted to it when it was planted upon the bluffs of Green river.

The patriotism which inspired, alike, the prophesies and the curses, can not be called in question. But Albert Sidney Johnson, while he felt the enthusiasm which was the concomitant of his perfect courage and high military genius, had trained himself to coolly examine, and carefully calculate every influence which could affect his plans. He had studied, and, I believe, he rightly estimated the popular feeling.

Revolutions may be inaugurated and accomplished by the unsworn, unarmed, unorganized masses; wars, once fairly commenced, must be won by soldiers. An entire population is frequently ripe for revolution, only a portion of it is available for, and will enlist for, war. Even had the most favorable accounts of the unanimity of the people of Kentucky, and their devotion to the Southern cause, reached General Johnson from credible sources, he would have been justified in still doubting that he would derive immediate benefit from it. There are no braver men than the Tennesseeans, they were then practically unanimous, except in the eastern portion of the State, they were very ardent, and yet the Tennesseeans took their time in flocking to the Confederate standard.

The gallantry and patriotism of the Mississippians are as bright as the light of day; and yet, in September, 1861, thousands of young Mississippians who afterward bled for the cause, were at home dealing out fiery denunciations against slaveholding States which would not secede. The same history is true of every other seceding State—States, unlike Kentucky, already embarked in and committed to the war. It was not because the men of these States lacked purpose—throngs of them who stayed at home until the news of our first disasters came, then enlisted, and fought and died with the quenchless valor which had descended to them from unconquered sires, and was traditional in a race which had believed itself invincible. It was because they knew little of war at all, and were utterly ignorant of the kind of war that was coming. The mighty conviction had not yet forced itself upon them. It is true that the Confederate Government had refused regiments raised and tendered by these States some time previously. Unable to arm them, it dismissed them, instead of placing them in camps of instruction until arms could be procured.

If, among the many errors which have been attributed to the great patriot, hero and statesman who was at the head of that Government, there was one really grave and fatal in its consequences, it was that he himself failed to appreciate the danger, failed to comprehend the magnitude of the struggle when it began, and failed therefore to arouse his people to an early and tremendous exertion, which might have triumphed. The absolute confidence of the Government blinded the people, and its policy tended rather to quiet, than to excite their enthusiasm. But whatever may have been the causes, it was for General Johnson to consider the effect. If, after the war had lasted four months, his immense department, composed of seceded States, could furnish him only six thousand troops, when he advanced to Bowlinggreen, with what show of reason could he count on obtaining from Kentucky—Kentucky that had not yet seceded, that was divided, distracted by conflicting opinions—the vast concourse of recruits, which so many professed to expect her to furnish, and which she was so indignantly denounced for not furnishing?

Could General Johnson have occupied Northern Kentucky without opposition, and have held it undisturbed for some months, it is highly probable that all dissensions would have been allayed, that the revolutionary fever would have spread through Kentucky (perhaps it might even have been propagated north of the Ohio), and thousands of Kentuckians would have joined the Confederate army, many of whom were subsequently its most formidable foes. But it must be remembered that the Federal Government had not been idle, that the North was on fire with the war spirit, that a host of sturdy volunteers had been gathered and organized for the special purpose of holding Kentucky, that, with the abundant means at its command, the Federal Government had already efficiently armed its soldiers, and provided all that was necessary for active and immediate service.

In forty-eight hours after Louisville had fallen, certainly before he could have brought up the forces to dispute its entrance at any point, an army from the North, vastly stronger than General Johnson's, could have been thrown into Kentucky. Could General Johnson have defeated this army? If defeated himself in such a situation, what would have been the consequences, not only to his hopes of revolutionizing Kentucky, not only to the army immediately under his command, but to the Confederate cause in the West? Would he, then, have been warranted in risking so much upon this throw? If General Johnson had been constrained to fight at once, and had been driven back, he would have sustained a disaster, perhaps fatal. The effect it would have had in Kentucky can easily be understood, and it would have had some and not a very cheering effect in more Southern latitudes. The patriotism and integrity of the mass of the people is undeniable, but for all that, "there is a great deal of human nature in man." Success is the most eloquent of arguments. He who appeals to the suffrages of an enlightened community after a victory will be better received then he who canvasses after a defeat. Again (it is a truth that will bear repetition) in revolutions, popular convulsions, political agitations—a method may be safely attempted which will be hazardous and of doubtful policy after actual war has commenced. In the former periods, enthusiasm runs higher, patriotism is more reckless and demonstrative than when the bayonets are about. The danger then is distant, and with the majority of men, when a general excitement is prevailing, the remote danger excites no fear. Many a patriot is willing to be Brigadier General of the peaceful militia, and to devote himself to a cause, from the stump, who would feel a strong and very natural reluctance to leave home, wife, children and property, to accept the hardships of a soldier's life, and be shot at whenever his officers feel enterprising.

If the sentiment of the people be not unanimous and very decided, the secret of success in revolutions is to captivate the popular fancy, give the first direction to the popular current. It is a struggle between the leaders, and the most audacious, not to say the least scrupulous, are apt to win.

It is unsafe, in such periods, to rely surely upon any sort of action from the people—it would be the mistake of supposing that every man, unshaken by any influence, had made up his mind, and knew what he was going to do, and that the majority by some instinct, would be immediately obeyed. A brave, honest, intelligent people will be likely, once convinced and committed, to abide gallantly by their decision. If their education has been wholesome, and their traditions unique, they will be stimulated by ordinary perils and disasters to increased energy and exertions.

But whether the revolutionary fermentation be in process, or the stand has been taken—it is easier to induce the masses of a people to vote for resolutions than to become soldiers.

It doubtless would have proven a successful policy, to have pushed Buckner instantly to Louisville, and Zollicoffer to Lexington, to stay as long as they were safe, and return with the recruits and the supplies that they could have collected, leaving behind them the positive assurance that the country was not inaccessible to Confederate troops. But to have taken the army into Northern Kentucky, upon the supposition that the unarmed population would arise and enable it to remain there—in the face of the threatening dangers and the almost positive certainty of instant battle—would have been a blind, unreasoning daring, which had no place among the qualities of General Johnson. The wisdom and prescience of the great commander were afterward so abundantly demonstrated, that we may be pardoned for believing his judgment right in this instance also.

In establishing his base at Bowlinggreen, he secured, as has been shown, a line well adapted to enable him to assume the offensive so soon as his army was sufficiently strong to do so with effect. The very fact of his moving into Kentucky at all was a pledge and guarantee to the people of his department, that, if sustained by them, he would keep the war out of their territory, and encouraged his army to hope for an active, dashing campaign. He placed himself where the more enterprising and determined of the Kentucky rebels could join him, and he spared no effort, no appeal, which could stimulate enlistment in his army among the young men of Kentucky, or of the States of his department.

That his appeals were neglected was not only his, but the Confederacy's deadly misfortune. Numerical weakness frustrated in September 1861, his plan to appear before the people, not only of Northern Kentucky, but of the Northwestern States, as the victor of a decisive battle, and, in the following February, forced him to retreat from Kentucky altogether. The first and most golden opportunity was lost; and the future history of the war in the West, was a series of terrible reverses to the Confederate arms, or of victories brilliant indeed, but, in the end, fruitless.

The condition of the Confederate troops was far better, in many respects, at this time, than at any subsequent period of the war.

There were, then, facilities and means for providing them with necessaries and comforts which more latterly did not exist. Provisions were abundant everywhere, and were regularly supplied.

The railroads, which were then, all in good repair and well provided with rolling stock, afforded sure means of supplying the troops which were stationed in those parts of the country through which they ran. The numerous navigable streams also afforded facilities, and practically shortened the routes of supply.

In all cases, however, in which neither the railways nor the rivers could be used to supply them, troops were compelled to depend for subsistence, in a great measure, upon the country immediately about their cantonments, and as they exhausted the surplus provisions in different neighborhoods, they would shift their encampments. This was owing to the great lack of wheel transportation. It was very difficult to procure wagons, except by purchase or impressment from the citizens, and those so gotten were of course inferior. Much less inconvenience was subsequently experienced on this score, after they began to be manufactured in the Confederate and were captured in great numbers from the enemy. At this time, many articles such as sugar, coffee, etc., indispensable to the comfort and conducive to the health of troops in the field, were plentifully furnished—after the first year of the war they were known among us only by camp-fire traditions. The men rarely suffered, then, from the want of clothing, blankets, shoes, etc., even when the quartermasters could not furnish them, for they could obtain them from home, or purchase them, wherever they happened to be quartered, at reasonable prices. There was, perhaps, no regiment in the army which had not its full complement of tents; they were manufactured at Memphis, and other points, in numbers adequate to the wants of all the troops.

Cooking utensils, also, could be had in abundance—the marching commands suffered, not from the want of them, but from the lack of transportation for them. It is true that those which were furnished us were not of the kind and pattern which experience has prescribed as most fitting for military use, but they were capital substitutes for flat stones and forked twigs.

In the medical department there was an almost total lack of the necessary material. The supply of medicines in the South at the outbreak of the war was barely sufficient for the wants of the population at that time. Some medicines were run through the blockade from the North, in small quantities, during the spring and summer of 1861. But the supply thus obtained by no means met the demand. The volunteers collected together in camps and crowded cantonments, subjected to a sudden change of diet and mode of living, sickened in great numbers. Diseases which had never before, or but in rare instances, proven dangerous, now assumed alarming types. The systems of the patients may have been relaxed and their vitality partially impaired, during the early period of camp life, when they were just foregoing their old habits and were not yet hardened to the new, or it may be that when men are congregated in great numbers, certain diseases, by transmission from one to another, may be cultivated into extraordinary malignancy—at any rate a large proportion of the inmates of every camp sickened and many died. At Bowlinggreen in the winter of 1861 and 1862, the mortality was dreadful, measles, typhoid fever, pneumonia and diseases of the bowels, carried off a host of victims—every sickness, however, seemed fatal at that time.

There was, consequently, a great and constantly increasing need of medicines; and, perhaps, some waste of them, when they were collected in large quantities and shipped from point to point, was unavoidable. But all these problems, all the difficulties of properly supplying the army, began to be solved and modified, as the genius of adaptation and substitution was developed among the troops themselves. If a man could not get a blanket, he made an old carpet, cut to the proper size and lined on one side with a piece of strong cotton cloth, serve him instead. The soldier who lacked shoes bid defiance to the rough roads, or the weather, in a pair of ox-hide buskins, or with complicated wrappings of rags about his feet. I have known more than one orderly sergeant make out his morning report upon a shingle, and the surgeon who lacked a tourniquet used a twisted handkerchief. Of the most necessary military material, arms and ordnance stores, there was the greatest scarcity. Perhaps one half of the entire western army (of all the troops in the department) were armed (at the time that General Johnson came) with shot-guns and squirrel rifles, and the majority of the other half with scarcely as serviceable flint-lock muskets.

The troops under General Bragg at Pensacola were perhaps better armed, but the rule held good with regard to the others. A few companies composed of young men from the cities, and of rich planters, were armed with fancy guns, Maynard rifles, etc., altogether unsuitable for the armament of infantry. In September of 1861, there were probably not one thousand Springfield and Enfield rifles in the army which General Johnson was trying to concentrate in Kentucky, and it was several months later before these unequaled weapons (the right arms for soldiers who mean to fight) could be supplied in numbers at all adequate to the need of them. In the advance to Bowlinggreen, more than three hundred able-bodied men of the Second Kentucky, and an equal, if not greater number of the Third Kentucky were left in the rear because arms could not be gotten for them. In November one or two regiments of the Kentucky brigade were given the Belgian in place of the flint-lock musket, and in December flint-lock guns, altered to percussion locks, were given the other regiments of the brigade. Proper accouterments were as scarce as guns. Cartridge-boxes, knapsacks, canteens, when they could be gotten at all, were very inferior. By great industry and effort, a considerable quantity of ammunition had been prepared and worked up into cartridges, but there was such a scarcity of lead and powder in the South, and such inferior facilities for the manufacture of the latter, that apprehension was felt lest, when the supply on hand was exhausted, it could not be replaced.

There was scarcely a percussion cap to be had (in the early part of the war) in the department, with the exception of some that were manufactured by an enterprising citizen of Nashville, and zealous Confederate, Mr. S.D. Morgan, an uncle of the General. But while so few of the Confederate soldiers were efficiently armed, almost every man of them, presuming that the Yankees were to be whipped in rough and tumble style, had his bowie-knife and revolver. The Arkansas and Texas troops, especially, carried enormous knives, that might have made a Malay's blood run cold, but in the end those huge weapons did duty far oftener as cleavers than as bayonets. The organization of the troops first put in the field was, of course, to some extent, imperfect. A good deal has been said about the evils of the system of electing officers, and much just censure has been passed upon it. It has been claimed that it gives rise to a laxity of discipline, and a disposition on the part of officers, who owe their positions to the suffrages of the men they command, to wink at irregularities and pardon gross neglect of duty.

This is undoubtedly true, in a great measure, and what is stranger, but equally as true, is the fact that troops which have been longest in the service, which know best what qualities are necessary to constitute a good officer, which appreciate perfectly the necessity of having good officers, not only to their efficiency and success in the field, but to their well-being at all times—just such troops seem least able to resist the temptation of electing some good-natured fellow, whom they will never respect, and will, perhaps, grow ashamed of, rather than men who will enforce their obedience, but promote alike their efficiency and their comfort. At all times they will look to and rely upon the good officer, but when they come to elect, the love of doing as they please, unchecked by the irksome restraints of discipline, is apt to make them vote for the man who will indulge them. But I believe that all those who observed these matters carefully will agree, that there was far less of this sort of feeling among the men who volunteered at the outbreak of the war than there was later.

The officers elected by the regiments first raised were, generally, about the best men that could have been selected. The men, at that time, in good faith, chose those they believed best qualified for the duties of command, and elected individuals who had manifested, or were thought to possess, courage, energy, and good sense. Of course some mistakes were made, and experience disclosed the fact, now well-established, that many men who figured respectably in times of peace, are unfitted for military responsibility, and weaken in the ordeal of military life.

No opportunity had been afforded then, for testing and discovering those qualified for positions of trust and importance—it was all a matter of experiment. Many injudicious selections were made, but it quite as often happened that the appointing system (as it was exercised at the beginning of the war) gave incompetent officers to the army. The graduates of West Point themselves, and even those officers who had served for years in the "Old Army," knew little or nothing of actual war. Their studies at the academy, and the reading appropriate to their profession, had instructed them in the theory of war.

They had the knowledge which the routine of camp and garrison duty teaches. Most of them had seen service in expeditions against the Indians on the Western plains. Some of them had served with distinction and benefit to themselves in Mexico, but this was an experience which they shared with many civilians. They had soldierly habits. They were well acquainted with, and knew the importance of the military etiquette and ceremonial so conducive to proper subordination and discipline, and without which neither can be maintained in an army. But beyond the necessity (permanently impressed upon them, and rendered a constant influence with them by long training and habit) of strictly obeying all the rules of discipline themselves, and of exacting the same obedience from others, they knew nothing which a quick mind, if endowed with a natural military aptitude and appreciation of military essentials, can not readily acquire. While the regulations prescribed clear and excellent rules of organization, the strictest conformity was not always had to them, and it was sometimes difficult to strictly apply them. Companies sometimes overran the maximum in a way that rendered them as embarrassing to the regiments in which they were placed, as they were painfully unwieldy to the unlearned Captains and Lieutenants who immediately commanded them.

When it was known that a very popular man was recruiting, the number of enlistments in his company was limited only by the number of able bodied men in his district who were inclined to enlist. As each volunteer had the right to select his Captain and company, and generally objected very decidedly to being transferred to any other, it was a delicate and difficult task to reduce these over-grown companies to proper proportions. Regiments frequently, on account of the popularity of their Colonels, or from other causes, swelled out of due bounds also. I knew one regiment, which in the early part of September, 1861, had in it seventeen companies and numbered, when all answered to roll call, more than two thousand men. There was at this time a very favorite, and very anomalous organization, known as the "Legion," which fortunately in a few months entirely disappeared. It was something between a regiment and a brigade, with all of a hybrid's vague awkwardness of conformation. It was the general supposition, too, for little was ever definitely known about it, that it was to be somewhat of an independent corps, something like the "Partisan Ranger" regiment of later date. When the army was in the first process of organization, these "Legions" could be heard of everywhere.

The idea doubtless originated with some officer who felt that he deserved a higher grade than that of Colonel, and could not obtain a Brigadier's commission.

As organization went on, and system prevailed, the "Legions," perhaps according to the merit of their commanders, or their numerical strength, sank into companies, were regularly organized as regiments, or were elevated into brigades. The brigades were from three to seven or eight thousand strong, and all arms of the service were represented in them; they included regiments of infantry and cavalry and batteries of artillery. It was in a measure necessary that this organization should be adopted, from the fact that for some months, each brigade commander was entrusted with supervision and defense of a large tract of territory, and it was impossible to dispense with either of the three arms. Divisions were not organized until late in the fall of 1861—the strength of the brigades was then, to some extent, equalized by the reduction of the larger ones; Army Corps were of still later creation.

A significant custom prevailed of denoting the companies of the first regiments which were raised, not by letter, but by some company denomination which they had borne in the militia organization, or had assumed as soon as mustered as an indispensable *nom-de-guerre*. They seemed to vie with each other in inventing titles of thrilling interest: "The Yellow Jackets," "The Dead Shots," "The Earthquakes," "The Chickasaha Desperadoes," "The Hell-roarers," are a few which made the newspapers of that day, in recording their movements, read like the pages of popular romance. So fondly did the professors of these appellations cling to them, that it was found almost as difficult to compel their exchange for the proper designations, as to effect far more harassing and laborious reforms. The spirit which prompted these particular organizations to adopt this method of distinguishing and identifying themselves, remained to the last characteristic of the Southern troops. Regiments, especially in the cavalry service, were quite as often styled by the names of their commanders, as by the numbers which they properly bore, and, if the commanders were popular, the former method was always the most agreeable.

In the latter part of the war, after every effort had been made to do away with this feeling, it was at length adjudged expedient to enjoin such a designation of brigades, by the names of their commanders, by order from the War Department. This peculiar affectation was but one form in which the temper of the Southern people was manifested—a temper which revolted against complete loss of individuality, and was prone to self-assertion. It is a temper which ought to be characteristic of a free and high spirited people, which, while for prudential reasons it will consent to severe restraints, seeks to mark the fact that the restraint is self-imposed. Few will doubt, upon reflection, that this feeling could have been turned to better account in the Southern army; that to have allowed commands to win distinctive and honorable appellations by extraordinary bravery would have elevated the standard of *morale*, as much as did promotion for personal gallantry and good conduct. The excellence of a command mentioned in general orders might be only partially known, but the fame conferred by the title of the "Stonewall Brigade" is universal. For the first year, there was, in the true sense of the word, no discipline in the Western army at all. The good sense and strong feeling of duty which pervaded the entire soldiery made them obedient, zealous, and tolerably patient. High courage and natural resolution made them fight well from the first, and, long exposure to the storms of battle taught them coolness in the midst of danger, and the comparative indifference to it, which become habitual with the veteran, and which are usually confounded with the effects of discipline, although they frequently exist where discipline has never obtained. A spirit of emulation induced them to readily learn the drill and all the more ostentatious duties of the soldier. A fortitude which, until they were put to the test, they were not themselves aware of, enabled them to endure without diminution of spirit, great hardship and privation. Pride and patriotism, in the midst of every suffering and temptation, kept them true and patient to the last. While all these influences combined to make excellent soldiers of the material of which that army was composed, it will be nearer the truth to say, that there was, in the true sense of the word, no discipline in the Western army, not only in the first year of the war, but at any time during the War. The rigid method introduced by General Bragg undoubtedly told with good effect upon the men of least pride and mettle, and kept all such men nearer the mark, but for the rest, Bragg's discipline improved the army rather by its operations upon the officers than upon the men.

No man who has intimately known the Southern soldiery can escape the conviction, that, while capable of acquiring any degree of instruction, and, if the word may be used, *veteranship*, they can not really be disciplined, that is, be converted, by the infliction and fear of punishment, into unreasoning machines. If there were no other proof of this, the reflection which was invariably shed upon the *morale* and tone of every command by the personal character, prowess and skill of its particular leader, would be sufficient proof of it, and the fact that the Southern troops almost always read their chances of success or defeat, not in the odds opposed to them, but in the reputation and character of their commander–it would be as wide of the truth to call this discipline, as it would be to speak of the perfect discipline of the Norman knights, who would insult a cowardly and indolent Prince upon his throne, and would, yet, obey with "proud humility" an heroic adventurer.

While no practical soldier will underrate the value of discipline and the marvels it works–still the experience of the late war will make many officers believe that it is no match for native intelligence, zeal, and pride–when those qualities have become trained and used to the requirements of war. Instruction and skill in military duties, are indispensable, although discipline is not always so. Give the high strung young soldier who has brains and good blood, some practice and knowledge of actual warfare, and the unthinking automaton, formed by routine and punishment, can no more stand before him than a tree can resist the stroke of the lightning, than the book general and paper tactician can resist the genius which throws his plans out of gear, and his mind into convulsions.

It will be well for those who read Southern histories of the war to keep in mind that the writers mean, when they use the word "discipline," the pride which stimulated the soldiers to learn their duties rather than incur disgrace, and the subordination which proceeded from self respect, and respect for an officer whom they thought worthy to command them. It was not the fault of the Southern men who took the field, that the efforts of the Southern people failed to establish, for themselves, a separate and independent Government.

Two great mistakes were made at the outset and were never retrieved. Mistakes which have lost battles and campaigns innumerable, and in this instance lost a war. The vigor and irresistible audacity which is gained by "taking the start" was lost to us by the defensive policy, and our troops were scattered so widely that even an energetic defense could nowhere be made, except in Virginia. The Government did not mass the troops for attack upon vulnerable points in the enemy's territory, nor to fall upon some one of his invading columns. Not only was the defensive strictly maintained, but an effort was made to defend every inch of the border. In the face of superior forces concentrating for invasion at certain points, a skirmish line, which employed all of our forces, was thrown out to hold all points from Richmond to the Western prairies.

But one original and cardinal error gave birth to all the others. The Confederate Government failed to invoke the only spirit which could have done its bidding. It ought, with out delay, to have stimulated the ardor and turned loose the tremendous energies of revolution, and have made the people drunken with its inspiration. The time was propitious, the Government was just established and was popular, the people were, practically, unanimous, and were irretrievably committed to the movement—they had never seen hostile troops or been daunted by the sights of war. The presence of formidable armed foes might have aroused prudence, but when Sumpter fell and war became inevitable, there were no armies in the field on either side. When the first gun boomed, the Government ought to have taken advantage of the glow of enthusiasm which was as yet unchilled by any fear of the yet distant danger. It ought to have asked for powers which the people in their, then, thorough confidence in their leaders would have readily granted. They felt, that if the struggle was really for important principles and vital rights, it was better to make rulers of their own choice, omnipotent for a short time, than to run the risk of defeat which would cause them entire, and, perhaps eternal, loss of liberty. The leaders knew that the temper of the people could be relied on—that if frankly told that success could be achieved only by prompt and enormous efforts and sacrifices—the efforts and sacrifices would be made. They were made later, when instead of universal hope and enthusiasm, there prevailed a feeling of almost despair. The strategy of revolution is identical, in principle, with that of war—the side which masses and marches fast wins. If, while it was yet a contest of peoples and not yet a conflict of armies, the entire white population of the South had been aroused, her territory converted into one vast camp, every male citizen between the ages of sixteen and sixty made a soldier, leaving to the President the power of exempting certain classes, and not regulating by law a matter so essentially discretionary, and every dollar's worth of property had been pledged to the cause, how different might have been the result? All this could have been done in the then condition of public sentiment; not a dissentient voice would have been heard. It would have been far more popular than the "Conscript Act" was a year later, and that caused little complaint.

Let any man think of what might have been done in May, 1861, with all the men, which were subsequently in the Confederate army, arrayed and pressed on the front. If unarmed, they would have met opponents also unarmed. Men followed the armies in Missouri and picked up guns on the battle field, while the Government was rejecting regiments because it had not arms to give them. Subsequently it found arms easier to be gotten than men.

If Jefferson Davis had possessed one tithe of the unscrupulous ambition of which he has been accused, he would not now be the inmate of a prison. He could have made, with all ease his Government a dictatorate—or turning off the useless and clamorous Congress, as an incumbrance to a Government which (until the war was won) was an experiment, have ruled during the war with a "committee of public safety."

To excite the energies of the people to the utmost, and then direct and employ them by means of some such machinery, was the way to win. But he preferred to believe that the danger was not great. He would have died sooner than assume unconstitutional power. The ardor of the people was rebuffed, and they sank into an apathy, from which they were awakened by terrible disasters, to find themselves encompassed by fierce and hostile armies.

CHAPTER V

In 1857, the company of volunteer militia called the "Lexington Rifles" was organized with John H. Morgan as Captain, it subsequently, upon the organization of the State-guard, became incorporated in that body. It was composed of the finest and most spirited young men of Lexington, and soon won a high reputation for proficiency in drill, and in all the duties taught in the camps of the State-guards, as well as for the intelligence and daring of its members.

From the hour of its organization the men of this company seemed to entertain the profoundest love and admiration for their Captain, and the influence and control they accorded him was not too strongly expressed in the words of their motto, which, written in large letters, framed and hung up in their armory, caught the eye of every visitor and announced, "Our laws the commands of our Captain."

It was with the forty-five or fifty men of this company who unhesitating followed his fortunes when he went to the Southern army, and a few other kindred spirits who immediately attached themselves to him, before he had won rank or fame, that Morgan began his career, and around them as a nucleus he gathered his gallant command. Although thoroughly Southern in sentiment, and frank to the last degree in its expression, the members of the company, with one or two exceptions, made no effort to go South until Captain Morgan signified his readiness to lead them, in this, as in all else, they awaited his decision and directions. The extreme illness of his wife, who died in July, 1861, required, during the early summer, his constant presence in Lexington, and he did not determine to act until after the troops, posted at Camp Dick Robinson and the Home guard organizations, began to give unmistakable evidences of hostility to all persons not "loyal."

When the order was issued for the disarming of the State-guard, Morgan determined to save his guns at all hazards. The State-guard was by this time virtually disbanded, many of its officers of high rank, elected under the impression that they were Southern men, had declared for the other side, and various other influences tended to cripple and demoralize it. An officer then, of that body, who decided to resist the edict, disarming his men and leaving them defenseless, in the reach of armed and bitter political opponents, could look for little backing from his comrades. His best chance was to make his way at once to the Confederate lines in Southern Kentucky. This Morgan resolved to do.

On Friday night, September 20, 1861, he confided to a few of his most reliable and trusted men his determination and plans, and taking the guns from the armory, loaded them into two wagons and started them out of Lexington on the Versailles road under a small guard. The men composing this guard left on such short notice that few of them had time to prepare and carry with them even necessary clothing, scarcely time to take leave of their families. They marched out of town with their cartridge-boxes belted on, their rifles on their shoulders, loaded, and their bayonets fixed. A regiment of Federal troops was encamped that night at the fair ground, about a mile from town, and many of the officers and men were in town at the time the guns were removed. In order to deceive as to his movements and lull any suspicion that might exist of his design to move the guns, Captain Morgan caused twelve or fifteen men to parade and tramp heavily about the armory for an hour or two after the wagons had been loaded and started, and so created the impression that his company was engaged in drilling.

The wagons were not stopped in the town, and only one soldier was encountered who was made prisoner by the escort, carried off some twenty miles, and then released.

Morgan accompanied the wagons for a short distance until it was apparent that there was no immediate danger to be apprehended, and returned to Lexington.

On the next day when it was ascertained that the guns had been taken away, and no trace of them could be discovered, a great excitement was gotten up. That very day had been appointed for their seizure by the authorities, and the authorities had been completely tricked and baffled.

The loyal citizens who had calculated upon witnessing the discomfiture of the "Rifles," and of all their backers, were disappointed, and had the farther mortification of learning that the wagons containing the coveted prizes had passed the night before, in the sight of them all, to a place where they dared not follow. Of course many taunts were flung at the fooled spies, and disappointed patriots; and at length the angry discussions brought on a shooting affray between some of the "Rifles," and a part of the troops and Home-guards. The regiment stationed at the fair grounds, was brought into town to quell this affair, and two pieces of artillery were planted to sweep the principal streets—and from that date, for four years, Lexington was under military rule.

Captain Morgan, for whose arrest an order was immediately issued, communicated during the day with such of his men as desired to follow him, and at nightfall left Lexington with them and rejoined those who had gone before. He passed through Anderson county to Nelson, and halted a few miles from Bardstown. Here he was joined by Captain John Cripps Wickliffe, subsequently Lieutenant Colonel of the Ninth Kentucky Infantry, and a very gallant officer. Captain Wickliffe had determined also to save his guns and take his company, or all that would follow him, to the Confederate army. The greater portion of his company, one of the finest in the State-guards, elected to go with him. Desirous, while about it, of doing a brisk business in guns, he confiscated those of a neighboring Home-guard company, and brought them to Morgan's camp—they were immediately placed in the hands of the unarmed men, who, finding an organized force making for the Confederate lines, attached themselves to it. Many such men, anxious to go South, but afraid to go without a leader, came to this camp during the four or five days that it was maintained.

On account of the kindness and liberality of the people who lived in that neighborhood, and who supplied its inmates with provisions of all kinds, this camp was entitled "Camp Charity," and long will it be remembered.

By the common wish and consent, Morgan took command of all the forces, and when, on Saturday evening, September 28th, he resumed his march, he was at the head of some two hundred men. He encountered no enemy. The Home-guards, who mustered strong in the region through which he passed, thought his force too formidable to attack and kept out of his path. When he would hear of two bodies of them, likely to give him trouble if united, he would pass between them and scare both.

After two days and nights hard marching, he reached Green river on Monday evening, September 30th. He received an enthusiastic welcome from the Confederate troops stationed there, most of whom were Kentuckians, and many of them knew him well.

Colonel Roger W. Hanson, the officer in command, was himself from Lexington, and was a warm personal friend of Morgan.

There were, at Green river, encamped on the Southern side of the stream, at this date, the Second Kentucky Infantry (Hanson's own regiment), six or seven hundred strong, Byrne's Battery, and four companies of Tennessee cavalry.

Colonel Thomas Hunt, an uncle of Captain Morgan, was also there with two companies of the regiment he was then organizing. Of all the general officers (he was made a General) which Kentucky gave to the Confederate service, least justice had been done by fame to Roger Hanson, and it is strange that such should be the case. Not only was he well known, constantly talked of, greatly loved, and ardently admired by the Kentuckians, but his name was familiar in all parts of the army. It is true that his early death blighted the reputation he was rapidly winning, but it is hard for those who knew him to understand how such a man could have failed to attract more general and more lively interest. While a very young man, he served with distinction in Mexico, returning home he indulged for a short period in an *erratic* career which astonished even the Kentuckians, and suddenly quitted it to beat all rivals at the bar, and become a leading politician. Friends and opponents agreed in pronouncing him one of the most effective speakers in the State. His youth was too much occupied in more agreeable pursuits, to admit of his employing profitably the educational advantages which were offered him, but his mind, although unused to the discipline of study, mastered all that it grappled with. He read less and comprehended more law than any member of the profession in Kentucky. His vigorous native intellect and acute sense, were perhaps more formidable, for this reason. Want of science made his method of attack more original and irresistible. In the contests of the bar and the hustings, he was a sort of heavy armed partisan, his irregular, rapid onslaught crushed opposition. The learning and eloquence of his ablest antagonists availed little against his manly logic, and often sounded like the merest folly after having been subjected to his telling ridicule. All of his ideas seemed clearly defined; his mind was never in a mist. His insight into character was extraordinary, and he had the most remarkable faculty of accurate observation and life-like reproduction, especially of ludicrous traits and scenes. His command of humorous, graphic, forcible expression was unequaled. He had very many noble traits of character. He was candid and truthful to bluntness. His scorn of dissimulation and affectation of any sort, gave his manner and speech a bluffness, and apparent want of sympathy with the feelings of other men, which caused him often to be misunderstood. I believe that he would rather that the whole world should have thought him a scoundrel, than have seemed for one moment, in his own eyes, a hypocrite. His will was dauntless, his resolution inflexible, his courage high. He had little opportunity, during his military life, to show the stuff that was in him, and to prove that he possessed other qualities befitting an officer beside courage and the strictest attention to the instruction, the comfort, and the discipline of his men. Notwithstanding that he was a very strict disciplinarian—and Kentucky troops have little love of discipline—he was very popular with his men. They retaliated by nick-naming him "Bench-leg," or "Old flint-lock," and admired him all the more intensely, the more frequently that he showed them that they could never deceive him nor attempt it with impunity. Once, thinking that the health of his regiment was getting too bad, and that many cases of illness, reported as severe, were but ruses to escape doing duty, he published an order that from that date "there should be but two sick men at the same time in each company," and caused it to be rigidly enforced. No one who ever saw Hanson can forget him. In stature he was a little under the medium hight, and he was powerfully but ungracefully built. His bulky and ungainly form indicated great but awkward strength. His shoulders were huge, round, and stooping, and he sat on his horse in the attitude in which a sick man bends over the fire. His head was large and perfectly round. His complexion was fair and florid, and his eyes gray and full of light. His strong and marked features, when he became excited, worked strangely and apparently without being moved by the same influences, and the alert movement of his head, at such moments, was in singular contrast to his otherwise heavy inactive manner. His face, when he was calm and giving careful attention to any thing said to him, wore a look of exceeding sternness, enhanced by a peculiar twitch of the muscles of the mouth and eye. He had a German face with all the Irish expressions. A wound received in a duel had shortened one leg and gave him a singular gait, something between a jerk and a roll. His voice was deep and guttural, and his utterance rapid, decided, abrupt, like that of a man who meant all that he said, and knew that it would produce an effect. No one could look him in the eye and fail to perceive that he was every inch a man—a strong, brave, manly nature looked out in every lineament of his face. Captain Wickliffe attached his company to the regiment which Colonel Hunt was organizing. Of the stragglers who had come out with Captain Morgan, some went one way and some another—only eight or ten remained with him. Although not yet in the Confederate service, he at once commenced the active and daring work which laid the foundation of his celebrity and brought him at once into general notice. The cavalry which had been stationed there previously to his coming, had confined themselves to doing picket duty, and had never sought or been required to do other service. This monotonous work, altogether devoid of excitement, did not accord with his nature, which demanded the stimulus of adventure; he, moreover, intuitively understood then, and declared the fact since so completely demonstrated, that cavalry can be employed to far better advantage, if kept well out upon the front or flanks of the army to which it belongs, and close upon the enemy, than by exacting of it the sort of duty which can just as well be performed by infantry. The Federal advanced forces were then stationed at Elizabethtown, and were soon pushed to Nolin Creek, distant about twenty-one or two miles from Munfordsville. Captain Morgan had at first not more than twenty mounted men of his own company, but with these and with volunteers from the other cavalry who were inspired by his example, he made frequent "scouts," and watched and reported every thing that transpired upon the front. These "excursions" were undertaken about four or five times in every week, and would usually occupy twenty-four hours. The scouting party would set out at or a little before dark; before reaching the lines of the enemy, some exciting chases would be had after the countrymen who were in Federal pay or sympathy, and who, always on the lookout for us, would start at break-neck speed for the camp of their friends, pursued by our foremost riders. At first they tried to do this courier duty on horseback, but finding that we were better mounted than they were, and that, when hard pressed and forced to take to the brush, their horses were abandoned for ever, they betook themselves to a less expensive mode of conveying information. They were fleet of foot and knew the paths through the thickets and hills perfectly, and it was difficult to follow and impossible to catch them. We, also, had many friends among the country people living near the enemy's camp, and as we would prowl all night around and among the Federal pickets and outposts, seeking to entrap the unwary, many were the secret conferences which we held in the shade of the woods with faithful informants, who generally closed their reports with emphatic adjurations that, "For the love of God," we would never breathe their names.

Once or twice Captain Morgan passed himself as a Federal officer, in close vicinity to their camps, but this ruse could not be repeated often with success. Once we were guided safely out of a very dangerous situation by an intensely "loyal" man who thought he was assisting some friends who had lost their way. When day returned the scouting party would take a position on the "line of retreat" at a convenient but safe distance from the enemy, rest and refresh men and horses, observe closely if there was any unusual movement in the hostile lines, and as the day declined and it became evident that all was likely to remain quiet, it would return to camp. After the first two or three weeks of this sort of service, and its advantages had become apparent, an order was given to turn over to Captain Morgan some thirty "condemned" artillery horses. With a little care and nursing they were rendered tolerably fit for his purposes, and he was thus enabled to mount, the better part of his company. I knew a scout to be performed, with most of the men riding these same rejected horses, of sixty-eight miles in twenty hours. Although these scouts and expeditions were not nearly so exciting as were subsequent ones, when the cavalry of both armies had become more accustomed to them and more enterprising, yet they were very pleasant episodes in the dull tedious life of the camp, and excellent preparation for really hard and hazardous service. Morgan himself derived great benefit from the experience they gave him, for he rarely if ever missed them. He always knew how to direct and how to estimate the scouting duty of his command, one of the most important, by the practical knowledge thus acquired. Nor will it injure any man who is called upon to exercise the duties of a General to take a few lessons in this school. The fatigue and discomfort from want of sleep attending these expeditions to those who went constantly upon them, was almost as great, as that suffered in later and far more difficult service.

The first skirmish in which Morgan's company or any portion of it was engaged, was a very insignificant and bloodless one, and served only to illustrate the character of the apprehensions which are apt to assail raw troops.

It was upon the second or third scout that Captain Morgan had taken, that we for the first time met the enemy. Contrary to the usual practice, the scouting party had started out early in the day; it consisted of some fifteen of Morgan's own company, twenty-five of the Tennessee cavalry, and ten or fifteen volunteers, about fifty in all. After proceeding some twelve miles in the direction of Nolin Creek, the advance of our party suddenly discovered a body of Federal infantry moving down the road toward us. Their bayonets glistening and just perceptible above a little rise three or four hundred yards off notified the videttes of their vicinity. They did not see us, and we immediately dismounted and posted ourselves in the thickets on both sides of the road, sending the horses to the rear under charge of eight or ten men. No plan of battle was adopted, although many were proposed—the various suggestions, however, that were thrown out, in the inspiration of the moment are lost to history. I remember, however, that one man gave it as his decided opinion, that we ought to charge them immediately on horseback, and he then rode rapidly back to Green river to report the situation to Colonel Hanson. Enjoining silence on the talkative, Captain Morgan went forward on foot to a house, about one hundred and forty or fifty yards in front of our position, and looked out from a window, which commanded a full view of their approach, upon the enemy. He saw a body of sixty or seventy, but this came so close upon him that he was compelled to leave the house before he could discover whether it was the advance of another and larger body, or was unsupported. Fortunately he effected his retreat from the house and rejoined his party without discovery by the enemy. The latter continued to march on, past the house, and toward our position, until, within forty or fifty yards of us, something discovered us to them and they halted. Captain Morgan immediately stepped out into the road, fired at and shot the officer riding at the head of the column. Without returning the fire his men fell back to the house before mentioned, situated on a long low knoll, through which, to the left of the house as we faced, was a cut of the railroad. This afforded a pretty good position and one which we should have taken ourselves. Here they deployed and opened a volley upon us, which would have been very fatal if we had been in the tops of instead of behind the trees. Both sides then continued to load and fire rapidly. With us, every man ought to have behaved well, for each acted upon his own responsibility. Captain Morgan with a few of the more enterprising, and one or two personal followers who always kept close to him, worked his way very nigh to the enemy, and did the only shooting that was effective. We had neither drill nor any understanding among ourselves. The fight was much like a camp-meeting, or an election row. After it had lasted about ten or twelve minutes, an intelligent horse-holder came up from the rear, breathless, and announced that the enemy was flanking us, and that he had been largely reinforced. The receipt of this important intelligence necessitated the withdrawal of the forces, and every man withdrew after his own fashion and in his own time. Our loss, was one man slightly wounded and several shot through the clothes. It was as bloody as an affair between Austrian and Italian outposts.

The horse-bolder who brought the information which led to our retreat, was evidently one who had carefully studied the military articles in the newspapers, and spoke from the influence of a sudden recollection of the "science" he had thus acquired, rather than from accurate observation. This may be safely asserted, as we were not pursued by the enemy, and next day, upon returning, learned that they had commenced retreating about the same time that we did, and that they were but a scouting party like ourselves. Two or three men who got first to Green river, before Captain Morgan's report was received there, stated that we had encountered a strong Federal column advancing to drive our forces away from Woodsonville; that we had attacked, and after a hard fight checked it, but that unless Captain Morgan was immediately reinforced it would probably resume its march. This statement created much excitement at Woodsonville, and was generally credited. But Colonel Hanson treated the gentlemen who brought it rather roughly, and said (with an unnecessary reflection on a gallant arm of the service) that it was a "Cavalry Story."

Several days after this affair, Morgan made his first narrow escape of capture. Hanson determined to send a force to the Nolin outposts sufficiently strong to drive them in and create serious confusion and alarm in the Federal camps. He accordingly ordered the Major commanding the battalion of Tennessee cavalry, to take his entire force, about two hundred and forty men, and, conducted by Morgan, who went with twenty of his men, to make the attack upon the outposts. This force started about nightfall. Morgan thinking that there were now men enough upon the road to accomplish some of his most favorite plans, was in high spirits. His own men, who had never in their lives seen so much cavalry on the march, believed the column invincible.

The Tennesseeans who had long murmured at the inaction to which they had been condemned, were anxious for a fight. The Major arranged the plan with Captain Morgan—the latter was to get, with his twenty men, in the rear of the pickets on post, and then fire a gun. At this signal, the Major was to dash down with his battalion, and, picking up the pickets, charge down upon the base and reserve. In the meantime, Morgan expected to entertain the latter with an unlooked-for volley. It was proposed to push the plan as far as possible, even, if the first features were successfully and quickly executed, to an attack upon the camps.

But it happened that some five miles from Nolin, one of the country fellows, who was in the habit of running into the Federal lines at our approach, was surprised and arrested by Captain Morgan who was in the advance.

The women of whom there were several in the house where he was taken, made a terribly outcry and noise, and would not be pacified.

Captain Morgan moved on, but was shortly afterward informed by one of the men, that the Tennessee battalion had turned back. He rode to the Major and urged, but unsuccessfully, that the plan should not be abandoned. Determined, then, to go forward himself, he proceeded to the point where the pickets on the extreme front had usually stood, but they were gone. He halted his detachment here, and taking with him one of his best and most trusted men (private, afterward Captain John Sisson), started down the road on foot to reconnoiter. He had been gone but a short time, when the rear guard of the Tennessee battalion, about twenty strong, came up; it was commanded by Captain, afterward Colonel, Biffel. It seemed that the Major had conceived that the shrieks of the women would notify the enemy of his coming, and prevent his plan of surprising the picket posts and base from succeeding.

Finding that Morgan had still gone on, Biffel took advantage of his position in the rear of the returning battalion and came to support him. As soon as he got up and learned why we were halted, he turned into the thicket with his detachment, on the side of the road, opposite to that occupied by Morgan's. Just as he was doing this, a Federal column of cavalry came up the road, and hearing the noise of horses forcing they way through the brush, halted about one hundred yards from the point where we lay. The night was clear, and we could easily distinguish them in the moonlight. I had been left in command of the detachment, and would not permit the men to fire, lest it should endanger Captain Morgan's safety, who, if we were driven off, would probably be captured. I ordered, therefore, that not a shot should be fired, unless they resumed their march and came right upon us.

They remained at the spot where they had halted for perhaps twenty minutes, apparently in consultation, when they countermarched and went off rapidly. In a few minutes after they had disappeared, Captain Morgan and Sisson returned and gave an account of what had happened to them. They had walked along the road for fifteen or twenty minutes, when suddenly they heard the tramp of cavalry. They were in a stretch of the road darkened for some distance by the shade of heavy timber. This column came upon them, and they slipped aside some ten or fifteen paces into the woods. Captain Morgan estimated it at about one hundred and twenty men. After it had passed, it occurred to him that his men would be attacked by it, and he started back rapidly to rejoin them. The fatigue of running through the woods was soon too much for him and he was compelled to desist.

As he drew near to the point where he had left us and heard no firing, he conceived a true idea of the situation. Stealing cautiously along, he came upon the enemy, who, at the halt, had gone into the woods also. He was then compelled to lie closely concealed and perfectly still until the road was left clear by the retreat of the enemy. Fortunately his proximity was not discovered by the enemy when in this last situation.

Captain Morgan continued actively engaged in this sort of service until the troops were withdrawn from Woodsonville, when he was also ordered to Bowlinggreen. There the men were sworn into the service, the company regularly organized and officers elected. John H. Morgan was of course elected Captain; I was elected First Lieutenant; James West, Second Lieutenant; Van Buren Sellers, Third, or, more properly, Brevet Second Lieutenant. The strength of the company was then a little above the "minimum" required for organization, numbering sixty-seven privates.

Immediately after reaching Bowlinggreen, excellent horses were purchased and turned over to the company, by General Buckner's order, and saddles, bridles, tents, etc., were issued to it. It was already provided with the best guns and accouterments, and when the fitting up at Bowlinggreen was completed, no command in the Confederate service was better equipped, in any respect.

At this period two other companies, one commanded by Captain Thomas Allen of Shelbyville, Kentucky, and the other by Captain James Bowles of Louisville, but principally recruited in the neighborhood of Glasgow, were assigned to Captain Morgan's command at the earnest request of their officers and men. Bowles' company was not full, and was consolidated with another fragment of a company commanded by Lieutenant Churchill—the latter becoming First Lieutenant of the new organization.

The three companies composed "Morgan's Squadron," a popular misnomer by which, however, the command came, in a short time, to be regularly designated. Morgan's company became A, of this organization; Allen's, B; Bowles', C. The squadron remained quietly in camp, at Bowlinggreen, for two or three weeks after its organization. This time was profitably spent in instructing the men in drill and teaching them something of discipline. The first expedition taken after this, was to Grayson county, on the north side of Green river, to collect and bring to Bowlinggreen a large drove of cattle which had been purchased, but could not be brought out without a guard.

The "Home-guards" held this county in strong force; they had long expected a Confederate inroad, and had sternly determined to punish the invaders when they came. The squadron reached the ferry, at which it was directed to cross at night. We found the boats sunken, but raised them, filled up the holes bored in their bottoms, bailed them out, and by eight o'clock next morning we had one company across. The day was spent in crossing the cattle to the southern side of the river.

On the following evening, the entire squadron was transferred to the north side of the river and passed the night agreeably in chasing the Home-guards, who did not make a hard fight, but ran off some twenty or thirty miles to a neighboring county to "rally."

Shortly after his return to Bowlinggreen, from this expedition, Captain Morgan was ordered to the front again, and reported to Brigadier General Hindman, who commanded a brigade of infantry and a strong force of cavalry, in all three thousand or thirty-five hundred men, upon the extreme front of our line.

General Hindman's headquarters were at Bell's tavern, twenty-five miles from Bowlinggreen, and thirteen from Woodsonville, then occupied by the enemy, who had advanced to Green river, ten or fifteen days after we left there.

It would, perhaps, be more correct to say, that the enemy held Munfordsville, for although Woodsonville was virtually in his possession, and completely at his disposal, there were, at that date, none of his regiments encamped on the southern side of the river.

A few days before Morgan's arrival, had occurred the fight, in which Colonel Terry, of the Eighth Texas Cavalry (better known then as Terry's Rangers), was killed, and of which so many contradictory versions have prevailed. The Northern account has often been published, and if the many later and more important events have not crowded it out of memory, is familiar to all who read the Northern newspapers at that time. Without presuming to give a minute account of the fight, for I did not witness it, nor have I ever seen a report of it, I can present, in a few words, the idea which I derived from the description of men who were present, and which was generally received, just after the fight, in our army.

General Hindman had received information that a strong body of the enemy had crossed the river, and desiring to ascertain if this movement was preliminary to an advance of the entire army, he moved forward with the greater part of his infantry, some artillery and Terry's regiment of cavalry, to reconnoiter, and, perhaps, contest an advance, if it were made. When he arrived at the ground upon which the fight commenced, about three miles from the river, he discovered the enemy, and, supposing his force to be not stronger than his own, determined to engage him.

I am not familiar with the plan or details of the fight, but am under the impression that, when first seen, the enemy was slowly advancing, unaware of Hindman's vicinity, and that the latter screened the bulk of his force behind a large hill, upon the eastern side of the Bowlinggreen road, the summit of which he occupied with skirmishers, and posted his artillery some distance farther back, where it was partially concealed, and could yet sweep the road and the ground over which the enemy was advancing.

Terry was instructed to skirmish in the enemy's front, and draw him on, until his flank should be exposed to the infantry, that was masked behind the hill. It was the intention then, I have always understood, to attack vigorously with all the infantry, throw a part of it in the enemy's rear, and between him and the river, while Terry charged him on the other flank. One part of Terry's regiment, under his own immediate command, was on the right of the road at a considerable distance from any support. Another, commanded by one of his Captains, was posted nearer the infantry.

Hindman's plan to bring his whole force into action and cut off and capture a part of the enemy's, if such was his plan, was frustrated by the impatient ardor of Terry, who, after a very brief retreat before Willich's regiment of infantry, turned and charged it furiously. The regiment was deployed in skirmish order, and had barely time to "rally by fours," when Terry, of whose command they had, up to that moment, seen only a very few, came down on them. The Texians rode around the groups of four, shooting the men down with their revolvers and shot-guns. Seeing his Colonel engaged, the officer commanding the other portion of the regiment, charged the enemy nighest him with similar success. Terry and six of his men were killed, and perhaps twice that number wounded. All the witnesses on the Confederate side concurred in saying that fifteen or twenty of the Federals were killed, and as many more, at least, wounded. I passed over the ground shortly afterward as bearer of a flag of truce, and heard the same account from the citizens living near the scene of the fight. Willich's regiment was a very fine one, and its commander a very superior officer.

General Hindman was an officer of great dash and energy, and very ambitious—he was, therefore, just the man to encourage an enterprising subordinate, and give him free rein in that sort of service which keeps up the *morale* of an army at a time when it must remain inactive, reflects credit upon the commanding officer who directs it, and which rank and duty forbid a commanding officer to undertake himself. Although his imperious and exacting temper made him many enemies, he had other qualities which gained him devoted friends. One was a disposition (proceeding either from a desire to attach to himself men whose friendship he thought would be valuable, or from a real feeling of regard—perhaps from both) to go all lengths for a friend. He entered heartily into all of Morgan's plans, encouraged and gave him every facility to extend his enterprises, and seemed to entertain a peculiar pride and pleasure in his success. There is no doubt that there was something in his nature which made him cordially sympathize with every thing that was daring and adventurous. Morgan became very fond of him, and always spoke with pleasure of this brief service with him. Although almost constantly close upon the outposts of the enemy, sometimes in small detachments, and occasionally with every effective man, the squadron had no engagement except the picket fights, which were of constant occurrence. The reason of this was that the Federals never came outside of their lines, except for very short distances, and then in bodies so strong that we dared not attack them. The practice of firing upon and attacking pickets was then much condemned by the Federal officers, but no valid reason has ever been assigned for this condemnation. It is true that killing and annoying pickets does not decide the result of campaigns, neither do the minor skirmishes and partial battles which so frequently occur in all wars, yet it is the means of affecting the general result, and assisting to make it successful as much as any other method of harassing an enemy. If war is to be confined to sieges, pitched battles, etc., then every method of wearying, annoying and discouraging an adversary, of keeping him in doubt, or goading him to desperation, must be equally condemned. All stratagem must be discarded, and a return may as well be had to the polite but highly ridiculous practice of lines of battle saluting each other and refusing to fire first. There are certain rules of war whose observance humanity and the spirit of the age demand. Prisoners ought not to be killed or maltreated, unless in retaliation; the terms of capitulations and surrenders ought to be honorably fulfilled and observed; war ought not to be made on non-combatants. But the soldier ought to be content to take his chance. It is more soldierly to teach pickets to fight when attacked, than to complain of it, and a picket who will allow himself to be surprised on his post ought to be shot. At the time of which I write the Federal army at Green river was provided with no cavalry, or cavalry that was useless. Its commander, therefore, unless informed by his spies, whose reports were, of course, infrequent, was ignorant of all that transpired even immediately outside of his advance videttes, and it was impossible for him to know whether an attack on his picket line was made by a scouting party, or premised a serious affair. He was, then, obliged either to prepare for battle every time any thing of the kind occurred, greatly harassing his troops, or to take the risk of an attack when unprepared. It was an excellent means, too, of judging of the strength of an infantry camp and the changes made from time to time in it, to attack the picket line at various points, hear the "long rolls" beaten, and see the troops turn out, as occasionally could be done.

One or two adventures of Captain Morgan at this period attracted a good deal of notice. One of them, the burning of Bacon creek bridge, took place before he reported to Hindman. This bridge had been destroyed at the time our forces fell back from Woodsonville. It was a small structure and easily replaced, but its reparation was necessary to the use of the road. The Federal army then lay encamped between Bacon and Nolin creeks, the advance about three miles from Bacon creek—the outposts were scarcely half a mile from the bridge. A few days labor served to erect the wood work of the bridge, and it was ready to receive the iron rails, when Morgan asked leave to destroy it. It was granted, and he started from Bowlinggreen on the same night with his entire command, for he believed that he would find the bridge strongly guarded and would have to fight for it. Halting at daybreak a short distance from the river, he waited until night fell again before resuming his march. He crossed the ford at Woodsonville, which was fortunately not guarded, and dispersed a party of Home-guards, which, ignorant of his vicinity, had assembled at Munfordsville to carry off some Southern sympathizers of that place.

Pressing on vigorously he reached the bridge at midnight, and to his surprise and satisfaction found it without a guard; that which protected the workmen during the day, having been withdrawn at night. The bridge was set on fire and in three hours thoroughly destroyed—no interruption to the work was attempted by the enemy. The damage inflicted was trifling, and the delay occasioned of little consequence. The benefit derived from it by Morgan was two-fold—it increased the hardihood of his men in that species of service, and gave himself still greater confidence in his own tactics. Shortly after Woodsonville had been included within the picket lines of the enemy and occupied with troops, Captain Morgan with two men went at night to Hewlett's station, on the railroad, about two hundred yards from the picket line, and found the small building which was used as a depot in the possession of five or six stragglers, who were playing cards and making merry, and captured them. He set fire to the building, and when the troops had been called out by the bright light, he sent in a message by one of his prisoners to the effect that in the following week he would come and burn them out of Woodsonville.

On the evening of the 20th or 21st of January, Captain Morgan with five men left his camp at Bell's tavern, crossed the Green river at an unguarded ferry, and on the following day rode into Lebanon, some sixty miles from his point of departure. Several hundred troops were encamped near this place, and a great many stores were in the town and in a large building between the town and the nearest camp. The soldiers off or on duty were frequently passing to and fro through the town. Morgan destroyed the stores, and made all the stragglers prisoners; some of them he was obliged to release after taking their overcoats, with which he disguised his own men and was thus enabled to get quietly through some dangerous situations. He brought back with him nine prisoners, a large flag and several other trophies. Two companies of cavalry followed him closely, but he gained the river first, crossed and turned the boat adrift, just as his pursuers reached the bank. Next day he marched into Glasgow with his five men and nine prisoners in column, and the United States flag flying at the front. He scared the citizens of the place and two or three straggling Confederates, who were there, horribly. The flag and blue overcoats demoralised them.

When he reached his own camp the prisoners were quartered with different "messes," but were not placed under regular guard. The inmates of each tent, in which prisoners were placed, were held responsible for them. On this occasion it happened that some of the men (by means in which they were learned and adroit) had obtained several bottles of wine—sparkling catawba—and the prisoners were assured that this sort of wine was regularly issued to the Confederate cavalry by their commissaries. They approved the wine and the practice of including it in soldiers' rations, and five of them next morning begged, with tears in their eyes, to be received into the Confederate service. These adventures are not related because it is thought that they will excite any especial interest, but because they fairly represent the nature of the service in which Morgan was constantly engaged during the occupation of Southern Kentucky by the Confederate army, in the fall of 1861, and the greater part of the succeeding winter.

Although greatly inferior in dash and execution to the subsequent cavalry operations of the West, this service of Morgan's was much superior, in both, to any thing which had, up to that time, been attempted by either side, and it served to educate Morgan's men and Morgan himself for the successful conduct of more daring and far more important enterprises.

A strong and mutual feeling of regard and friendship commenced (during the period that we served with General Hindman), between the Eighth Texas (Terry's Rangers), and the squadron, which continued to the close of the war, growing warmer as Morgan's command grew in numbers, and, doubtless, it exists, now, in the hearts of the men, who composed the two organizations. This feeling interfered in some degree with discipline, for most of the men of both were young and wild, and inclined, when they could evade the vigilance of camp guards, to rove nocturnally and extensively, and neither, when on picket, would arrest or stop their friends from the other command.

The gallant Rangers paid dearly for their proud record, and few of those who used to roam and fight so recklessly then, are, I fear, living now, to recall the events which we witnessed together. The squadron remained with the forces under command of General Hindman until the evacuation of Bowlinggreen and the retreat from Kentucky. Then we left the scenes and the region with which we had become so familiar with sad hearts. We had hoped that when the signal for departure was sounded, it would be also the order to advance; that we would press on to recover the whole of Kentucky, and win victories that would give her to us forever, and the retreat seemed to us like a march to our graves. But a feeling of regret at leaving the country in which we had passed months of such pleasant and stirring service, was natural, even without other reasons for it. Men are apt to become attached to the localities where they have led free and active lives, and to connect with them agreeable associations. This country had many such for us, and that part especially between Bell's tavern on the one side of Green river, and Nolin on the other. For many miles to the right and left there was scarcely a foot of the ground which we had not traversed, nor a thicket in which we had not hidden; from almost every hill we had watched the enemy, and at almost every turn in the road shot at him. These are not precisely the kind of reminiscences that the poetical and romantic sigh over, but every man has a right to be sentimental after his own fashion, and Morgan's men were always mightily so about the Green river country.

CHAPTER VI

In the latter part of January, 1862, it became evident that General Johnson, with the inferior force at his disposal, could not hold his line in Kentucky. Crittenden, upon the right flank, had sustained a serious disaster at Mill Springs, near Somerset, and had been forced back across the Cumberland, which he had crossed to attack Thomas. In this battle General Zollicoffer was killed—his death was in itself an irreparable loss. Crittenden retreated first upon Monticello and subsequently to Gainesville in Tennessee. He lost his artillery and trains, and his troops could be relied on to oppose no effective resistance—for the time—to the farther advance of the enemy. The superiority of the latter in numbers had been not more marked than their superiority in arms and equipment. The fatigue and privation endured by Crittenden's men upon their retreat had contributed greatly to impair their efficiency. The expeditions against Forts Henry and Donelson were vigorously pressed, and scarcely had full confirmation arrived of the defeat of Crittenden, when we got the first rumors of the fall of Fort Henry. General Johnson had never been able to collect at all the points of defense in Kentucky, exclusive of Columbus, more than twenty-four thousand men. In this force were included sixty-days' men and all the minor garrisons. He had at Bowlinggreen in January and the first of February about ten thousand.

Buell had organized, during the period that the two armies lay inactive and confronting each other, fifty or sixty thousand men, and they were, at the time when General Johnson commenced his retreat, concentrated, mobilized, and ready to fall upon him. Therefore, even before it became evident that Donelson must fall, before the capture of Nashville was imminent, by an enemy moving from either flank, and before his line of retreat was endangered, but just so soon as Buell put his army in motion General Johnson evacuated Bowlinggreen. Then began the campaign, in which more than in any other of the war, was displayed the profoundest strategy, the most heroic decision, the highest order of generalship.

General Johnson had long foreseen the storm of difficulties which now assailed him. His resources were scanty and the emergency was terrible, but he did not despair of fighting through it to victory. Upon one flank of his line, he had sustained a crushing defeat, the forces protecting it had been driven off. Nashville might be taken by the victors. One of the forts protecting the great water lines which led right into the heart of his department, and away to the rear of his army, had been taken. If the other fell the fate of Nashville was sealed, but far worse, he would be inclosed at Bowlinggreen, should he remain there, between three armies each much stronger than his own. If he lingered around Nashville, he could not protect the city, but gave his enemy the opportunity of cutting him off completely from the only territory whence he could hope to obtain recruits, and of preventing his junction with the reinforcements which he had ordered to his assistance. He did not hesitate a moment.

Price and Van Dorn were ordered from Arkansas, Bragg was ordered from Pensacola, all the available troops at New Orleans, and every point in the department where troops were stationed, were called into the field, and the concentration of all at Corinth, in Northern Mississippi, was arranged. Here he would have every thing massed and in hand, and in his rear would be no danger, nor indefensible line by which danger could menace him. His adversaries on the contrary would be separated from each other; rivers and all the perils of a hostile population would be between them and safety, if they were defeated or forced to turn and retreat; energy and promptness would enable him to strike them heavy blows before they could unite; if every detail of his plan worked right, he might hope to outnumber them at every collision.

This plan would require the evacuation of Columbus, even if the occupation of New Madrid did not; but there was no longer any use of holding Columbus, after a retreat to Mississippi had been decided upon. Its garrison would help to swell the ranks of the army for the decisive battle—and if that battle were won, territory far North of Columbus would be gained. Therefore, braving censure and remonstrance more general, energetic, and daring, than was ever encountered by any Confederate officer, before or since, General Johnson turned his back upon Kentucky and commenced the retreat which culminated in the battle of Shiloh. When the dangers from which this retreat extricated him, the favorable position in which it placed him for offensive operations, the exact calculation of the proper time to turn retreat into attack, and the electric rapidity and courage with which the latter was done—when all the features are considered, is it claiming too much to say that no conception of the war was more magnificent?

The evacuation of Bowlinggreen was commenced on the 14th of February, and notwithstanding the discontent of the troops, was accomplished in perfect order. On the day after it was all over, the enemy arrived upon the opposite bank of Barren river—the bridges had all, of course, been burned—and shelled the town which he could not immediately enter.

The weather for the week following the evacuation, was intensely cold, and the troops accustomed, for the most part, to comfortable quarters during the winter, and exposed for the first time to real hardships, suffered severely. Still, after the first murmuring was over, they were kept in high spirits by the impression, assiduously cultivated by their officers, that they were marching to surprise and attack Thomas, who was supposed to have compromised himself by an imprudent pursuit of Crittenden.

The news from Donelson, where the fight was then raging, was very favorable, and the successful defense of the fort for several days encouraged even General Johnson to hope that it would be held and the assailants completely beaten off.

As the army neared Nashville, some doubts of the truth of the programme which the men had arranged in their imaginations began to intrude, and they began to believe that the retreat meant in good earnest the giving up of Kentucky—perhaps something more which they were unwilling to contemplate. While they were in this state of doubt and anxiety, like a thunder-clap came the news of the fall of Donelson—the news that seven thousand Confederate were prisoners in the hands of the enemy.

General Johnson, himself, was thoroughly surprised by the suddenness of the disaster, for, six hours before he received information of the surrender, he had been dispatched that the enemy had been signally repulsed, and were drawing off, and until the intelligence came of the fate of the garrison, he had learned of no new attack. The depression, which this information produced, was deepened by the gloom which hung over Nashville when the troops entered. It is impossible to describe the scene. Disasters were then new to us, and our people had been taught to believe them impossible. No subsequent reverse, although fraught with far more real calamity, ever created the shame, sorrow, and wild consternation which swept over the South with the news of the surrender of Donelson. And in Nashville, itself sure to fall next and speedily, an anguish and terror were felt and expressed, scarcely to be conceived by those who have not witnessed a similar scene. All the worst evils which follow in the train of war and subjugation seemed to be anticipated by the terrified people, and the feeling was quickly communicated to the troops, and grew with every hour until it assumed almost the proportions of a panic. The Tennessee troops were naturally most influenced by the considerations which affected the citizens, but all shared the feeling. Some wept at the thought of abandoning the city to a fate which they esteemed as dreadful as utter destruction, and many, infuriated, loudly advocated burning it to the ground that the enemy might have nothing of it but its ashes.

During the first night after the army reached Nashville, when the excitement and fury were at the highest pitch, and officers and privates were alike influenced by it, it seemed as if the bonds of discipline would be cast off altogether. Crowds of soldiers were mingled with the citizens who thronged the streets all night, and yells, curses, shots rang on all sides. In some houses the women were pale and sobbing, and in others there was even merriment, as if in defiance of the worst. Very soon all those who had escaped from Donelson began to arrive.

Forrest had cut his way through the beleaguering lines and brought off his entire regiment. He reached Nashville on the day after it was entered by the army. It was impossible for the infantry men who escaped to make their way from the scene of disaster, except in small detachments. They were necessarily scattered all over the country, and those who reached Nashville in time to accompany the army upon its farther march, came in as stragglers and without any organization. Neither men nor officers had an idea of how or when they were to do duty again. The arrival of these disbanded soldiers, among whom it was difficult to establish and enforce order, because no immediate disposition could be made of them, increased the confusion already prevailing. Rumors, too, of the near approach of the enemy were circulated, and were believed even by officers of high rank.

Buell's army, which was really not far south of Bowlinggreen, was reported to be within a few miles of the city, and the Federal gunboats, which had not yet reached Clarksville, were confidently declared to be within sight of Fort Zollicoffer, only seven miles below Nashville.

Upon the second day matters had arrived at such a state, and the excitement and disorder were so extreme, that it became necessary to take other precautions to repress the license that was prevailing, besides the establishment of guards and sentinels about the camps where the troops lay, and General Johnson ordered the establishment of a strong military police in Nashville. The First Missouri infantry, one of the finest and best disciplined regiments in the service, was detailed for this duty, and Morgan's squadron was sent to assist it. Our duty was to patrol the city and suburbs, and we were constantly engaged at it until the city was evacuated. General John B. Floyd, of Virginia, was appointed commandant of Nashville, and entrusted with the enforcement of discipline and with all the details of the evacuation. His task was one of no ordinary difficulty. It was hard, at such a time, to know how to begin the work. In such a chaos, with such passions ruling, it seemed folly to hope for the restoration of order. Those who remember the event, will recall the feeling of despair which had seized upon the soldiery—the entire army seemed, for the time, hopeless of any retrieval of our fortunes, and every man was thoroughly reckless. Few excesses were committed; but, with such a temper prevailing, the worst consequences were to be apprehended, if the influence of the officers should be entirely lost and the minds of the men should be directed to mischief. General Floyd would have found the demoralization and license which had grown apace among the troops, and the terrors of the citizens, serious impediments to his efforts to remove the valuable stores which had been collected in Nashville, even if he had possessed abundant facilities for their removal. But of such facilities he was almost entirely destitute. The trains with the army were needed for transportation of supplies for immediate use. The scanty wheel transportation which belonged to captured and disorganized commands, and had been brought to the city, could scarcely be made available. When it could be discovered and laid hold of, the wagons and teams were usually found to be unserviceable. General Floyd's first care (after satisfying himself by active scouting, that there was no truth in the reports of the proximity of the enemy, and burning the bridge at Edgefield junction), was to make arrangements for saving as many of the stores as was possible, giving the preference to ordnance stores. For this purpose he ordered an impressment of transportation in Nashville and the vicinity, making a clean sweep of every thing that ran on wheels. In this manner some eighty or ninety vehicles were gotten together, with teams, and as many loads of ordnance stores were saved for the army. He issued orders that the citizens should be permitted to help themselves to the remaining stores, and a promiscuous scramble for clothing, blankets, meat, meal, and all sorts of quartermaster and commissary stores, commenced and lasted three days. Occasionally, a half-drunken, straggling soldier, would walk into the midst of the snatchers, with gun on shoulder and pistol at his belt, and the citizens would stand back, jackall like, until he had helped himself. Crowds would stand upon the pavements underneath the tall buildings, upon the Court House Square, while out of their fourth and fifth-story windows large bales of goods were pitched, which would have crushed any one upon whom they had fallen. Yet numbers would rush and fasten upon them, while other bales were already in the air descending. Excitement and avarice seemed to stimulate the people to preternatural strength. I saw an old woman, whose appearance indicated the extremest decrepitude, staggering under a load of meat which I would have hardly thought a quartermaster's mule could carry. Twice during the first day of these scenes, orders were received by a portion of Forrest's regiment, drawn up on the Square, to stop the appropriation of stores by the citizens, and they accordingly charged the crowd (deaf to any less forcible reason) with drawn sabers; several men were wounded and trampled upon, but fortunately none were killed. Nothing could have been more admirable than the fortitude, patience and good sense which General Floyd displayed in his arduous and unenviable task. He had, already, for ten days, endured great and uninterrupted excitement and fatigue; without respite or rest, he was called to this responsibility and duty. Those who have never witnessed nor been placed in such situations, can not understand how they harass the mind and try the temper.

General Floyd soon found that he could (with no exertion) maintain perfect order, or rescue more than a fragment from the wreck, and he bent all his energies to the task of repressing serious disorders, preventing the worst outrages, and preserving all that was most absolutely required for the use of the army, and that it was practical to remove.

It was easy for officers who respectively saw and considered but one matter, to advise attention to that in particular, and to censure if their advice was not taken. But the very multiplicity of such counsellors, embarrassed rather than assisted, and showed the utter impossibility, in the brief time allowed, of attending to every thing. I saw a great deal of General Floyd, while he was commanding in Nashville, and I was remarkably impressed by him. I was required to report to him almost every hour in the twenty-four, and he was always surrounded by a crowd of applicants for all sorts of favors, and couriers bringing all sorts of news. It was impossible in the state of confusion which prevailed to prohibit or regulate this pressing and noisy attendance, or to judge, without examination, of what was important to be considered. Many matters which ordinarily a general officer would not permit himself to be troubled with, might need attention and action from him at such a time. Irascible and impetuous as General Floyd seemed to be by nature—his nerves unstrung, too, by the fatigues of so many busy days and sleepless nights—and galled as he must have been by the constant annoyances, he yet showed no sign of impatience. I saw him give way but once to anger, which was, then, provoked by the most stupid and insolent pertinacity. It was interesting to watch the struggle which would sometimes occur between his naturally violent temper and the restraint he imposed upon it. His eye would glow, his face and his lips turn pale, and his frame shake with passion; he would be silent for minutes, as if not daring to trust himself to speak, looking all the while upon the ground, and he would then address the man, whose brusqueness or obstinacy had provoked him, in the mildest tone and manner. He was evidently endowed with no common nerve, will, and judgment.

At last the evacuation was completed, the army was gotten clear of Nashville, the last straggler driven out, all the stores which could not be carried off, nor distributed to the citizens, burned, and the capitol of Tennessee (although we did not know it then) was abandoned finally to the enemy. Morgan's squadron was the last to leave, as it was required to remain in the extreme rear of the army and pick up all the stragglers that evaded the rear guards of the infantry. Our scouts left behind, when we, in our turn, departed, witnessed the arrival of the Federals and their occupation of the city.

The army was halted at Murfreesboro', thirty miles from Nashville, where it remained for nearly a week. Here it was joined by the remnant of Crittenden's forces. After a few days given to repose, reorganization and the re-establishment of discipline, General Johnson resumed his retreat. He concluded it with a battle in which he himself was the assailant, and which, but for his death, would have advanced our banners to the Ohio. It was fruitless of apparent and immediate results, but it checked for more than a year the career of Federal conquest, infused fresh courage into the Southern people, and gave them breathing time to rally for farther contest. His death upon the field prevented vast and triumphant results from following it then—the incompetency of his successors squandered glorious chances (months afterward) which this battle directly gave to the Confederacy. When the line of march was taken up, and the heads of the columns were still turned southward, the dissatisfaction of the troops broke out into fresh and frequent murmurs. Discipline, somewhat restored at Murfreesboro', had been too much relaxed by the scenes witnessed at Nashville, to impose much restraint upon them. Unjust as it was, officers and men concurred in laying the whole burden of blame upon General Johnson. Many a voice was then raised to denounce him, which has since been enthusiastic in his praise, and many joined in the clamor, then almost universal against him, who, a few weeks later, when he lay dead upon the field he had so gallantly fought, would have given their own lives to recall him.

Crossing the Tennessee river at Decatur, Alabama, and destroying the immense railroad bridge at that point, General Johnson pressed on down through the valley, through Courtland, Tuscumbia, and Iuca, to Corinth. This was for a short time, until he could concentrate for battle, the goal of his march. Here all the reinforcements at his command could reach him, coming from every direction. He only awaited their arrival to attack the enemy, which, flushed with the successes at Henry and Donelson, lay exposed to his blows, ignorant of his vicinity.

The force with which he crossed the Tennessee river was a little over twenty thousand men. It was composed of the troops which had held the lines in Kentucky—those which had been stationed at Bowlinggreen, all that was left of Crittenden's command, all that were left of the garrisons of Donelson and Henry. The garrisons of minor importance in Tennessee contributed, as the State was evacuated, to strengthen the army. He was very soon joined by the forces from Pensacola, about ten thousand strong, and a splendid body of men. They were superior in arms, equipment, instruction and dress, to all of the Western troops, and presented an imposing appearance and striking contrast to their weather-stained, dusty and travel-worn comrades. Nothing had ever occurred to them to impair their morale; they seemed animated by the stern spirit and discipline which characterized their commander, and a fit reserve with which to turn the tide of fortune. Beauregard brought with him some troops from New Orleans and other parts of Louisiana. General Polk came with the troops which had held Columbus. Several hurriedly raised and organized regiments came from the various States of the department. Price and Van Dorn, having between them fifteen thousand veterans, did not arrive in season to participate in the immediate movements which General Johnson had determined upon. A knowledge that the retreat had been brought to a close and that a battle was about to be fought in which we would attack, did more to inspirit the troops and restore to them soldierly feeling and bearing, than any efforts in behalf of discipline. The spirit of the men who had come from Florida and other points not surrendered to the enemy had a favorable influence upon the remainder, whose pride was aroused by the comparison and example. The sudden and seemingly magical change from despondency to highest hope, from a sullen indifference to duty to the most cheerful alacrity and perfect subordination, showed how wonderfully susceptible was the material which composed our army to the hopes inspired by a daring policy. The same men who had dragged themselves reluctantly along, as if careless of reputation and forgetful of the cause they had to fight for, were now full of zeal, energy and confidence. Those who had almost broken out into open mutiny, now rendered the promptest obedience to every order. The denunciations they had uttered against General Johnson, were silenced just so soon as they learned that he was about to lead them to instant battle, and his name was never mentioned except with becoming respect, and often with praise. In short, every trace of demoralization disappeared—courage, pride and efficiency, returned; and, from a condition not much better than that of an armed mob, the army became again disciplined, valiant and reliable. While the masterly ability and soldierly vigor and decision of General Johnson must excite the profoundest admiration, those who remember him may be pardoned for dwelling quite as much upon the grandeur, the loftiness, the heroism of his character. In this we may look in vain for his peer, except to the great Virginian, his immortal comrade, the man whom every former Southern soldier must feel it is his religious duty to venerate. Through all that period of sickening doubt, amidst all the reverses, in the wide spread demoralization which attacked all ranks, General Johnson towered like a being superior to the fears and fate of other men. The bitter censure which was cast at him from all sides, could move him to nothing weak or unworthy of his high nature. He gave way to no anger or scorn—he deigned no argument or apology. When the President, his devoted friend and warm admirer, urged him to supersede the officers who had suffered defeat, he answered that they were brave, although inexperienced men, and that he preferred to trust them until he could find better.

He defended unsuccessful generals with his generous warmth, and reposed in them a confidence, which saved them, but directed all the clamor against himself. He entertained with courtesy and listened with patience, to importunate, censorious civilians, while he had in his pocket copies of dispatches which they had sent to Richmond furiously denouncing him. Not one word was he ever heard to say in comment or rebuke, while censure and detraction were most frequent against him, and his zealous, paternal care for his army was never relaxed. His majestic presence, calm and noble face and superb dignity, might themselves—it would seem—have overawed and hushed the cavilers. Surely, there never suffered a nobler, purer, braver martyr to senseless prejudice and unjust, inconsiderate reproach.

While the enemy was retreating through Tennessee, Morgan's squadron remained in the neighborhood of Nashville until all the detachments which had been left in the rear to protect and ship off by rail the stores and supplies (which could be hastily collected) at Murfreesboro', Shelbyville, and other points, had gotten through with their work and departed after the army. Morgan encamped his command at La Vergne, a station upon the railroad, about half way between Nashville and Murfreesboro'. This little place became quite famous in the subsequent annals of the war. Morgan first brought its name into men's mouths, Forrest and Wheeler kept it notorious.

Here, for the first time, we met the Fourth Ohio Cavalry—our acquaintance afterward became more intimate, and lasted as long as that gallant regiment was in the field. The Fourth was encamped at the "Lunatic Asylum"—I asked one of the officers of the regiment (subsequently) why they were sent *there*, but he did not seem to know—eight miles from Nashville, on the Murfreesboro' pike, and seven miles from La Vergne. Our respective "bases" were consequently pretty close to each other. Our pickets used to stand in sight of theirs during the day, and in hearing distance at night. The videttes treated each other with respect and consideration, but the scouts were continually slipping around through the woods and shooting some one. On one occasion an officer of the Fourth placed some men in ambush in a thicket upon the side of the road, and then with a small party rode down near to our pickets, fired, turned and galloped away again, hoping that some of us would be induced to follow and receive the fire of his ambuscade. The night was dark, and by an unaccountable mistake the men in ambush fired into their own friends as they passed—no damage was done, I believe, except to horses.

One morning our pickets came rushing in with a party of the enemy in pursuit (no unusual occurrence), and as we stood to arms, we noticed—they were three or four hundred yards off—one of the pickets some distance in the rear of the others, and almost in the clutches of the enemy, who were peppering away at him. It was private Sam Murrill, of Co. C., (afterward chief of my couriers, and a first rate soldier to the end of the war), his horse was slow and blown, and the foremost pursuer had gotten along side of him and presented his pistol at his head. Murrill, too quick for him, fired first, and as his enemy dropped dead from the saddle, seized pistol and horse, and, although closely pushed, until the guns of his comrades drove back his daring pursuers, brought both in triumph into camp. These small affairs were of daily occurrence, but at last our opponents became more wary and circumspect, and to obtain decided advantages, we had to go far into their lines. We noticed finally that they adopted a practice of withdrawing their pickets at night, from the points where they stood during the day, some miles to the rear. Captain Morgan after making this discovery, resolved to anticipate them at the place where they made their picket base at night. He remained with a few men demonstrating all day in sight of the outpost pickets, and just before nightfall made a circuit which carried him far to their rear, previously to their withdrawal. He reached the place (where he learned that a party of twenty-five or thirty stood nightly), about the time that it was fairly dark.

It was a small house, in a yard some eighty or ninety feet square, surrounded by a picket fence of cedar. He had with him nine men, of these he detailed five to hold horses, and with the other four; all armed with shot guns loaded with buck-shot, he lay down behind the low fence. The horses were sent back some distance into the bushes. Captain Morgan instructed his party to hold their fire until he gave the signal. It was his intention to permit the party, which was expected, to pass and then fire upon the rear—hoping thus to drive it down the road toward his own camp and, following rapidly, capture it. When it arrived, however, about twenty-five strong, the officer in command halted it before it reached the point where we lay, but at a distance of not more than thirty feet from us, so that we could distinctly hear every word which was uttered. The officer in command talked with his guide for some minutes, sending men to reconnoiter upon each side of the road in the meantime. At length the officer ordered his men to enter the little yard, and they came right up to the fence, and just upon the opposite side from our position. Captain Morgan shouted the word "Now," and each man arose and fired one barrel of his gun. The roar and the flash so near, must have been terrible to men taken completely by surprise. The officer fell immediately, and his party, panic stricken, filed toward their camp. Another volley was delivered upon them as they ran. A chain picket was established between the point where this happened and the camp at the asylum; and we could hear shots fired at rapid intervals, for minutes, as the fleeing party passed the men on post. Several wounded men fell in the road, after they had fled a short distance.

A short time before he left La Vergne, Captain Morgan selected fifteen men for an expedition to Nashville. Avoiding the high roads, he made his way through the woods to the Lebanon pike, which he struck only a mile from the city.

The vicinity of the city favored rather than endangered him, and he rode down into the streets without attracting hostile observation. A patrol of twenty or thirty cavalry, were making the round of the streets, and he rode in the rear of this party. After reconnoitering for a short time, he determined on his plan of operations. He sent all but five or six of his men out into the thickets, a short distance from the city, and, with those whom he kept, he made his way, dismounted and leading the horses along the river bank, until he came near the reservoir, about opposite to which, and a little out in the river, a steamboat was anchored. This boat was one which was in the employ of the Federal Government. It was Captain Morgan's desire to set her on fire, and let her drift down into the midst of a number of other transports, which lay a few hundred yards below, and were crowded with troops, hoping she might fire them also. Three gallant young fellows volunteered to do the work, and boarded the boat in an old canoe, which was found, bottom upward, on the shore. They fired her, but could not cut her adrift, as she was made fast at stem and stern, with chain cables, and thus the best part of the plan was frustrated. The work was done in full view and notice of the troops on the other transports, and the engineer and workmen, on board of the boat, were brought to the shore. The names of the young men, or rather boys, who did this, were Warfield, Garrett and Buckner—the latter was soon afterward killed at Shiloh. The canoe was so unmanageable that its crew came near falling into the hands of the enemy—but accident favored them at the most perilous moment. A long line of panel fence had drifted out into the river, one end still being attached to the bank. When their paddles failed them in the swift current, they fortunately came in reach of this, and they were enabled to pull in by it to the shore. As soon as the land was gained, all remounted their horses, watched for a while the rising flames and the consternation of the fleet, and then, with three cheers for Morgan, rode rapidly to rejoin their comrades.

Cavalry was sent in pursuit, but was left far behind. Captain Morgan went straight across the country to the Murfreesboro' pike. As he gained it he encountered a small body of Federal cavalry, attacked and drove it into town. He lost only one man, but he was a capital soldier, Peter Atherton by name.

He got back to La Vergne about twelve at night. After the thorough and final evacuation of Murfreesboro', Captain Morgan withdrew to that place with his command. He almost directly afterward sent the bulk of it to the Shelbyville and Nashville road, with instructions to encamp about twenty miles from Nashville, and picket and scout the adjacent country, and all the neighboring roads. He retained with him at Murfreesboro', about forty of his own men, and some fifty of Colonel Wirt Adams' regiment of cavalry, under command of Lieutenant Colonel Wood, of that regiment. This officer was exceedingly fond of the sort of service which Morgan was performing, and had been with him constantly for ten or twelve days. He preferred to remain with and report to him, although his superior in rank, rather than accompany his own regiment on the retreat of the army, and see no active work.

A day or two after he had made this disposition of this command, Captain Morgan taking with him thirty-two of the men he had kept at Murfreesboro', penetrated by bridle paths and traces through the woods, to the immediate vicinity of the enemy's encampments at the Lunatic Asylum.

At this time, Mitchell's entire brigade was encamped there. Stationing his men in the thickets along the road, at various points, Captain Morgan went systematically to work to catch every thing that should come into sight. There was, of course, a great deal of passing to and from the headquarters of the commanding officers and between the various camps. No one anticipated danger there, and stragglers, couriers, escorts, and guards, went carelessly and unsuspectingly along, into the same bag. In the course of an hour or two eighty odd prisoners were taken.

Colonel Wood went off with twenty-eight of them, and, by some oversight, sixty were started to Murfreesboro', later, guarded by only ten men. A number of wagons had been also captured and burned. The teams were used to mount the prisoners. One staff officer was captured and sent off with the large hatch of prisoners. Captain Morgan remained behind with one man, after he had sent off all the others. This sort of service always gave him great pleasure, and he was loth to give it up. As the number of passengers fell off, he rode down the road with his companion, dressed like himself in a blue overcoat, to a point where a guard of ten men were stationed under a Sergeant for some purpose. He placed himself between them and their guns, made his follower put his pistol to the head of the Sergeant and began to rate them for neglect of duty. He represented himself as a Federal officer of high rank and reminded them sternly and reproachfully that such careless guard as they were then keeping had enabled Morgan to play all of his tricks. They had been careless and were overwhelmed with just shame and mortification at his rebuke. He at length ordered them all under arrest, and taking the Sergeant's weapons from him and leaving the guns stacked—he could not have carried them off without entrusting them to the prisoners—he marched the whole party away. They were under the impression that they were going to Mitchell's headquarters, but he got them mounted and carried them to Murfreesboro'. In the meantime the smoke from the wagons which were burned within half a mile of Mitchell's headquarters, attracted attention and led to inquiry, and it was not long before what was going on was discovered. Troops were at once dispatched to put a stop to the mischief and beat off or follow the perpetrators. The Fourth Ohio got on the track of the party guarding the sixty prisoners, and, as its progress was necessarily slow, it was soon overtaken. Nothing could be done but release the prisoners and run for it, and the whole escort went off in rapid flight. One prisoner had, by a strange mistake, been allowed to retain a loaded gun. As one of the guard who had been in the extreme rear of the column dashed past this man, the latter fired and grazed his face. The other turned in his saddle, fired and shot his unexpected assailant dead. The pursuers had gotten close before they had been perceived, and they pressed the chase vigorously. Over fences and gulches, through fields and thickets, as hard as their horses could go, fled the one party and followed the other for ten miles. One of our men was killed, two or three wounded, and as many captured. Thirty-eight prisoners were secured by Morgan—twenty-eight brought off by Wood, and ten captured and escorted by himself. On the evening of the same day a party of eighteen men were dispatched from the camp on the Shelbyville road to push as close to Nashville as possible, and learn the position of the Federal troops in that quarter. I was myself in command of the party, and had an accurate knowledge of the points at which guards and pickets had been previously stationed. On arriving in the vicinity of these points—around which, without creating an alarm, it was desirable to pass, in order to get near to the encampments and observe them closely—they were found unoccupied. The party moved some three miles further down the road without coming upon an enemy, although a day or two before the picket posts had been thick in this quarter.

It was apparent that some plan for our benefit had caused this change, and unusual caution became necessary. I had hoped to find some officers quartered at the houses well in the rear of the reserve pickets, where they would believe themselves secure, and to capture them, but I now approached the houses, not with the expectation of making prisoners, but of getting information. None of the citizens in that neighborhood had ever seen any man in my party, and they would tell nothing, but their alarm at seeing us, and evident anxiety to get rid of us, showed plainly that they knew of the proximity of danger. At length, when in about six hundred yards of the Cross-roads near "Flat Rock," I think it is called, four miles from Nashville, and where it was confidently reported by our informants that McCook's division was encamped, I halted and secreted men and horses in the thick brush on the right hand side of the road, and, with the guide, went forward on foot about a quarter of a mile, until I suddenly heard the challenge of a picket. I judged from the words I caught that it was the officer of the day making his rounds. Soon a negro came down the road toward us, whom we caught and questioned. He answered very glibly, and evinced too little fear, not to excite suspicion that he came out to be captured with a made-up tale. He said that there were ten men on picket at the Cross-roads. As a large encampment was only a few hundred yards on the other side of this point, his story did not seem credible. However, we had at last found an enemy.

Leaving five men to take care of the horses, in the thicket where they were already concealed I carried the others through a wide meadow on the right of the road which we had traveled (the Shelbyville and Nashville pike) to the road which crossed it at "Flat Rock," striking the latter about two hundred yards from the point of intersection. I was convinced that the withdrawal of the pickets was part of a plan to entrap just such scouting parties as ours, and that a strong force was in ambush at the Cross-roads. There was little hope of accomplishing the objects of the expedition, but the trap could, at least, be sprung, and there was a chance of surprising the ambuscade. My men were armed with shot-guns and pistols, the proper weapons for such an affair. I ordered them to follow me in single-file in the direction of the enemy, instructing them to hold their fire until we were challenged, and to then discharge their weapons, and, without stopping to reload, make their way back to the horses. The moon had just gone down as we began to move slowly down the road. We made little noise, and were soon convinced by a chorus of coughing, which broke on our ears as we neared them, that a pretty good crowd was before us. When we had almost reached the point where the roads cross, a Sergeant, with five or six men at his back, sprang up, so near to us that I could have touched him by making another step, and ordered "halt," in a low voice, evidently taking us for friends. Our answer was a shot, and he fell dead. His comrades returned our fire, and at once a line of men rose from the fence corners on the opposite side of the road which we had just descended—we had passed them unseen in the darkness. Many of them must have been asleep until alarmed by the firing. The bulk of the force, however, was stationed upon the other road, and, as they sprang up at the sudden uproar, and aimed at the blaze of the guns, they endangered their own friends more than us. My men sank at once upon their knees, and the enemy firing wildly and high, did not touch one of them. They pointed their shot-guns low, and every flash was followed by a groan, and, by the quick vivid light, we could see the men we hit writhing on the ground. The curses and commands of the officers, shouts of the combatants, and yells of the wounded were mingled together. The breadth of the road, only, separated us, and the blaze from the guns met. When our weapons were emptied, we sprang over the fence and ran at top speed for our horses. A chain picket which had been posted on the left of the Shelbyville road, a short distance from it, rushed forward and opened upon us, and the enemy we had just bidden farewell redoubled his fire. When we regained the horses, we were nearly surrounded. Parties had come out from the woods behind us, as we passed down the road, and our retreat by the way we had come was blocked. Our signals to call in the laggards, as we prepared to leave, were answered from every direction by the enemy. But the woods befriended us, as they had often done before, and we escaped under its shelter. On that same night a similar adventure befell some Confederates (I think of Starne's command) on the Franklin pike, and some pickets were killed on the side of Nashville entirely opposite to that into which all of these roads (which have been mentioned) run. Of course every thing was attributed to Morgan, and the Federals were puzzled and uncertain, whether to believe him really *ubiquitous*, or the commander of two or three thousand men.

A day or two after these occurrences, Morgan went with a flag of truce to Mitchell's encampment to endeavor to exchange some of his prisoners for his own men who had been captured. Colonel Wood, who was with him, was asked confidentially how many men Morgan had, and was told that the mischief he was doing could only be accounted for upon the supposition that he had control of a large force. Wood answered, also *in confidence*, that although he had co-operated with Morgan for two or three weeks, he was entirely ignorant of the strength of his command. That he knew, only, that Morgan was controlling the motions of men whom he (Morgan) rarely saw; and that, although he himself was intimately cognizant of all that occurred under Morgan's immediate supervision, he was frequently astonished by hearing from the latter, accounts of enterprises which had been accomplished by his orders in quarters very remote from where he was in person operating. Wood saw the impression which prevailed, and shaped his answers to confirm it. In reality, there were not in the vicinity of Nashville, at that time, on all sides, more than three hundred Confederate soldiers. Of this number, Morgan could control only his own three companies and the fifty men with Wood, although the others, who were stragglers, and furloughed men from the Texas Rangers, Starne's, McNairy's and other cavalry regiments, often joined him upon his expeditions.

Many of the Federal soldiers killed around Nashville, and whose deaths were, charged to Morgan's men, were killed by the *independent* partisans, most of them men who lived in the neighboring country, and had obtained leave to linger, for a while, about their homes. Great zeal and activity, however, was displayed by all parties.

When the flag of truce party mentioned above got to the picket line, it was met by an expedition consisting of cavalry, artillery and infantry, riding in wagons, *en route* for Murfreesboro', with the expectation of capturing Morgan's entire band. General Mitchell was very angry when the arrival of the flag was announced, and complained that Morgan had taken that method of defeating his plans, that otherwise would have been assuredly successful. This charge created a good deal of amusement, when Morgan told the story later to his brother officers of Johnson's array. Even if Morgan (as Mitchell thought), had known that an expedition was on foot for his capture, he still would have had a perfect right to transact at that time—if listened to—any matter of business which required to be done under flag of truce. It is legitimate to send them even while battles are going on.

During the entire war, both sides used to send flags of truce for quite other purposes than the ostensible ones. Morgan was the commanding Confederate officer in all that region, and had a right to send flags of truce for any purpose whatever, so long as he observed the usages which govern them. The flag of truce need not have stopped the expedition.

It was Mitchell's own fault if it was allowed to go far enough to see what he wished to conceal. It is the right and positive duty of an officer in charge of a flag, to go as far as he is permitted. General Mitchell could have refused to receive it, and have ordered it back. Morgan's friends somewhat doubted whether this expedition (even if it had not been met and checked by the flag of truce), would have resulted in Morgan's capture. General Mitchell was a profound strategist, but he was going to travel by daylight through a country full of Morgan's friends, and upon a road constantly watched by his scouts, to surprise Morgan. At any rate, it may be safely asserted that the fond hope which General Mitchell cherished, could never have been realized, after Morgan had gotten such timely information of an expedition intended for his capture, that he was able to meet it with a flag of truce as it was just setting out.

The country around Nashville, in which Morgan did the service, which I have attempted to describe, is one admirably adapted to it. It is one of the most fertile and wealthy portions of Middle Tennessee, a region unsurpassed in productiveness. Yet teeming as it is with every crop which the farmer wishes, one would think, in riding along the fine turnpikes which enter Nashville upon all sides, that a comparatively small proportion of the land is cultivated. A dense growth of timber, principally cedar, stretches, sometimes for miles, along the roads, and runs back from them, occasionally, to considerable distances. The cedar glades, are, some of them, of great extent, and are penetrated in all directions by roads. Springs, and small watercourses, are frequent. It is indeed a beautiful country, and the paradise of partisan cavalry, who can find in it, every where, supplies for men and horses, shelter to hide them, going against and escaping from an enemy, and, stop where they will, all that makes a camp happy.

The people who live in this country are worthy to possess it. They are brave, frank, generous and hospitable—true to their friends, kind to the distressed. They are just and honorable, and uphold through all trials and evils, the right, as they understand it, and their plighted word. Come what will upon this country, may God bless the people of Middle Tennessee.

Two or three days after the flag of truce affair, Morgan determined upon an expedition to a different quarter from that in which he had been hitherto employed. It was high time that, in accordance with the instructions he had received, he followed and rejoined the army, and he desired to leave an impression upon the enemy of his "ubiquity," which would be useful, after he himself was gone.

Upon the north side of the Cumberland, and about eight miles from it in a direct line, is the little town of Gallatin, in Sumner County, Tennessee. It is situated on the Louisville and Nashville road, about thirty miles from Nashville. This place was one of no military importance at that time, but it was right upon the line of communication between Louisville and Nashville—the roads running from Kentucky, as well as the railroad, all passing through it—and the line of telegraph. This place is about fifty miles from Murfreesboro', by the most direct route. Morgan resolved to hold this place for a day or two, and get the benefit of the "communication" himself. He left Murfreesboro' about midday, passed through Lebanon that evening, and encamped for the night near that place. Crossing the Cumberland next morning at Canoe-branch ferry, he reached Gallatin about ten o'clock. He found the town ungarrisoned, two or three clerks to take care of unimportant stores, and a telegraph operator, constituting all the force there was to oppose him. The citizens of this place were always strongly attached to the Confederate cause, and devoted friends of Morgan and his command—for which they subsequently suffered no little—and they received him enthusiastically. This neighborhood was always noted for good cheer, and, on this occasion, dainties of all kinds appeared as if by magic, and bouquets were showered by the score. Desiring the latest information from Nashville, Morgan, accompanied by Colonel Wood, went straight to the telegraph office, where they were kindly received by the operator, to whom they introduced themselves as Federal officers just from the interior of Kentucky. The operator immediately placed himself in communication with Nashville and got the last news for their benefit. The conversation then turned on Morgan. "The clerk of the lightning" said that he had not yet disturbed them at Gallatin, but that he might be expected any day: "However," he continued, "let him come, I, for one, am ready for him." He told the story of Morgan's coming to Mitchell's lines with the flag of truce (which, it seems, had raised great excitement), and declared that he ought to have been shot then and there. "Had I been there," said he, fiercely, and brandishing his revolver, "the scoundrel would have never left alive."

"Give me that pistol," Morgan said quietly; and, taking it, much to the fellow's surprise, "I am Morgan."

The consternation of the operator was extreme, and his apology, when he found his tongue, polite. It was accepted, and so was he and placed under guard. He was badly scared, at first, but he was treated kindly, and in a few days became domesticated and even playful. An engine and a few cars, found standing at the depot, were taken possession of—the cars were immediately burned. Morgan got on the engine with two or three companions, and run some miles up the railroad to visit two or three points of interest. He desired especially to ascertain if the tunnel could readily be destroyed, but found that it would be a work of more time than he had to spare. While he was absent, several Federal officers and soldiers came into the town and were made prisoners. When he returned, the engine was run off the track, over a steep bank, and destroyed. On the next morning he sent the bulk of his command across the river again, with instructions to remain near and guard the ferry. He, himself, with ten or fifteen men, remained at Gallatin two days longer with the hope of catching some of the trains. He was disappointed, the news got around and none came. Twenty or thirty wagons which were coming from Scottsville, under a small guard, were also turned back—the escort getting the alarm after he had made all his preparations to capture them—so that his expedition was more barren of the spoils of war than he had hoped. But his main object—to persuade the enemy that they could never safely count upon his being "gone"—was perfectly accomplished. While his men on the south side of the river were waiting for him, six transports, loaded with troops from Monticello, passed down toward Nashville. The men on the boats did not know who the cavalry were, and our men were afraid to fire upon them, lest they might endanger Captain Morgan and their comrades with him, on the other side. Immediately after his return to Murfreesboro', he set out to rejoin the army, and met at Shelbyville that portion of his command which had been encamped on the Shelbyville and Nashville road, and which, in obedience to his orders, had also repaired to the former place.

Here we remained for two or three days and then marched on in the track of the army. While at Shelbyville, the first and only causeless stampede of our pickets and false alarm to the camps which occurred during our squadron organization, took place. Ten or fifteen men were posted on picket some eight miles from the town toward Nashville, near a small bridge, at the southern end of which the extreme outpost vidette stood. From tales told by the citizens, these pickets had conceived the idea that the enemy contemplated an attack to surprise and capture them, and (perhaps for the very reason that they had so often played the same game themselves) they became very nervous about it. Late in the night, two men came down the road from toward Nashville in a buggy, and drove rapidly upon the bridge without heeding the vidette's challenge—he, taking them to be the enemy, shot both barrels of his gun at them and fled to alarm the other videttes and his comrades at the base. The whole party became so alarmed by his representation of the immense number and headlong advance of the enemy, that, without stopping to fight or reconnoiter, they all came in a hand-gallop to camp. The officer in charge sent the vidette who had given the alarm, in advance, to report to me. I immediately got the command under arms and then questioned him. He stated that the enemy's cavalry came on, at the charge, in column of fours, that they paid no attention to his challenge, and that when he fired, they dashed at him, making the air ring with their yells and curses. He said that "the road seemed perfectly blue for more than half a mile," so great was their number.

It was a moonless night, and a slight rain was falling, making the darkness intense. I asked him if he might not have been deceived and if he was not scared. "No, sir," said he, "not a bit, but I was somewhat *arrytated*."

Leaving Shelbyville, we marched through Fayetteville to Huntsville; every where along the route the people flocked to see Morgan, and his progress was one continual ovation. When we reached Huntsville, the most beautiful town in Alabama (and now that Columbia is in ashes) perhaps in the entire South, we were received with the kindness and hospitality which characterize that generous, warm-hearted population. Huntsville, the birth-place of Morgan, greeted him like a mother indeed. For ten days we remained there; every man in the command the recipient of unwearying attention. It was very injurious to good soldierly habits, but served, as many other such instances did, to show the men that they were fighting for a people who loved to be grateful, and to prove it—and unavailing as the struggle was, it is still a thought of pride and satisfaction, that the labors and sacrifices were made for a people worthy of them all.

Crossing the Tennessee river at Decatur and marching just in the track of the army, we reached Byrnesville, a few miles from Corinth, on the third of April, and found there the division of General Breckinridge, to which we were attached. The whole army was then astir, and forming to march to attack the enemy who lay at Pittsburg Landing on the southern bank of the Tennessee some twenty miles from Corinth.

Morgan's services were much talked of, and he was complimented by General Johnson in terms that were very grateful to him. He was given the commission of Colonel, to take effect from the fourth of April, and he received (what he valued much more highly) an assurance, or what he construed to be such, that he would be permitted to act independently again, and follow his favorite service with a stronger force and upon a larger scale.

None among the many ardent and high-strung men who went with so much zeal into that fight, felt more hope and enthusiasm than Morgan, for he saw beyond it, a career of excitement, success, and glory, that might satisfy the most energetic and most daring nature.

CHAPTER VII

On the 3rd of April, the army, leaving its cantonments around Corinth, commenced its advance, and the heads of the columns were directed toward Pittsburg, on the Tennessee river, where, unconscious of the gathering storm, lay the Federal host under General Grant, which had conquered at Donelson. Flushed with that victory and insolent with triumph, the enemy rested for the long march of invasion which he believed would lead him (unchecked, even if opposed) to easy, speedy and decisive conquest. No thought of danger to himself, disturbed these pleasant anticipations.

The suggestion that an attack from the Confederate forces at Corinth was imminent, would have been dismissed as the idlest and weakest of apprehensions. The different corps moved from their respective positions, on the railroads which enter Corinth, by the most direct roads to the point indicated for their concentration.

General Johnson had declared, some weeks previously, with prophetic judgment, that upon that very spot, "the great battle of the Southwest would be fought."

Breckinridge's division, to which Morgan's squadron was now attached, moved from Byrnesville. The roads were narrow and miry, and were not improved by a heavy rain which fell during the march, and by the passage of successive trains of wagons and batteries of artillery. The march was slow and toilsome. The infantry labored along with mud-clogged feet, casting sour looks and candid curses at the cavalry and couriers, who bespattered them. The artillery often stuck fast, and the struggling horses failed to move the pieces, until the cannoneers applied themselves and pushed and strained at the heavy wheels.

On the 5th, about three or four in the afternoon, every thing was concentrated upon the ground, where General Johnson proposed to establish his line, and the disposition of the forces, in accordance with the plan of battle, was at once commenced. On account of some accident, or mistake, this concentration was effected one day later than had been contemplated, causing a corresponding delay in the attack. It has frequently been asserted that this was occasioned by the failure of General Polk's corps to arrive at the appointed time.

General Polk's report demonstrates the injustice of this statement, and it is probable that the condition of the roads was the sole cause of the delay.

A want of promptness upon the part of General Polk, no doubt would have produced a suspension of the attack. A corps so strong and efficient, could have been ill-spared from an army, already inferior in numbers to the antagonist it was about to assail, and the absence of the brave old Bishop from the field, would have been, of itself, a serious loss. This delay was the cause of grave apprehensions to many of the

Confederate Generals, and, as matters were managed, was really unfortunate.

It was known that Buell was marching rapidly to the support of Grant, and General Johnson wished to crush the latter before their junction was effected.

General Beauregard was of opinion that the attack, having been so long delayed, ought to be abandoned altogether; that it would now be extremely hazardous, and that the safety of the army would be compromised if it did not retire promptly to Corinth.

General Johnson listened courteously to every argument, but was moved by none to relinquish his plan. His resolution to fight, after placing his army in front of the enemy, was fixed. He believed, "the offensive once assumed, ought to be maintained at all hazards." He trusted that vigor and audacity would enable him to accomplish victory on the first day, before the fresh troops came, and his designs were too profoundly considered, his gallant faith in his soldiers, too earnest, for his purpose to be shaken. In answer to an anxious inquiry from his aide, Colonel William Preston, he said, quietly, "I would fight them were they a million."

The ground selected for battle was that inclosed between Owl and Lick creeks, which run nearly parallel with each other, and empty into the Tennessee river. The flanks of the two armies rested upon these little streams, and the front of each was just the distances, at their respective positions, between the two creeks. The Confederate front was, consequently, a little more than three miles long. The distance between the creeks widens somewhat, as they approach the river, and the Federal army had more ground upon which to deploy. The position which the enemy occupied next morning, is five or six miles from the river, and his advance camp was perhaps a mile southward of Shiloh Church. He had, as yet, established no line; the attack next morning took him completely by surprise, and he formed after the fight had commenced.

General Johnson's effective strength, including all the forces available for that battle, was about thirty-five thousand men. That of the enemy was, perhaps, forty-five thousand men. The advantages of attack and surprise would, General Johnson thought, more than counterbalance his numerical inferiority. If Buell brought reinforcements to his opponents, by forced marches, in advance of his army, he would feel their effect only in a stronger line, and more stubborn resistance upon the front—his flanks would be safe in any event. The array of his forces evinced a resolution to break through and crush, at any cost, whatever should confront him in the narrow space where the whole conflict would be crowded.

The troops were bivouacked that night upon the ground which it was intended that they should occupy in line of battle. No disposition which could be made that evening was delayed; every precaution was taken to guard against a further procrastination of the attack. The men laid down to sleep in the order in which they were to rush upon the enemy.

General Hardee had command of the first line, General Bragg of the second, and General Polk of the third. General Hardee's line extended from the one creek to the other, and as his corps (fully deployed) could not properly occupy the entire distance, he was reinforced by a fine brigade under Brigadier General Gladden. To Hardee was given the honor of commencing the battle, and he was ordered to push his whole line rapidly forward, at early dawn. General Bragg's line was formed similarly to General Hardee's, and about a quarter of a mile in its rear. Bragg was ordered to advance simultaneously with Hardee, and to support him when he needed assistance. Then, at the distance of eight hundred yards, came General Polk's corps, not deployed, but formed in column of brigades. General Breckinridge's division (over six thousand strong) constituted the reserve, and was close in the rear of Polk's corps. The cavalry was promiscuously disposed—indeed, no one in authority seemed to think it could win the battle. Morgan's squadron was formed with the Kentucky troops, and occupied the extreme left of Breckinridge's division. This disposition of the forces and the energetic conduct of the Confederate commanders, explain the striking features of the battle, which have been so often remarked—the *methodical* success of the Confederates, upon the first day, the certainty with which they won their way forward against the most determined resistance; the "clock-like" regularity of their advance, the desperate struggle, the Federal retreat, repeated again and again through the day. Taking into consideration the circumstances under which the collision occurred, military *savants* will, some day, demonstrate that success ought, with mathematical certainty, to have resulted from the tactics of General Johnson. An army moving to attack (an enemy, surprised and unprepared), in three lines, supported by a reserve, and with its flanks perfectly protected, ought to have delivered crushing and continuous blows. Such a formation, directed by consummate skill and the finest nerve in a commander, of troops who believed that to fight would be to win, promised an onset well nigh irresistible.

The afternoon wore away and no sign in the enemy's camps indicated that he had discovered our presence. The night fell, and, the stern preparations for the morrow, having been all completed, the army sank to rest. The forest was soon almost as still as before it had been tenanted with the hosts of war. But, before the day broke, the army was astir; the bugles sounded the reveille on all sides, and the long lines began to form. About five o'clock, the first gun rang on the front—another and another, succeeding, as our skirmishers pressed on, until the musketry grew into the crackling, labored sound, which precedes the roar of real battle. The troops seemed excited to frenzy by the sound. It was the first fight in which the majority of them had ever been engaged, and they had, as yet, seen and suffered nothing to abate the ardor with which the high-spirited young fellows panted for battle. Every one who witnessed that scene—the marshaling of the Confederate army for attack upon the morning of the sixth of April—must remember more distinctly than any thing else, the glowing enthusiasm of the men, their buoyancy and spirited impatience to close with the enemy. As each regiment formed upon the ground where it had bivouacked, the voice of its commander might be heard as he spoke high words of encouragement to his men, and it would ring clearer as he appealed to their regimental pride, and bade them think of the fame they might win. When the lines began to advance, the wild cheers which arose made the woods stir as if with the rush of a mighty wind. No where was there any thought of fear—every where were the evidences of impetuous and determined valor.

For some distance the woods were open and clear of undergrowth, and the troops passed through, preserving their array with little difficulty; but as the point, where the fight between the pickets had commenced, was neared, the timber became dwarfed into scrubby brush, and at some places dense thickets impeded the advance. The ground, too, grew rugged and difficult of passage in unbroken line. Frequent halts to reform and dress the ranks became necessary, and at such times General Johnson's magnificent battle order was read to the regiments, and its manly, heroic language was listened to with the feeling it was intended to evoke. The gray, clear morning was, ere long, enlivened with a radiant sunrise. As the great light burst in full splendor above the horizon, sending brilliancy over the scene, many a man thought of the great conqueror's augury and pointed in exultation and hope to the "Sun of Shiloh." Breckinridge's division went into the fight last, and, of course, saw or heard a great deal of it, before becoming itself actively engaged. Not far off, on the left and center, the fight soon grew earnest, as Hardee dashed resolutely on; the uneasy, broken rattle of the skirmishers gave way to the sustained volleys of the lines, and the artillery joined in the clamor, while away on the right, the voice of the strife swelled hoarser and angrier, like the growl of some wounded monster—furious and at bay. Hardee's line carried all before it. At the first encampment it met not even the semblance of a check. Following close and eager upon the fleeing pickets, it burst upon the startled inmates as they emerged, half clad, from their tents, giving them no time to form, driving them in rapid panic, bayoneting the dilatory—on through the camp swept, together, pursuers and pursued. But now the alarm was thoroughly given, the "long roll" and the bugle were calling the Federals to arms; all through their thick encampments they were hastily forming.

As Hardee, close upon the haunches of the foe he had first started, broke into another camp, a long line of steel and flame met him, staggering, and for a little while, stopping his advance. But his gallant corps was still too fresh for an enemy, not yet recovered from the enervating effects of surprise, to hold it back long. For a while it writhed and surged before the stern barrier suddenly erected in its front, and then, gathering itself, dashed irresistibly forward. The enemy was beaten back, but the hardy Western men who filled his ranks (although raw and for the first time under fire) could not be forced to positive flight. They had once formed, and at this stage of the battle, they could not be routed. They had little discipline, but plenty of staunch courage. Soon they turned for another stand, and the Confederates were, at once, upon them. Again they gave way, but strewed the path of their stubborn retreat with many a corpse in gray as well as in blue. At half past seven the first lines began to give signs of exhaustion, and its march over the rough ground while struggling with the enemy, had thinned and impaired it. It was time for Bragg's corps to come to the relief, and that superb line now moved up in serried strength. The first sign of slackening upon the part of the Confederates seemed to add vigor to the enemy's resistance. But bravely as they fought, they never recovered from the stun of the surprise. Their half of the battle was out of joint at the beginning, and it was never gotten right during that day. They were making desperate efforts to retrieve their lost ground when Bragg's disciplined tornado burst upon them. The shock was met gallantly but in vain. Another bloody grapple was followed by another retreat of the Federals, and again our line moved on.

Those who were in that battle will remember these successive contests, followed by short periods of apparent inaction, going on all the day. To use the illustration of one well acquainted with its plan and incidents: "It went on like the regular stroke of some tremendous machine." There would be a rapid charge and fierce fight—the wild yell would announce a Confederate success—then would ensue a comparative lull, broken again in a few minutes, and the charge, struggle and horrible din would recommence.

About half past ten Polk's corps prepared to take part in the fight. He had previously, by order personally given by General Johnson (who was all the time in the front), sent one brigade to reinforce General Bragg's right, where the second line had been most hotly engaged. He had also sent, by order of General Beauregard, one brigade to the left. The fight at this time was joined all along the line, and urged with greater fury, than at any period of the day. Almost immediately after parting with these two brigades, General Polk became engaged with the remainder of his corps. The enemy had, now, disposed his entire force for resistance—the men fought as if determined not to accept defeat—and their stern, tenacious leader was not the man to relinquish hope, although his lines had been repeatedly broken and the ground was piled with his slain. The corps of Hardee, Bragg and Polk, were now striving abreast, or mingled with each other.

In reading the reports of the Confederate Generals, frequent allusion will be found to regiments and brigades fighting without "head or orders." One commander would sometimes direct the movements of troops belonging to another. At this phase of the struggle, the narrative should dwell more upon "the biographies of the regiments than the history of the battle." But the wise arrangement of the lines and the instructions given subordinate commanders, ensured harmonious action and the desired result.

Each brigade commander was ordered (when he became disengaged), to seek and attack the nearest enemy, to press the flank of every stubborn hostile force which his neighbors could not move, and at all hazards to press forward. General Johnson seemed to have adopted the spirit of the motto, "When fighting in the dark, strike out straight." He more than once assumed command of brigades which knew not what to do, and led them to where they could fight with effect. Our successes were not won without costly sacrifices, and the carnage was lavish upon both sides.

While all this was going on in front, Morgan's squadron moved along with Breckinridge's division, and we listened to the hideous noise, and thought how much larger the affair was than the skirmishes on Green river and around Nashville. We soon learned to distinguish when the fight was sharp and hotly contested, and when our lines were triumphantly advancing, and we wondered if those before us would finish the business before we got in.

We had not marched far, before we saw bloody indications of the fierce work that had been done upon the ground over which we were passing. The dead and the wounded were thick in the first camp, and, thence, onward. Some of the corpses (of men killed by artillery), showed ghastly mutilation. In getting up our glowing anticipation of the day's programme, we had left these items out of the account, and we mournfully recognized the fact, that many who seek military distinction, will obtain it posthumously, if they get it at all. The actual sight of a corpse immensely chills an abstract love of glory. The impression soon wears off, however, and the dead are very little noticed. Toward ten or eleven o'clock we wandered away from the infantry to which we had been attached, and getting no orders or instructions, devoted ourselves to an examination of the many interesting scenes of the field, which we viewed with keen relish.

The camps whence the enemy had been driven, attracted especial and admiring attention. There was a profusion of all the necessaries, and many of the luxuries of military life. How we wondered that an army could have ever permitted itself to be driven away from them.

While we were curiously inspecting the second or third encampment, and had gotten closer, than at any time previously, to the scene of the fighting, a slight incident interrupted, for a moment, the pleasure of the investigation. Some of the enemy's shells were bursting over our heads, and as we were practically ignorant of artillery, we were at first puzzled to know what they were. In the general thunder of the fight, no special reports could be heard, to lead to a solution of the particular phenomena. Suddenly a short yell of mingled indignation and amazement, announced that one of the party had some practical information on the subject. He had been struck by a fragment on the shoulder, inflicting a severe gash and bruise. Not knowing how the missile had reached him, he seemed to think himself a very ill-treated man.

Just as Breckinridge's division was going into action, about 12 P.M., we came upon the left of it, where the Kentucky troops were formed. The bullets were beginning to fly thick about us. Simultaneously, the squadron and the regiment nearest to us, struck up the favorite song of the Kentuckians, "Cheer Boys, Cheer"—the effect was animating beyond all description.

About this time our advance was receiving its first serious check.

While the right and the left were advancing, the left-center was repulsed before a strong position which the enemy held in force. They were posted upon an eminence, in front of which were thickets and underbrush. Plenty of artillery strongly supported, crowned this eminence, and Hardee's utmost efforts to carry it had been foiled. So furiously played the batteries of the enemy, that nothing could be seen of the position, but sheets of flame and clouds of smoke. When an advance was attempted against it, a shower of minnie balls would be felt. It was finally taken, after the impetus given the line by the arrival of the reserve under Breckinridge, had sent our forces forward on both sides so far, that it was completely flanked. While the advance, at this point, was thus suspended, the squadron happened to approach, and General Hardee sent an aide to know "what cavalry that was?" Upon learning that it was Morgan's, he expressed himself much pleased, and said that he would use it to "take that battery." When informed of this truly gratifying compliment, the men bore themselves with becoming sobriety, and as they formed for the charge, which we were told would be immediately ordered, they indulged in no unseemly or extravagant expressions of joy. Indeed, it is an historical fact, that while we were ready enough to go, we were not so sanguine of the result as General Hardee seemed to be. The General sat on his horse near Schoup's gallant battery which was replying, but ineffectually, to the vicious rain of grape and shell which poured from the hill. He seemed indifferent to the terrible volleys, and only anxious to capture the guns.

The order, we were expecting, was never given us. At the first slackening of the fire from the hill, some of the infantry regiments, which were lying down, dashed forward, but the enemy left the position because he was in danger of being surrounded. Many of the guns were abandoned.

The right was now checked, meeting the fiercest resistance. The left and center bore rapidly forward.

From a passage in General Bragg's report, it would seem that it had been part of the plan to press more strongly upon our right and drive the enemy down the river, "leaving the left open for him to escape." But it was already apparent that he was being hemmed in and forced from all sides, toward Pittsburg Landing.

General Hardee, at this time, ordered Colonel Morgan to take his command to the extreme left, and "charge the first enemy he saw." Colonel Morgan immediately proceeded in the direction indicated as rapidly as his column could gallop. The left of our line was moving so swiftly to the front that, leaving to go some distance by a bridle path in the rear, before turning to overtake it, we did not reach it until nearly one o'clock in the afternoon. Just as we approached, we saw, on the extreme left, a body of men dressed in blue uniforms, going through with some strange evolutions. Their dress was much like that of the enemy, but there were troops, evidently Confederate, not far from them that were paying them no attention. Colonel Morgan ordered a platoon of Company A, to dismount and approach them cautiously, to fire into them if satisfied that they were the enemy, and it was his intention to then charge them. We drew very near to them unnoticed. A little man flourishing a portentous saber, was directing their movements with off-hand eloquence. We forbore to fire, because, although we did not understand what he said, we thought from the emphasis of the speaker, his volubility, and the imprecatory sound of the language, that it was French, and that his party were Louisianians. This surmise was correct. They were members of Colonel Mouton's fine regiment, the Eighteenth Louisiana. Their uniform cost them dearly before the fight was over. They were frequently fired into by Confederate regiments, and received, in that way, smart loss. At length they retaliated whenever they received a volley. This caused some complaint, but it is related that the Louisianians gave sound military reasons for their conduct, saying: "We fire at any body, what fire at us—G-d d-m." Shortly after we made this discovery, we saw this regiment and a portion of the Kentucky brigade, charge across a wide field on the extreme left of our line. Here a ravine which had protected our left flank suddenly terminated, and when the line had dashed across this field and had entered the woods beyond, it was entirely uncovered. A strong force of the enemy was formed in the middle of this field (where one of the camps was situated), and the Confederates rushed so closely upon them, that it seemed as if the bayonets must cross, before they gave way. The volume of musketry in this charge was tremendous, and drowned the crash of the artillery. When the Federals turned to retreat they still preserved their array, and went off in perfect order.

They frequently faced about to fire on their pursuers, who poured continuous volleys into them, and thus fighting they disappeared in the woods. Our squadron and the Texian rangers—Eighth Texas—were following behind the infantry, and had been unable to get past them, or (on account of the ravine) to the left of them. Now, however, an opportunity of actively participating in the battle occurred, which we had not expected. As we were pressing across the field, some Federal skirmishers appeared in the edge of the woods upon the left of the field, not more than eighty yards from us. They directed their attention principally to Byrne's battery, which was also crossing the field, and prevented the cannoneers from unlimbering the guns. Colonel Morgan at once ordered the charge, and the squadron dashed at full gallop into the woods. The skirmishers ran back, but as we forced our way in a crowded mass (all line lost) through the thickets, we came suddenly upon the infantry regiment to which these skirmishers belonged. Fortunately for us, this regiment, in scrambling through the brush, had lost the compactness of its formation. We came close upon them before the Federals fired—they delivered one stunning volley, the blaze almost reaching our faces, and the roar rang in our ears like thunder. The next moment we rode right through them—some of the men trying to cut them down with the saber, and making ridiculous failures, others doing real execution with gun and pistol. We lost only three men killed, but they were noble, gallant soldiers—Lieutenant James West and privates Samuel Buckner and James Ghiselin. We lost several others wounded. Twelve of the enemy were killed and a few made prisoners. The affair was over directly, and the Federals retreated. The Texians, as we prepared to charge, asked what we were going to do. "To go in," was the answer, "Then we will go in, too," they shouted, and galloping down the rear of our line, until they reached the right of it, they turned short to the left and charged into the woods. They struck the rest of the brigade to which the regiment we had met belonged, and drove it back for some distance. They were never checked until they reached a high fence, which they could not pass. Their loss was then severe, and many of their riderless horses came galloping over the ground where our wounded lay.

Our infantry had pressed on beyond this point, and there was no Confederate force near except this cavalry. It was impossible to conjecture how strong the enemy was just here, but Colonel Morgan, fearing that he might come in force sufficient to endanger this flank, disposed his command on foot, to make all possible resistance in such an event. Our skirmishers, thrown forward, could not find him, and the receding din of the battle seemed to promise perfect safety against all such dangers. About half-past one or two o'clock, occurred the great calamity which rendered unavailing all of the sacrifices and successes of the day. General Johnson was killed. He had exposed himself with almost culpable recklessness. From the commencement of the fight he had been in the van—cheering the struggling men—adding fresh spirit to the charge—stimulating to new energy the battalions that were checked. His clothing had been torn by balls which were unheeded.

Once he had ridden along the rear of a brave Arkansas Regiment, which had just recoiled from a terrible fire. "Where now," he said, striking some of the men encouragingly upon the shoulder, "are the Arkansas boys, who boasted that they would fight with their bowie knives? You have a nobler weapon in your grasp—will you dare to use it?" He spoke to men who could not hear such words in vain—they rushed forward and won the position.

Statham's magnificent brigade had at length faltered. General Johnson, bare-headed and with his hand elevated, rode out in front of the brigade, and called on it to follow. His dress, majestic presence, imposing gesture and large gray horse, made him a conspicuous mark. A ball pierced his leg, severing the artery. He paid no notice to the wound, but continued to follow the troops, who, incited by his example, had charged successfully. Suddenly he grew faint and reeled in his saddle. His staff came to his assistance, but too late. They bore him into a ravine for shelter, and in a few moments he died. I cannot venture to speak of General Johnson in the ordinary terms of eulogy—such applied to him would seem frivolous and profane. He was too great for it in life—and it would little accord with the veneration, silent, but profound, with which we, his people, cherish his memory. If he had lived but a few days more! Shortly after this great disaster the lines were pressed forward rapidly again at all points. Our troops were still instinct with the spirit of the lost leader. His genius had prepared effects, accomplished after he was gone. The left had swept far around—the center, where the latest check had been felt, was a little behind—the right driving everything before it, when, by hard fighting the resistance opposed to it at noon had been overcome, was approaching the river.

Now the word was passed through the army, "Let every order be forward." In the last determined stand which the enemy made, Major General Prentice and two thousand of his division were captured. His troops stood, until the advancing Confederates closed in on two sides, and escape had become impossible.

Our army was now near the river, and a victory absolutely complete and decisive, was just within its grasp. The fighting had been hard and our success blood-bought but brilliant. For many miles (through his encampments, piled up with rich spoils) we had driven the enemy. His brave resistance had at length been completely broken, and after immense losses, he seemed ready to yield. It is an indisputable fact, that for an hour, at least, before the Confederate advance was checked by order of the Commanding General, it was meeting with no sort of check from the enemy. The Northern writers, who shortly after the battle described it, one and all depicted a scene of utter confusion and consternation as prevailing in the Federal army, crowded upon the bank of the river. Scarcely a semblance of resistance (according to these writers), was maintained—while thousands (all discipline and confidence gone), were prepared to surrender. Hundreds, unable to force their way upon the boats, plunged into the river and were drowned.

The head of Buell's column commenced to arrive late in the afternoon, and the troops were crossed as rapidly as they came up. Nelson's division crossed first. The leading brigade was compelled to force its way through the mass of fugitives. On that afternoon, the second chance which the Confederacy had, to win the war, was thrown away.

All night long, the huge pieces upon the gunboats thundered at intervals, with a roar which seemed like that of a bursting firmament. They had been opened during the afternoon, but, on account of the great elevation necessary to enable them to shoot over the bluffs, the shells had gone high in the air. These huge missiles came screaming louder than a steam whistle, striking off the tops of trees, and filling the air with dense clouds of smoke when they burst, but doing no damage.

During the night little was done to reorganize the Confederate soldiery. Only Bragg's corps maintained its discipline. Thousands of stragglers (from the other corps) roamed over the field to plunder and riot. The Federal Generals strained every nerve to repair their disaster. The fugitives were collected and placed again in the ranks. The boats plied steadily, bringing over Buell's fresh and undiscouraged forces, and at six o'clock next morning the victors were in their turn assailed by an army larger than the one they had confronted on the day before, and half of which was fresh and unwearied. General Beauregard disposed his tired troops to receive this storm—and although his line was thin—weakened (from the superb array of the day before) by the dead and wounded and those who had straggled from their colors—it could not be driven.

General Beauregard in his report of the battle, says:

"On his right and center the enemy was repulsed in every effort he made with his heavy columns in that quarter of the field. On the left, our line was weakest, and here the enemy drove on line after line of fresh troops with unremitting fury." Our troops stood firm, but General Beauregard feared that they must eventually break, and at 12 P.M. (all of his scanty reserves having been put in) he ordered a withdrawal of the line.

After a repulse of a desperate attack the troops began to retire, and accomplished the movement without trouble. General Beauregard says: "The lines of troops established to cover this movement had been disposed on a favorable ridge—commanding the ground of Shiloh Church, from this position our artillery played upon the woods beyond, but upon no visible enemy, and without a reply. Soon satisfied that no serious pursuit was, or would be attempted, this last line was withdrawn, and never did troops leave a battlefield in better order."

General Breckinridge (whose heroic conduct on both days had almost repaid the Kentuckians—in their pride in it—for the loss of the battle) was left as rear guard, just in front of the intersection of the Pittsburg and Hamburg roads—upon the ground occupied by the army upon Saturday night. On the next day he was withdrawn three miles to Mickey's, and remained there undisturbed for five or six days. Our cavalry occupied the ground several miles further to the north. Morgan's squadron, and other cavalry commands, were posted for more than a week upon a portion of the field won from the enemy on the first day, during which time only two or three trifling skirmishes occurred.

The army marched to Corinth on the 7th and 8th.

It is a point conceded, now, on all sides, that had the Confederate army pursued its success on the evening of the first day, the army under General Grant would have been annihilated, and Buell never could have crossed the river. Had General Johnson survived, the battle would have been pressed vigorously to that consummation. Then, what would have been the situation? The army, remaining upon the banks of the Tennessee for a few days, would have been reorganized and recovered from the exhausting effects of the battle. The slightly wounded returning to the ranks would have made the muster-roll full thirty thousand effectives.

Price and Van Dorn coming with about fifteen thousand and the levies from all quarters, which were hastening to Corinth, would have given General Johnson nearly sixty thousand infantry. Buell, unable to cross the river or to use it for obtaining supplies, his communications with Nashville in constant danger, and hourly interrupted by the five or six thousand cavalry which General Johnson could have thrown upon them, would have been suspended without the ability to obtain foothold or prop anywhere. If nothing else could have made him retreat, a menace to Nashville, from the troops in East Tennessee, would have served the purpose. Then General Johnson could have crossed the river, and the cavalry have been pushed on to operate between Nashville and Louisville. General Buell would not have halted to fight. With the odds against him, to do *that* (in the heart of a hostile population and far from support) would have been too hazardous. But retreat would have been almost as disastrous as defeat, and, closely pressed, would have resulted in the partial disintegration of his army. Military men, who understand the situation, and the topography of the country, will concur in the opinion that General Buell could not have halted with safety at Nashville, nor, indeed, until he had reached Munfordsville.

Gentlemen who were upon General Johnson's staff, and in his confidence, state that it was his intention to have attempted no march into Kentucky, but that if Buell retreated beyond the Cumberland river, he designed (while keeping his cavalry on the railroad between Nashville and Louisville) to have marched his army, rapidly, along the South bank of the Cumberland to the Ohio river, and, crossing that stream, to have pushed into Illinois, and (destroying the great trunk lines of railroads) have marched to Kentucky by way of Ohio. He could have made the march in less time than troops could have been organized to oppose him. The plan appeared daring to rashness, but where were the forces to endanger such a march? The militia could not have stopped it a moment. General Johnson believed that, his army would have increased as it advanced, and that vacillation and disaffection removed from Kentucky and Missouri, would be transferred to the Northwestern States, and that negotiations for peace would be entertained by those States separately.

But the battle of Shiloh was, after all, a Confederate success. The army of invasion was crippled and reduced to a cautious offensive, little better than inactivity. The Federal arms were stayed and blunted, and the Southern people, reanimated, prepared for fresh and vigorous resistance.

When relieved from duty on the field of Shiloh, Colonel Morgan sought and obtained permission to dash into Tennessee, with a force adequate to important results. While the army lay in the entrenchments around Corinth, which the Federal forces under Halleck were tediously approaching, he wished to pounce upon the rich prizes in their rear. He assembled the troops, with which he was about to make the contemplated expedition at Byrnesville, on or about the twenty-third of April.

His own command, Companies A, B and C, respectively commanded by Lieutenants Sellers, Chadburn and Churchill, had been augmented by a fourth company, or rather nucleus of a company, some twenty-five strong, commanded by Captain Brown—a gallant officer. Detachments from Colonel Wirt Adams' regiment and McNairy's battalion had, also, been assigned him. These were commanded by his friend, Lieutenant Colonel Wood, and Captain Harris. The entire force at his disposal numbered three hundred and twenty-five effectives. Colonel Morgan was detained at Byrnesville for several days, having his horses shod, arms put in order, rations cooked, and other necessary arrangements for the expedition perfected. When all was ready, the command commenced its march on the 26th. Extra ammunition and rations were carried on pack mules—one being allowed to each section, or four to a company.

These mules were led by men, detailed from the section to which they were attached, and the "train" was placed under charge of private Frank Leathers—called by courteous reminiscence of his former rank in the Kentucky militia, and as ex-legislator—Colonel. This gallant gentleman will pardon me for complimenting the energy and diligence he displayed, by recording the grumbling acknowledgment of one of those he "put in motion," who declared that "he made a bigger row in driving his mules than was necessary to align a division of cavalry for action."

Passing through Iuka, that day, the command encamped six miles from the Tennessee river, and reaching it early next morning, immediately commenced to cross. The river was high, and there was nothing with which to effect the crossing, but one boat—a small horse-ferry, capable of holding ten or twelve. Efforts were made (unsuccessfully), to cross a portion of the command at other points. Two days and nights of hard work were occupied in getting every thing across. One of the men who was actively engaged in the work, describes an apprehension which rendered it more disagreeable. "We had," he says, "the gunboat fever very badly, at that time, and expected every minute to see one come in sight, for they were patroling the river for some miles above this point."

Leaving the river on the morning of the 30th, Colonel Morgan reached Lawrenceburg, in Lawrence county, Tennessee, on that afternoon, and encamped for the night. It was a fertile country, settled by hospitable people. Rations and forage in abundance were procured, and a good deal more whisky than was good for the men. Early on the next morning the march, was resumed, and about 10 A.M. (not far from Pulaski), Colonel Morgan learned that four hundred Federal troops had just passed through on the road to Columbia. They were principally convalescents, employed in putting up a line of telegraph from Columbia to Huntsville, Alabama, and other "light work." Colonel Morgan determined to relieve them. The command was pressed on to the town in a gallop. Captain Mitchell (son of the Federal General of that name), was captured here, and paroled, that he might effect his exchange for Colonel Morgan's brother—Captain Charlton Morgan—who had been wounded at Shiloh, and captured at Huntsville—whither he had gone to convalesce in the smiles of the fair ladies of that beautiful place. Moving on rapidly, Colonel Morgan overtook the enemy a short distance beyond the town, and at once attacked. Learning his approach, the Federals had hastily thrown up some slight breastworks in a field on the side of the road (in which a part of them were posted)—others occupied a wood on the left of the road. Colonel Morgan formed his command, and—the ground permitting—charged on horseback, carrying the entire line. Many prisoners were captured, the remnant of the Federal force rallied after retreating about a mile, leaving wagons. They were flanked by Co. A, and surrendered.

At this juncture, a body of cavalry appeared, approaching from the direction of Columbia. Not knowing their strength, Colonel Morgan engaged them with skirmishers. Finding them not strong, he ordered Captain Brown to charge them, who routed and drove them six or seven miles. They were about fifty strong. Colonel Morgan's loss in this affair was slight. A few, only, of the enemy were killed. The prisoners (nearly four hundred), were taken back to Pulaski. The citizens were enthusiastic in their reception of Colonel Morgan and his soldiers—the men were wild with excitement, and the women were in tears. Colonel Morgan's celebrated mare, "Black Bess"—came in for her share of admiration and attention. The ladies crowded around to caress and feed her with dainties (for which she had a weakness), and her glossy tresses were in great request. It is recorded that upon this occasion, for the first and only time in his life—Colonel Morgan opposed the wishes of his lady friends. Fearing that Bess would be completely shorn, he "tore her away," and sent her to the stable. Guards and pickets were posted, and the command encamped. Twenty wagons—six loaded with cotton—were captured, here, and burned. On the next morning—the 2nd—the officer commanding pickets on the Huntsville road, reported that a train of wagons was approaching. The command was drawn up to receive them, but learning that they were escorted by a strong regiment, Colonel Morgan decided not to attack. Moving on in the direction of Murfreesboro', the command encamped that night in a loyal neighborhood, and mindful always of a decorous respect for the opinions of other people, Colonel Morgan made all of his men "play Union." They were consequently treated with distinguished consideration, and some were furnished with fresh horses, for which they gave their kind friends orders (on the disbursing officers at Nashville), for their back pay.

On the 3rd the column reached Harrington—fifteen miles from Shelbyville. Some lots of cotton were burned on that day. General Beauregard (in accordance with the instructions of the War Department) had issued orders that all cotton (likely to fall into the enemy's hands) should be burned. The command remained at Harrington during the night. Over one store the stars and stripes were floating resplendent. The men were so much pleased with this evidence of patriotism that they would patronize no other store in the place. Reaching the vicinity of Murfreesboro', on the night of the 4th, Colonel Morgan drove in all the pickets (next morning) and made a circuit about the town, striking the Nashville and Murfreesboro' pike, about five miles from Stone river. The advance guard captured a few of the enemy's videttes on this road.

Some cotton was burned, and the telegraph wires were cut, after a dispatch had been sent to Nashville to the effect that Morgan had captured Shelbyville, and Murfreesboro' wanted reinforcements. Colonel Morgan (anticipating brilliant feats in that line in the future) carried a telegraph operator (provided with a pocket instrument) upon this expedition. That night (at dark) the column reached Lebanon, in Wilson county. The entire command was quartered in the town. Companies A, B and C (of the Squadron) were placed at the college. The horses were tied in the large yard and the men occupied the building. The detachments under Colonel Wood, Captain Harris and Captain Brown were quartered at the livery stables. Colonel Morgan's headquarters were at the hotel. Colonel Wood, who had been left in the vicinity of Murfreesboro', with a small party, to observe if the enemy followed, came in, some hours after nightfall, and reported that all was quiet.

It was Colonel Morgan's intention to have moved at an early hour next morning, and to have crossed the Cumberland river at Canoe-branch ferry, about ten miles from Lebanon. Orders were issued that the men should saddle their horses at four o'clock, and that the command should form immediately afterward. These orders were not communicated to the company commanders. The night was rainy and bleak. The enemy, advancing upon the Murfreesboro' road, came to the picket stands a little before daybreak.

The pickets were all at a house. This criminal neglect of duty was disastrous. Before the videttes discovered the consequences of their bad conduct, at least one whole regiment had passed. Then one of them, named Pleasant Whitlow, a brave and (always before) excellent soldier, declared that he would retrieve his fault, or die. He was mounted upon a fleet mare, and dashed at full speed along the road, passing the Federal column, unstopped. He reached the hotel where Colonel Morgan was quartered, just as the foremost Federal approached it. As Whitlow called loudly to alarm the Colonel, the enemy fired and killed him. The men at the college had just commenced to saddle, when the enemy approached. They hurriedly formed—Company C, which was quartered in the part of the grounds nearest where the enemy entered the town, were attacked and driven pell-mell through the others, before it was fairly aligned. The three companies became mingled together, and fell back into the town and upon the road, across which Company A (extricating itself from the others) formed, under charge of its cool and gallant Orderly Sergeant, Zelah Bowyer.

Colonel Morgan soon came up, and his presence reinspirited the men. He desired to join with the other detachments, but the enemy occupied the intervening space. A strong column was approaching Company A. Colonel Morgan ordered the men to dismount, reserve their fire, and drive it back when they did open. When the enemy was close, the order to fire was given. A good many men and horses fell and the column recoiled. Several Federal officers in the confusion of this fight rode into the ranks of Colonel Morgan's command. Colonel Woolford was made a prisoner in this way. General Dumont, commanding the entire force, was very nearly made prisoner.

A Chaplain, who made this mistake, asked, upon becoming undeceived, that he might be permitted to rejoin his command—"to pray for his men." "The h—ll you say," responded a member of Co. A; "Don't you think Morgan's men need praying for as well as Woolford's?" The detachments in the center of the town were completely surrounded. Colonel Morgan made his way, with about one hundred men, to the Rome and Carthage road, upon which he commenced his retreat at a steady gait. Suddenly his rear was attacked. The enemy dashed upon it, sabering the men. In the excitement, Colonel Morgan's mare broke the curb of her bridle, and he was unable to restrain her, or reform his men. Two or three taking hold of the reins strove to hold her in, but uselessly. She went like a tornado. No effort was made, then, at concerted resistance—a few men turned and fought, and then resumed their flight. A horse falling near the center of the column, caused many others to fall, and added—if any thing could add—to the wild confused rattling hurricane of flight. Colonel Morgan instructed the men (by courier, for Black Bess would not let him go in person) to take to the woods when their horses gave out. Many escaped in this way. The enemy (Kentucky regiments) were mounted on fine horses, comparatively fresh, which enabled them to press the pursuit so vigorously. One man gives a graphic account of his part in the race. "I was riding," he says, "a horse captured from General Dumont, and kept up with the Colonel until my horse threw his shoes, which put me in the rear. The men had all passed me with the exception of Ben Drake. When Ben went by, he said, 'Tom, Dumont will get his horse.' I said, 'Yes, catch me a horse, Ben.' About a mile from that point, I found Bole Roberts' horse, with the saddle under his belly, and the stirrups broken off. As I did not have time to change saddles, I fixed Bole's saddle, led the horse to the fence, jumped on, used the spurs, and soon passed Ben again, whose horse was now played out. I overtook Colonel Morgan, passed him, and found another horse with a saddle on. I stopped and changed saddles. When we got to Rome, thirteen miles from Lebanon, I traded horses again, and stayed in the rear with Colonel Morgan, who had gotten Black Bess pulled up. A short distance from Rome, the Yanks came within about one hundred yards of us, and told us to stop. I told them 'to go to ——.' The Colonel then told me to ride forward and make the men push on, as fast as possible. I was the first to reach the ferry, twenty-one miles from Lebanon. The boat was luckily on our side of the river. We got into it, as quickly as possible, and left our horses on the shore. We wanted the Colonel to take Black Bess, but he said no, if time was allowed he would send for all." This magnificent animal has never been mentioned, as I am aware, in any official report, and she was too completely identified with Morgan's early career, to be dismissed without a description. She was the most perfect beauty I have ever beheld—even in Kentucky. Not fifteen hands high, the immense power of her short back, broad tilted loins, and thighs—all muscle—enabled her to carry Colonel Morgan's one hundred and eighty-five pounds as if he were a feather-weight. Her head was as beautiful as a "poet's dream"—is popularly supposed to be. Wide between the eyes, it tapered down, until her muzzle was small enough to have picked a lady's pocket.

The way it was set on her matchless throttle, might well "haunt the imagination for years." Her straight superbly proportioned neck, her shoulder and girth, might have fascinated the eye for ever!—but for her beautiful hind quarters and the speed and power they indicated! The arch of her back rib, her flank, her clean legs, with firm, dry muscle, and tendons like steel wires, her hoofs, almost as small as a clenched fist, but open and hard as flint, all these utterly baffle description. Her hide was glossy black, without a hair of white. From her Canadian sire she had inherited the staunchest constitution, and her thoroughbred dam dowered her with speed, game, intelligence and grace. An anchorite might have coveted such an animal. When Colonel Morgan lost her, on this day, he naturally hoped that she would be subjected to no ignoble use. The civilized world will scarcely credit that a Yankee subsequently traveled her about the country, showing her at twenty-five cents a sight. Poor Bess—her spirit must have been broken, or she would have kicked the brute's brains out.

Some fifteen men crossed in the ferry-boat. Sergeant Tom Quirk sprang into a canoe and paddled back to bring the mare over. When about half way across, the enemy arrived on the shore to which he was returning, and fired upon him, riddling the canoe with balls. But he escaped uninjured.

Efforts were made to obtain Colonel Morgan a horse. A fine one was selected, but an old woman (the owner) stood in the door-way with an axe, and prevented all attempts "to trade." In vain was it represented to her that she should certainly be paid—she declared that "unless she were first shot, the horse should not be taken," and the "assessors" were compelled to beat a retreat. When Colonel Morgan halted that night, he had scarcely twenty men with him, and shed tears, as he speculated upon the probable fate of the rest. Only six men were killed. A number of others were wounded, and some one hundred and twenty were captured. The men of the detachments (which were surrounded in Lebanon) were nearly all made prisoners. Colonel Wood held out for hours, until the enemy threatened to burn the town, if he did not surrender. Among the killed was Captain Brown. The enemy lost more in killed and wounded than did Colonel Morgan.

On the 6th, Colonel Morgan reached Sparta, Tennessee, and remained there until the 9th. In those three days a good many of his men came in. This inspirited and decided him to assume the offensive. Shoeing the horses and equipping the men as he best could (under the circumstances) he left Sparta on the 9th with nearly one hundred and fifty men—for the most part badly armed. He directed his march toward the territory of his former service, the country about Bowlinggreen. He hoped to find points of importance, slenderly guarded, and the garrisons careless, under the impression that his severe defeat—four days previously—had finished him. His forces were miscellaneous. He had not quite fifty of his own men, but Captains Bledsoe and Hamilton (commanding companies which operated exclusively in that district) joined him, and Champ Ferguson reported as guide with four or five men. The men of Hamilton's and Bledsoe's companies were, either new recruits or had never been subjected to any sort of discipline. Hamilton's ferry, sixty miles from Sparta, was reached that night, and the command crossing the river, encamped on the northern bank.

Colonel Morgan had no difficulty in traveling expeditiously, for every inch of the ground, for many miles beyond the river, was well known to his Tennessee guides, and when their knowledge failed, he had reached a country familiar to many of his own men. Marching by roads unfrequently traversed, and bridle paths, he would have kept his motions perfectly secret but for a system of communicating intelligence adopted about this time, by the Home-guards of Southern Kentucky. Conch shells and horns were blown, all along his route, by these fellows, the sound of which, transmitted a long distance, traveled faster than his column.

On the next day, reaching the vicinity of Glasgow, the command was halted, and John Hines, a clever, daring scout and native of the place, was sent to Bowlinggreen, to ascertain the strength of the garrison and condition of affairs there.

Colonel Morgan desired to capture the town and burn the stores.

Hines returned in a few hours with the information that five hundred fine troops were in the town, and it was determined not to attack. Colonel Morgan immediately determined then, to strike the Louisville and Nashville railroad between Bowlinggreen and the river, and attack and capture, at all hazards, the first train which passed. He was not likely to encounter one with many troops upon it, and the Bowlinggreen garrison would not come out to fight him. Traveling all night, he passed through Glasgow, and early next day reached Cave City, twelve miles distant—the point elected at which to make his venture. Going in advance, himself, with five men, he had the good luck to discover a long train approaching, and immediately took measures to stop it. It seemed to be loaded with troops, who turned out, upon capture, to be employees on the road. His entire command soon arrived. Forty freight cars and a fine engine were captured in this train, and destroyed.

Colonel Morgan was especially hopeful that he would be able to catch the train conveying his men—captured at Lebanon—to prison, but they had been sent off by the river.

In a short time the passenger train from Louisville was heard coming. A cow-gap was filled with upright beams to stop the train, and a party was detailed to lie in ambush, some distance up the road, and throw obstructions on the road as soon as the train had passed, to prevent its return. Some women notified the conductor of his danger, but instead of backing, he pressed on more rapidly. Suddenly becoming aware of the blockade in front, he checked his train and tried to return, but there was already a barrier behind him. Some Federal officers were on the train, among them Majors Coffee and Helveti, of Woolford's regiment.

"Major Coffee," said an eye witness, "came out upon the platform and opened upon us with a battery of Colt's pistols. Ben Bigstaff dismounted and took a shot at him with his minnie rifle; the bullet struck within an inch of the Major's head and silenced his battery." A great many women were upon the train, who were naturally much frightened. Colonel Morgan exerted himself to reassure them. The greatest surprise was manifested by the passengers when they learned that it was Morgan who had captured them. It was generally believed that he had been killed, and his command utterly destroyed.

One officer captured, was accompanied by his wife. The lady approached Colonel Morgan, weeping, and implored him to spare her husband. "My dear Madam," he replied, bowing debonairly, and with the arch smile which none who knew him can forget, "I did not know that you had a husband." "Yes, sir," she said, "I have. Here he is. Don't kill him." "He is no longer my prisoner," said the Colonel, "he is yours," and he released the officer unconditionally, bidding him console his wife. About eight thousand dollars in greenbacks—Government funds—were captured. The train was not burned, but Colonel Morgan begged the ladies to "accept it as a small token," etc.

After all was over, the men sat down to a fine dinner prepared at the Cave City Hotel, for the passengers.

Colonel Morgan now directed his march toward the Cumberland again. He had retaliated, in some degree, for the injury he had received, and could meet his comrades in the South, fresh from a success instead of a disaster. The column marched steadily and encamped at twelve o'clock at night, fifteen miles from Glasgow. An incident happened at this place well illustrative of Colonel Morgan's kindness, and of the manner in which he could do things which would have been undignified in other officers and destructive of their authority. It was customary for each officer of rank, to have his horses attended to by his negro, and the men were rarely required to perform such duties. Colonel Morgan's groom, however, had been captured. "When we dismounted," said the man who related to me the story, "Colonel Morgan gave his horse to Ben Drake, requesting him to unsaddle and feed him. As Ben had ridden twelve hours longer than the rest of us, he thought this very unkind, to say the least, in the Colonel. He, however, paid no attention to Ben's sour looks, as the latter took the horse and obeyed the order. When Ben returned to the house, Colonel Morgan had reserved a place by the fire for him to sleep in. The next morning Ben was awakened by the Colonel, who told him to get up and eat his breakfast, as the command was ready to move. "Why did you not have me roused sooner, Colonel?" asked Ben, "my horse has not been fed." "I wished you to sleep longer," answered the Colonel, "and fed, curried and saddled your horse, myself." Would any other Colonel in the army have done the same for a "poor private"?

Major Coffee was paroled, on condition that he would exert himself to procure his own exchange for Lieutenant-Colonel Wood, and that he would report again as prisoner if he failed.

Passing through Burkesville on county-court day, capturing a few Federals, and making many horse trades, the command passed on to a ford of the Cumberland, twelve miles from the little town, and crossed. Sparta was reached on the next day, where the Tennessee companies were left—and Colonel Morgan marched on toward Chattanooga, which place he reached by easy marches. Some twenty or thirty more refugees and survivors of the "Lebanon races" soon joined him here. Leaving these men at Chattanooga—to recruit and refit as well as was possible there, he immediately set out for Corinth to see what could be effected in the way of obtaining guns and the necessary equipment for his men, and to obtain permission to make another expedition into Kentucky—that he might recruit his regiment. About the middle of May two fine companies of Texas cavalry, commanded by Captains R.M. Gano and Jno. Huffman, both native Kentuckians, arrived at Corinth, and requested to be assigned to Morgan, that they might see service in Kentucky. Their application was granted, and they at once marched for Chattanooga.

I had been severely wounded at Shiloh, and left behind when the command started upon the expedition just described. Upon my return to Corinth, I collected some thirty men of the squadron (who for various reasons had not accompanied Colonel Morgan into Tennessee), and marched with Captain Gano to Chattanooga. We marched through a country, where the people were friendly and hospitable, and had no difficulty in supplying the men and horses. We had a few skirmishes with Federal troops posted along the Tennessee river, in one of which Captain Gano took some prisoners, and burned a good deal of cotton, collected by the Federals for transportation to Huntsville. The last two days of our march showed us the grandest and most beautiful scenery. We traversed the ridgy summit of the mountain range, which runs just along the southern bank of the Tennessee and connects with the group of bold mountains around Chattanooga. At one point the view is exceedingly striking. From the immense hight we occupied, we could see a vast and varied expanse of country. In our front and to the right, the mountains rose like blue domes, piled closely together—a tremendous gulf—the bottom of which eyesight could not fathom—spread between the range (where we were), and their hazy, azure sides. Directly before us "Lookout"—giant chief of all—loomed high toward heaven.

Sheer down, hundreds of feet beneath us, flowed the Tennessee—I could almost believe that my horse could leap from the top of the precipice to the opposite bank of the river. On the other side the land was low and nearly level. The green fields ran back from the river's brink, in a gentle imperceptible ascent, until miles away, the eye lost them in the horizon. The noisy cavalrymen were hushed by the scene, and the grand silence was not disturbed.

CHAPTER VIII

At Chattanooga we found and were welcomed by Colonel Morgan and our gallant comrades, and never did brothers meet after separation and danger, with more hearty joy. For the first time, then, we learned who had been lost, and as we talked it over, the pleasure and congratulation, so natural at our reunion, gave way to sadness as we named the dead and counted up the captives. Although much reduced in numbers, the squadron was unbroken in spirit and courage; the men who had safely gone through the dangers of the late expedition, were more eager than ever for another, and burned to wipe out any stain that might dim their reputation and to avenge their comrades. They had completely recovered from the fatigue of the raid, and their first thought (when they welcomed the accession to the command that we brought), was of instant march to Kentucky.

Gano and his Texians were greeted with enthusiasm, and were delighted with the choice they had made of a leader and brothers-in-arms. The work of reorganization was immediately commenced. The three companies of the squadron, much depleted, were filled nearly to the maximum by recruits who came in rapidly—and became (of course), the three first companies of the regiment which was now formed.

Some three hundred men of the First Kentucky infantry (which had been just disbanded in Virginia, their term of service having expired), came to Chattanooga to join Morgan. A good many of them went into the old companies, and the remainder formed companies under officers known to them in their original regimental organization. Captain Jacob Cassell was appointed by Colonel Morgan (who now began to exercise in good earnest the appointing power), to the command of Company A. Captain Thomas Allen resigned (on account of extreme ill health), the Captaincy of Company B. and his brother, John Allen (once Colonel in Nicaragua under Walker), was appointed to command it. Captain Bowles remained in command of Company C. John B. Castleman, who had just come out of Kentucky (fighting as he came) with a number of recruits, was made Captain of company D. John Hutchinson, formerly Lieutenant in the First Kentucky infantry, was made Captain of Company E. Captain Thomas B. Webber, who had served at Pensacola, under General Bragg, during the past year, brought with him from Mississippi, a company of most gallant soldiers, many of them his former comrades. This company was admitted into the regiment as Company F., and glad was Colonel Morgan to welcome it. Captain McFarland, of Alabama, brought with him a few men, and was promised that so soon as his company was recruited to the proper standard, it should take its place in the regiment as Company G.

Thus it will be seen that Morgan's old regiment was composed of the men of his old squadron, of veterans from Virginia, and men (from nearly all the Southern States) who had, with few exceptions, seen service. These six companies, and the fragment of the seventh, numbered in all not quite four hundred men. The field and staff, were immediately organized. I became Lieutenant Colonel; G.W. Morgan, formerly of the Third Tennessee infantry, better known as Major Wash, was appointed Major. Gordon E. Niles once editor of a New York paper, and a private of Company A., was appointed Adjutant. He was a gallant soldier, and died, not long afterward, a soldier's death. Captain Thomas Allen, formerly of Company B., was appointed Surgeon—Doctor Edelin, the Assistant Surgeon, performed for many months the duties of both offices, on account of the illness of the former. D.H. Llewellyn and Hiram Reese, both members of the old squadron, were appointed respectively, Quartermaster and Commissary.

While we were at Chattanooga, General Mitchell came to the other side of the river and shelled and sharpshot at the town. The commandant of the place General Leadbetter, had two or three guns in battery, and replied—when the gunners, who were the most independent fellows I ever saw, chose to work the guns. The defense of the place was left entirely to the individual efforts of those who chose to defend it; nothing prevented its capture but the fact that the enemy could not cross the river. Very little loss was sustained, and the damage done the town by the shells was immaterial. We tried to keep our men in camp, but some joined in the fight; one only was hurt. He volunteered to assist in working one of the guns and had part of his tongue shot off by a rifleman upon the opposite bank. About five, P.M., the enemy seemed to be withdrawing. The artillery was still playing on both sides, and the enemy occupied the hights where their battery was planted, but the infantry and sharpshooters had disappeared from the low land, just opposite to the city. Colonel Morgan (desirous to ascertain certainly if they had gone) crossed the river in a canoe. I was unwilling to see him go alone, and, after trying in vain to dissuade him, very regretfully accompanied him. Several shells flew over the canoe and one burst just above it, some of the fragments falling in it. We landed just opposite the wharf, and stole cautiously through a straggling thicket to the position which the enemy had occupied. We stood upon the very ground which they had held only a short time before, and as nothing could be seen of them, we concluded that they had drawn off entirely. I was very much relieved by this reflection. Such a situation—without a horse—and with no means of escape but a canoe, if indeed we could have gotten back to the river at all—was not to my taste, and I devoutly thanked Providence that the enemy had left.

As we returned, we met Jack Wilson (the trustiest soldier that ever shouldered a rifle) who had paddled us over, on his way to look for us; unable to endure the suspense, he had left the canoe, over which he had been posted as guard.

After a week or ten days sojourn at Chattanooga, we set out for Knoxville. The better-part of the men were mounted, and those, who were not, had *great hopes*. When we reached Knoxville, the Second Kentucky (as our regiment was designated in the rolls of the War Department) and the Texas squadron were encamped in close vicinity, and for two or three weeks both were drilled strictly, twice a day, and mightily distressed by guard-mounting and dress-parades. These dress-parades presented a graceful and pleasing spectacle on account of the variegated appearance of the ranks.

The men were all comfortably clad, but their clothing was uniform, only, in its variety. Strange as it may seem to the unexperienced, dress has a good deal to do with the spirit of soldiers. The morale of troops depends, in a great measure, upon pride, and personal appearance has something to do with pride. How awful, for instance, must it be to a sensitive young fellow, accustomed at home to wear good clothes and appear confidently before the ladies, when he is marching through a town and the girls come out to wave their handkerchiefs, to feel that the rear of his pantaloons has given way in complete disorder. The cavalryman, in such cases, finds protection in his saddle, but the soldier on foot is defenseless: and thus the very recognition, which, if he has a stout pair of breeches, would be his dearest recompense for all his toils, becomes his most terrible affliction. Many a time, have I seen a gallant infantryman, who would have faced a battery double-shotted with grape and canister with comparative indifference, groan and turn pale in this fearful ordeal. It was a touching sight to see them seek to dispose their knapsacks in such a manner that they should serve as fortifications.

The ideas which the experience of the past eight months had suggested, regarding the peculiar tactics best adapted to the service and the kind of fighting we had to do, were now put into practical shape. A specific drill, different in almost every respect from every other employed for cavalry, was adopted. It was based upon a drill taught in the old army for Indian fighting, called "Maury's skirmish tactics for cavalry," I believe; but as that drill contemplated the employment of but a very few men, and ours had to provide for the evolutions of regiments, and eventually brigades, the latter was necessarily much more comprehensive. The formation of the company, the method of counting off in sets, and of dismounting and deploying to the front, flanks, or rear, for battle, was the same as in Maury's tactics; but a great many movements necessary to the change of front, as the kind of ground or other circumstances required it to be made in various ways, to the formations from column into line, and from line into column, the methods of taking ground to the front, or rear, in establishing or changing line, the various methods of providing, as circumstances might require, for the employment of all, or only part of a regiment or brigade, or for the employment of supports and reserves, all these evolutions had to be added. It would be uninteresting to all but the practical military reader, and unnecessary, as well, to enter into a minute explanation of these matters.

If the reader will only imagine a regiment drawn up in single rank, the flank companies skirmishing, sometimes on horseback, and then thrown out as skirmishers on foot, and so deployed as to cover the whole front of the regiment, the rest of the men dismounted (one out of each set of four and the corporals, remaining to hold horses) and deployed as circumstances required, and the command indicated, to the front of, on either flank, or to the rear of the line of horses—the files two yards apart—and then imagine this line moved forward at a double-quick, or oftener a half run, he will have an idea of Morgan's style of fighting.

Exactly the same evolutions were applicable for horseback, or foot fighting, but the latter method was much oftener practiced—we were, in fact, not cavalry, but mounted riflemen. A small body of mounted men was usually kept in reserve to act on the flanks, cover a retreat, or press a victory, but otherwise our men fought very little on horseback, except on scouting expeditions. Our men were all admirable riders, trained from childhood to manage the wildest horses with perfect ease; but the nature of the ground on which we generally fought, covered with dense woods, or crossed by high fences, and the impossibility of devoting sufficient time to the training of the horses, rendered the employment of large bodies of mounted men to any good purpose, very difficult. It was very easy to charge down a road in column of fours, but very hard to charge across the country in extended line, and keep any sort of formation. Then we never used sabers, and long guns were not exactly the weapons for cavalry evolutions. We found the method of fighting on foot more effective—we could maneuver with more certainty, and sustain less and inflict more loss. "The long flexible line curving forward at each extremity," as an excellent writer described it, was very hard to break; if forced back at one point, a withering fire from every other would be poured in on the assailant. It admitted, too, of such facility of maneuvering, it could be thrown about like a rope, and by simply facing to the right or left, and double-quicking in the same direction, every man could be quickly concentrated at any point where it was desirable to mass them.

It must be remembered that Morgan very rarely fought with the army; he had to make his command a self-sustaining one. If repulsed, he could not fall back and reform behind the infantry. He had to fight infantry, cavalry, artillery; take towns when every house was a garrison, and attack fortifications with nothing to depend on but his own immediate command. He was obliged, therefore, to adopt a method which enabled him to do a great deal in a short time, and to keep his men always in hand, whether successful or repulsed. With his support from forty to five hundred miles distant, an officer had better learn to rely on himself.

If General Morgan had ever been enabled to develope his plan of organization as he wished, he would have made his division of mounted riflemen a miniature army. With his regiments armed as he wished them—a battalion of two or three hundred men, appropriately armed, and attached to each brigade, to be used only as cavalry, and with his battery of three-inch Parrots, and train of mountain howitzers, he could have met any contingency. The ease and rapidity with which this simple drill was learned, and the expedition with which it enabled all movements to be accomplished, chiefly recommended it to Morgan, I have seen his division, when numbering over three thousand men, and stretched out in column, put into line of battle in thirty minutes. Regular cavalry can no doubt form with much more dispatch, but this was quicker than it is often done in this country.

The weapon which was always preferred by the officers and men of the command, was the rifle known as the "medium Enfield." The short Enfield was very convenient to carry, but was deficient both in length of range and accuracy. The long Enfield, without any exception the best of all rifles, was unwieldy either to carry or to use, as sometimes became necessary, on horseback. The Springfield rifle, nearly equal to the long Enfield, was liable to the same objections, although in a less degree. Now that the military world has finally decided in favor of breech-loading guns, it may seem presumptuous to condemn them; but, so far as my own experience goes, they are decidedly inferior. When I say inferior, I mean not so much that they will not carry far, nor accurately, although a fair trial of every sort I could lay my hands upon with the Enfield and Springfield, convinced me of the superiority, in these respects, of the two latter; but that for other reasons they are not so effective as the muzzle-loading guns. Of the two best patterns, the Sharp and the Spencer—for the Maynard is a pop-gun, and the others are so contrived that, generally, after one shot, the shell of the cartridge sticks in the chamber—of these two, I have seen the Sharp do the most execution. It has been the verdict of every officer of the Western Confederate cavalry with whom I have talked upon the subject, and it certainly has been my experience, that those Federal cavalry regiments which were armed with breech-loading guns did least execution. The difference in the rapidity with which men dropped when exposed to the fire of an infantry regiment, and the loss from that of a cavalry regiment of equal strength, even when the latter fought well, ought of itself to go far to settle the question, for the federal infantry were all armed with muzzle-loading guns.

A close study of the subject will convince any man that the very fact of having to load his gun will make a soldier comparatively cool and steady. If he will stay to load at all, and will fix his mind upon what he is doing, he will become cool enough to take aim. While if he has only to stick in a cartridge and shoot, or turn a crank and pull trigger, he will fire fast, but he will fire wildly. I have seen some of the steadiest soldiers I ever knew, men who were dead shots with an Enfield, shoot as if they were aiming at the sun with a Spencer. The Spencer rifle would doubtless be an excellent weapon for a weak line to hold works with, where the men were accustomed to note the ground accurately, and would, therefore, be apt to aim low, and it is desirable to pour in a rapid, continuous fire to stagger an attacking line.

It is perhaps a first-rate gun for small skirmishes on horseback, although for those, our cavalry decidedly preferred the revolver. But in battle, when lines and numbers are engaged, accurate and not rapid firing is desirable. If one fiftieth of the shots from either side were to take effect in battle, the other would be annihilated. If rapid firing is so desirable, why do the same critics who advocate it also recommend that troops shall hold their fire until they can pour in deadly volleys? Why do they deprecate so much firing, and recommend the use of the bayonet?

It is folly to talk to men who have seen battles, about the moral effect of rapid firing, and of "bullets raining around men's heads like hail stones." That is like the straggler's excuse to General Lee that he was "stung by a bomb." Any man who has ever heard lines of battle engaged, knows that, let the men fire fast or slow, the nicest ear can detect no interval between the shots; the musketry sounds like the incessant, unintermitted crash of a gong—even cannonading, when one or two hundred guns are working, sounds like the long roll of a drum—and the hiss of bullets is perfectly ceaseless. Good troops will fight well with almost any sort of guns. Mean troops will not win, no matter how they are armed.

If the matter were investigated, it would probably be found that the regiments which won most distinction, in the late war on this continent, on both sides, fired the fewest number of rounds.

At one time—when Morgan's command was somewhat demoralized—the men were loud in describing the terrific effect of the Spencer rifle, when it was notorious that, at that time, it was an unusual occurrence to lose a man—they subsequently became ashamed of their panic, and met the troops carrying Spencer rifles, with more confidence than those armed in any other way. It would be very convenient to attribute every whipping we ever got to the use of breech-loading rifles by our antagonists, but it would be very wide of the truth. It was impossible, however, to obtain, when we were organizing at Knoxville, the exact description of guns we wished. One company, was armed with the long Enfield, another had the medium, and Company A got the short Enfield. Company C was furnished with Mississippi rifles and Company B retained the shot-guns which they had used for nearly a year. Company E was provided with a gun, called from the stamp upon the barrel, the "Tower gun;" it was of English make, and was a sort of Enfield carbine. Its barrel was rather short and bore immense; it carried a ball larger than the Belgian. Its range and accuracy were first rate. The roar of this gun was almost as loud as that of a field piece and the tremendous bullet it carried would almost shatter an ordinary wall.

It was some months before each company of the regiment was armed with the same or similar guns. Nearly every man had a pistol, and some two. Shortly afterward, when they were captured in sufficient numbers, each man was provided with a pair. The pistol preferred and usually worn by the men, was the army Colt furnished to the Federal cavalry regiments—this patent is far the best and most effective of any I have ever seen. At this time two mountain howitzers were sent from Richmond for Morgan's use. It is unnecessary to describe a piece so well known, but it may be as well to say, that no gun is so well adapted in all respects to the wants of cavalry, as these little guns. With a large command, it is always well enough to have two or four pieces of longer range and yet of light draught, such as the three-inch Parrot—but if I were required to dispense with one or the other, I would choose to retain the former. They can be drawn (with a good supply of ammunition in the limbers), by two horses over any kind of road. They can go over ravines, up hills, through thickets, almost any where, in short, that a horseman can go; they can be taken, without attracting attention, in as close proximity to the enemy as two horsemen can go—they throw shell with accuracy eight hundred yards, quite as far as there is any necessity for, generally in cavalry fighting—they throw canister and grape, two and three hundred yards, as effectively as a twelve pounder—they can be carried by hand right along with the line, and as close to the enemy as the line goes—and they make a great deal more noise than one would suppose from their size and appearance. If the carriages are well made, they can stand very hard service, and they are easily repaired, if injured. These little guns were attached to the Second Kentucky, and the men of that regiment became much attached to them. They called them familiarly and affectionately, the "bull pups," and cheered them whenever they were taken into a fight. They remained with us, doing excellent service, until just before the Ohio raid; and, then, when General Bragg's ordnance officer arbitrarily took them away from us, it came near raising a mutiny in the regiment. I would, myself, have gladly seen him tied to the muzzle of one of them and shot off. They were captured by the enemy in two weeks after they were taken from us.

Just before Morgan left Knoxville to go on the expedition known as "the First Kentucky raid," he was joined by a gentleman "from abroad," whose history had been a curious and extraordinary series of exciting adventures, and who now came to see something of our war. This was Lieutenant Colonel St. Leger Greenfell, of the English service, and of all the very remarkable characters who have figured (outside of popular novels) in this age, he will receive the suffrages of our Western cavalrymen, for pre-eminence in devil-may-care eccentricity. He had commenced life (I believe) by running away from his father, because the latter would not permit him to enter the army, and in doing so, he showed the good sense that he really possessed, for the army was the proper place for him—provided they went to war often enough. He served five years in some French regiment in Algeria, and then quitting the service, lived for a number of years in Tangiers, where he did a little business with the Moorish batteries, when the French bombarded the place. He served four years with Abd-El-Kader, of whom he always spoke in the highest terms, as having been every thing that he ought to have been, except a member of the Church of England. Having exhausted life in Africa, he looked elsewhere for excitement, and passed many years of his subsequent life in great happiness and contentment, amid the pleasant scenes of the Crimean war, the Sepoy rebellion, and Garibaldi's South American service.

When the war broke out over here he came of course—and taking a fancy to Morgan, from what he had heard of him, came to join him. He was very fond of discussing military matters, but did not like to talk about himself, and although I talked with him daily, it was months before he told any thing of his history. He was a thorough and very accomplished soldier—and may have encountered something in early life that he feared, but if so, it had ceased to exist.

He became Morgan's Adjutant General and was of great assistance to him, but sometimes gave trouble by his impracticable temper—he persisted, among other things, in making out all papers in the style he had learned in the English service, the regulations and orders of the War Department "to the contrary notwithstanding."

He was always in a good temper when matters were active—I never saw him hilarious but once—and that was the day after the battle of Hartsville; he had just thrashed his landlord, and doubled up a brother Englishman, in a "set-to" about a mule, and was contemplating an expedition on the morrow, with General Morgan to Nashville. He was the only gentleman, I ever knew, who liked to fight with his fists, and he was always cheerful and contented when he could shoot and be shot at.

After he left Morgan he was made Chief Inspector of Cavalry, and became the terror of the entire "front." He would have been invaluable as commander of a brigade of cavalry, composed of men who (unlike our volunteers) appreciated the "military necessity" of occasionally having an officer to knock them in the head. If permitted to form, discipline, and drill such a brigade of regular cavalry after his own fashion, he would have made gaps in many lines of battle, or have gotten his "blackguards well peppered" in trying.

Sometime in the latter part of June, Colonel Hunt of Georgia arrived at Knoxville with a "Partisan Ranger" regiment between three and four hundred strong, to accompany Morgan upon his contemplated raid.

When the entire force of able bodied and mounted men was estimated, it was found eight hundred and seventy-six strong. Hunt's regiment numbering about three hundred and fifty; mine, the Second Kentucky, about three hundred and seventy, and Gano's squadron making up the balance.

Fifty or sixty men, from all the commands, were left at Knoxville for lack of horses. Perhaps two hundred men of this force, with which Morgan commenced the expedition, were unarmed, and a much larger number were badly mounted and provided with the most indifferent saddles and equipments.

The command set out from Knoxville on the morning of the 4th of July, 1862, and took the road to Sparta (a little place on the confines of the rugged mountainous country which separates Middle Tennessee from the rich valley of East Tennessee) in which Knoxville is situated. Sparta is one hundred and four miles from Knoxville. We reached it, after tolerably hard marching, for the road was terribly rough, on the evening of the third day, and encamped five miles beyond it on the road to Livingston.

While traversing the region between Knoxville and Sparta, we were repeatedly fired upon by bushwhackers, but had only one man killed by them—a Texian of Gano's squadron. We made many unsuccessful attempts to capture them, but they always chose the most inaccessible points to fire from and we could never get to them. Frequently they would shoot at us from a ledge of rocks not forty feet above our heads, and yet to get to it we would have had to go hundreds of yards—they consequently always escaped.

At Sparta, Champ Ferguson reported himself as a guide, and I, for the first time, saw him, although I had often heard of him before. He had the reputation of never giving quarter, and, no doubt, deserved it (when upon his own private expeditions), although when with Morgan he attempted no interference with prisoners. This redoubted personage was a native of Clinton county, Kentucky, and was a fair specimen of the kind of characters which the wild mountain country produces. He was a man of strong sense, although totally uneducated, and of the intense will and energy, which, in men of his stamp and mode of life, have such a tendency to develope into ferocity, when they are in the least injured or opposed. He was grateful for kindness, and instinctively attached to friends, and vindictive to his enemies. He was known as a desperate man before the war, and ill-treatment of his wife and daughter, by some soldiers and Home-guards enlisted in his own neighborhood, made him relentless in his hatred of all Union men; he killed all the parties concerned in the outrage upon his family, and, becoming then an outlaw, kept up that style of warfare. It is probable that, at the close of the war, he did not himself know how many men he had killed. He had a brother, of the same character as himself, in the Union army, and they sought each other persistently, mutually bent on fratricide. Champ became more widely known than any of them, but the mountains of Kentucky and Tennessee were filled with such men, who murdered every prisoner that they took, and they took part, as their politics inclined them, with either side. For a long time Ferguson hunted, or was hunted by, a man of his own order and nearly as notorious on the other side, namely, "Tinker Dave Beattie." On the evening of the 7th, we encamped in the vicinity of Livingston. Leaving early next morning, by midday we reached the Cumberland river at the ford near the small village of Selina. Here Colonel Morgan received positive information of the strength and position of the enemy at Tompkinsville, eighteen miles from Selina. He had learned at Knoxville that a Federal garrison was at this place, and had determined to attack it. One battalion of the 9th Pennsylvania, under command of Major Jordan, about three hundred and fifty strong, constituted the entire force. It was Morgan's object to surprise and capture the whole of it. He accordingly sent forward scouts to watch and report every thing going on at their camp, while he halted the bulk of the command until nightfall. The men employed the interval of rest in attention to their horses, and in bathing in the river. At eleven o'clock the March was resumed; the road was rough and incumbered at some points with fallen timber, so that the column made slow progress. When within four or five miles of Tompkinsville, Gano's squadron and Hamilton's company of Tennessee Partisan Rangers, which had joined us the evening before, were sent by a road which led to the right to get in the rear of the enemy and upon his line of retreat toward Glasgow. The rest of the command reached Tompkinsville at five o'clock. It was consequently broad daylight, and the enemy had information of our approach in time to form to receive us. Colonel Hunt was formed upon the left, and my regiment upon the right, with the howitzers in the center. It was altogether unnecessary to form any reserve, and as our numbers were so superior, our only care was to "lap around" far enough on the flanks to encircle the game.

The enemy were posted on a thickly wooded hill, to reach which we had to cross open fields. They fired, therefore, three or four volleys while we were closing on them. The Second Kentucky did not fire until within about sixty yards of them, and one volley was then enough. The fight did not last ten minutes. The enemy lost about twenty killed and twenty or thirty wounded. Thirty prisoners, only, were taken on the ground, but

Gano and Hamilton intercepted and captured a good many more, including the commander, Major Jordan. Our force was too much superior in strength for them to have made much resistance, as we outnumbered them more than two to one.

Our loss was only in wounded, we had none killed. But a severe loss was sustained in Colonel Hunt, whose leg was shattered and it was necessary to leave him; he died in a few days of the wound. Three of the Texians also were wounded in their chase after the fugitives. The tents, stores, and camp equipage were destroyed. A wagon train of twenty wagons and fifty mules were captured and a number of cavalry horses. Abundant supplies of coffee, sugar, etc., etc., were found in the camp. The guns captured were useless breech-loading carbines, which were thrown away.

Leaving Tompkinsville at three o'clock in the afternoon, after paroling the prisoners, we reached Glasgow about one o'clock that night. This town was unoccupied by any garrison, and its people were very friendly to us. Company C, of the old squadron had been principally recruited here. The command rested at Glasgow until 9 A.M. next day; during the time, the ladies busied themselves in preparing breakfast for us, and before we left, every man had taken in a three days' supply. A straggler captured at Glasgow gave us some "grape vine" intelligence which annoyed us no little. He stated that McClellan had taken Richmond. When we left Knoxville, the battle of the seven days was going on, and we had, of course, heard nothing after we started. Our prisoner, however, was gravely assured, just before he was paroled, that a courier had just reached us with the information that McClellan was in Richmond, but as a prisoner, and with half his army in the same condition. This fellow, who represented himself to be an officer, turned out to be one of the buglers of the Ninth Pennsylvania, and all the information he gave was as reliable as the McClellan story. A halt of two or three hours was made at Bear Wallow, to enable Mr. Ellsworth (popularly known as "Lightning"), the telegraphic operator on Colonel Morgan's staff, to tap the line between Louisville and Nashville, and obtain the necessary information regarding the position of the Federal forces in Kentucky. Connecting his own instrument and wire with the line, Ellsworth began to take off the dispatches. Finding the news come slow he entered into a conversation with Louisville and obtained much of what was wanted. He in return communicated such information as Colonel Morgan desired to have the enemy act upon. One statement, made at hap hazard, and with no other knowledge to support it, except that Forrest was in Middle Tennessee, was singularly verified. Morgan caused Ellsworth to telegraph that Forrest had taken Murfreesboro' and had captured the entire garrison. Forrest did exactly what was attributed to him on that or the next day. A heavy storm coming on caused them, after several fruitless efforts to continue, to desist telegraphing.

The column was put in motion again immediately upon Colonel Morgan's return, and marching all night got within about fifteen miles of Lebanon by 11 A.M. next morning. Here Company B was detached, to push rapidly to the railroad between Lebanon and Lebanon junction, and ordered to destroy it, so that troops might not be thrown into Lebanon in time to oppose us. The march was not resumed until three or four in the afternoon, so that when we reached Rolling Fork river, six miles from Lebanon, it was dark. Colonel Morgan, who was riding with his staff in front of the advance guard, was fired upon as he entered the small covered bridge across the stream, by a party of the enemy stationed at the other end of it. His hat was shot from his head, but neither he nor any of his staff were touched. One of the howitzers was immediately run up and a shell was thrown into the bridge. A platoon of the leading company was dismounted and carried at a double-quick to clear it. When they reached it, the enemy, alarmed by the shell, which had killed one man, had retreated, the bottom of the bridge was found to have been torn up, and a short time was spent in repairing it. This was a strong position and one which the enemy ought, by all means, to have occupied with his entire force.

There was no ford for six or eight miles above or below; the bridge was the only means of crossing without a wide detour; and not twenty yards from the mouth of the bridge (on the side held by the enemy), and perfectly commanding it, was a steep bluff (not too high) covered with timber, and affording an admirable natural fortification. As soon as the bridge was repaired, the column crossed and pressed on to Lebanon. Within a mile of the town, skirmishing commenced with the force which held it. Two companies (E and C of the Second Kentucky) were thrown out on foot, and advanced at a brisk pace, driving the enemy before them. Two or three of the enemy were killed; our loss was nothing. The town was surrendered by its commandant about ten o'clock; some two hundred prisoners were taken.

Pickets were immediately posted on every road, and the whole command encamped in such a manner that it could be immediately established in line. It was necessary to remain at Lebanon until the large quantity of stores of all kinds, which were there, were disposed of, and, as we were now in the midst of enemies, no precaution could be omitted. Captain Allen, who, as has been mentioned, was detached with Company B of the Second Kentucky to prevent the train from bringing reinforcements to Lebanon, struck the railroad at New Hope Church and had just commenced to destroy it, when a train came with a large number of troops on board for Lebanon. He attacked it, and a skirmish of a few minutes resulted in the train going back. The night was very dark, and little loss, if any, was inflicted on either side.

On the next day, an examination of the stores showed an abundance of every description. A sufficient number of excellent guns were gotten to arm every man efficiently, and some thousands were destroyed. A large building was found to be filled with cartridges and fixed ammunition. An abundant supply of ammunition for small arms was thus obtained, and a fresh supply of ammunition was also gotten for the howitzers. After taking what was needed, all this was destroyed. There was also a stone magazine not far from the depot, which was full of powder. The powder was all taken out of it, and thrown into the stream near by.

Very large supplies of provisions were found—meat, flour, sugar, coffee, etc.—which were turned over to the citizens, and when they had helped themselves, the remainder was burned. A great deal of clothing had also been collected here, and the men were enabled to provide themselves with every thing which they needed in the way of under-clothing. While at Lebanon, copies of a flaming proclamation, written and published at Glasgow, were circulated.

After the destruction of the stores had been completed, and Ellsworth had closed his business at the telegraph office, the command was again put in motion. It left the town about two P.M., on the Springfield road. Before leaving Knoxville, Colonel Morgan, appreciating the necessity of having an advance-guard which could be thoroughly relied on, and disinclined to trust to details, changed every day, for that duty, had organized a body of twenty-five men, selected with great care from the entire force under his command, to constitute an advance-guard for the expedition. So well did this body perform the service assigned it, that the men composing it, with some additions to make up the tale as others were taken out, were permanently detailed for that duty, and it became an honor eagerly sought, and a reward for gallantry and good conduct second only to promotion, to be enrolled in "the advance." The non-commissioned officers were chosen with the same care, and First Lieutenant Charles W. Rogers of Company E, formerly of the First Kentucky Infantry, was appointed to command it. This officer possessed in an eminent degree the cool judgment, perfect fearlessness, command of men, and shrewdness of perception requisite for such an office.

This guard habitually marched at a distance of four hundred yards in front of the column; three videttes were posted at intervals of one hundred yards between it and the column. Their duties were to transmit information and orders between the column and the guard, and to regulate the gait of the former, so that it would not press too close on the latter, and, also, to prevent any straggling between the two. Six videttes were thrown out in front of the guard—four at intervals of fifty yards, and with another interval of the same distance from the fourth of these, two rode together in the extreme front. These two were consequently at a distance of two hundred and fifty yards in front of the body of the guard. At first these videttes were regularly relieved, but it was afterward judged best to keep the same men always on the same duty. The advance videttes were required to examine carefully on all sides, and report to the officer of the guard the slightest indication which seemed suspicious. When they came to by-roads or cross-roads one or both, as the case might require, immediately galloped some two or three hundred yards down them, and remained until relieved by men sent for that purpose from the head of the column, when they returned to their posts.

As soon as they notified the officer of the guard (by calling to the videttes next behind them), that they were about to leave their posts, he took measures to supply their places. The two videttes next to them in the chain galloped to the front, the other two, also moved up, respectively, fifty yards, and two men were sent from the guard to fill the places of the last.

When the videttes, regularly in advance returned, the original disposition was resumed. If an enemy was encountered, men were dispatched from the guard to the assistance of the videttes, or the latter fell back on the guard, as circumstances dictated. If the enemy was too strong to be driven by the advance, the latter endeavored to hold him in check (and was reinforced if necessary), until the command could be formed for attack or defense. Scouting parties were of course thrown out on the front and flanks, as well as to the rear, but as these parties were often miles away in search of information, a vigilant advance guard was always necessary. During an engagement, the advance was generally kept mounted and held in reserve.

Passing through Springfield without a halt, the column marched in the direction of Harrodsburg. Late in the evening, some of the scouts had an engagement at a little place called Macksville, with a Home-guard organization, in which two or three were wounded and two captured. During the night, finding that it would be impossible to ferret out the captors, we negotiated an exchange of prisoners. On the next morning, about nine o'clock we entered Harrodsburg,. another stronghold of our friends, and were warmly welcomed.

It was Sunday, and a large concourse of people were in town. We found that the ladies, in anticipation of our coming, had prepared the most inviting rations, and the men after attending to their horses and supplying them with forage, a "superabundance of which," to use the old forage-master's expression, was stacked close by, fell to themselves, and most of them were eating, with short intervals employed in sleeping, until the hour of departure. Harrodsburg is twenty-eight miles from Lexington, the headquarters then of the Federal forces of the region. Gano, with his squadron, was detached at Harrodsburg to go around Lexington and burn the bridges on the Kentucky Central Railroad, in order to prevent troops from being thrown into Lexington from Cincinnati. Captain Allen was sent to destroy the bridges over Benson and other small streams on the Louisville and Lexington road, to prevent the transmission of troops by that road, and also to induce the impression that the command was making for Louisville. About dark the column moved from Harrodsburg on the Frankfort pike. It was Morgan's wish to induce the belief that he intended to attack Frankfort, but to suddenly turn to the right and make for Lexington, capture that place if he could, and if he could not, at least enjoy the fine country in its vicinity.

At one P.M. that night we encamped at Lawrenceburg, the county seat of Anderson county, twenty miles from Harrodsburg and about fifteen from Frankfort. A scouting party was sent immediately on in the direction of Frankfort, with instructions to drive in the pickets after daybreak, and to rejoin us at Versailles. The command had now marched three hundred and odd miles in eight days, but the men, despite the fatigue usually resulting from night marching, were comparatively fresh, and in the most exultant spirits. So far, every thing had gone well; although encompassed by superior forces, celerity of movement, and skillful selection of route, had enabled us to elude them; a good many little affairs had occurred with the Home-guards, which I have not mentioned, but they had been expected, and the damage from them was trifling. Leaving Lawrenceburg next morning at daybreak, the column took the road to Versailles, but was compelled to halt at Shryock's ferry, seven miles from Versailles. On account of the ferry-boat having been sunk, it was necessary to raise and repair it, so that the howitzers might be crossed. This delay prevented us from reaching Versailles before night fell. It was now deemed good policy to march more slowly, obtain perfectly accurate information, and increase the confusion already prevailing by threatening all points of importance. This policy was not a hazardous one, under the circumstances, for although the forces surrounding the point where we now were, were each a superior to our own, yet by getting between them and preventing their concentration, and industriously creating the impression to which the people were, at any rate disposed, that our force was four or five thousand strong, Morgan had demoralized them, and they were afraid to come out and meet him. The ease with which he had, hitherto, pressed right on, without a momentary check, confirmed the belief that he was very strong.

The command remained encamped at Versailles during the night. Scouts were sent in every direction, and upon their return next day reported that a very general consternation prevailed, as well as uncertainty regarding our movements. The Home-guards and little detachments of troops were running, on the one side for Lexington, and on the other for Frankfort. Leaving Versailles next day about 10 A.M., the column moved toward Georgetown.

Before leaving Versailles, the scouting parties which had been dispatched to Frankfort rejoined the command. Frankfort was by this time relieved of all fear of immediate attack, and Colonel Morgan became apprehensive that the troops there might be marched out after him, or that communication might be opened with Lexington which might lead to a simultaneous attack upon him by the forces of the two points. He hoped that the detachment under Captain Allen returning, after the destruction of the bridge between Frankfort and Louisville, and necessarily marching close to the former (in doing so), would produce the impression there, that an attack was again imminent. We reached Midway (about 12 P.M.), a little town on the railroad, and equi-distant from Lexington and Frankfort. What took place at Midway is best described in Ellsworth's language. He says, "At this place I surprised the operator, who was quietly sitting on the platform in front of his office, enjoying himself hugely. Little did he suspect that the much-dreaded Morgan was in his vicinity. I demanded of him to call Lexington and inquire the time of day, which he did. This I did for the purpose of getting his style of handling the 'key' in writing dispatches. My first impression of his style, from noting the paper in the instrument, was confirmed. He was, to use a telegraphic term, a 'plug' operator. I adopted his style of telegraphing, and commenced operations. In this office I found a signal book, which proved very useful. It contained the calls of all the offices. Dispatch after dispatch was going to and from Lexington, Georgetown, Paris and Frankfort, all containing something in reference to Morgan. On commencing operations, I discovered that there were two wires on the line along this railroad. One was what we term a 'through wire,' running direct from Lexington to Frankfort, and not entering any of the way offices. I found that all military messages were sent over that line. As it did not enter Midway office I ordered it to be cut, thus forcing Lexington on to the wire that did run through the office. I tested the line and found, by applying the ground wire, it made no difference with the circuit; and, as Lexington was Head-Quarters, I cut Frankfort off. Midway was called, I answered, and received the following:

'LEXINGTON, *July 15, 1862.*

'*To J.W. Woolums, operator, Midway*:

'Will there be any danger in coming to Midway? Is every thing right?

'TAYLOR—*Conductor*.'

"I inquired of my prisoner (the operator) if he knew a man by the name of Taylor. He said Taylor was the conductor. I immediately gave Taylor the following reply:

'MIDWAY, *July 15, 1862.*

'*To Taylor, Lexington*:

'All right; come on. No sign of any rebels here.

'WOOLUMS.'

"The operator in Cincinnati then called Frankfort. I answered and received about a dozen unimportant dispatches. He had no sooner finished than Lexington called Frankfort. Again I answered, and received the following message:

'LEXINGTON, *July 15, 1862.*

'*To General Finnell, Frankfort*:

'I wish you to move the forces at Frankfort, on the line of the Lexington railroad, immediately, and have the cars follow and take them up as soon as possible. Further orders will await them at Midway. I will, in three or four hours, move forward on the Georgetown pike; will have most of my men mounted. Morgan left Versailles this morning with eight hundred and fifty men, on the Midway road, moving in the direction of Georgetown.

'BRIGADIER-GENERAL WARD.'

"This being our position and intention exactly, it was thought proper to throw General Ward on some other track. So, in the course of half an hour, I manufactured and sent the following dispatch, which was approved by General Morgan:

'MIDWAY, *July 15, 1862.*

'*To Brigadier-General Ward, Lexington*:

'Morgan, with upward of one thousand men, came within a mile of here, and took the old Frankfort road, marching, we suppose, for Frankfort. This is reliable.

'WOOLUMS—*Operator*.'

"In about ten minutes Lexington again called Frankfort, when I received the following:

'LEXINGTON, *July 15, 1862*.

'*To General Finnell, Frankfort*;

'Morgan, with more than one thousand men, came within a mile of here, and took the old Frankfort road. This dispatch received from Midway, and is reliable. The regiment from Frankfort had better be recalled.

'BRIGADIER-GENERAL WARD.'

"I receipted for this message, and again manufactured a message to confirm the information General Ward received from Midway, and not knowing the tariff from Frankfort to Lexington, I could not send a formal message; so, appearing greatly agitated, I waited until the circuit was occupied, and broke in, telling them to wait a minute, and commenced calling Lexington. He answered with as much gusto as I called him. I telegraphed as follows:

'*Frankfort to Lexington*:

'Tell General Ward our pickets are just driven in. Great excitement. Pickets say the force of enemy must be two thousand.

'OPERATOR.'

It was now two P.M., and General Morgan wished to be off for Georgetown. I ran a secret ground connection, and opened the circuit on the Lexington end. This was to leave the impression that the Frankfort operator was skedaddling, or that Morgan's men had destroyed the telegraph.

While at Midway, dispositions were made for the capture of the trains coming from both ends of the road; but they were not sent. The command reached Georgetown just at sundown. A small force of Home-guards had mustered there to oppose us. Morgan sent them word to surrender, and they should not be hurt. The leader of this band is said to have made his men a speech of singular eloquence and stirring effect. If he was reported correctly, he told them that "Morgan, the marauder and murderer—the accursed of the Union men of Kentucky," was coming upon them. That, in "his track every where prevailed terror and desolation. In his rear, the smoke of burning towns was ascending, the blood of martyred patriots was streaming, the wails of widowed women and orphan children were resounding. In his front, Home-guards and soldiers were flying." That "Tom Long reported him just outside of town, with ten or twelve thousand men, armed with long beards and butcher-knives;" and the orator thought that they "had better scatter and take care of themselves." They accordingly "scattered" at full speed. Several prisoners (Southern sympathizers) were confined in the court-house; among them, a man whom many Kentuckians have a lively recollection of—poor Will Webb. He, upon seeing the Home-guards flee, thrust his body half out of a window, and pointing to the stars and stripes still flying, apostrophized the fugitives in terms that ought to have made a sutler fight. "Are you going to desert your flag?" he said. "Remain, and perform the pleasing duty of dying under its glorious folds, and afford us the agreeable spectacle that you will thus present." This touching appeal was of no avail.

The geographical situation of Georgetown with relation to the towns of that portion of Kentucky—especially those occupied by Federal troops—made it an excellent point for Colonel Morgan's purposes. He was in a central position here, nearly equi-distant from all points of importance, and could observe and checkmate movements made from any of them. Georgetown is twelve miles from Lexington, and eighteen from Frankfort, the two points from which he had chiefly to anticipate attacks. Although not directly between these two places, Georgetown is so nearly on a line with them, that its possession enabled him to prevent communication of any kind between the troops occupying them.

As the command greatly needed rest, Colonel Morgan remained here (where he felt more secure, for the reasons I have mentioned) during two days. He was not entirely idle, however, during that time. He sent Captain Hamilton, with one company, to disperse a Home-guard organization at the Stamping Ground, thirteen miles from Georgetown. Hamilton accomplished his mission, and burned the tents, and destroyed the guns. Detachments were kept constantly at or near Midway, to prevent any communication by the railroad between Lexington and Frankfort. Captain Castleman was sent to destroy the bridges on the Kentucky Central Railroad between Lexington and Paris—which he did; and was instructed to rejoin the command in three or four days at Winchester, in Clark county. For other than strategic reasons, Georgetown was an admirable selection as a resting point. The large majority of the people throughout this region were, even at that time, strongly Southern in sentiment and sympathy, and their native inclination to hospitality was much enhanced by the knowledge that they were feeding their friends, when we would suddenly descend upon them. There was a drawback in the apprehension of a visit from some provost-guards, to investigate the circumstances of this profuse and practical sympathy with armed rebels. But they hit upon an expedient which they thought would obviate all the unpleasant after-claps. They *would give nothing of their own free will and accord*; but forced us to "impress" every thing that we needed. Many a time have I seen an old farmer unlock all the closets and presses in his house—press the keys of his meat-house into the hands of the Commissary, point out to the Quartermaster where forage could be obtained, muster his negroes to cook and make themselves generally useful, protesting all the time that he was acting under the cruelest compulsion, and then stand by, rubbing his hands and chuckling to think how well he had reconciled the indulgence of his private sympathies with his public repute for loyalty. The old ladies, however, were serious obstacles to the establishment of these decorous records. They wished not only to give but to talk freely, and the more the husband wisely preached "policy" and an astute prudence, the more certainly were his cob-webs of caution torn into shreds by the trenchant tongue of his wife.

Of all the points which we could have reached just at that time, Georgetown was the one where this sympathy for us was strongest. There were only a very few Union men living in the town, and these had run away; and the county (Scott) was the very hot-bed of Southern feeling. To Owen and Boone we did not contemplate paying a visit. We had not yet reached Harrison; but in halting in Scott county and at Georgetown, we felt that our situation would not need to be improved. A good many recruits had been obtained at various points in the State, and at Georgetown a full company was raised, of which W.C.P. Breckinridge, a young lawyer of Lexington, was elected Captain. He had just run the blockade established around the latter town.

While lying at Georgetown the command was encamped in line of battle, day and night, and scouting parties were sent three or four times a day toward Lexington—which were instructed to clear the road of the enemy's pickets and reconnoitering parties. While here, Gano and Allen rejoined the column, having accomplished their respective missions.

Gano (in making a detour around Lexington) had driven in the pickets on every road—creating a fearful amount of confusion in the place among its gallant defenders, and causing the order that all rebel sympathizers, seen on the streets should be shot, to be emphatically reiterated. As Gano had approached Georgetown, after leaving Lexington and on his way to burn the bridges below Paris, an assemblage of a strange character occurred. He had formerly lived near Georgetown and knew nearly every man in the county. He stopped at the house of an intimate personal friend, who was also a notorious "sympathizer," who lived four or five miles from Georgetown, and "forced" him to feed his men and horses. While there, two or three of the Southern citizens of Scott, among them Stoddard Johnston (afterward Lieutenant Colonel on General Breckinridge's staff) came to the house, and were immediately and with great solemnity, placed under arrest.

Shortly afterward the assistant provost marshal of Georgetown (who was a very clever fellow), came out to protect the house and grounds from any disorder that the troops might be inclined to indulge in—thinking (in his simplicity) when he heard that troops were quartered there, that they must be "Union." The owner of the house (of course) interceded for him, and Gano pleased with the motive which had actuated him, promised to detain him, only until he himself moved again. In a short time another arrival was announced. The most determined, deeply-pitted, high-colored and uncompromising Union man in Georgetown, came galloping up the road to the house, and asked in a loud and authoritative tone for the commander of the detachment. Gano walked forth and greeted him. "Why how are you, Dick," said the new comer, "I didn't know that you were in the Union army; I've got something for you to do, old fellow." Gano assured him that he was delighted to hear it. "Where is the commander of these men," continued the "dauntless patriot." "I am their commander," said

Gano. "Well then here's an order for you," said the bearer of dispatches handing him a communication from the Home-guard headquarters, in Georgetown. Gano read it. "Oliver," he then said, slowly and very impressively, "I should be truly sorry to see you injured, we were school mates, and I remember our early friendship." Oliver's jaw fell, and his intelligent eye grew glassy with a "wild and maddening" apprehension, but his feelings would not permit him to speak. "Oliver," continued Gano after a pause (and keeping his countenance remarkably) "isn't it possible that you may be mistaken in these troops. To which army do you think they belong?" "Why," gasped Oliver; "ain't they Union?" "Union!" echoed Gano with a groan of horror, "don't let them hear you say so, I mightn't be able to control them. They are Morgan's Texas Rangers." He then led the half fainting Oliver, who under the influence of this last speech had become "even as a little child," to the house, and placed him with the other prisoners.

Saddest and most inconsolable of these were the sympathizers who had come purposely to be captured. When the hour drew near for Gano's departure, he held a brief conference with the "secesh," and then paroled the whole batch, including his host, binding them not to divulge any thing which they had seen or heard. All were impressed with the solemn nature of this obligation, but the melancholy gravity of Johnston (who had suggested it) was even awful.

Colonel Morgan finding how strongly Lexington was garrisoned, gave up all thought of attacking it, but it was high time that he made his arrangements to return to Dixie. He determined to make a dash at Cynthiana, the county seat of Harrison county, situated on the Kentucky Central Railroad, thirty-two miles from Lexington, and about twenty-two by turnpike from Georgetown. By moving in this direction, and striking a blow at this point, he hoped to induce the impression that he was aiming at Cincinnati, and at the same time thoroughly bewilder the officer in command at Lexington regarding his real intentions. When he reached Cynthiana he would be master of three or four routes, by either of which he could leave Kentucky, completely eluding his pursuers, and he did not doubt that he could defeat whatever force might be collected there.

He left Georgetown on the morning of the 18th, having first dispatched parts of two companies to drive all scouts and detachments of every kind into Lexington. While moving rapidly with the bulk of his command toward Cynthiana, these detachments protected his march and prevented it from being discovered too soon. Cynthiana was occupied by three or four hundred men of Metcalfe's regiment of cavalry, and about the same number of Home-guards, all under command of Lieutenant-Colonel Landrum, of Metcalfe's regiment. There was but one piece of artillery in the town, a brass twelve-pound howitzer. This was under charge of a company of firemen from Cincinnati, under command of "Captain Billy Glass of the Fourth Ward," and they went to work when the fight opened as if they were "putting out a fire." We struck the pickets a mile or two from the town, and the advance guard chased them in, capturing three or four.

General Morgan had previously determined upon his dispositions for the attack, well knowing the country, and they were made immediately after the alarm to the pickets. Between us and the town was the Licking river, crossed at the Georgetown pike, which we were traveling, by a narrow, covered bridge. Just by the side of the bridge, there was a ford about waist-deep. Nowhere else, in the then stage of water, was the river fordable in that immediate vicinity. But above and below about a mile, respectively, from the bridge, were fords, and to these were sent, Gano above, and the Georgians below, with instructions to cross and attack the town upon the respective quarters by which they approached it. The Second Kentucky was ordered to attack upon the road by which we had advanced.

The enemy held all the houses upon the opposite bank of the river, which runs close to the town, and opened a smart fire of musketry upon the regiment as it advanced. Companies A and B were deployed upon the right of the road, E and F upon the left, and C was held in reserve, mounted; the advance-guard had been sent with Gano. The recruits, most of whom were unarmed, were also, of course, kept in the rear. The howitzers were planted near the road, about three hundred and fifty yards from the bridge, and were opened at once upon the houses, evidently filled with the enemy.

The enemy's single piece of artillery swept the bridge and road, and commanded the position where the howitzers were stationed. Companies E and F advanced to the river's edge and poured such a fire across the narrow stream that they compelled the troops exposed to it to throw down their guns and surrender. They were then made to swim the river in order to join their captors. In the meantime, Company A, after having been repulsed two or three times in attempting to rush across the bridge, plunged into the river and, holding their guns and ammunition above their heads, crossed at the ford above-mentioned, and effected a lodgment on the other side. For awhile those first over were compelled to take shelter behind a long warehouse near the bridge, and even when the entire company had gotten over, and assistance had been sent to it, it seemed that the enemy, who concentrated to oppose us here, and redoubled his fire, would drive all back. The adjacent houses and yards were filled with sharpshooters, who poured in telling volleys as the men sought to close with them.

The lines were at this point not more than forty yards apart, and most of our loss was sustained here, and by Company A.

The howitzers were brought up, and posted on the corner, but the close fire drove the gunners away from them. One gunner named Talbot loaded and fired his piece two or three times by himself, while the balls were actually striking it. He was afterward made a Lieutenant. The team of one of the pieces, smarting with wounds, ran away with the limber, and carried it into the midst of the enemy. This check did not last more than three or four minutes. Company C charged across the bridge and up the principal street, on horseback, losing three or four men only, and distracting the enemy's attention. Company B got a position on the other bank where they could shoot right into the party which was holding Company A in check. The latter made a determined rush, at the head of which were Sergeants Drake and Quirk and private James Moore, of Louisiana, a little fellow, not yet sixteen years old, who fell with two severe wounds, but recovered, to make one of the most gallant officers of our command. In this dash, Sergeant Quirk, out of ammunition, and seeing his friend, Drake, in imminent peril, knocked down his assailant with a stone. The enemy then gave way; the other companies were, in the mean time, brought up to press them.

Gano came in on the one side, and the Georgians on the other, each driving all opponents before them. The Texians, Georgians, and Kentuckians arrived simultaneously at the piece of artillery, which the enemy had kept busily employed all the time. It was immediately taken, each claiming its capture.

The enemy immediately evacuated the town, and retreated eastwardly, but were closely pressed, and the better part captured. Greenfell headed a charge upon the depot, in which some of them took refuge. He received eleven bullets through his horse, person, and clothes, but was only slightly hurt. A curious little scarlet skull cap, which he used to wear, was perforated. It fitted so tight upon his head that I previously thought a ball could not go through it without blowing his brains out.

Colonel Landrum was chased eight or ten miles. Little Billy Peyton, a mere boy (Colonel Morgan's Orderly), but perfectly fearless, followed him closely, and exhausted two pistols without hitting him. The Colonel was riding a superb horse, which attracted attention to him, but which saved him. The enemy's loss was about ninety in killed and wounded; ours was about forty. Four hundred and twenty prisoners were taken.

It would be an unfair description of this fight if mention were omitted of the gallant conduct of the recruits. Although the most of them, as has been stated, were unarmed, they all "went in" like game cocks. Plenty of fine guns, with ammunition, were captured; also a large quantity of stores, and two or three hundred horses.

Cynthiana, like Georgetown and Versailles, was full of our devoted friends, and we felt satisfied that the wounded we were obliged to leave behind us would be well taken care of. Two men who subsequently died of their wounds, privates George Arnold and —— Clarke, behaved with such conspicuous gallantry, and were always so noted for good conduct, that their loss caused universal regret. Arnold was a member of the advance-guard, and volunteered to accompany Company C in the charge through the town. He fell with an arm and a thigh broken. Clarke undertook to carry an order through the enemy's line to Gano, who was in their rear, and fell pierced through the body with five balls. The best men were among the killed. Private Wm. Craig, of Company A, first to cross the river, was killed as he mounted the bank. All of the other officers having been wounded, the command of Company A devolved upon the Third Lieutenant, S.D. Morgan.

Leaving Cynthiana at one or two P.M., the command marched for Paris. About five miles from that place, we encountered a deputation of citizens, coming out to surrender the town. We reached Paris about sundown, and rested there during the night. I have omitted to mention that at Georgetown, Lieutenant Niles was appointed by Colonel Morgan upon his staff, and P.H. Thorpe, formerly Captain in the First Kentucky Infantry, was made Adjutant in his stead. I mention these appointments as if they were regular and valid, because they were all so in the end. The War Department made some trouble about them, as was expected, and perfectly proper, but as the appointees were borne on the muster and pay rolls as officers, there was nothing to be done but recognize them.

R.A. Alston, formerly a member of a South Carolina regiment of cavalry, but a member and private at the time of Company A, Second Kentucky, had been selected at Knoxville by Colonel Morgan to perform the duties of Adjutant-General, on account of his superior fitness for that position. He was permitted to recruit a company during the raid, in order that he might obtain the rank of Captain. He got his commission, and his company was divided between some others, and he was continued upon staff duty, although Greenfell, immediately after the conclusion of this raid became Adjutant-General.

The next morning after our arrival at Paris, a large force came down the Lexington road, and about eight A.M. gave us strong reasons for resuming our march. This force, about twenty-five hundred or three thousand men, was commanded by General G. Clay Smith. Our scouts had notified us of its approach the previous night, and as the command was encamped on the Winchester road, the one which we wished to travel, there was no danger of its cutting us off. It came on very slowly, and there was at no time any determined effort made to engage us. If a dash had been made at us when we prepared to leave, we could have been compelled to fight, for although the prisoners had all been paroled, we were very much incumbered with carriages containing wounded men, brought off from Cynthiana and other points.

Morgan always made it a point to carry off every wounded man who could be safely moved; in this way he prevented much of the demoralization attending the fear the men felt of falling, when wounded, into the hands of the enemy. I was once seriously told that a belief prevailed with some people, that Morgan killed his own wounded to prevent the enemy from making them prisoners.

The command reached Winchester about 12 P.M. and remained there until 4 P.M., when the march was taken up again and we crossed the Kentucky river just before dark. Marching on, we reached Richmond at 4 the next morning. Here we met with another very kind reception, and were joined by a company of recruits under Captain Jennings. It was admitted into the Second Kentucky as Company K. Leaving Richmond at 4 P.M. that day we marched toward Crab Orchard, and reached that place about day break next morning.

It had, at first, been Colonel Morgan's intention to make a stand at Richmond, as the whole population seemed inclined to join him, but his real strength was now known to the enemy, and they were collecting to attack him in such numbers, that he concluded that it was too hazardous. He would have had to have fought three battles at least, against superior forces, and have won all before he would have been safe.

Clay Smith was following him, Woolford was collecting forces to the southward to intercept him, and troops were coming from Louisville and other points to push after him. In the march from Paris to Crab Orchard, a good many wagons and a large number of guns were captured, and all—wagons and guns—that were not needed were burned. The horses captured with the twelve pounder at Cynthiana gave out and died before we reached the Kentucky river.

Leaving Crab Orchard at 11 A.M., the command moved toward Somerset and reached that place about sundown. The telegraph was again taken possession of, and Colonel Morgan instructed Ellsworth to countermand all of General Boyle's orders for pursuit. At Crab Orchard and Somerset one hundred and thirty Government wagons were captured and burned. At Somerset a great many stores of all kinds, blankets, shoes, etc., were found. Several wagons were loaded with as much as could be conveniently carried away, and the rest were destroyed. Arms, and ammunition for small arms and artillery, were also found in abundance, and were destroyed.

From Somerset the column marched to Stagall's ferry on the Cumberland river, and crossed there. We reached Monticello twenty-one miles from the river that night, but all danger was over when we had gotten safely across the river. The next day we proceeded leisurely toward Livingston, having a little excitement with the bushwhackers, but suffering no loss.

For several days after leaving Somerset, and indeed after reaching Livingston, we suffered greatly for want of rations, as this country was almost bare of provisions. Colonel Morgan's objects in making this raid, viz; to obtain recruits and horses, to thoroughly equip and arm his men, to reconnoiter for the grand invasion in the fall, and to teach the enemy that we could reciprocate the compliment of invasion, were pretty well accomplished. Enough of spare horses and more than enough of extra guns, saddles, etc., were brought out, to supply all the men who had been left behind. A great many prisoners were taken, of whom I have made no mention. But the results of the expedition are best summed up in the words of Colonel Morgan's report—

"I left Knoxville on the 4th day of this month, with about nine hundred men, and returned to Livingston on the 28th inst. with nearly twelve hundred, having been absent just twenty-four days, during which time I have traveled over a thousand miles, captured seventeen towns, destroyed all the Government supplies and arms in them, dispersed about fifteen hundred Home-guards and paroled nearly twelve hundred regular troops. I lost in killed, wounded and missing of the number that I carried into Kentucky, about ninety."

One practice was habitually pursued, on this raid, that may be remembered by some of our friends in the state for whose benefit it was done. Great pains were always taken to capture the most bitter Union man in each town and neighborhood—the one who was most inclined to bear down on Southern men—especially if he were provost marshal. He would be kept, sometimes a day or two, and thoroughly frightened. Colonel Morgan, who derived infinite amusement from such scenes, would gravely assure each one, when brought into his presence, that one of the chief objects of his raid was to catch him. It was a curious sight to see the mixed terror and vanity this declaration would generally excite—even in the agonies of anticipated death, the prisoner would be sensibly touched by the compliment. After awhile, however, a compromise would be effected; the prisoner would be released upon the implied condition that he was, in the future, to exert himself to protect Southern people. It was thought better to turn all the captured provost marshals loose and let them resume their functions, than to carry them off, and let new men be appointed, with whom no understanding could be had.

Ellsworth wound up his operations at Somerset, with complimentary dispatches from Colonel Morgan to General Jerry Boyle, Prentice, and others, and concluded with the following general order on his own part to the Kentucky telegraphic operators:

'HEADQUARTERS, TELEGRAPH DEPT. OF KY.,
CONFEDERATE STATES OF AMERICA.
'*General Order No. 1.*

'When an operator is positively informed that the enemy is marching on his station, he will immediately proceed to destroy the telegraphic instruments and all material in his charge. Such instances of carelessness, as were exhibited on the part of the operators at Lebanon, Midway, and Georgetown, will be severely dealt with. By order of

G.A. ELLSWORTH,
General Military Supt. C.S. Telegraphic Dept.'

At Livingston Colonel Morgan left the Second Kentucky and proceeded to Knoxville, taking with him the Georgians, Gano's squadron, and the howitzers—which needed some repairs. After remaining at Livingston three days, I marched the regiment to Sparta, where more abundant supplies could be obtained, and facilities for shoeing horses could be had. While at Livingston, the men suffered extremely with hunger, and one man declared his wish to quit a service in which he was subjected to such privations. He was deprived of his horse, arms, and equipments, and "blown out" of the regiment; that is, upon dress parade, he was marched down the front of the regiment (after his offense and the nature of the punishment had been read by the Adjutant), with the bugler blowing the "Skedaddle" behind him amid the hisses of the men, who were thoroughly disgusted with him; he was then driven away from the camp. At Sparta we found a better country and the kindest and most hospitable people.

CHAPTER IX

As soon as the Second Kentucky was placed in camp at Sparta, a much stricter system was adopted than had ever prevailed before. Camp-guards were regularly posted in order to keep the men in camp; and as staying in camp closely was something they particularly disliked, the guard had to be doubled, until finally nearly one half of the regiment had to be put on to watch the rest. Guard-mounting, dress-parades, and drills (company and regimental, on foot and on horseback), were had daily, much to the edification and improvement of the recruits, who rapidly acquired instruction, and quite as much to the disgust of the old hands, who thought that they "knew it all." In one respect, however, they were all equally assiduous and diligent that was in the care of their horses and attention to their arms and accouterments—no man had ever to be reproved or punished for neglect of these duties. The regiment now numbered about seven hundred men, nearly all of the recruits obtained in Kentucky having joined it.

It was then in the flush of hope and confidence, composed of the best material Kentucky could afford, and looked forward to a career of certain success and of glory. The officers were (with scarcely an exception), very young men; almost every one of them had won his promotion by energy and gallantry, and all aspired to yet further preferment. The men were of just such staff as the officers, and all relied upon (in their turn), winning promotion.

The character of Kentucky troops was never better illustrated than in this regiment and at that time. Give them officers that they love, respect, and rely on, and any thing can be accomplished with them. While almost irrepressibly fond of whisky, and incorrigible, when not on active service, about straggling through the country and running out of camp, they, nevertheless, stick to work at the time when it is necessary, and answer to the roll-call in an emergency unfailingly, no matter what may be the prospect before them. Aware too that (in quiet times), they are always behaving badly, they will cheerfully submit to the severest punishment—provided, always, that it is not of a degrading nature. They can not endure harsh and insulting language, or any thing that is humiliating. In this respect they show the traits which characterize all of their Southern brethren—the Irish are of a similar disposition. I have frequently known the efficiency of fine companies greatly impaired by officers who were offensive in their language to them, and yet rarely punished, while other officers, who never indulged in such language, but were accustomed to punish severely, were not only more promptly obeyed, but were infinitely more liked. While the regiment was at Sparta, Colonel Jno. Scott also came with his own fine regiment the First Louisiana, and a portion of our old friends, the Eighth Texas.

Colonel Scott was one of the most active, efficient, and daring cavalry officers in the Western Confederate army. He had performed very successful and brilliant service, during the spring, in North Alabama, and had lately served with Forrest in the latter's dashing operations in Middle Tennessee. While we were all at Sparta together, Buell's army began to commence to concentrate, and a large part of it under Nelson came to McMinnville.

McMinnville is twenty-eight miles from Sparta, and a force of infantry, preceded by two or three hundred cavalry, came one day to the bridge over Calf Killer creek, on the McMinnville road, within five miles of Sparta. Colonel Scott sent Major Harrison (afterward Brigadier General), of the Eighth Texas, with two or three companies of the First Louisiana, and as many of the Eighth Texas, to drive them back. Harrison fell on them in his usual style, and they went back immediately. One or two of them were killed, and a few prisoners were taken. I sent Lieutenant Manly, of my regiment, about this time, to ascertain the disposition of Buell's forces. He reported, in a few days, that there were three thousand and six hundred men at Nashville, a great many of them convalescents, four thousand at Columbia, three thousand at Pulaski, and three thousand at Shelbyville. At McMinnville twelve thousand. At points on the Tennessee river, in Alabama, about two thousand. Generals Bragg and Smith were then preparing for the invasion of Kentucky. Bragg lay at Chattanooga with about thirty thousand men. We confidently expected that he would dash across the river, while Buell's army was thus scattered, break through it and take Nashville, and pick up the fragments at his leisure. He gave Buell a little time, and the latter concentrated with a quickness that seemed magical, protected Nashville, and was ready for the race into Kentucky. Buell's own friends have damned him pretty thoroughly, but that one exhibition of energy and skill, satisfied his enemies (that is, the Confederates) of his caliber, and we welcomed his removal with gratification. Manly also reported, that rolling stock was being collected, from all the roads, at Nashville, and that wagon trains were being gotten together at convenient points. This indicated pretty clearly that a concentration was contemplated for some purpose. After remaining a few days at Sparta, Colonel Scott received orders to report with his command to General Kirby Smith, whose Headquarters were at Knoxville. Shortly afterward, Colonel Morgan reached Sparta, bringing with him Gano's squadron and Company G. Gano's two companies, numbered now, however, only one hundred and ten effectives; he had left a good many sick at Knoxville, who did not rejoin us for some time. The howitzers, to our great regret, were left behind. A day or two after Colonel Morgan's arrival, we set out to surprise the Federal garrison at Gallatin, distant about seventy or eighty miles. Morgan had received instructions to break the railroad between Louisville and Nashville, in order to retard Buell's retreat to Louisville as greatly as possible, also to occupy the Federal cavalry, and prevent them from paying attention to what was going on in other quarters. Gallatin seemed to him an excellent point at which to commence operations with all these views. On the way, he was joined by Captain Joseph Desha (formerly of the First Kentucky infantry), with twenty or thirty men. Captain Desha's small detachment was received into the Second Kentucky, and he was promised recruits enough to make him a full company. He soon got them, and his company was duly lettered L of the regiment. Crossing the Cumberland at Sand Shoals ford, three miles from Carthage, on the day after we left Sparta, we reached Dixon Springs, about eight miles from Gallatin, about 2 or 3 P.M., and, as our coming had been announced by couriers sent on in advance, we found that the friendly and hospitable citizens had provided abundant supplies for men and horses. Crowds of them met to welcome us, bringing every delicacy. It was a convincing proof of the unanimity of sentiment in that region, that while hundreds knew of our march and destination, not one was found to carry the information to the enemy. Just before dark the march was resumed, and we reached Hartsville, sixteen miles from Gallatin, about 11 o'clock at night. Pressing on through Hartsville without halting, the column turned off from the turnpike a few miles from Gallatin, entirely avoiding the pickets, which were captured by scouts sent after we had gained their rear. As we entered Gallatin, Captain Desha was sent forward with a small party to capture Colonel Boone, the Federal commander, who, as we had learned, was in the habit of sleeping in town. Desha reached the house where he was quartered, and found him dressed and just about to start to camp. It was now about daybreak. Colonel Morgan immediately saw Boone and represented to him that he had better write to the officer in command at the camp, advising him to surrender, in order to spare the "effusion of blood," etc. This Boone consented to do, and his letter was at once dispatched to the camp under flag of truce. It had the desired effect, and the garrison fell into our hands without firing a shot. Two companies had been sent off for some purpose, and escaped capture. About two hundred prisoners were taken, including a good many officers. As these troops were infantry, no horses were captured with them, but during the forenoon, a train arrived with some eighty very fine ones, *en route* for Nashville. Two or three hundred excellent Springfield rifles were captured, with which all the inferior guns were replaced. Some valuable stores were also captured, and wagoned off to Hartsville.

The prisoners were paroled and sent off Northward, during that and the following day. The Government freight train seized, numbered nineteen cars, laden with forage for the cavalry at Nashville. Efforts were made to decoy the train from Nashville into our possession, but unsuccessfully. Ellsworth was immediately put in possession of the telegraph office, and went to work with even more than his ordinary ingenuity. It was the peculiarity of this "great man" to be successful only in his own department; if he attempted any thing else he was almost sure to fail. At Crab Orchard, for instance, on the late raid, he had taken it into his head to go after a notorious and desperate bushwhacker, whom our best scouts had tried in vain to capture.

Telling no one of his intention, he took Colonel Greenfell's horse, upon which was strapped a saddle that the owner valued very highly, and behind the saddle was tied a buff coat equally as much prized, and in the coat was all the gold the Colonel had brought from Richmond, when he came to join us—and thus equipped he sallied out with one companion, to take the formidable "Captain King."

He went boldly to that worthy's house, who, seeing only two men coming, scorned to take to the brush. To Ellsworth's demand to surrender, he answered with volleys from shot gun and revolver, severely wounding the friend and putting Ellsworth himself to flight. King pressed the retreat, and Ellsworth, although he brought off his wounded companion, lost horse, saddle, coat and gold. St. Leger was like an excited volcano, and sought Ellsworth to slay him instantly.

Three days were required to pacify him, during which time, the great "operator" had to be carefully kept out of his sight. But when Ellsworth was seated in the telegraph office he was always "master of the situation." No man could watch him at work, see him catch, without a boggle, "signals," "tariff," and all the rest, fool the regular operators, baffle with calm confidence their efforts to detect him, and turn to his own advantage their very suspicions, and not unhesitatingly pronounce him a genius. As if to demonstrate incontestably his own superiority, he has (since the war closed) invented a plan to prevent just such tricks, as he used to practice at way stations, from being played.

When he "took the chair" at Gallatin, he first, in accordance with Colonel Morgan's instructions, telegraphed in Colonel Boone's name, to the commandant at Bowlinggreen to send him reinforcements, as he expected to be attacked. But this generous plan to capture and parole soldiers, who wished to go home and see their friends, miscarried. Then he turned his attention to Nashville. The operator there was suspicious and put a good many questions, all of which were successfully answered.

At length the train he wished sent, was started, but when it got within six miles of Gallatin, a negro signaled it and gave the alarm. A railroad bridge between Gallatin and Nashville, was then at once destroyed, and the fine tunnel, six miles above, was rendered impassable for months. The roof of the tunnel was of a peculiar rock which was liable at all times to disintegrate and tumble down; to remedy this, huge beams, supported by strong uprights, had been stretched horizontally across the tunnel, and a sort of scaffolding have been built upon these beams. A good deal of wood work was consequently put up. Some of the freight cars were also run into the tunnel and set on fire when the wood work was kindled. This fire smouldered on, after it had ceased to burn fiercely, for a long time, and it was weeks before any repairs could be attempted, on account of the intense heat and the huge masses of rock which were constantly falling. This tunnel is eight hundred feet long.

In the "History of the Louisville and Nashville Railroad during the war," the Superintendent, Mr. Albert Fink, whose energy to repair, was equal to Morgan's to destroy, says of the year commencing July 1, 1862, and ending July 1, 1863, "the road has been operated for its entire length only seven months and twelve days." He says, moreover, "All the bridges and trestlework on the main stem and branches, with the exception of the bridge over Barren river and four small bridges, were destroyed and rebuilt during the year; some of the structures were destroyed twice, and some three times. In addition to this, most of the water stations, several depots, and a large number of cars were burnt, a number of engines badly damaged, and a tunnel in Tennessee nearly filled up for a distance of eight hundred feet." This shows a great activity to destroy, but wonderful patience and industry to repair. It was by this road that the Federal army in Tennessee got its supplies and reinforcements, almost altogether, during the greater part of the year. In the same report the writer goes on to say: "General Morgan took possession of the Louisville and Nashville road at Gallatin, in August, 1862, and this, with other causes, forced General Buell's retreat to Louisville."

Before giving up the wires, and after Colonel Morgan permitted him to reveal himself, Ellsworth told some first-class romances. He made Morgan's force out about four thousand, and did it with a skill that carried conviction. He would speak, in dispatches to various well-known Federals, of certain imaginary commands, under men whom they well knew. He telegraphed Prentice that Wash. Morgan was at Gallatin, with four hundred Indians, raised especially to seek for his (Prentice's) scalp.

Lieutenant Manly, and a few men, were left at Gallatin to burn the amphitheater at the fair-grounds, where Boone's regiment had been quartered. The command left Gallatin about 12 o'clock at night, and returned to Hartsville. Gallatin was taken on the 12th of August. We remained encamped at Hartsville until the 19th. During that time, men and horses were entirely recruited. The citizens supplied all the rations and forage that we needed, and frequently we would have whole stacks of hams, turkeys, chickens, etc. (all cooked) piled up in our camps.

On the 13th of August, the day after we left Gallatin, a Federal force of about twelve hundred men, with four pieces of artillery, came there, and drove Lieutenant Manly and his party away. Manly was killed, and, we learned, after he had surrendered. Sergeant Quirk, of Company A, was sent, with fifteen men, on a scout to Gallatin, next day. He found, when he got there, that this force had left, on the way to Nashville again. He followed, and overtook it, about three miles from Gallatin, as it was preparing to get on the cars. He attacked it immediately, and killed two or three, and captured a few prisoners. The artillery was opened upon him, with canister, but did him no damage. He brought his fifteen men upon them through a cornfield, and got close before he fired. John Donnellan, a soldier who was always in the extreme front in every fight, exerted a powerful voice, in issuing orders to the "Texians" to go one way, the "Indians" another, and "Duke's regiment" to fall on their rear, until he had ostensibly and vociferously disposed in line enough troops to have frightened the "heroes of Marengo."

On the 19th, Colonel Morgan received information that a force of some three hundred infantry had come to Gallatin, and on that evening he started out in pursuit. He had hoped to surprise them in the town, but learned, on the road, that they had left at midnight, and were on their way back to Nashville. Captain Hutchinson, of Company E, of the Second Kentucky, was sent, with his company, to intercept them, if possible, at a point seven miles below Gallatin, where a bridge had been burned, on the railroad, and where it was thought that, probably, a train would be waiting to take them back. The rest of the command pushed on to Gallatin, and reached that place about 8 o'clock on the morning of the 20th. We found that the enemy had taken off nearly every male inhabitant of the place above the age of twelve, and the women were all in terrible distress when we came in. This had been done on account of the kind reception which had been given us in the place, on the 12th. We also found the corpse of one of our men, killed the night before, and the citizens told us that he had been kicked and cuffed after he was shot. As we passed out of town, on the Nashville pike, we saw on the bridge the stain of Manly's blood. The men became very much excited, and could scarcely be kept in the ranks. As we pressed on down the road, we reached the point where Hutchinson had been directed to intercept the party which had been to Gallatin. He had failed to do this, but had captured a stockade garrisoned by forty or fifty men. He came upon the party after which he started, but they had passed the point at which he could have checked them.

Another garrison of fifty men was captured at a stockade still lower down, and we came soon after upon the men we were looking for. We could not prevent the escape of the greater portion, who got on hand cars and ran down the road, but we killed some forty, and released all the prisoners. At Edgefield junction, First Lieutenant Jas. Smith who reached that point first, with a part of his Company (A of the Second Kentucky), attacked the stockade, there, supported by Captain Breckinridge who shortly afterward arrived. The inmates of the stockade made fight, and Smith lost three of his men, and was himself shot through the head, of which wound he soon died. Lieutenant Niles, of Morgan's staff, was also killed at this point, shot through the body with five or six balls. I came up at the time that these officers were shot and ordered the men back. I saw no chance of reducing the work, even with great loss, in the time that would be allowed us.

These stockades were built with heavy upright timber, ten or twelve feet high. They were surrounded by ditches and pierced for musketry. Assailants when right at this bases, were as far from taking them as ever. There was a plan, which I am satisfied would have been successful against them, but I never saw it tried, viz.: to construct bundles of bushwood large enough to shelter a man and compact enough to stop a musket ball, and place a sufficient number of them in the hands of the men, who holding them in front, should advance and press them against the loop-holes—of course riflemen would have to be posted in range, to prevent a sally on the bundle-carriers. The fire from the stockade having been thus stopped, the walls could be chopped down with axes, or brush, in large quantities, could be set on fire and tossed over among the defenders, until they concluded to surrender. This plan, however, would require plenty of time, and that is just what partisan cavalry have least of on such occasions.

Colonel Morgan was much attached to both Smith and Niles, and it was with great difficulty that he could be dissuaded from continuing to attack until the stockade was taken. Lieutenant Smith had been one of the best soldiers in the squadron, and had given universal satisfaction by his conduct as an officer. He was more than ordinarily brave, intelligent and zealous, and would certainly have been made a field-officer if he had lived a few months longer. His men were devotedly attached to him. The repulse at this stockade made us more than ever regret the absence of the howitzers. With them we could have battered it down directly. It was lucky that Hutchinson had caught the garrison of the first one captured, outside of its walls, and as they attempted to enter, his men rushed in with them. The other stockade taken, surrendered without firing a shot. This was a very exciting day; the chase and succession of skirmishes made the whole affair very interesting.

Returning to Gallatin, we met the people of the adjacent country coming with vehicles of every description to convey their recaptured friends back home. The latter weary and footsore, were plodding along as best they might, except when our men would take them behind them or dismount and let them ride their horses. There was a scene of wild congratulation in town, that evening, when they all got in. That night the entire command encamped in the fair grounds. About 12 o'clock, Colonel Morgan received information that a formidable Federal force had passed through Hartsville on the previous afternoon, and was encamped at Castalian Springs, ten miles from Gallatin. He ordered the pickets to be strengthened in that direction, and shrewd scouts were put out to watch their movements closely, but he did not disturb the command, wishing that it should be rested for the next day's work. He had been informed that infantry and artillery composed this force, as well as cavalry, and he knew that if the latter waited on the former, he was in no danger of being forced into a fight that it might be imprudent to make. In the morning the scouts came in, saying that the enemy were rapidly advancing. The column was immediately put in motion, moving toward the enemy, but it was Colonel Morgan's intention to decline battle until more positively informed of the enemy's strength, and when he reached the junction of the Hartsville and Scottsville turnpikes, at the eastern edge of the town, he turned off on the Scottsville pike, which runs nearly at right angles to the other, and northeast.

The enemy, in the meantime, were pressing on vigorously, driving in the scouts and pickets. Colonel Morgan and myself had taken position at the junction of the two roads, as the column filed past, and fearing that we would be taken in flank, or that our rear would be attacked after the entire command had taken the Scottsville road, I advised him to form and fight, saying that I believed we could whip them. He answered that he could "get fights enough, but could not easily get such a command again, if he lost this one." Immediately afterward, seeing the enemy come galloping down the road, he added, with a half smile, "We will have to whip these fellows, sure enough. Form your men, and, as soon as you check them, attack. Gano, who was in the extreme rear, was ordered, as soon as his squadron arrived at the junction of the roads, to charge and drive back the enemy's advance. He did so in his usual dashing, impetuous style. The enemy's advance guard was strong and determined, and met Gano's charge gallantly. As he led on his men, the enemy directed their fire principally at him, but with the good fortune which attended him during four years of dangerous and incessant service, he escaped unhurt, losing, by the shots aimed at him, only his hat and a few locks of hair, which latter was a loss he could well stand, although the other was a serious matter. After a brief struggle, Gano drove back the advance, killing and wounding several. Our entire force, deducting one hundred men used as a guard for the prisoners taken the day before, and other details, was about seven hundred strong. That of the enemy was about the same. On the right of the Hartsville road, as our line faced, was a cornfield. This was immediately occupied by Companies I and K. On the left of the Hartsville pike, and just east of the Scottsville road, was a woodland of some twenty acres. Company D was deployed in this, and immediately cleared it of the enemy, who had entered it, and kept it until the line advanced. To the left of this woodland was a long meadow, five or six hundred yards in extent, and some three hundred broad; to the left of this, again, was another cornfield. The column had gotten some distance upon the Scottsville pike before the command to halt and face toward the enemy had been transmitted to its head, and when these companies mentioned had been formed, there was a gap of nearly two hundred yards opened between them and the others that were further to the front. Toward this gap the enemy immediately darted. Believing that we were seeking to escape upon the Scottsville road, he had thrown the bulk of his force in that direction, at any rate, and it was formed and advanced rapidly and gallantly. Throwing down the eastern fence of the meadow, some three hundred poured into it, formed a long line, and dashed across it, with sabers drawn, toward the line of horses which they saw in the road beyond. Companies B, C, E and F were by this time dismounted, and had dropped on their knees behind the low fence on the road-side, as the enemy came rushing on. They held their fire until the enemy were within thirty yards, when they opened. Then was seen the effect of a volley from that long thin line, which looked so easy to break, and, yet, whose fire was so deadly. Every man had elbow-room and took dead aim at an individual foe, and, as the blaze left the guns, two thirds of the riders and horses seemed to go down. The cavalry was at once broken, and recoiled. Our men sprang over the fence and ran close up to them, as they endeavored to retreat rapidly through the gaps in the fence, by which they had entered, and poured in such another volley that the rout was completed. However, they reformed and came back, but only to be repulsed again. By this time the companies on the right had driven off their opponents in that direction, and had gotten a position where they could enfilade the enemy's line as it strove to advance, and in a little while it was forced back at all points. Gano charged again, and pressed them closely. After retreating about half a mile, the enemy halted and reformed upon a hill which ran for some hundreds of yards parallel with their former line, and on the crest of which were high fences and timber.

As we had repulsed them the last time, some interesting incidents occurred. Captain Leabo, of the Second Indiana, dashed down upon our line, and, coming on himself after his men turned back, was made prisoner. Another individual was made prisoner in the same way, although he did not come with the same intent which inspired the gallant Captain. The wildest looking fellow perhaps in the Federal army came rattling down the pike on a big sorrel horse, which he could not hold, his hair standing on end, his mouth wide open, his shirt collar flying by one end like a flag of truce, and his eyes glazed. He was caught by the greatest wag in the command, and perhaps in the Western Army—the celebrated Jeff. Sterritt. With a look of appalling ferocity, the captor exclaimed: "I don't know whether to kill you now, or to wait until the fight's over." "For God's sake," said the captive, "don't kill me at all. I'm a dissipated character, and not prepared to die."

Company A and the advance-guard had been held until this time in reserve on the extreme left. When our whole line was pressed forward after the retreating enemy, I carried them rapidly in advance of the rest of the line, and through a woods which concealed the movement upon the flank of the enemy's new line just as it was formed. The effect of their fire, then delivered at short range, was decisive, and the enemy instantly broke again, and this time made, at full speed, for the road, and went off in full retreat. The bulk of the command was too far from the line of horses to mount and pursue promptly, but Gano pressed them closely again. Adjutant Wyncoop, son of the Colonel of that name, was killed in this retreat, as he was trying to rally his men. His body was removed to the side of the road, and lay there as we passed, with a coat thrown over his face as if he were unwilling to look upon the rout of his command.

The enemy fell back about three miles, and halted again. Their loss had been very heavy, and perhaps two hundred horses had been killed for them. Nearly all of the men thus dismounted were made prisoners. Colonel Morgan now learned that the officer in command of the troops he had been fighting, was Brigadier-General Johnson, and became satisfied that the infantry and artillery with which the force had been at first provided was not in supporting distance. We subsequently learned that it had been sent back to McMinnville a day or two before.

Just as the horses were brought up and the men were mounted, a flag of truce came from General Johnson proposing an armistice in order that he might bury his dead. Colonel Morgan answered that he could entertain no proposition except unconditional surrender, but shortly afterward sent offering to parole officers and men if a surrender were made. General Johnson replied that "catching came before hanging." Colonel Morgan resolved upon immediate and vigorous pursuit, and believing that in the broken and demoralized condition of the enemy he could safely attempt such a plan, he divided his force into three columns, directing each in a special direction, in order to more certainly encounter the enemy, who had now more than three miles the start of us. Five companies were placed upon the left of the road under Major Morgan. Colonel Morgan himself kept the road with Gano's squadron, while I had the right, with Companies A, B, and E, and the advance-guard, in all about two hundred and twenty-five men. The road bends to the left at about the point where General Johnson had last halted, and as he turned off just there, in order to make for the river, the other two columns missed him altogether, and mine, pressing on rapidly in the direction indicated, was so fortunate as to soon overtake him.

The three companies were formed in parallel columns of fours, with full distance between them, and the advance-guard, thrown out as skirmishers in front. When the enemy was neared, the whole force was thrown into line, and advanced at a gallop. We were not more than fifty yards from the enemy when this was done, but there was a high stone wall between us, which our horses could not leap. This prevented us from closing with them, and enabled them to get some distance ahead of us. As we passed the wall, the original formation was resumed, and we followed at good speed. Soon the advance guard, sent on again in front, reported that the enemy had halted and formed for a fight.

A short reconnoisance showed that they were dismounted and drawn up under a long hill, and about forty yards from its crest, but their formation was defective, in that, instead of presenting a straight, uniform line, so that their numbers could tell, they were formed in the shape of a V, perhaps to meet any movement to flank them. The hill was one of those gentle undulations of the blue-grass pastures, which present perfectly smooth surfaces on either side, and yet rise enough to conceal from those on the one side what is being done on the other.

The three companies and the advance were immediately brought into line and dismounted under cover of the brow of the hill, and moved to a position which would bring the apex of the enemy's formation about opposite the center of our line. When we, then, charged over the hill, although the enemy had some advantage in firing upward, it was more than counterbalanced by the fact that the men upon their flanks could not fire at us at all, while our whole line could fire without difficulty upon any portion of their formation. After a short but sharp fight they gave way again. Our loss in this skirmish was two killed. We captured General Johnson, his Adjutant General, Major Winfrey and several other officers and twenty or thirty privates. In the two engagements the enemy left sixty-four dead on the field, and a number of wounded. About two hundred prisoners were taken.

This force had been selected with great care from all the cavalry of

Buell's army, and placed under General Johnson, regarded as one of their best and most dashing officers, for the express purpose of hunting Morgan. It was completely disorganized and shattered by this defeat. A great deal of censure was cast at the time upon these men, and they were accused of arrant cowardice by the Northern press. Nothing could have been more unjust, and many who joined in denouncing them, afterward behaved much more badly. They attacked with spirit and without hesitation, and were unable to close with us on account of their heavy loss in men and horses. They returned two or three times to the attack until they found their efforts unavailing. They could not use their sabers, and they found their breech-loading carbines only incumbrances. They may have shown trepidation and panic toward the last, but, to an enemy (while they were evidently trying to get away) they appeared resolute although dispirited. I have seen troops much more highly boasted than these were before their defeat, behave not nearly so well. Johnson had been very confident. He had boasted as he passed through Hartsville, that he would "catch Morgan and bring him back in a band-box."

Hearing the day before the fight that Forrest was in his rear, he had, very properly, pressed on to fight Morgan before the former came up. His attack was made promptly and in splendid style, his dispositions throughout the first fight were good, and he exhibited fine personal courage and energy. I could never understand his reason for giving battle the second time, without fresh troops, when his men were already dispirited by defeat, and pressed by an enemy flushed with recent victory. He could have gotten off without a fight by a prompt retreat, immediately after his last message to Morgan, and protected, by a judicious use of detachments composed of his best men as rear guards. He was evidently a fine officer, but seemed not to comprehend the "new style of cavalry," at all.

Our loss, in both engagements, was seven killed and eighteen wounded. The conduct of men and officers was unexceptionable. Captains Cassell and Hutchinson and Lieutenant White, of the Second Kentucky, and Lieutenant Rogers of the advance guard, were especially mentioned. Nothing could have exceeded the dash and gallantry of the officers and men of Gano's squadron. The junior Captain Huffman had his arm shattered early in the action, but went through it all, despite the suffering he endured, at the head of his men.

Colonel Morgan in his address to his men, thus summed up the results of the last two days:

"All communications cut off between Gallatin and Nashville; a body of infantry, three hundred strong, totally cut to pieces or taken prisoners the liberation of those kind friends arrested by our revengeful foes, for no other reason than their compassionate care of our sick and wounded, would have been laurels sufficient for your brows. But soldiers, the utter annihilation of General Jonson's brigade, composed of twenty-four picked companies, sent on purpose to take us, raises your reputation as soldiers, and strikes fear into the craven hearts of your enemies. General Johnson and his staff, with two hundred men taken prisoners, sixty-four killed, and one hundred wounded, attests the resistance made, and bears testimony to your valor."

Having burned all the bridges the day before that were under his then immediate supervision, and preferring Hartsville as a place for a somewhat lengthened encampment, he returned to that place on the evening of the 21st. A good writer and excellent officer of Morgan's old command very truly says, in reference to the choice of Hartsville in this respect:

"The selection of this little unknown village was a proof of Morgan's consummate strategic ability." It was a point where it was literally impossible to entrap him. While here, a deserter taken in arms and fighting, was tried by court-martial, sentenced and shot in presence of the command. Forrest reached Hartsville on the 22nd with a portion of his command. He had hurried on to reinforce Morgan before the latter fought Johnson, fearing that the entire original force of infantry, artillery and cavalry, which had left McMinnville with Johnson, would be too much for us. Learning that he was no longer needed in Sumner county, he crossed the river without delay, and in a day or two we heard of his sweeping every thing clean around Nashville. So demoralizing was the effect of the system of immediately paroling prisoners, and sending them off by routes which prevented them from meeting troops of their own army, which had been instituted and practiced, for some time previously to this date, that General Buell found it necessary to issue an order on the subject.

Morgan and Forrest inaugurated the system, and hundreds of prisoners were induced to fall into their hands, by the facilities thus offered them of getting home, who, otherwise, would never have been captured. A man, thus paroled, was lost to the Federal army for months at least, for, even if not inclined to respect his parole, it was hard for the authorities to find him. His gun and equipments, also, became ours. In his order, General Buell said: "The system of paroles as practiced in this army has run into an intolerable abuse. Hereafter no officer or soldier belonging to the forces in this district will give his parole not to take up arms, for the purpose of leaving the enemy's lines, without the sanction of the General commanding this army, except when by reason of wounds or disease, he could not be removed without endangering his life. Any parole given in violation of this order will not be recognized, and the person giving it will be required to perform military duty, and take the risks prescribed by the laws of war," etc.

This order was issued on the 8th of August, before the surrender of Boone. While we were at Hartsville a case of types and printing press had been found in the deserted room once occupied as a printing office, and were immediately put to use. Poor Niles, who had once been an editor, went to work and organized a corps of assistants from among the practical printers, of whom there were several in the Second Kentucky, and issued a small sheet which he called the *Vidette*. It was printed on any sort of paper that could be procured, and consequently, although perfectly consistent in its politics, it appeared at different times in different colors. Sometimes it would be a drab, sometimes a pale rose color, and, my recollection is, that Boone's surrender was recorded upon a page of delicate pea-green. Colonel Morgan finding the pleasure that it gave the men, took great pains to promote the enterprise. The *Vidette* was expected with as much interest by the soldiers of the command, and country people, as the *Tribune* or *News*, by the reading people of New York. General orders were published in it, promotions announced, and complimentary notices made by Colonel Morgan of the deserving. Full accounts of all our operations were published, and the reports of the various scouting parties filled up the column devoted to "local news." The editors indulged in the most profound and brilliant speculations on the political future, and got off the ablest critiques upon the conduct of the war. As every thing "good" was published, some tremendous and overwhelmingly decisive Confederate victories, of which the official records make no mention, even by name, were described in the *Vidette*, and the horrors of Federal invasion were depicted in terms which made the citizen reader's blood freeze in his veins.

Contemporary papers were encouraged, or rebuked, as the case might require, with becoming zeal, and the "pestilent opposition sheets" were attacked with that felicitous but inexorable sarcasm which distinguishes editorial contests. The rhetorical expression of contempt or indignation, and the large share which these passions had in the leading articles, justly entitled the "*Vidette*" to an eminent place among the journals of the period.

About this time there had recently been another call for some hundreds of thousands of men by the Federal Government, and Morgan hoped to avail himself of the disinclination of the Kentuckians to be drafted, to increase his own force. He had dispatched many recruiting agents into the counties of Southern Kentucky, and had instructed them to inform all young men who wished to avoid the draft, that the best way to do it effectually, was to join him. As a great many preferred (of the two armies) the Confederate, they came, when forced to a decision, to the latter. Many, too, had long hesitatingly contemplated "joining Morgan," and the imminent danger of being placed, forcibly, in the other army, quickened their wits and resolution, and they came.

Adam R. Johnson and Woodward, who were at this time operating very successfully in Southwestern Kentucky, got a large number of recruits seeking to avoid the draft. A great many came to Morgan—enough to fill up Desha's company, and, besides increasing all the old companies, to add another company to the regiment. This one was lettered M, and was commanded by Captain W.H. Jones, who became a fine officer, although he had then seen no service. To remedy all trouble from the inexperience of the Captain, Colonel Morgan, in accordance with his usual policy, appointed, as First and Second Lieutenants, Sergeants Thomas Quirk and Ben Drake of Company A. Both had previously distinguished themselves, and both made their mark as officers. Henry Hukill, another Sergeant of Company A, and an excellent soldier, was appointed First Lieutenant of

Company L. Gano, also, recruited another company for his squadron at this time. It was a large and fine one, and was commanded by Captain Theophilus Steele, formerly Surgeon of the Second Kentucky infantry, but he was one of that kind of Surgeons, who, in war, prefer inflicting wounds to curing them.

A short repose at Hartsville was interrupted by the most welcome and stirring summons we had ever received. This was an order from General Kirby Smith to Colonel Morgan, to meet him at Lexington, Kentucky, on the 2nd of the coming month (September).

It will be impossible for the men, whose history I am writing, to ever forget this period of their lives. The beautiful country in which it was passed, the blue-grass pastures and the noble trees, the encampments in the shady forests, through which ran the clear cool Tennessee waters, the lazy enjoyments of the green bivouacs, changing abruptly to the excitement of the chase and the action, the midnight moonlit rides amidst the lovely scenery, cause the recollections which crowd our minds, when we think of Gallatin and Hartsville, to mingle almost inseparably with the descriptions of romance. In this country live a people worthy of it. In all the qualities which win respect and love, in generosity, honesty, devoted friendship, zealous adherence to what they deem the right, unflinching support of those who labor for it, in hospitality and kindliness, the Creator never made a people to excel them. May God bless and prosper them, and may they and their children, only, at the judgment day, "arise from that corner of the earth, to answer for the sins of the brave."

CHAPTER X

Bidding our friends at Hartsville farewell, we set out for the heart of Kentucky on the morning of the 29th. Never were men in higher and more exultant spirits, and cheer after cheer rang from the front to the rear of the column, and when these evidences of enthusiastic joy at length ceased the way was enlivened with laugh, jest, and song. Passing by the Red Sulphur Springs, we reached Scottsville, in Allen county, Kentucky, on that night and encamped at 12 o'clock a few miles beyond. Stokes' and Haggard's regiments of Federal cavalry were reported to be in that section of the country, and the necessity for somewhat careful scouting could not be ignored. We saw nothing of them, however, and resuming our march early the next morning, reached Glasgow about 10 A.M.

At Glasgow we found rumors prevailing, as yet undefined and crude, of Kirby Smith's advance through Southeastern Kentucky. Our friends in Glasgow welcomed us with their usual kindness and after enjoying their hospitality for some hours, we marched off on the Columbia road. Encamping that night at Green river, we reached Columbia, in Adair county, on the next day about 12 P.M., and remained there until the next morning.

The reason for the slow marching of the last two days, had been Colonel Morgan's anxiety to obtain some information of the two howitzers, which were being escorted from Knoxville, under charge of his brother and Aide-Campe Captain C.H. Morgan, with an escort of seventy-five men. This escort was composed of men who had been granted furloughs, and of convalescent sick and wounded men, returning to the command. These men were all well armed, and were under the immediate command of Captain Allen, who was assisted by several excellent officers. When this party reached Sparta, it marched, in accordance with instructions sent there for its guidance, to Carthage, and thence to Red Sulphur Springs, following, then, directly in the track of the column. Stokes' cavalry heard of them, and pursued. Once, this regiment came very near falling foul of them. The party had encamped late at night, and as a measure of precaution, the horses were taken back some distance into the woods, and the men were made to lie down in line, concealed by the brush—the howitzers were planted to sweep the road. No fires were lighted. Shortly afterward, the regiment in pursuit of them passed by, moving not more than twenty yards from the line, without discovering it; whether a discovery would have benefited the said regiment, will never be known, although there are many private opinions about the matter.

When the party reached Glasgow—it was in the middle of the night—Captain Morgan could get no information about the whereabouts of the command for some time. He was supposed to be a Federal officer. At last he was recognized and, at once, got the necessary information.

On the same occasion, an incident occurred, which illustrated well the coolness and self-possession which characterized the men of Morgan's command, in the peculiar service to which they were inured. A party of some twenty men had been sent, before Colonel Morgan left Hartsville, to carry dispatches to Johnson and Woodward, inviting them to co-operate with Morgan. In returning, this party learned that Colonel Morgan was on the march for Central Kentucky, and immediately changed route to join him the more speedily, and this change brought them to Glasgow at this time. Neither of these parties knew of the other's presence, or anticipated any such meeting, until they suddenly encountered in the streets of Glasgow. Fortunately, the party coming from the West was under the command of a young officer of more than ordinary coolness and shrewdness, as well as daring—Lieutenant Houston Hopkins. Each of these detachments had every reason to believe that the other was an enemy. The bulk of the command had long passed this point, so long that the rear-guard, scouts, every thing of the kind, ought to have been gone, and the enemy in considerable numbers was not far off. Yet, with a sort of instinct, each forbore to fire, until more positively assured of what the other was. They came within twenty yards of each other—so close that the officers of each, could hear the muttered speculations of the others as to their probable character.

The larger detachment, under Captain Allen, immediately formed across the road, and advanced slowly, with guns at a "ready." The other wheeled rapidly, and fell back about two hundred yards, halted, and also formed. Lieutenant Hopkins then rode back to within a short distance of Captain Allen, and entered into a parley with him, which, of course, soon ended in recognition. When it is remembered that the first wish and impulse of both parties, when two hostile detachments meet, is, generally, to get the first fire, and make the quickest dash, it will be conceded that on this occasion there was exhibited rare coolness and discretion.

Captain Morgan had dispatched a courier to his brother, informing him of his line of march, which courier reached Columbia soon after the command had gone into camp there. Gano's squadron was immediately sent back to reinforce the escort, and met it shortly after it had left Glasgow. The necessary delay for the arrival of the guns caused us to remain at Columbia for two days. Resuming the march on the day after they came, at an early hour the command moved in the direction of Liberty, in Casey County. In the vicinity of this place, we saw, in the brief time that we remained, more active and business-like bushwhacking than ever before in our entire service. The hills along the road seemed alive with them, and from behind every fourth or fifth tree apparently, they were blazing away at us. Every Southern reader will understand at once what sort of individual is meant by a "bushwhacker"—that he is a gentleman of leisure, who lives in a wild and, generally, a mountainous country, does not join the army, but shoots, from the tops of hills, or from behind trees and rocks, at those who are so unfortunate as to differ with him in politics. It is his way of expressing his opinions. His style of fighting is very similar to that of the outlying scouts of partisan cavalry, except that he esteems it a weakness and an unnecessary inconvenience to take prisoners, and generally kills his captives. Sometimes, and especially toward the latter part of the war, these fellows would band together in considerable numbers, make certain portions of the country impassable, except to strong detachments, and even undertake expeditions into neighboring sections.

There were "Union bushwhackers" and "Southern bushwhackers;" in Kentucky, the former were more numerous. "It is a gratifying reflection," to use the language of one of Colonel Clarence Prentice's official reports, "that many of them will 'whack' no more." In the Northern mind, bushwhackers and guerrillas are confounded together, an egregious error in classification. It is probable that the bushwhacker of this country would answer exactly to the guerrilla of European warfare; but the guerrilla of North America is, or rather was (for happily he is almost, if not quite extinct), an animal entirely distinct from either. Formerly the Northern press styled all the Southern cavalry guerrillas, because they traveled about the country freely, and gave their enemies some trouble. This, however, was when the Federal cavalry used to still ride with pillows on their saddles, were put to bed carefully every night by the General commanding, and encamped on the march in the midst of infantry regiments, who were instructed to see that their horses did not hurt them, etc. When the hardy, dashing regiments of the latter part of the war—after, indeed, the first eighteen months—began to do real service, the Northern writers found that they would be called on to record as cavalry operations the very kind of affairs which they had been accustomed to chronicle as guerrilla irregularities.

A guerrilla was, properly speaking, a man who had belonged to some army, and had deserted and gone to making war on his private account. He was necessarily a marauder, sometimes spared his former friend, and was much admired by weak young women who were afflicted with a tendency toward shoddy romance.

On this march through Casey county, the bushwhackers were unusually officious. The advance-guard, which for some reason had gone on some distance in front, reached Liberty about two hours before the column, and during that time were fairly besieged in the place. Colonel Morgan himself made a narrow escape. One fellow, more daring than the others, had come down from the hills, and had approached within seventy yards of the road. He fired at Morgan, missing him, but wounded a little negro boy, his servant, who was riding by his side, receiving some order. The man, who fired, at once ran back to the hill, followed by one or two of our fellows from the head of the column. He was killed by private, afterward Captain Thomas Franks, who made an excellent shot, hitting the bushwhacker in the head while he was running at top speed, and Franks himself was going at a rapid gallop.

That night we reached Houstonville, about fourteen miles from Danville, and learned there of General Smith's complete victory at Richmond, and of the probability that he was already at Lexington. This news excited the men very much, and sleep was banished from the camp that night. Early on the next morning we started for a good day's march, and reached Danville about ten A.M., halted there some three hours, and, resuming the march, reached Nicholasville, twenty-three miles distant, and twelve from Lexington, at dusk.

On the next day, the 4th of September, the command entered Lexington about 10 A.M., amid the most enthusiastic shouts, plaudits, and congratulations. Colonel Morgan (as has been said) and many of his officers and men, were formerly citizens of Lexington, and many others came from the vicinity of the place; relations and friends, therefore, by the score, were in the crowd which thronged the streets of the town.

The people of this particular section of Kentucky, known as the Blue-grass region, had always been strongly Southern in their views and sympathies, and this occasion, except that of General Smith's entrance a day or two before, was the first chance they had ever had to manifest their political proclivities. Some of them shortly afterward were very sorry, doubtless, that they had been so candid. The command, at this time, numbered about eleven hundred men. The Second Kentucky had been greatly increased, and, after deducting all losses, was nearly, if not quite nine hundred strong. Gano's squadron numbered about two hundred effectives. The rapidity with which recruits came to Morgan was astonishing. Captain Breckinridge was immediately granted authority, by General Smith, to raise a battalion of four companies, to serve in Morgan's brigade. He was permitted to take his own company (I) out of the Second Kentucky, as a nucleus for his battalion organization, and in a very short time he had gotten three other large and fine companies, and he could (if he had been permitted) have recruited a regiment with as little trouble.

Gano was granted authority to raise a regiment, and in a very short time had recruited three companies. Active service, which necessitated rapid and continuous marching, interfered for a time with the organization of his regiment, but it was eventually completed. Second Lieutenant Alexander, of Company E, Second Kentucky, was given permission to raise a company, in the vicinity of Harrodsburg, Mercer county, and in four or five days returned with a company of over sixty men, which was admitted into the Second Kentucky, and lettered H, a letter which had been in disuse in the regiment, since the partition of the company which bore Alston into a Captaincy. Lieutenant S.D. Morgan, of Company A, was also authorized to recruit a company, and soon did it. It was admitted into the Second Kentucky as Company I, in place of Breckinridge's. The Second Kentucky now numbered twelve companies, and nearly eleven hundred effective men. Almost immediately, upon arriving at Lexington, Captain Desha resigned the Captaincy of Company L. He was a very fine officer, and we all regretted to part with him. He received authority to recruit a regiment of infantry, and had partially succeeded, when the retreat from Kentucky commenced. He then entered Colonel Thomas Hunt's regiment, the Fifth Kentucky infantry. In the last year of the war he was offered a Brigadier's commission, but declined it upon the ground that ill-health would not permit him to exercise the duties required of him, in such a station, without delay. Private John Cooper, of Company A, was appointed Captain in his stead—he had previously been elected color-bearer of the regiment, when Colonel Morgan had directed the officers to choose the best man in the regiment to bear a flag presented to him by the ladies of the State.

Every company of the Second Kentucky was increased by recruits, during the first week after our arrival. Two gentlemen, Colonels Cluke and Chenault, were authorized to recruit regiments for Morgan's brigade, and immediately went to work to do so.

As soon as the first greetings had been passed with our friends, every man was curious to learn the particulars of General Smith's march through Southeastern Kentucky, and of the fight at Richmond. General Smith had collected at Knoxville, and other points in East Tennessee, some twenty thousand men, and leaving eight thousand, under General Stephenson, in front of Cumberland Gap, then occupied by the Federal General G.W. Morgan, with eight or nine thousand men, he, with twelve thousand men, and thirty or forty pieces of artillery, pressed through the Big Creek and Rogers gaps (of the Cumberland mountains), and marched rapidly for the Blue-grass country. Master of Lexington, he would have the terminus of the two railroads, and, indeed, one half of the State of

Kentucky. A complete defeat of the forces, then in that region, would clear his path to Louisville, in the one direction, and to Covington in the other. He would be in no danger, until forces were collected and organized in sufficient strength at Cincinnati, to march against and push him away. As for Buell's army, it was General Bragg's duty to take care of that. General Smith had with his army about one thousand cavalry. This force, under Colonel John Scott, advancing some distance in his front, fell upon Metcalfe's regiment, eleven or twelve hundred strong, on the Bighill, fifteen miles from Richmond, and thoroughly defeated and dispersed it. Even after this affair, the Federal commander remained in ignorance of any force, besides the cavalry under Scott, having approached in that direction, until General Smith, having pressed on with wonderful celerity and secrecy, had gotten within a few miles of Richmond.

Then every available man was concentrated at Richmond and pushed out to meet the invading column. The collision occurred on the 29th of August. General Smith had marched so rapidly, his men had fared so badly (having subsisted for ten days on green corn), and their badly shod feet were so cut by the rough stony way, that his column was necessarily somewhat prolonged, although there was little of what might be called straggling. Consequently, he could put into the fight only about six thousand men. Heath was some distance in the rear. He attacked as soon as he came upon the enemy, drove them, and although three several stands were made, his advance was never seriously checked. The last stand, and hardest fight, was made in the outskirts of the little town of Richmond itself, and when the enemy was driven from the town, his route was complete. The Federal commander General Nelson was wounded. The enemy's loss was over one thousand in killed and wounded, and six thousand prisoners were taken and paroled. General Smith's loss was nine hundred in killed and wounded.

Scott with the cavalry, pressed the fugitives for many miles. The route and disintegration of the Federal army was such, that perhaps not a single command maintained its organization, and the stream of fugitives poured through Lexington all Saturday night and Sunday, toward Louisville and Cincinnati. This decisive victory finished General Smith's part of the programme, and closed his campaign, for the time, with the possession of all that part of Kentucky. On the 1st of September, General Smith took possession of Lexington, and on the 2nd or 3rd he dispatched General Heath with five or six thousand men toward Covington. General Smith issued the strictest orders for the maintenance of order and discipline, and the prevention of excesses or mal-conduct among his troops, of any description. Such was the state of discipline that he had brought his army to before, that these orders were little needed. He also went energetically to work to encourage enlistments in his ranks, to organize every department, necessary to the subsistence and equipment of his army, and to collect supplies.

Notwithstanding the efforts that were made to induce the Kentuckians to enlist as infantry, very few would do so, and those who did, joined regiments which came in with General Smith; not a single infantry regiment was raised during the time that the Confederate army was in the State. All of the Kentuckians who joined at that time, wanted to ride. As a people, they are fond of horses, and if they went to war at all, they thought it a too great tax upon them to make them walk.

A brigadier's commission was given to Captain Abram Buford (formerly of the regular army), a man well known and very popular in this portion of Kentucky, and he was authorized to recruit a mixed brigade of infantry and cavalry. He got three fine regiments of cavalry, under Colonels Butler, Smith and Grigsby, without any trouble, but not an infantryman. The two last of the above named regiments, were subsequently assigned to Morgan. One reason why so many enlisted in cavalry (independently of the decided preference of the Kentuckians for that branch of the service), was the fact, that companies and regiments had, in many instances, their men bespoken and ready to enlist with them as soon as a favorable opportunity should occur. Many (also), had made up their minds to join Morgan when he next came through the country. Men who expected to become soldiers (under such circumstances), would of course wish to join the cavalry, and made all their preparations to enlist in that arm of the service.

Had a decisive battle been fought and won by General Bragg, there is little doubt but that the majority of that class of men, who were waiting for that event before they enlisted, would then have enlisted as infantry. Two or three days after we reached Lexington, four companies of the Second Kentucky were sent with the two howitzers, to capture the stockade at the bridge over Salt river, on the Louisville and Nashville Railroad, and burn the bridge. The expedition was under command of Captain Hutchinson. This officer had some days previously been made, at my request, Acting Lieutenant Colonel of my regiment (the Second Kentucky), and he was always afterward addressed by that title, and was subsequently given the position. Hutchinson was a singularly active and energetic officer, and possessed the shrewdness as well as daring which eminently qualified him for the command of detachments. He made a tremendous march, and arrived at his destination, before any Federal force, which could have intercepted him or have marched to prevent his purpose, heard of his coming.

The garrison of the stockade was some one hundred and fifty strong. He placed his men in position around it, and planted his howitzers to command it. He then sent Captain Bowles to demand the surrender of the garrison, telling him that he would allow but twenty minutes for the negotiation.

Captain Bowles approached under flag of truce and entered into a parley with the enemy. They were quite willing to surrender in less than twenty minutes, provided that one strange stipulation should be conceded, viz: that the bridge would not be burned. While Bowles was endeavoring to prove to them the folly of such a proposition, the twenty minutes expired. Hutchinson, who was very literal in observing all that he said, immediately caused his artillery to open without waiting for the return of his envoy, and two shells were bursted just above the stockade, wounding one of the inmates. This might have caused the death of the bearer of the flag, as the garrison had, then, a perfect right to shoot him. The effect of it on Bowles, however, who was one of the very few men I have known, who, I believe, never felt fear, was to render him indignant that his embassy should be interrupted, just as he thought that it was about to be successful, and he came galloping back at full speed, waving his flag at his own friends, and shouting at the top of his voice, "don't shoot any more, they'll be all right directly."

The inmates of the stockade at the same time poured out, without regard to rank, waiving pocket handkerchiefs, portions of their nether garments hastily torn off, and whatever else, they could lay hold of, that would serve the purpose. As soon, however, as the howitzers opened, the skirmishers advanced, in accordance with Hutchinson's previous instructions, firing also, and their fire drove the enemy back into the stockade.

Soon, however, all mistakes were rectified and an amicable adjustment of the difficulty arrived at. The prisoners were immediately paroled, the bridge thoroughly destroyed, and the detachment returned. It was absent only a few days. The bridge destroyed was four hundred and fifty feet long, and forty-six feet high.

Almost immediately after Colonel Hutchinson returned to Lexington, he was sent with Companies B, C, D, E, L and M to report to General Heath, who had advanced to within five miles of Covington, and withdrawing, needed cavalry. The utmost consternation prevailed in Cincinnati during the time that Heath was in the vicinity of Covington; the city was placed under martial law, and every citizen was required to report himself for military duty. So persistent were the detectives in their search for treason, that all the business houses in the town had to be shut up, and it became so frequent a matter to construe thoughtless words into expressions of disloyal sentiment, that it was unsafe to speak any other language than Dutch. Thousands of respectable citizens, nightly left their comfortable homes, to cross the river, and shiver and ache with apprehension and fatigue, in the ditches around Covington. Many a tradesman torn from his shop, got the manual mixed up with his accounts, and lost the run of both; and as he sat in a rifle-pit, with only one pontoon bridge (and that narrow) connecting him with Cincinnati, he had to console him—the reflection that he was performing a patriotic, duty, and letting his business go to the devil.

The most telling maneuver against such an army, would have been to send emissaries to stir up the street boys in Cincinnati to an attack on the ungarrisoned shops; in such an event a precipitate retreat would most probably have occurred from the Kentucky side of the river.

For several days after Heath was close enough to have made a dash at Covington, at any hour, there were no other defenders in the works around the place than these extempore soldiers. A very few only of their guns mounted were in a condition to be worked, and the ammunition first provided was not of the proper caliber. On the first, Gen. Heath came within sight of the works, that he had prepared to attack, and just before he moved upon them, received dispatches from Gen. Smith, instructing him not to do so, but to be prepared to return at short notice. General Smith expected to be soon called, to reinforce General Bragg, with his whole force to fight Buell's army before it reached Louisville; he therefore wished every thing kept well in hand, and esteemed the maintenance of the mobility of the troops under Heath as of more importance than the capture of Cincinnati. In the course of a few days, however, regular troops began to arrive at Cincinnati, and they came in rapidly. When Heath fell back, there was a formidable veteran force, there, of perhaps twelve or fifteen thousand men. Hutchinson reported to him at Walton twenty-five miles from Covington, and was at once ordered to duty on the front. For some days he was very actively engaged immediately upon the ground which Heath had just left. He was engaged in scouting for some distance above and below Covington, to ascertain if there was any movement by the river, as well as having to carefully watch all roads leading out of the place. His various detachments had several skirmishes, the most successful of which was made by a party under command of Lieutenant Allensworth, who routed a much larger body of the enemy and captured a number of prisoners.

Just before General Heath came down into that country, fifteen young men of Boone county who had long wished to join Morgan, hearing that Confederate troops might shortly be expected in their neighborhood, banded together and attacked a train of twenty-seven wagons guarded by fifty-one Federal soldiers, dispersed the guard and burned the wagons. This party with some twenty-five of their friends then equipped themselves and set out to join us.

They were placed in the new Company I. In the service done at this time, Hutchinson's loss was slight, and he inflicted a good deal upon the enemy. He took a number of prisoners. The railroad was destroyed—track torn up and bridges burned—for a good many miles. General Heath continued to fall back toward Georgetown. After Hutchinson had been in command upon the Covington front six or seven days, I sent him Company A, and the next day followed myself with Company I. Colonel Morgan was ordered to go to Eastern Kentucky and intercept the Federal General Geo. W. Morgan on his march from Cumberland Gap to the Ohio river. General Morgan had evacuated the gap and gained two days march on the force watching it on the other side. It was General Smith's desire that Colonel Morgan should blockade the roads in his front, and use every exertion to retard his progress. By uniting with General Marshall's forces, it was hoped that Colonel Morgan, in the rugged, almost impassable country, through which the Federal column had to march, might stop it altogether, until another body of troops could be thrown upon its rear, and thus literally starve it into surrender. As it was, Marshall remained inactive, and Morgan after felling trees across the road, climbing up and down mountains, and sticking close to the front of the column for six days, was compelled to suffer the mortification of seeing it get away triumphantly.

While Colonel Morgan was employed in the mountains, General Smith directed me to annoy the enemy as much as possible in the direction of Covington. On the evening that I arrived at Walton, where Hutchinson had been encamped, I found him in retreat, pressed by a superior force of the enemy. We soon found that we could not efficiently check the enemy's advance, and accordingly fell back to Crittenden, a little place seven miles from Walton. The enemy encamped five miles from the place. On the next morning we were driven out of Crittenden, and as the enemy continued to advance, I dispatched General Heath that I believed it was an advance upon Lexington. The enemy's force consisted, as we afterward ascertained, of about seven thousand infantry, one thousand cavalry, or, perhaps a little more, and eight pieces of artillery. Skirmishers were thrown out, in strong lines, for a mile or more on each side of the road. The country was open and easily traversed by troops, enabling them to strengthen any part of the line that might need it. We could therefore hope to effect little; and after carefully reconnoitering, without finding a convenient opening, we recontented to move slowly in their front, forcing them to keep up their troublesome precautions.

About 1 or 2 P.M., leaving scouts to observe them, I marched rapidly to Williamstown. This place is just upon the northern edge of the rugged Eagle hills. Thence I moved eastwardly to Falmouth, a small town on the Central Kentucky Railroad, about forty miles from Covington, and twenty miles from Williamstown—indeed nearly equi-distant from the Dry-ridge road, or Cincinnati and Lexington pike (upon which the enemy were moving), and the Maysville and Lexington pike, which also needed some watching. I was then in a position to observe every movement upon the entire front, and was, so to speak, in the center of the web commanding all the avenues which should be guarded. If the enemy continued upon the road upon which he was then advancing, he would have to force his way through General Heath's forces, advantageously posted amid the hills of the Eagle creek. If he turned to the left to seek a road not so well defended, he would have to come by Falmouth, and therefore Falmouth was the point where the cavalry watching him should be.

On the road, however, and before I reached Falmouth, scouts brought the information that the enemy had fallen back to Walton, and also informed me of what his strength apparently was. It was plain that no force of that size would attempt to march on Lexington. Shortly afterward, other scouts, which had been sent to watch the Ohio river, came from Warsaw, a little town on its banks, and reported that a number of boats laden with troops had gone down the river toward Louisville. This information explained every thing. Finding that Heath had withdrawn, and Cincinnati was no longer threatened, this force, which had driven us away from Walton, had been sent to clear the country of troublesome detachments, and also to attract attention in that direction, and conceal the concentration of troops at Louisville. Walton is twenty-five miles from

Falmouth. On the day after reaching the latter, I sent a flag of truce to Walton, with dispatches, which General Smith had instructed me to forward to Cincinnati. The flag was borne by Captain S.D. Morgan, who betted with the Aide of the commanding General, that he (Morgan), would drive in his pickets within forty-eight hours—he won the wager. The entire strength of the six companies, which Colonel Hutchinson had taken to this country, was not quite five hundred men—the two additional companies A and I, did not swell the total effective to six hundred men. All of those were large ones, but many men (from four or five of them) were on furlough. When the flag of truce returned, Captain Morgan gave me such an account of the enemy that a desire, previously conceived, to visit him was greatly increased. Morgan could, of course, see but little; he was, however, vigilant and shrewd, and drew accurate inferences from what he saw. He was satisfied that, while careful and systematic guard was kept, the troops were all green and could be easily surprised. He said that so far as he could learn, there was no attempt made at scouting, and that a total ignorance prevailed among them of what was going on, a few hundred yards even, beyond the outposts. This latter information was confirmed by the reports of all my scouts, and was in accordance with the habits of raw men and officers. He thought, moreover, from something he had heard, that cavalry were encamped a mile or two from the infantry, and the country people, some of whom from that neighborhood visited us, stated that the cavalry were encamped a mile and a half from the main body, and nearer Walton. We had tried in vain to get hold of the cavalry on the day we were driven away from Walton; it kept carefully behind the infantry.

Moving from Falmouth late in the afternoon, with nearly the entire command, I marched until about twelve o'clock at night, and halted at a point on the Independence road, about ten miles from the enemy's encampment. Scouts were immediately sent out to ascertain as nearly as possible the exact location of the pickets, and the condition of every thing about the encampments. They were instructed not to fire upon, or in anywise alarm the pickets, or do anything which might make them suspect our vicinity.

The scouts observed their instructions closely, and did not see the pickets at all, but inquired of the people who lived near the encampment, and were told that no change had occurred in the last day or two, in any respect, in the posts on the different roads. After this information I was satisfied that I would be able to get upon the Georgetown and Covington pike, upon which the enemy was encamped, by a country road which runs into it from the Independence pike, without alarming the main body. I could then move rapidly to the point where the cavalry was encamped, and defeat it before the infantry came to the rescue. The infantry encampment was about two miles north of Walton, and this by-road comes into the pike about one thousand yards from the site of the encampment, and between it and Walton.

The column was accordingly put in motion again at daybreak, and marched rapidly. Just at sunrise we reached the Georgetown and

Covington pike, and saw standing, in sight of the point where we would enter, ten cavalry pickets. The column was at once halted, and arrangements made to capture them. They had not yet seen us. A brief reconnoisance showed an infantry regiment on post, some three hundred yards further down the road. There was now no hope of passing this point without discovery by the main body, and it only remained to make the most out of the situation.

Lieutenant Messick, of Company A, was sent with ten men to take in the cavalry videttes, and Lieutenant Roberts, commanding the advance-guard, was sent with a portion of it to try the same game with the infantry. He went right into the midst of it. The column was moved forward at a gallop, as soon as the pickets were disturbed, and turned in the direction of Walton; the rear company, however, being carried at full speed to the assistance of Lieutenant Roberts. One of the howitzers which had been brought along, was planted at the point where we entered the pike, to cover our retreat, if it were pressed. When I reached the little squad of Lieutenant Roberts with the company which I took to assist it, I found it, or rather a fragment of it, in a situation which perhaps was never paralleled daring the war.

Lieutenant Roberts was still further down the road, and toward the encampment, with a portion of the detachment, picking up stragglers. Sergeant Will Hays stood with six men in the midst of a company of sixty-nine Federal infantry. The infantry seemed sullen and bewildered, and stood with their rifles cocked and at a ready. Hays had his rifle at the head of the Lieutenant commanding, demanding that he should order his men to surrender, and threatening to blow his brains out if he encouraged them to resist. Hays' six men were grouped around him, ready to shoot down any man who should raise a gun against him. I thought it the finest sight I had ever seen. The arrival of the company decided the infantry to surrender, and the caps and bayonets having been taken off of their guns, they were sent off, guarded by the men which had been brought up to complete their capture. Lieutenant Roberts had gone, with his mere corporal's guard, into the infantry regiment, had captured one company, and run the balance back into camp.

The men of this regiment were very raw and green. Hays had persuaded them for some time, that he was an officer of their own cavalry, and it was only when he peremptorily ordered them to follow him to Walton, that they suspected him. After sending off the prisoners, four or five of us rode on down the road to join Lieutenant Roberts, and soon found him, bringing back more prisoners. We were now farther in toward the encampment, than the regiment on picket had stood, and had a fair view of it. We saw the whole force form, and it was a very pretty sight. The regiments first formed on their respective campgrounds, and then took their positions in line of battle, at a double-quick. They were finely drilled, although very raw. The artillery was run into position, and behind every thing, peeping over the shoulders of the infantry, were our friends the cavalry, that we had taken so much pains to see.

While we were looking on, a staff officer came galloping toward us, evidently not knowing who we were, and taking us for some of his pickets not yet driven in. He came right up to us; thinking his capture certain, Captain Morgan, who thought that he recognized in him, the officer with whom he had made the bet two days previously, rode forward, saluted him, and told him he was a prisoner. He, however, did not seem to be of that opinion for he wheeled his horse, coming so close to us in doing so as to almost brush the foremost man, and dashed back at full speed, despite the shots that were fired at him.

The skirmishers, who were not more than two hundred yards off, soon induced us to leave, and we galloped after the column. Eighty or ninety prisoners were taken, and were sent on to Lexington, as soon as we got back to Falmouth. The enemy did not know for some hours, that we were entirely gone, and indeed rather expected during that time to be attacked in force. I perhaps ought to have attacked, but the disparity of forces, and the knowledge that the enemy could detect it as I advanced, deterred me.

On the next day I sent Captain Castleman with Company D, to Foster's landing on the Ohio river. He fired upon a Government transport loaded with troops, but could not bring her to with his rifles. He captured the regular packet, and was shelled by one of the river gun boats, suffering no loss.

At this period the Home-guard organizations were disbanding, or being incorporated into the Federal army. At Augusta, a town in Bracken county, about twenty-five miles from Falmouth, and situated on the river, forty odd miles above Cincinnati, there was a regiment being formed out of some Home-guard companies. This organization had already begun to give trouble, and one or two of its scouting parties had even ventured within a short distance of Falmouth. I was also informed that all sorts of men, whether willing or not, were being placed in its ranks. I determined therefore to break it up, before it became formidable. There was a ford, moreover, just below Augusta, by which the river could be crossed at that season without difficulty. I wished to take the town, if possible, with little loss, and cross into Ohio, and marching toward Cincinnati, so threaten the city that the troops at Walton would be hurried back to protect it.

Leaving Falmouth in the morning of one day, I could (if allowed to cross the river without opposition) have been in the vicinity of Cincinnati at daylight of the next day. Two days, therefore, after the expedition to Walton, I started from Falmouth with about four hundred and fifty men—leaving Company D and some details behind to observe the enemy at Walton and for other purposes.

On the way to Augusta, I came upon a large scouting party from that place but it dispersed before I could attack—it was cut off, however, from Augusta and prevented from taking part in the fight there. We marched through Brookville and about 7 A.M. reached the high ground in the rear of Augusta and which perfectly commanded the town. Two small stern wheel boats lay at the wharf, to assist in the defense of the place. A twelve pounder was mounted on each of them; their sides were protected by hay bales and they were manned by sharpshooters in addition to the gunners. These boats commanded the turnpike which led into the town from Brookville (by which road we were advancing) but about a mile from the town I turned the column from the road and approached the hill (upon which I took position) through the fields. The crest of this hill is perhaps two hundred feet above the level of the river (at low water) and about six hundred yards from its bank. The town runs back to the foot of the hill. From our position on the summit of this hill we could distinctly see the Home-guards going into the houses and preparing for fight, but a portion of them were already ensconced in the houses near the head of the street by which we entered the town a little while afterward. These latter kept themselves concealed while we remained on the hill and our ignorance of their location cost us dearly. Seeing that the boats commanded the street by which I wished to enter the town, I determined to drive them away before moving the bulk of the command from the hill.

Accordingly, having dismounted and formed Companies B, C, E, I and M, and planted the howitzers on the highest point I could find, where they could probably chuck every shell into the boats, I ordered Company A, and the advance-guard to cross the Germantown pike and take position near the bank of the river in the eastern end of the town. Here they would be enabled to annoy the troops on the boats very greatly with their rifles and would also be in position to assist in reducing the garrisoned houses, when the fight in town commenced. In that part of the town there were no houses occupied by the enemy. Captain Cassell of Company A, was instructed to dispose of his own company and the advance-guard in accordance with these views and to take command of both. I especially charged him to let no man approach that part of the town where I expected to have to fight on horseback, but to bring the men on foot when he heard firing.

As soon as Cassell had gotten into position, the howitzers were opened upon the boats. Several shells burst near them and one penetrated the hull of the "Flag Ship," as I suppose I may term the boat upon which the Captain commanding both of them had his quarters. Cassell's riflemen, also made themselves very disagreeable, and after firing only three shots, the "fleet" withdrew. As long as the boats were in range the "Bull pups" kept after them and they steamed up the river and out of sight. Having driven off these gun boats, upon which I knew the officer commanding in the town chiefly relied for the defense of the place, I believed that I would have no more trouble and that the garrison would surrender without more fighting. I immediately entered by the principal street with Companies B and C. After these two companies had gotten well into the town and in front of the houses into which the defenders of the place had gone unseen by us, a sharp fire was suddenly opened upon them, killing and wounding several. I at once ordered the men to gather on the right hand side of the street, although the fire came from both sides, and to take shelter as they best could.

A fierce fight at once began. I sent for Companies E, I, and portions of L and M, leaving three sections of each to guard the road in our rear. I made the men force their way into the houses, whence they were fired upon. Captain Cassell came to join me as soon as he heard the firing, but unfortunately Lieutenant Roberts forgot, in his ardor, the order that no men should enter the town mounted, and he dashed up to the scene of the fight with his men on horseback, greatly increasing the confusion. The Sergeant, who had charge of the howitzers, opened upon the town, when he heard the firing, and his shots did us as much harm as they did the enemy. Lieutenant Roberts was killed almost instantly, two or three men and several horses of his guard were also shot, and the crowding of horses into the street added to the disorder. In a few minutes, however, some method was restored. Details of men were posted in the middle of the street in front of every house, to fire at the inmates when they showed themselves, and prevent them from maintaining an accurate and effective fire. Other details were made to break in the doors of the houses and enter them. The artillery was brought into the town and turned upon the houses in which the most stubborn resistance was kept up. Planted about ten paces from a house, aimed to strike about a yard below the sills of the windows, beneath which the defenders were crouched (except when taking aim), and double-shotted with grape and canister, the howitzers tore great gaps in the walls. Two or three houses from which sharp volleys were kept up were set on fire. Flags of truce, about this time, were hung out from several windows, and believing that a general surrender was meant, I ordered the fires to be extinguished. But only those who shook the white flags meant to give up, and the others continued to fight. One or two men putting out the fires were shot. I immediately ordered that every house from which shots came should be burned. A good many were soon in flames, and even then the fighting continued in some of them. My men were infuriated by what they esteemed bad faith, in a continuance of the fight after the flags of truce were displayed, and by the loss of their comrades and of some favorite officers. I never saw them fight with such ferocity. Few lives were spared in the houses into which they forced their way. Several savage hand-to-hand fights occurred. As private James March, of Company A, was about to enter a house after battering down the door with the butt of his rifle, a Home-guard, armed with musket and bayonet, sprang out and lunged at him. March avoided his thrust, knocked him down with his clubbed gun, and then seizing the other's musket, pinned him to the ground with the bayonet. A somewhat similar affair happened to a private of Company B. whose name I have forgotten. As he, also, was forcing his way into a house, a strong, active fellow bounded out and cut at him with a large heavy knife, made from a blacksmith's file, such as were formerly often seen in Kentucky. He closed quickly with his assailant, whose blow consequently missed him, and in a moment they were locked in each other's arms. The Home-guard could not use his knife, for his right arm was stretched over the other's shoulder in the position in which it had fallen with the blow. The other wore one of the largest sized, heaviest, army pistols. He had dropped his gun, and as he drew his pistol, his enemy clasped the lock with his left hand, and he could not cock it. Both were powerful men, and fighting for life, because quarter was not thought of by either. At length the Confederate raised the pistol to a level with the other's head, and although he could strike only by the inflection of the wrist, inflicted blows with the heavy barrel upon his enemy's temple, which stunned him. Then dashing him to the ground, the Confederate beat in his skull with the butt of his pistol. The fighting lasted about fifteen or twenty minutes, when Colonel Bradford, the commander of the organization, surrendered. It was with great difficulty that his life, or the lives of his men, could be saved. Fighting in narrow streets, close to their opponents, the loss in my command was, of course, severe, and a great many wounds proved mortal, on account of the balls coming from above, ranging downward.

My loss was twenty-one killed, and eighteen wounded. I had about three hundred and fifty men engaged. Among the killed were some matchless officers. Captain Samuel D. Morgan (a cousin of Colonel Morgan) killed several men with his own hand before he fell. He had been a good soldier, and gave promise of unusual merit as an officer. His gallantry and devotion were superb, and he was always urgent to be placed on perilous service. He was a mere boy. Lieutenant Greenberry Roberts had been made First Lieutenant of Company A after Lieutenant Smith's death. He much resembled his predecessor. He had been placed in command of the advance-guard when Lieutenant Rogers was compelled to return to his company (E) upon the promotion of Captain Hutchinson. He was nineteen years old when killed; gay, handsome, and a universal favorite. His courage was untempered by any discretion or calculation, and unless bound by positive instructions, he would go at any thing. Lieutenant Rogers was a model officer and gentleman. He was killed while exerting himself to save the inmates of a house from which the shot which killed him came.

Lieutenant King, a gallant boy, brevet Second Lieutenant of Company E, fell dead the moment afterward across Rogers' body, and, a rather singular circumstance, an old man of that company, devotedly attached to both these officers, private Puckett (one of the few old men in the regiment) rushed to raise them and was instantaneously killed, falling upon them. Captain Kennett, of Company B, just made Captain in the place of Captain Allen, who was elected Lieutenant-Colonel of Butler's regiment, and Lieutenant George White, of the same company, were mortally wounded, and died very soon. Both were veterans of the old squadron, and very brave men.

Most of the casualties occurred in the first few minutes of the street fight, before proper dispositions were made to reduce the garrisons of the houses, and while the latter were taking deadly aim.

Captain Cassell's bold attack on the gunboats saved us much greater loss. Some of the women came (while the fight was raging) from the part of the town where they had retired for safety, to the most dangerous positions, and waited upon the wounded, while the balls were striking around them. The majority of the people of this town, or a large proportion at least, were Southern sympathizers. The regular members of the Home-guard regiment were collected from the country for miles around. A number of the Southern men were also pressed into the service.

The last house set on fire was that of James Armstrong. After the garrison in it were disposed of, efforts were made to save it. The owner bade me "let it burn," but urged me to collect and destroy all the arms of the Home-guards, that they might not give trouble again. During the fight a boat, coming from Cincinnati, hove in sight of the town, but did not come on. It was reported, but incorrectly, that she carried troops.

This fight prevented the excursion into Ohio. All of the ammunition for the howitzers was shot away. I was anxious to remove my wounded and dead, and had two hundred prisoners whom I wanted to carry off. About four P.M., employing all the carriages and light wagons that I could find about the town and neighborhood to carry the wounded, who could stand transportation, and the dead bodies, which were not too much mutilated, I went back toward Falmouth. That night we reached Brookville after dark, and passed the night there, the gloomiest and saddest that any man among us had ever known.

Brookville is a little hamlet, nine miles from Augusta, and eighteen from Maysville. This latter place had been taken by Gano, a week or two before, without a shot. He left next day, and the Union men there became belligerent, sent for regular troops, collected Home-guards, "resolved" that they would fight, bleed, and die, if they got another chance, and distinguished themselves very much in that way. News reached Maysville of the fight at Augusta on the same evening that it occurred, and about four o'clock next morning troops left there to march to the relief of Augusta. At seven A.M. of that morning, I sent off the train of dead and wounded, and all of the prisoners, except about eighty, whom I intended, to parole. As soon as they were fairly started, I ordered Colonel Hutchinson to follow with the command. I retained Sergeant Hays and ten men of the advance-guard with me. Most of the prisoners left were Southern men, who had been forced to fight, and a few others were men paroled at Armstrong's request.

About 9 or 10 A.M., while engaged in writing out paroles, I was informed by my orderly that a force of Federals was coming into town on the Maysville pike. I had placed no pickets after the regular detail had been withdrawn upon the march of the column, and nearly all of the ten men left with me were in the court-house at the time by my side. We immediately passed out and mounted our horses. Sargeant Hays formed seven men and we dashed through the enemy. There were perhaps fifty or sixty cavalry in the town—they were scattered about, and had no chance to stop us. Several shots were fired upon both sides. None of my party were hurt. One of the enemy was killed and three seized by the bridle reins, as we went through them, and carried off prisoners. A few men were still unparoled when the alarm was given. Private Conrade remained and paroled them all, then followed us through the enemy. He was subsequently promoted for other instances of the coolest daring. A recruiting officer had been captured that morning and placed in charge of Privates Franks and McVae. They were eating breakfast when the enemy entered the town and were nearly captured. They placed their prisoner on a bare-backed horse and carried him off across the country, taking fences and every thing else at a gallop.

We lost one man taken prisoner, he could not get to his horse. The enemy's force was composed of the cavalry which first entered and about four hundred infantry, with two pieces of artillery. After we had gotten out of the town, we turned and galloped back to it again, to create, if possible, a diversion in favor of the three men I supposed to be still there. The infantry, however, immediately drove us off. As we then moved rapidly after the command, we met the rear-guard, which always marched a good distance in the rear of the column, coming back at a gallop to reinforce us. The officer in charge of it, one of the very best in the regiment—Lieutenant Ash Welsh, had returned as soon as he heard the firing. His men and himself were dressed in dark clothing, and I thought when they first came in sight, that they were a part of the enemy which had cut us off. They also mistook us for the enemy, and we charged each other at full speed. When within about fifty yards of each other and just about to fire, a mutual recognition fortunately prevented it.

Soon afterward, I met Hutchinson coming with the command, but I turned him again. The enemy shelled the road after we were all gone. Learning that Captain Castleman had fallen back from Falmouth (in anticipation of an advance from Walton), to Cynthiana, I went to that place also. It turned out that the rumor of the intended attack upon Falmouth was altogether unfounded. I placed the command in camp at Cynthiana, and sent the prisoners and all of the wounded who were not too much exhausted to travel, to Lexington.

On the next day the funeral of Lieutenant Rogers was celebrated. He was a native of Cynthiana, and the citizens of that place had loved him and were proud of his record. They came, the true, warm-hearted yeomanry, to witness his soldier-burial, and sympathize in the sorrow of his aged and heart-broken father. The men remained in camp at Cynthiana from the 30th of September until the night of the 4th of October. During that time I made several promotions which were confirmed by an exercise of General Morgan's appointing power.

Thomas Franks, private in the Mississippi company and "member in high standing" of the advance guard, was made Captain of Company I. He was a worthy successor of Captain Morgan. By a series of gallant acts and uniform good conduct and assiduous and thorough discharge of his duty, he had well won his preferment. Brevet Second Lieutenant William Messick (of whom a great deal remains to be said), was made First Lieutenant of Company A. Privates Parks and Ashbrook were made respectively First and Second Lieutenants of Company E. They were gallant, and had fought in the front of every fight since the organization of the regiment. Sergeant Wm. Hays was offered his choice of Captaincy of Company B, or the First Lieutenancy of the same company, with the privilege of commanding the advance-guard. He choose the latter—like the gallant man that he was, loving danger honestly encountered and honor fairly won.

General Morgan unhesitatingly approved all of these appointments—complimenting the appointees and declared that he had contemplated their promotion earlier. In pure, unflinching courage, soldierly desire for personal distinction, devotion to the interests of the service, pride in the reputation of their own corps, respect for and zealous obedience to their own commanders, energy and intelligence—these officers had no superiors.

I have already said that Colonel Morgan had been sent to Eastern Kentucky, to intercept the Federal General Morgan on his march to the Ohio river—I can not do better than copy *verbatim* a description, given of his operations by an excellent writer. "Succeeded in collecting about a thousand cavalrymen, all recruits except Gano's Texians, Company F, of Duke's regiment, and such of our battalion (Breckinridge's) as had seen service—many insufficiently armed and not well organized. We reached Richmond on the morning of the 20th, and received information that the Federals were moving from Manchester, via Booneville to Mt. Sterling, so as to strike the Ohio at Maysville. Morgan concentrated at Irvine on the 21st and moved toward Proctor, turned to the right, and, the head of his column was at Campton, Wolfe county. It became necessary to make a detour, and by rapid marches head them near Hazel Green. Colonel Ashby and General Stephenson were to press them in rear; General Humphrey Marshall was to move to Mt. Sterling, and either stop their march or strike them in flank. Our part was merely to delay them until Stephenson or Marshall could strike. The enemy beat us to Hazel Green; another detour and night march and we headed them near West Liberty.

"On the afternoon of the 26th, Morgan sent two companies under Captain Will Jones to strike the flank of the marching column. He knew that the column must be stretched out, for some miles; that a vigorous attack would cause the halt of the leading command, so that the column might close; this delay would help us. Jones attacked on foot, striking the rear-guard of the second advance brigade, and utterly surprising them; killed several, captured some dozen prisoners, scattered a drove of cattle through the woods, and gave warning of our presence. Morgan and his staff and Major Breckinridge had ridden along to see Jones' fight, though Jones had complete command, and is entitled to the credit.

"After this little brush was over, Morgan rode with some others, to the main road to get some information. Doctor Tom Allen had the wounded (all Federals) moved to a church near by, to dress their wounds. Morgan, Breckinridge, Alston, and others rode a few hundred yards forward to where a beautiful creek crossed the road, and beyond the creek was a short, steep, wooded hill. With culpable carelessness the whole party stopped to water the horses, and one or two dismounted, and kneeling upon rocks were drinking, when suddenly a regiment in line of battle, made its appearance upon the crest of the hill, not a hundred yards distant, and fired a full volley at us. Fortunately the hill was so steep they overshot us. Behind was a long lane with high fences and cleared fields on each side. Death or capture seemed inevitable. But with perfect coolness Morgan shouted. 'Tell Colonel Breckinridge to advance; Major Jones, open your guns.' The regiment fell back over the hill, and we in greater hurry evacuated those premises. The country being Union, it was very difficult to get reliable information, which General Morgan said must be had.

"While we were talking we saw some mountaineers with guns approaching: Morgan said instantly, 'I'll pass for Colonel De Courcey' (a Federal Colonel about Morgan's size). When the men came up they asked who we were; Alston said 'That's Colonel De Courcey.' 'Why, the boys told us De Courcey's brigade was behind, and we were mighty glad to see you.' It had been raining, and we had on gum cloths, which assisted the plan. Morgan asked, 'Wouldn't you like to join us?' 'Oh no,' answered one of the scoundrels, 'We can do you more good at home, killing the d——d secesh.' With a sweet approving smile, Morgan said, 'Oh, have you killed many secesh?' 'I reckon we have. You'd have laughed if you had seen us make Bill (I have forgotten the last name) kill his brother.' 'What did you do it for?' 'Why you see Bill went South, and we burned his house, and he deserted; we arrested him, and said we were going to hang him as a spy: he said he'd do any thing if we let him off, that his family would starve if we hung him. Last Wednesday we took him, and made him kill his brother Jack. He didn't want to do it, but we told him we'd kill them both if he didn't, and we made him do it.'

"Morgan kept his face unchanged, and drew from these murderers full accounts of other crimes; and from one of them, who had watched our column, a pretty fair account of our own strength. They gave us all they knew of the Federal strength, of the politics of the citizens on the road, and of the roads and country. After getting from them all he wanted, he said, 'I am John Morgan, and I'm going to have you hung.' Unfortunately, however, General Morgan's leniency, which always got the better of him when he paused to think, induced him to spare them."

The writer goes on—"Upon the 27th, another skirmish, and captured a few prisoners; the enemy evidently waiting for the column to close up. On the 28th, through the treachery of a guide, we were led into an ambush, out of which we extricated ourselves with small loss. Upon the 29th, Company A, Breckinridge's battalion, and Company F, Duke's regiment, under Major Breckinridge, ambushed the enemy from the side of a semicircular bluff, around which the road runs. The column came to within twenty yards of the line of ambush, and its head was nearly beyond the extreme flank of the two companies; in advance were seventeen cavalrymen, some sitting with, their legs thrown over the pommels of the saddle, some eating pawpaws; the *insignia* of rank upon their shoulders could be easily distinguished. Suddenly over a hundred rifles belched forth death and fire—again their volley echoed through the mountains; when the smoke cleared away, the head of the column had disappeared like a wave broken upon a rock, and before a line could be formed or a gun unlimbered, we were gone, and laughed as we marched to the music of their guns shelling the innocent woods over the mountain from us.

"After this they changed their tactics, and marched with a heavy line of skirmishers in front and upon both flanks. After shelling the woods for hours, we fought vigorously with the axe and torch, felling trees, barricading the road, destroying bridges, and making every barricade cost a skirmish and time, for with us time was every thing. The country was not fit for cavalry operations. The 30th passed away; the 1st of October was half gone. From the morning of the 26th to noon of the 1st, over five days, the Federals had marched not over thirty miles, less than six miles a day. We had done our work, but where was Marshall or Stephenson? Since the morning of the 29th, we had been anxiously looking for news from them. Couriers had been constantly sent to both, and to General Smith. We knew that the enemy were living on meat alone, for we, in their front, went without bread for over three days, living on fresh beef, without salt, half-ripe corn, and the luscious pawpaws. If Marshall or Stephenson had attacked, the army of the gap would have been prisoners. Whoever was to blame, let him be censured. Morgan, with raw recruits, badly armed, accomplished his part of the task. About noon, October 1st, Morgan received an order from General Smith to withdraw from George Morgan's front, not to attempt further to impede his progress, but rather assist him to leave the State, and rejoin the main army at Lexington, or *wherever it might be*."

This writer tells well the story of the campaign in the mountains, and the reader can derive from it a vivid idea of what it was like. Toward the latter part of the expedition, the bushwhackers became very troublesome, and wounded several men. Little Billy Peyton, the Colonel's orderly, once rode down on one of them and tried to scare him into surrender with an empty pistol. The fellow had two guns—he had just fired one at Peyton, and the other was loaded. He answered Peyton's demand to surrender with a shot from the latter. Throwing himself along his horse's side, Billy escaped being killed, but was slightly wounded. His chief regret, however, was that his assailant escaped.

On the afternoon of the 4th, Colonel Morgan reached Lexington. Before he got in, he became satisfied that an immediate evacuation was imminent, and he was induced to believe that the enemy were nearer than was actually the case. Anxious to get his command together again, and learning where I was, he, with characteristic promptitude, dispatched me a courier, bidding me keep a careful lookout, and if "cut off, come by way of Richmond and Lancaster." He knew that I would be mightily exercised by such a dispatch. I had heard nothing of the meditated evacuation of Lexington, and without waiting for orders from General Smith, I at once moved with my command, and marched all night. When I reached Lexington, I found that preparations were being made for its evacuation. I hoped, as did thousands of others, that it would be only a temporary one, and that we could return after a decisive victory, which should give us fast possession of Kentucky. I mentioned this hope to Colonel Morgan, and I shall never forget his laugh, and the bitter sarcasm with which he spoke of the retreat, which he seemed to certainly expect. As he rapidly mentioned the indications which convinced him that we were going to give up the stakes without an effort to win them, my faith, too, gave way, and my heart sank. He generously defended General Bragg, however, saying, that his course was perfectly consistent, inasmuch as he had come into Kentucky to escape a fight, and was now about to go out for the same reason, and that, moreover, a commander-in-chief always did well to avoid battle, no matter what was the spirit of his troops, when he felt demoralized himself.

On the 6th of October, Colonel Morgan left Lexington on the track of General Smith's infantry forces, with Cluke, Gano and the Second Kentucky. It was thought probable that the enemy would advance from the direction of Frankfort, and an engagement in the vicinity of Versailles, where a portion of General Smith's infantry were stationed, was anticipated. Morgan, whose entire force amounted to some fifteen hundred effective men, was ordered to take position between Versailles and Frankfort, and attack the enemy if he made his appearance. The bulk of General Smith's command was eight or ten miles farther to the southwest, in the vicinity of Lawrenceburg.

Breckinridge's battalion had been detached on the 4th, and was ordered to report first to Buford, then to Wharton, and finally to Ashby. It was engaged in the skirmishing which the two latter officers successfully conducted with the enemy, on the road between Lawrenceburg and Harrodsburg, and Harrodsburg and Perryville. The movements of Buell had completely mystified General Bragg, and the latter was not only reduced to the defensive, but to a state of mind pitiable in the extreme. He acted like a man whose nerves by some accident or disorder, had been crazed; he was the victim of every rumor; he was alternately exhilarated and dejected. If the enemy dallied, or the distance between them *happened* to be increased, he became bold and confident; when a collision was imminent, he could contemplate nothing but defeat and disaster. Of that kind of fear which induces provision against dangers which are far in the future, he knew nothing, and he was equally as ignorant of the courage which kindles highest when the hour of final issue has arrived. General Bragg, had, as a subordinate, no superior in bravery—he had, as a commander, no bravery at all. While I shall make no sort of comment upon General Bragg's character or his conduct, which I do not thoroughly believe to be correct, and just and warranted by the record and by the circumstances of that time and of this—I yet deem it my duty to candidly warn my readers to receive with due allowance every line written about Bragg by a Kentuckian.

The wrongs he did Kentucky and Kentuckians, the malignity with which he bore down on his Kentucky troops, his hatred and bitter active antagonism to all prominent Kentucky officers, have made an abhorrence of him part of a Kentuckian's creed. There is no reason why any expression of natural feeling toward him should be now suppressed—he is not dead, nor a prisoner, nor an exile.

General Bragg came to the western army with a most enviable reputation. He had already displayed those qualities as an organizer, a disciplinarian, and a military administrator, in which he was unrivaled. His dashing conduct at Shiloh, and the courage and ability (there exhibited in perfection), in which (as a corps commander), no man excelled him, had made him a great and universal favorite. The admirable method which (when second in command at Corinth, and really at the head of affairs), he introduced into all departments; the marvelous skill in discipline, with which he made of the "mob" at Corinth a splendidly ordered, formidable army, and his masterly evacuation of the place (totally deceiving Halleck in doing so), caused him to be regarded, almost universally, as the fit successor of Albert Sydney Johnson, and the coming man of the West.

The plan of retiring altogether from Mississippi, and of suddenly moving the army, by the Southern railroads, away around into Tennessee again—losing the slow, dull-scented Halleck—if conceived by a subordinate, was, at least, attributed to him. It was brilliant in itself, and was successfully executed. Men waited, in breathless interest, the consummation of such a career. But right there he began to fail, and soon he gave way entirely. It is almost impossible now to realize that the Bragg of the spring and the Bragg of the autumn of 1862, are identical. When he reached Chattanooga, he showed for the first time vacillation and a disposition to delay. He crossed the river on the 28th of August with twenty-five thousand infantry, beside artillery and cavalry. He moved over Waldron's ridge, up the Sequatchy valley, through Sparta, into Kentucky, seeking to beat Buell to Munfordsville. The disposition of Buell's forces has already been given in a former chapter. His army, about forty or forty-five thousand strong, was scattered over a wide extent of territory, in small detachments (with the exception of the forces at Battle creek and at McMinnville—each about twelve or fourteen thousand strong).

This disposition was rendered necessary by the difficulty of obtaining supplies—it was also requisite to a thorough garrisoning of the country. Had General Bragg, as soon as he crossed the river, marched straight on Nashville, General Buell could not possibly have met him with more than twenty thousand men. General Buell did not issue orders for the concentration of his troops until the 30th of August, although preparations had been made for it before. This concentration was effected at Murfreesboro'. It then became apparent to him that General Bragg was pushing for central Kentucky, and it became necessary that Buell, to save his communication, should march into Kentucky also. General Bragg had the start and the short route, and reached Glasgow on the 13th of September; then taking position on the main roads at Cave City, while Buell, with all the expedition he could use, had gotten only so far as Bowlinggreen, he cut the latter off from Louisville and the reinforcements awaiting him there.

General Buell's army had been decreased by the detachment of a garrison for Nashville. After an unsuccessful attack (with the loss of two or three hundred men), by a small Confederate force upon Munfordsville—the garrison of that place, over four thousand strong, subsequently surrendered on the 17th. What now was to hinder General Bragg, holding the strong position of Munfordsville, from stopping Buell, calling Kirby Smith, with his whole force, to his assistance, and out-numbering, crush his adversary? This question has been asked very often. How long would the raw troops at Louisville have withstood the attack of Bragg's veterans when their turn came? General Bragg discovered that the country was barren of supplies—that one of the richest, most fertile regions of Kentucky, could not support his army for a week, and he withdrew to Bardstown. Buell finding the road clear, marched on to Louisville. His immense wagon train, more than twenty miles long and the flank of his army were exposed, and with impunity by this movement.

It was certainly not expecting too much of General Bragg, as commander-in-chief of the Confederate forces in Kentucky, to expect that he would (after this was done) make up his mind whether he was going to fight or not, without farther delay. If he did not intend to fight, would it not have been wiser to have marched back on Nashville, while Buell was marching on Louisville, to have taken that place and to have established himself on the banks of the Cumberland with less of loss, fatigue, and discontent among his troops, than existed when after his long, harassing, wearying marches through the mountains, he halted at Murfreesboro' much later? Kirby Smith could have remained in Kentucky long enough to collect and secure all the supplies—he had demonstrated that he could take care of himself, and if he had been hard-pressed, he could have retreated more rapidly than any pursuer could follow. If General Bragg did intend to fight, why did he not concentrate his army and fight hard?

After Buell marched to Louisville (which he reached on the 29th of September), Bragg took position at and about Bardstown. Our line, including General Smith's forces, may be described as running from Bardstown, on the extreme left, through Frankfort and Lexington, to Mount Sterling on the right flank. It was an admirable one. However threatened on front or flanks, the troops could be marched to the threatened points, by excellent roads. The base at Bryantsville was perfectly secure—roads ran from it in every direction—and it was a place of immense natural strength. The force available, for the defense of this line, was quite forty-nine thousand infantry, General Bragg's Staff officers represent the force of infantry (which entered the State with General Bragg) to have been twenty-five thousand. General Smith's infantry forces (including Marshall) numbered twenty-four thousand [so estimated by General Smith himself]. There were perhaps one hundred and thirty pieces of artillery in all. The cavalry, all told, was about six thousand Strong (including Morgan and Buford), making a grand total of about fifty-six thousand men.

Buell moved out from Louisville on the 1st of October. His advance was made just as might have been anticipated, and as many had predicted.

Not caring to involve his whole army in the rough Chaplin and Benson hills, he sent detachments toward Frankfort and Lawrenceburg, to guard against any movement on Louisville, and to distract Bragg's attention from his (Buell's) main design, and make him divide his army. In this latter intention he perfectly succeeded. The bulk of his army marched through Bardstown and Springfield to Perryville, to get in Bragg's rear and upon his line of retreat. The force sent to Frankfort, five or six thousand strong, under Dumont, broke up the inaugural ceremonies of the Provisional Government, which General Bragg, as if in mockery of the promises he had so lavishly and so confidently made to his own Government, and to the people of Kentucky, and of the hopes he had excited, had instituted. He made one of the first and best men of the State, a man of venerable years and character, held in universal respect for a long life of unblemished integrity, beloved for his kind, open, manly nature, and especially honored by the Southern people of Kentucky for his devotion to the cause—General Bragg made this old man, who had been unanimously indicated as the proper man for Provisional Governor of Kentucky, tell the people, who crowded to listen to his inaugural address, that the State would be held by the Confederate army, cost what it might. At the very time that General Bragg so deceived Governor Hawes, and made him unwillingly deceive his people, the Confederate army had already commenced to retreat.

This force, which came to Frankfort, was the same which General Smith was prepared to fight at Versailles, its real strength not being at first known. A day or two afterward it came out upon the Versailles road, and was ambushed by Colonel John Scott, and driven back with smart loss. General Smith, hearing that the enemy were advancing in force to Lawrenceburg, and that they had occupied that place with an advance guard, ordered Buford to drive them out with his cavalry, and followed with his whole force. The establishment of the enemy at Lawrenceburg, and upon the road thence to Harrodsburg, would have completely cut off General Smith from General Bragg. The force advancing toward Lawrenceburg, was Sill's division, perhaps six or seven thousand strong in effectives. This division had diverged from the main army at the same time with Dumont's.

General Smith's forces were arranged at Lawrenceburg (which was not occupied by the enemy) and on the road thence to Harrodsburg on the 6th. Sill's division fell back across Salt river and into the rugged Chaplin hills, pressed by a portion of General Smith's infantry, Colonel Thomas Taylor's brigade in advance. Several hundred prisoners were taken. The position of General Smith's forces was not materially changed during that day and the next, although they continued to draw nearer to Harrodsburg. The main body of the enemy had in the mean time concentrated its marching columns and moved to the vicinity of Perryville, 58,000 strong, on the evening of the 7th.

The detachments which advanced to Frankfort and toward Lawrenceburg, were not more than 12,000 strong in all. So rugged and difficult of passage is the country through which these detachments had to pass, that a comparatively small force could have prevented their junction at Lawrenceburg and held both at bay, leaving the bulk of the Confederate army free to concentrate at Perryville. Even had their junction been permitted, three thousand such cavalry as Bragg had at his disposal could have retarded their march to Harrodsburg for several days. They could not have forced their way along the road in less than two or three days, and as many would have been required to make a detour and join Buell. In that time the battle of Perryville could have been decided. But so completely was General Bragg in the dark about Buell's movements that, when he first heard of the advance from Louisville, he supposed it was a movement of the whole Federal army upon Frankfort, and he ordered General Polk "to move from Bardstown, by way of Bloomfield, toward Frankfort, to strike the enemy in flank and rear," while General Smith should take him in front. This order was evidently issued under an unaccountable and entire misapprehension of the true state of affairs, but showed a nerve and purpose which promised well. General Bragg must certainly, when he issued it, have supposed that General Buell's whole army was coming from that direction. How strange is it that a commander who could thus resolve to fight his foes, when he believed them to be united, should fear to encounter them separately. Whatever may be the verdict upon General Polk's disobedience of orders, whether it was one of those cases in which a subordinate can rightfully exercise this discretion or not, the fact of General Bragg's incompetency looms up in unmistakable proportions.

The most remarkable feature of General Bragg's conduct was this strange, unexampled vacillation. There was perhaps never afforded such an instance of perfect infirmity and fickleness of purpose. He had, there can be little doubt, resolved to retreat without delivering battle before the 1st of October. He nevertheless sought to fight at Frankfort (as has been seen) a few days afterward. Again, immediately afterward, he did his best to avoid battle when it could have been delivered (as all but himself thought) under far more favorable circumstances. No one now doubts, I presume, that General Bragg fought at Perryville with a fragment of his army, not to win a victory, but to check the enemy and cover his retreat.

After General Polk moved to Perryville, General Bragg, of course, learned of the advance of the enemy in that direction, and must have known that it was in strong column, or he would not have permitted sixteen thousand troops to collect there to oppose it. He was still in error regarding the other movements, and left the larger part of his army to confront the forces maneuvering about Lawrenceburg and Frankfort. One glance at the map will show the reader that, if the enemy was really advancing in heavy columns by these different routes, it was clearly General Bragg's best policy to have struck and crushed (if he could) that body threatening him from the south. If he crushed that his line of retreat would be safe, and he could have fought the other at his leisure, or not at all, as he chose. He could have fought (if it had continued to advance) at Bryantsville, or gone after and attacked it. If, on the contrary, he had concentrated to fight at Frankfort or Lawrenceburg, defeat, with this other force on his line of retreat, would have been ruinous. Even complete and decisive victory would have left him still in danger, having still another army to defeat or drive away. He would have been, in either case, between his foes, preventing their junction, and in a situation to strike them in succession; but in the one case his rear was safe, and in the other it was threatened.

With the true trimming instinct, he elected to take a middle course; he divided his army, and sought to meet both dangers at the same time. Is it saying too much that he was saved from utter destruction by the heroic courage, against vast odds, of that fragment of his army which fought at Perryville? It is the popular idea that a commander is out-generaled when he is deceived. Military phraseology can mystify the popular mind, but it can not eradicate from it this idea. Buell certainly deceived Bragg, and by sending detachments, numbering in all not more than twelve thousand, through a country from which a mere handful of men could have prevented them from debouching, he kept thirty thousand men, the bulk of General Bragg's army, idle, and rendered them useless until the game was decided.

After the battle of Perryville (where he certainly got the better of the forces opposed to him)—an earnest of what might have been done if the whole army had been concentrated—and after an accurate knowledge had been obtained, of how Sill's and Dumont's detachments had deceived him into the belief that they were the whole Federal army—General Bragg had his entire army concentrated at Harrodsburg. The two armies then fairly confronted each other, neither had any strategic experiments to fear, on flank or rear, for Sill's division was making a wide and prudent circuit to get to Buell, and Dumont was stationary at Frankfort. It would have been a fair, square, stand up fight. It is, now, well known that there was not the disparity in numbers which General Bragg and his friends claimed to have existed. There was less numerical inequality, between the armies, than there has been on many battlefields—where the Confederate arms have been indisputably victorious. Buell's strength was less than at any other period of the eight or ten days that a battle was imminent. Sill had not gotten up—the Federal army was fifty-eight thousand strong—minus the four thousand killed and wounded at Perryville, and the stragglers. Buell had in his army, regiments and brigades, of raw troops, thirty-three thousand in all. Bragg had not more than five thousand; most of them distributed among veteran regiments. There were no full regiments, nor even full companies of recruits in Bragg's army, except in the Kentucky cavalry commands. The two armies faced each other, not more than three miles apart. The belief was almost universal, in each army, that next morning we would fight. The troops thought so, and, despite the pouring rain, and their uncomfortable bivouacs, were in high and exultant spirits. I know, for I saw them late in the night, that some officers of high rank confidently looked for battle, and were cheerful, and sanguine of victory.

What General Bragg really intended to do that night—perhaps he himself only knows—and it is quite as probable that even he does not know. He retreated on the next morning to Bryantsville. There was no undignified haste about this movement—the troops moved off deliberately, and in such order, that they could have been thrown quickly, if it had become necessary, into line of battle. General Bragg manifested no great anxiety to get away from the vicinity of his enemy, and Buell certainly manifested no strong desire to detain him.

On the next day (the 12th), the army remained at Bryantsville, and took up its march for Lancaster about ten o'clock of that night. It reached Lancaster on the morning of the 13th, and divided. General Smith going to Richmond, and over the Big hill, to Cumberland Gap, General Bragg with the troops which had come into Kentucky under his immediate command, passing through Crab Orchard.

It was hoped, and thought probable, that Buell would overtake and force Bragg to fight at Crab Orchard. He did, indeed, come very near doing so. Sending one division to Lancaster, he moved with the bulk of his army toward Crab Orchard. He failed, however, to intercept Bragg, and the latter moved on out of Kentucky.

Thus ended a campaign from which so much was expected, and which, had it been successful, would have incalculably benefited the Confederate cause. Able writers have exerted all their skill in apologies for this campaign, but time has developed into a certainty, that opinion then instinctively held by so many, that with the failure to hold Kentucky, our best and last chance to win the war was thrown away.

Let the historian recall the situation, and reflect upon the influences which in the, then, condition of affairs were likely to control the destinies at stake, and he will declare, that with this retreat the pall fell upon the fortunes of the Confederacy.

All the subsequent tremendous struggle, was but the dying agony of a great cause, and a gallant people. At that period the veteran Federal army of the West was numerically much inferior to what it ever was again; and even after the accession of the recruits hastily collected at Louisville, it was much less formidable than it subsequently became.

The Confederate army was composed of the veterans of Shiloh, and the soldiers formed in the ordeal of Corinth. It was as nearly equal to the Federal army, in numerical strength, as there was any chance of it ever being, and the character of its material more than made up for any inequality in this respect. No man, who saw it in Kentucky, will doubt that it would have fought up to its full capacity. Never was there a more fiery ardor, a more intense resolution pervading an army, than that one felt, when expecting a battle which should decide whether they were to hold Kentucky, or march back again, carrying the war once more with them to their homes and firesides. Not even on the first day of Shiloh, when it seemed that they could have charged the rooted hills from their bases, were those troops in a temper to make so desperate a fight. But a doting Æolus held the keys which confined the storm. It will be difficult for any one who will carefully study the history of this period, to avoid the conclusion that it was the crisis of the war. First let the military situation be considered. While at almost every point of subordinate importance the

Confederates were holding their own, they were at those points, where the war assumed its grand proportions, and the issue was vital, carrying every thing before them.

The Confederate Government had at length adopted the policy of massing its troops, and the effect was instantly seen. In Virginia, General Lee's onset was irresistible. His army burst from the entrenchments around Richmond, like the lava from the volcano, and the host of McClellan, shrank withered, from its path. Driving McClellan to his new base, and leaving him to make explanations to his soldiery, "Uncle Robert" fell headlong upon Pope, and Pope boasted no more. Forcing the immense Federal masses disintegrated and demoralized back to Washington, General Lee crossed the Potomac and pushed into Maryland. Jackson took Harper's Ferry, while General Lee fought the battle of Antietam with forty thousand men, and again crippled McClellan.

Although the Confederate army recrossed the Potomac on the 18th of September, McClellan did not follow, but remained inactive and by no means certain (as his dispatches show) that his great adversary would not return to attack him. It was not until late in October, that the Federal army again advanced, and its march was then slow and irresolute. It will be seen then, that on the 17th, the day on which Bragg took Munfordsville, General Lee was fighting in Maryland. Ought not General Bragg to have risked a battle (with his superior force) in Kentucky, which (if successful), would have ruined the army opposed to him and have laid the whole Northwest open to him, unless McClellan had furnished the troops to oppose him, and have placed himself at the mercy of Lee?

General Bragg did not (of course) know, on the 17th of September, 1862, that the battle of Antietam was being fought, but he knew that General Lee had achieved great successes, and that he was marching into Maryland. Again, what effect are we at liberty to suppose that a decisive victory won by General Bragg, at Perryville, on the 6th of October, would have had upon the general result. General Buell, pressed by Bragg's entire army, would have had some trouble to cross the Ohio river, after reaching Louisville; and the defense of the Western States would have been then intrusted with many misgivings to his shattered army. And yet the West would have been left with no other defense, unless the army of the Potomac had (in the event of such a necessity) been weakened and endangered, that reinforcements might go to Buell. It may be said that all this is hypothetical. Of course it is. But what General ever yet inaugurated and conducted a campaign, or planned and fought a battle, and banished such hypotheses altogether from his calculations? Why then should they be forbidden in the criticism of campaigns and battles? It is not infallibly certain that General Bragg could have defeated Buell. Nothing is positively certain in a military sense, not even the impregnability of a work built by a West Pointer, and pronounced so by a committee of his classmates. War is a game of various and varying chances. What I mean to urge, is, that General Bragg should, under all the circumstances, have, by all the rules of the game, risked the chances of a battle. But if there were strong military reasons why an effort should have been made to accomplish decisive results in this campaign, there were other and even stronger reasons for it, to be found in the political condition, North and South. The Confederacy, alarmed by the reverses of the winter and spring, had just put forth tremendous and almost incredible efforts. The South had done all that she could be made to do by the stimulus of fear. Increased, aye, even sustained exertion could have been elicited from her people, only by the intoxication of unwonted and dazzling success. No additional inducement could have been offered to the soldiers, whom pride and patriotism had sent into the field, to remain with their colors, but the attraction of brilliant victories and popular campaigns. No incentive could have lured into the ranks the young men who had evaded the conscription and held out against the sentiment of their people, but the prospect of a speedy and successful termination of the war. But there are few among those who were acquainted with the people of Tennessee, Alabama, and Mississippi, and their temper at that time, who will not agree with me, that a great victory in Kentucky, and the prospect of holding the State, perhaps of crossing the Ohio, would have brought to Bragg's army more Tennesseeans, Alabamians and Mississippians, than were ever gotten into the Confederate service, during the remaining two years and a half of the war. Such a victory would have undoubtedly added more than twenty thousand Kentuckians to the army, for accurate computation has been made of that many who were ready to enlist, as soon as Bragg had won his fight. Five thousand did enlist while it was still uncertain whether the Confederate army would remain in the State. It is not perfectly certain that more than five thousand volunteers were ever obtained, in the same length of time, in any seceded State. All of these men, too, followed the army away from Kentucky. Some of General Bragg's friends have assigned, as one reason, why he left Kentucky without an effort to hold her, that he was disappointed in not receiving more recruits from the State. It is highly probable that such was the case. If an able General had marched into his enemy's territory, depending upon fighting an early and hardly contested battle against a veteran army, with the assistance of recruits just obtained, and whom he could not have yet armed, his friends would have concealed (if possible) his design, or if unable to do so, would have confessed it a weakness unworthy of their chief, for which they blushed. But it is not difficult to believe that General Bragg entertained just such a plan. The Kentuckians had not the confidence in the ultimate success of the Confederate cause, to induce them to enlist in the Confederate service, risking every thing, immediately sacrificing much, as they did so, when they saw a magnificent Confederate army decline battle with a Federal force, certainly not its superior. General Bragg was not only a very shrewd judge of human nature, but even he might have known that the irresolution and timidity he showed from the first day he put foot in Kentucky, was not the way to inspire confidence in any people—it certainly was the worst method he could have adopted to win the people of Kentucky.

And now, to consider the effect which such a Confederate success would have in the North: I do not allude to the effect it would have had upon the wishes and plans of President and Cabinet, upon the views of the Congress, nor upon the arrangements of politicians and the patch work of their conventions, but to the direction it might have given the popular mind and the popular feeling. Men who were then serving in the Confederate army, know little, of course, of the temper of the Northern people, at that time, but many were impressed with the idea, then, strengthened by conversation with Northern men since, that, if ever the Northern people doubted of subjugating the South, it was at that period.

Immense efforts had been made, immense sums had been expended, immense armies had been sent against them, and still the Southern people were unconquered, defiant, and apparently stronger than ever. Would it have been possible to strengthen this doubt into a conviction that the attempt to subdue the Southern people was hopeless, and the war had better be stopped? Volunteering was no longer filling the Federal armies. Now, if the Confederate arms had been incontestably triumphant, from the Potomac to the Ohio, if Northern territory had been in turn threatened with general invasion, and if the option of continuing a war, thus going against them, or making peace, had been submitted at the critical moment to the Northern people, how would they have decided? Would they have encouraged their Government to draft them—or would they have forced the Government to make peace? The matter was, at any rate, sufficiently doubtful to make it worth while to try the experiment. When that scare passed off, it is the firm conviction of more than one man who "saw the war out" that the last chance of Confederate independence passed away.

The Northern people then learned, for the first time, their real strength; they found that bounties, and the draft, and the freedmen, and importations from the recruiting markets of the whole world, would keep their armies full, and nothing could have made them despond again. The war then became merely a comparison of national resources. Something was undoubtedly gained by the march into Kentucky, but how little in comparison with the golden opportunity which was thrown away. Had the combatants been equally matched, the result of this campaign might have been a matter for congratulation; but when the Confederacy was compelled, in order to cope with its formidable antagonist, to deal mortal blows in every encounter, or come out of each one the loser, the prisoners, artillery, and small arms taken, the recovery of Cumberland Gap and a portion of Tennessee, and the supplies secured for the army, scarcely repaid for the loss of prestige to Confederate generalship, and the renewal of confidence in the war party of the North.

When Bragg moved out of Kentucky, he left behind him, uncrippled, a Federal army which soon (having become more formidable than ever before) bore down upon him in Tennessee. The inquest of history will cause a verdict to be rendered, that the Confederacy "came to its death" from too much technical science. It is singular, too, that the maxims which were always on the lips of the military *savants*, were often neglected by themselves and applied by the unlettered "irregulars." The academic magnates declared in sonorous phrase that struck admiration into the very popular marrow, the propriety of a General "marching by interior lines, and striking the fragments of his enemy's forces with the masses of his own;" while Forrest, perhaps, after doing that very thing, would make it appear a very ordinary performance, by describing it as "taking the short cut, and getting there first with the most men."

It was a great misfortune to the Confederacy, too, that Fabius ever lived, or, at least, that his strategy ever became famous. Every Confederate General who retreated, when he might have fought successfully, and who failed to improve an opportunity to punish the enemy, had only to compare his policy to that of Fabius, and criticism was silenced. Perhaps, if history had preserved the reports of Hannibal, the "Fabian policy" would not have become so reputable. At any rate, it is safe to assume that, had Rome been situated on the same side of the Mediterranean as Carthage, and had she been a seceded state, inferior in wealth, numbers, and resources, which the latter was trying to "coerce," Fabius would have been a most injudicious selection as commander-in-chief. Historians are agreed, I believe, that if the advice of this classic "Micawber," to the consuls Livius and Nero, had been followed by them, the battle of "The Metaurus" would not have been fought, the two sons of the "Thunder-bolt" would have effected their junction, and would, in all probability, have forced the legions to another and final "change of base."

This campaign demonstrated conclusively the immense importance to the Confederacy of the possession of East Tennessee, and the strategic advantage (especially for offenso-defensive operations) which that vast natural fortress afforded us. While that region was firmly in the Confederate grasp, one half of the South was safe, and the conquests of the Federal armies of the rest were insecure. It is apparent at a glance that so long as we held it, communication between the armies of Northern Virginia and of Tennessee would be rapid and direct; co-operation, therefore, between them would be secure whenever necessary. While these two armies could thus practically be handled almost as if they were one and the same, communication between the Federal army of the Potomac and that of the Ohio was circuitous, dilatory, and public. No advance of the enemy through Tennessee into Georgia or Alabama could permanently endanger the integrity of the Confederate territory, while the flank and rear of his army was constantly exposed to sudden attack by formidable forces poured upon it from this citadel of the Confederacy.

Not only would the safety of invading armies be compromised, and their communications (even if confined to the Tennessee rivers), be liable at any time to be destroyed, but a sudden irruption from East Tennessee might (unless an army was always ready to meet it), place the most fertile portions of Kentucky, perhaps, even a portion of the territory of Ohio, in the hands of the Confederates. The success clearly attending the Confederate strategy in the first part of this campaign, would seem, too, to establish the fact, that, until the concentration for decisive battle becomes necessary, an army may (under certain circumstances), be moved in two or more columns, upon lines entirely independent of each other, and even widely apart, but which lead to a common goal—and its operations will be more efficient—than if it be marched *en masse*, by one route.

The advantages to be derived from such a disposition (as regards freedom, and rapidity of movement, and facility of obtaining supplies), are at once apparent, but certain strategic advantages besides, may, in some cases, be thus secured. To attempt it, in moving against a strong enemy, already posted at the objective point, would be to give him the opportunity of attacking and crushing the columns separately. But when, as was the case in this campaign of General Bragg, two armies make a race for the occupation of a certain territory which is to be fought for, the army which is divided, while on the march, if the columns are all kept on the same flank of the enemy, can be worked most actively and as safely. More can be accomplished by such a disposition of forces, in the partial engagements and lighter work of the campaign, and the morale of the troops will be all the better when the detachments are again combined. Such campaigns might be made more frequently than they are, and with success.

When the army was concentrated at Harrodsburg, on the night of the 10th of October, Colonel Morgan was ordered to take position about six miles from the town, on the Danville pike, and picket the extreme left flank. Desirous of ascertaining what was before him—as he could see the camp-fires of the enemy stretching in a great semi-circle, in front of Harrodsburg—Colonel Morgan during the night, sent Captain Cassell to reconnoiter the ground in his front. The night was rainy and very dark. The position of both armies, of the main body of each, at least, was distinctly marked by the long lines of fires which glared through the gloom, but we had not lighted fires, and Morgan thought that any body of the enemy which might be confronting him, and detailed upon similar duty, would exercise the same prudence. Cassell returned about daylight, and reported that he had discovered, exactly in front of our position, and about a mile and a quarter from it, a small body of cavalry on picket, and a few hundred yards to their rear, a force of infantry, perhaps of one regiment. He stated positively, also, that one piece of artillery had passed along a narrow lane, which connected the point where the cavalry was stationed with the position of the infantry. The intense darkness prevented his seeing the tracks made by the wheels, but he had satisfied himself, by feeling, that, from the width of the tire, and the depth to which the wheels had sunk into the soft earth, they could only have been made by artillery. This report was verified on the next day, in every particular.

Colonel Morgan, at an early hour, attacked the cavalry, with a portion of his command, drove them back to the point indicated by Captain Cassell, as that one where he had seen the infantry, and sure enough, as he rode down upon it, he received a volley from a regiment of infantry posted behind a stone fence, and was opened upon by a single piece of artillery. The perfect accuracy with which Captain Cassell, under circumstances peculiarly unfavorable, noted every detail of the enemy's strength, position, etc., elicited the admiration of all of his comrades, and among them, were perhaps, as shrewd, practiced, and daring scouts as ever lived.

About 1 or 2 P.M., learning that General Bragg was falling back to Bryantsville, Colonel Morgan sent pickets to Harrodsburg; these soon sent word that the enemy had entered that place. About the same time our scouts brought us information that the enemy were in Danville also—about four miles from our position. Having an enemy, now, upon three sides of him, and finding that General Bragg's rear was unmolested, Colonel Morgan concluded, in the absence of instructions to fall back also. He accordingly struck across the country to Shakertown, reaching that place, about 4 P.M. Colonel Morgan had always respected the peaceful and hospitable "Shakers," and had afforded them, whenever it became necessary, protection, strictly forbidding all members of his command to trespass upon them in any way. We were consequently great favorites in Shakertown, and on this occasion derived great benefit from the perfect rectitude of conduct which we had always observed—"in that part of the country." The entire community resolved itself into a culinary committee, and cooked the most magnificent meal for the command. It was with deep regret that we tore ourselves away on the next morning.

Colonel Morgan received orders, on the 12th, to proceed to Nicholasville and remain there until the next day. On the 13th we followed the army and reached Lancaster about midday. In the afternoon the enemy, with whom General Wheeler had been skirmishing all day, advanced upon Lancaster, and opened upon the troops, collected about the place, with artillery. A little sharp shooting was also done upon both sides. Two guns belonging to Rain's brigade of infantry, which was General Smith's rear-guard, were brought back and replied to the enemy's fire. One man of this section killed, was the only loss sustained upon our side. The cannonading was kept up until dark. We held the town during the night. Only one division of Buell's army (as has already been stated), was sent to Lancaster.

On the morning of the 14th, we moved slowly away from Lancaster, our command forming (with Colonel Ashby's) the extreme rear-guard of General Smith's corps. We were not at all pressed by the enemy, and on the 15th halted at Gum Springs twenty-five miles from Richmond. Colonel Morgan obtained permission from General Smith to select his own "line of retreat" from Kentucky, with the understanding, however, that he should protect the rear of the infantry until all danger was manifestly over. He represented to General Smith that he could feed his men and horses, and have them in good condition at the end of the retreat, by taking a different route from that pursued by the army, which would consume every thing. He explained, moreover, how in the route he proposed to take, he would cross Buell's rear, taking prisoners, capturing trains, and seriously annoying the enemy, and that establishing himself in the vicinity of Gallatin again, he could, before he was driven away, so tear up the railroad, once more, as to greatly retard the concentration of the Federal army at Nashville. It was perfectly apparent to General Smith, that all this could be done, and that, when Morgan reached the portion of Tennessee which he indicated, he would be in exactly the proper position to guard one flank of the line, which Bragg's army would probably establish. He accorded him, therefore, the desired permission, and on the 17th, when the infantry had gotten beyond Big Hill and were more than thirty miles from an enemy, Colonel Morgan turned over to Colonel Ashby the care of "the rear" and prepared to leave Kentucky in his own way. Colonel Ashby had proven himself competent to the successful discharge of even more important duty.

Colonel Morgan's force consisted at this time, counting troops actually with him, of the Second Kentucky (with the exception of one company), Gano's regiment (the Third Kentucky), and Breckinridge's battalion which had rejoined us at Lancaster—in all about eighteen hundred men. Cluke's and Chenault's regiments had gone with General Smith. The time and situation were both propitious to such an expedition as he contemplated. No such dash was looked for by the enemy who believed that every Confederate was anxious to get away as rapidly as possible by the shortest route. The interior of Kentucky and the route Morgan proposed to take were clear of Federal troops, excepting detachments not strong enough or sufficiently enterprising to give him much cause for apprehension.

CHAPTER XI

On the 17th of October, Colonel Morgan marched from Gum Springs in the direction of Lexington. The command was put in motion about 1 P.M. Gano and Breckinridge were sent to the Richmond pike, by which it was intended that they should approach the town, and full instructions regarding the time and manner of attack, were given them. Information had been received that a body of Federal cavalry had occupied Lexington a day or two previously, and Lieutenant Tom Quirk had been sent to ascertain some thing about them; he returned on the evening of the 17th, bringing accurate information of the strength and position of the enemy. Colonel Morgan accompanied my regiment (the Second Kentucky), which crossed the river below Clay's ferry, and moved by country roads toward Lexington.

The immediate region was not familiar to any man in the regiment, nor to Morgan himself, and, as it was strongly Union, some difficulty was at first anticipated about getting guides or information regarding the routes. This was obviated by Colonel Morgan's address. It was quite dark by the time the column was fairly across the river, and he rode to the nearest house, where, representing himself as Colonel Frank Woolford, of the Federal service, a great favorite in that neighborhood, he expressed his wish to procure a guide to Lexington. The man of the house declared his joy at seeing Colonel Woolford, and expressed his perfect willingness to act as guide himself. His loyal spirit was warmly applauded, and his offer cordially accepted. Under his guidance we threaded the country safely, and reached the Tates-creek pike, at a point about ten miles from Lexington, a little after midnight. About two o'clock we had gotten within three miles of the town, and were not much more than a mile from the enemy's encampment. We halted here, for, in accordance with the plan previously arranged, a simultaneous attack was to be made just at daylight, and Gano and Breckinridge had been instructed to that effect.

The guide, now, for the first time, learned the mistake under which he had been laboring, and his amazement was only equaled by his horror. All during the night he had been saying many hard things (to Woolford as he thought), about Morgan, at which the so-called Woolford had seemed, greatly amused, and had encouraged him to indulge himself in that way. All at once, the merry, good-humored "Woolford" turned out to be Morgan, and Morgan, seemed for a few moments, to be in a temper which made the guide's flesh creep. He expected to be shot, and scalped perhaps, without delay. Soon finding, however, that he was not going to be hurt, he grew bolder, and actually assumed the offensive. "General Morgan," he said, "I hope you wont take my horse under the circumstances, although I did make this here little mistake?" He was turned loose, horse and all, after having been strongly advised to be careful in future how he confided in soldiers.

The force encamped near Lexington, which we were about to attack, was the Fourth Ohio cavalry—our old friends. The main body was at Ashland, about two miles from the town, encamped in the eastern extremity of the woods, in which the Clay mansion stands, on the southern side of the Richmond pike. One or two companies were in town, quartered at the court-house. As daylight approached, I put my regiment in motion again, detaching two companies to enter the town, under command of Captain Cassell, and capture the provost-guard, and to also picket the road toward Paris. Two other companies, under Captain Bowles, were sent to take position on the Richmond pike, at a point between the town and the camp, and about equi-distant from them. This detachment was intended to intercept the enemy if they attempted to retreat from Ashland to the town before we could surround the encampment, also to maintain communication between the detachment sent into town and the bulk of the regiment, in the event of our having to engage other forces than those we had bargained for.

Quirk had furnished very full and positive information, as has already been mentioned, but he had also stated that the Federal General Granger was at Paris (eighteen miles from Lexington), and it was not impossible that he might have been marching to Lexington within the past fifteen hours. Colonel Morgan instructed me to move with the remainder of my regiment, upon the enemy's encampment. Just as we entered the woods, and were within some five hundred yards of the enemy, a smart firing was heard upon the Richmond pike. It turned out to be a volley let off at a picket, whom Gano had failed to capture, and who ran into the camp. We thought, however, that the fight had begun, and instantly advanced at a gallop. In accordance with the plan previously arranged, Breckinridge was to attack on foot, and Gano was to support him, mounted, keeping his column on the pike. Breckinridge was in line and advancing (when this firing occurred), directly upon the enemy's front, and he opened fire just as my men formed in column of platoons, came charging upon the rear. I was upon elevated ground, about one hundred yards from the enemy's position on one side; Breckinridge was about the same distance off on the other side, and the enemy were in a slight depression between us. Consequently, I got the benefit of Breckinridge's fire—in great part at least. I saw a great cloud of white smoke suddenly puff out and rise like a wall pierced by flashes of flame, and the next instant the balls came whizzing through my column, fortunately killing no one. This volley settled the enemy and repulsed me!

Not caring to fight both Yankees and Rebels, I wheeled and took position further back, contenting myself with catching the stragglers who sought to escape. Breckinridge, however, did not enjoy his double triumph long. The howitzers had been sent to take position on the right of the enemy—to be used only in case of a stubborn resistance; they happened, on that occasion, to be under command of Sergeant, afterward First Lieutenant Corbett, a capital officer, but one constitutionally unable to avoid taking part in every fight that he was in hearing of. About the time that Breckinridge's men were taking victorious possession of the encampment, Corbett opened upon it, and shelled them away. The chapter of accidents was not yet concluded. While my regiment was watching a lot of prisoners, and was drawn up in line parallel to the pike, the men sitting carelessly on their horses, it was suddenly and unaccountably fired into by Gano's, which moved down and confronted it. Again, and this time almost miraculously, we escaped without loss. Unfortunately, however, one prisoner was shot. Colonel Morgan rushed in front of the prisoners, and narrowly escaped being killed in trying to stop the firing. His coat was pierced by several balls.

The Second Kentucky began to think that their friends were tired of them, and were plotting to put them out of the way. Gano's men stated, however, that shots were first fired at them from some quarter. My Adjutant, Captain Pat Thorpe, as gallant a man as ever breathed, came to me after this affair was over, with a serious complaint against Gano. Thorpe always dressed with some taste, and great brilliancy, and on this occasion he was wearing a beautiful Zouave jacket, thickly studded, upon the sleeves, with red coral buttons. He justly believed that every man in the brigade was well acquainted with that jacket. He stated with considerable heat that, while he was standing in front of the regiment calling, gesticulating, and trying in every way to stop the firing, Colonel Gano, "an officer for whom he entertained the most profound respect and the warmest friendship," had deliberately shot twice at him. I bade him not to think hard of it—that it was barely light at the time, and that, of course, Gano did not know him. "Ah, Colonel," he answered, "I held up my arms full in his sight, and although he might not have recognized my face, he couldn't have failed to know these buttons." Just before this occurred, Major Wash Morgan was mortally wounded by the last shot fired by the enemy. The man who hit him, was galloping toward town, and fired when within a few paces of him. This man was killed by one of the Second Kentucky, immediately afterward. All of the enemy who made their escape from the camp were intercepted by Bowles. The provost-guard made some show of fight, but were soon induced to surrender. Our force was too superior, and our attack, on all sides, too sudden, for much resistance to be offered, either at the camp or in the town. Between five and six hundred prisoners were taken, very few were killed or wounded. The most valuable capture was of army Colt's pistols, of which a large supply was obtained. Our horses were so much better than those which were captured, that few of the latter were carried off. Such of the men who had not good saddles, and blankets, provided themselves with both, in the camp.

Lexington was thrown by this affair into a state of extreme excitement and equal bewilderment; no one could exactly understand what it meant. The Union people feared, and our people hoped that it portended the return of the Confederate army. There lived (and still lives) in Lexington, an old gentleman, who was Union and loyal in his politics, but who, to use his own expression, "never saw any use in quarreling with either side which held the town." His kindness and benevolence made him very popular with people of both sides. As Colonel Morgan rode into town, this old gentleman stopped him, and said, with the strong lisp which those who know him can supply, "Well, John, you are a curious fellow! How are Kirby Smith and Gracie? Well, John, when we don't look for you, it's the very time you come."

The previous evening, the loyal people had decorated their houses with flags and many pretty ornaments, in honor of the arrival of the Federal troops; and had met them as gayly as the mythological young women used to dance before Bacchus. On the morning of the 18th, all of these symbols of joy were taken in. The Southern people, in their turn, were jubilant—"which they afterward wished they hadn't."

Resuming our march at 1 P.M., on that day, the brigade passed through Versailles, and went into camp at Shryock's ferry. Gano and Breckinridge crossed the river and encamped on the southern side; my regiment remained on the other side. About 1 o'clock at night we were awakened by the bursting of two or three shells in my camp. Dumont had learned that we had passed through Versailles, and had started out in pursuit. He sent his cavalry on the road which we had taken, and pressed his infantry out from Frankfort to Lawrenceburg. Shryock's ferry is four miles from Lawrenceburg; the country between the two points is very broken and difficult of passage.

Had every thing been kept quiet until the infantry had occupied

Lawrenceburg, our situation would have been critical indeed. With this disposition in our front, and the road closed behind us, we would have been forced to take across the country, and that would have been something like climbing over the houses to get out of a street. Colonel Morgan had hesitated to halt there in the first instance, and was induced to do so only by the fatigue of men and horses after a march of over sixty miles, and the knowledge that no fit ground for camping was within some miles. It was a generous act of the officer, who came in our rear, to shell us, and it saved us a vast deal of trouble, if nothing worse. He had not even disturbed our pickets, but turning off of the road, planted his guns on the high cliff which overlooks the ferry on that side, and sent us an intimation that we had better leave. Colonel Morgan comprehended his danger at once, and as he sprang to his feet, instructed one of the little orderlies, who always slept near him, to gallop to Colonel Gano and Major Breckinridge, and direct them to move at once to Lawrenceburg; the one, who formed first, taking the front, and picketing and holding the road to Frankfort, as soon as the town was reached. The boys, who were his orderlies, were intelligent little fellows, well known, and it was our habit to obey orders brought by them, as promptly as if delivered by a staff officer. The officers to whom the orders were sent, were the promptest of men, and although my regiment formed rapidly, the others were marching by the time that it was ready to move. The howitzers were sent across the river first (fortunately it was shallow fording at that season), and the regiment immediately followed. The pickets on the road to Versailles were withdrawn as soon as the regiment was fairly across, and the officer in charge of them was instructed to make a rear-guard of his detail. The entire brigade was hurrying to Lawrenceburg, in less than twenty minutes after the first shell awakened us. We reached Lawrenceburg a little after 2 o'clock, and passed through without halting, taking the Bloomfield road. I have heard since, but do not know if it be true, that General Dumont reached Lawrenceburg about half an hour after our rear-guard quitted it. Marching on steadily until 12 or 1 o'clock of the next day, we reached Bloomfield, a little place whose every citizen was a warm friend of "Morgan's men." They met us with the utmost kindness, and at once provided supplies of forage and provisions. We halted only about an hour to enjoy their hospitality, and then moved on toward Bardstown.

Colonel Morgan, at this time, received information that there was at Bardstown a force of infantry strong enough to give a good deal of trouble, if they chose to ensconce themselves in the houses. They were stationed there to protect sick and wounded men, and hospital stores. As there was nothing in prospect of their capture to repay for the delay, and probable loss it would cost, he determined to make a circuit around the town. This was done, the column moving within about a mile of the town (the pickets having been previously driven in), and crossing the Louisville road, two miles from the town.

We encamped that night not far from the Elizabethtown road, and some five or six miles from Bardstown. During the night Lieutenant Sales, with Company E, of the 2nd Kentucky, was sent some miles down the Louisville road, and captured one hundred and fifty wagons, the escort and many stragglers. The wagons were laden with supplies for Buell's army. They were burned, with the exception of two sutlers' wagons, which Sales brought in next morning. These wagons contained every thing to gladden a rebel's heart, from cavalry boots to ginger-bread. The brigade moved again at 10 A.M., the next day, the 20th, and reached Elizabethtown that evening. Here the prisoners picked up around Bardstown, and upon the march, who had not been paroled during the day, were given their free papers. The command went into camp on the Litchfield road, two miles from Elizabethtown. About 3 o'clock of the next morning a train of cars came down the railroad, and troops were disembarked from them. A culvert, three miles from town, had been burned the night before, in anticipation of such a visit and the train necessarily stopped at that spot. Our pickets were stationed there, and the troops were furnished a lively greeting as they got off of the cars. After a good deal of fussing with the pickets, these troops entered the town about 5 A.M., and at 6 A.M., we moved off on the Litchfield road.

The brigade encamped at Litchfield on the night of the 21st, and on the next day "crossed Green river at Morganton and Woodbury," almost in the face of the garrison of Bowlinggreen, "who pretended to try to catch us, and who would have been very much grieved if they had," as has been truthfully written. My regiment was in the rear on the morning of the 23rd, when we marched away from Morganton, and I placed it in ambush on the western side of the road, upon which the enemy were "figuring," for they could not be said to be advancing.

The road which the rest of the brigade had taken ran at right angles to this one, and my left flank rested upon it. To my astonishment, about half an hour afterward, the enemy, also, went into ambush on the same side of the road, and a few hundred yards from the right of my line. After they had gotten snug and warm, I moved off quietly after the column, leaving them "still vigilant." We crossed Mud river that night at Rochester, on a bridge constructed of three flat boats, laid endwise, tightly bound together, and propped, where the water was deep, by beams passing under the bottoms of each one and resting on the end of the next; each receiving this sort of support they mutually braced each other. A planking, some five feet wide, was then laid, and the horses, wagons, and artillery were crossed without trouble. The bridge was built in about two hours.

On the 24th we reached Greenville; that night a tremendous snow fell—tremendous, at least, for the latitude and season. After crossing Mud river, there was no longer cause for apprehension, and we marched leisurely. Colonel Morgan had found the country through which he had just passed filled, as he had expected, with detachments which he could master or evade, and with trains, which it was pleasant and profitable to catch. He and his followers felt that they had acquitted themselves well, and had wittingly left nothing undone. If there was any thing which they could have "gone for" and had not "gone for," they did not know it. A very strong disposition was felt, therefore, to halt for a few days at Hopkinsville, situated in a rich and beautiful country, the people of which were nearly all friendly to us. We knew that we would receive a hospitality which our mouths watered to think of. Colonel Morgan felt the more inclined to humor his command in this wish, because he himself fully appreciated how agreeable as well as beneficial this rest would be.

Before commencing the long and rapid march from Gum Spring to Hopkinsville, we had all been engaged in very arduous and constant service. This last mentioned march was by no means an easy one, and both men and horses began to show that fatigue was telling upon them. Many of the men were then comparatively young soldiers, and were not able to endure fatigue, want of sleep, and exposure, as they could do subsequently, when they had become as hardy and untiring as wild beasts. On this march I saw more ingenious culinary expedients devised than I had ever witnessed before. Soldiers, it is well known, never have any trouble about cooking meat; they can broil it on the coals, or, fixing it on a forked stick, roast it before a camp fire with perfect ease. So, no matter whether the meat issued them be bacon, or beef, or pork freshly slaughtered, they can speedily prepare it. An old campaigner will always contend that meat cooked in this way is the most palatable. Indeed it is hard to conceive of how to impart a more delicious flavor to fresh beef than, after a hard day's ride, by broiling it on a long stick before the right kind of a fire, taking care to pin pieces of fat upon it to make gravy; then with pepper and salt, which can be easily carried, a magnificent meal can be made, if enough is issued to keep a man cooking and eating half the night. Four or five pounds of fresh beef, thus prepared, will be mightily relished by a hungry man, but as it is easily digested he will soon become hungry again. It is the bread about which there is the trouble. Cavalry, doing such service as Morgan's did, can not carry hard tack about with them very well, nor was bread ready cooked generally found in any neighborhood (south of the Ohio) in sufficient quantities to supply a brigade of soldiers. Houses were not always conveniently near to the camps where they could have bread cooked, and as they would have it, or would not do without it many days in succession, they were thrown upon their own resources, and compelled to make it themselves, notwithstanding their lack of proper utensils. I had often seen bread baked upon a flat rock, or a board, or by twisting it around a ramrod or stick, and holding it to the fire, but one method of baking corn bread was practiced successfully upon this march which I had never witnessed before. It was invented, I believe, in Breckinridge's battalion. The men would take meal dough and fit it into a corn-shuck, tying the shucks tightly. It would then be placed among the hot embers, and in a short time would come out beautifully browned. This method was something like the Old Virginia way of making "ash cake," but was far preferable, and the bread so made was much sweeter. The trouble of making up bread (without a tray) was very readily gotten over. Every man carried an oil-cloth (as they were issued to all of the Federal cavalry), and wheaten bread was made up on one of these. Corn meal was worked up into dough in the half of a pumpkin, thoroughly scooped out. When we were in a country where meat, meal, and flour were readily obtained, and we were not compelled to march at night, but could go regularly into camp, we never had trouble in feeding the men, although on our long marches and raids we never carried cooking utensils.

At Hopkinsville, Colonel Woodward came to see Morgan; his command was encamped not far off. He had been doing excellent service in this section of the State for several months, and Colonel Morgan was very anxious to have him attached to his brigade. We remained at Hopkinsville three days, and then resumed our march.

At "Camp Coleman" we were the guests of Woodward's regiment, and their friends, in that neighborhood, brought in whole wagon loads of provisions, ready cooked—hams, turkeys, saddles-of-mutton were too common to excite remark—we realized that we were returning to "Dixie," and were not far off from Sumner county, Tennessee. We reached Springfield, Robertson county, Tennessee, on the 1st or 2nd of November.

We remained here two days. During this stay, a printing press, type, etc., having been found in the town, the "*Vidette*" made its appearance again. A full account of the Kentucky campaign was published, telling what everybody did, and hinting what was going to be done next time. Prentice and Horace Greely were properly reprimanded, and the "*London Times*" was commended and encouraged. A heavy mail had been captured, on the march through Kentucky, containing many letters denunciatory of Buell—all these were published. We were glad to do any thing which might push out of the way, the man we thought the ablest General in the Federal service.

While at Springfield, Gano's regiment was increased by the accessions of two full companies under Captains Dorch and Page. Captain Walter McLean, of Logan county, Kentucky, also joined us with some thirty or forty men. This fragment was consolidated with Company B, of the Second Kentucky, and McLean was made Captain. He was junior Captain of the regiment until Lieutenant Ralph Sheldon was promoted to the Captaincy of Company C, vice Captain Bowles promoted to the Majority, after Major Morgan's death.

On the 4th of November, we arrived at Gallatin, and were received by our friends there with the warmest welcome. We had been absent two months and a half, and we were now to perform the same work to retard the return of the Federal army into Tennessee, as we had previously done to embarrass its march into Kentucky. While at Hopkinsville, Colonel Gano had been sent with his regiment to destroy the railroad between Louisville and Nashville, and also on the Russellville branch. The bridges over Whippoorwill and Elk Fork, and the bridge between Russellville and Bowlinggreen, three miles and a half from Russellville, were burned. Captain Garth of Woodward's command joined Gano and was of great assistance to him. Some portion of the road between Bowlinggreen and Gallatin was destroyed. Lieutenant Colonel Hutchinson burned the trestle near Springfield, and the two long trestles between Springfield and

Clarksville which finished the work on that end of the road. On the 31st the trestle at the ridge, and the three small bridges between the ridge and Goodletsville were destroyed. So it will be seen that the road was scarcely in running condition when Morgan got through with it. I have thus far neglected to mention a circumstance, which should by no means be omitted from the narration of this period of Morgan's history.

A courier came from General Smith, while we were at Lexington, on the 18th of October, countermanding his permission previously given Colonel Morgan to go out of Kentucky by the Western route, on account of an order received from General Bragg instructing him to send Morgan to guard the salt works in Virginia. General Smith regretted it, but he ordered Colonel Morgan to proceed at once to that point. A staff officer who saw the order before the courier could deliver it to Colonel Morgan, pocketed it and dismissed the courier. The officer reasoned that the salt works were in no danger, that if they were, it was Marshall's peculiar province to guard them. That it was more important to operate upon the railroads, in front of Nashville, than to look after salt works, and that therefore it was better not to mention the matter.

Whether it was General Bragg's intention or not, it is certain that if we had gotten into Western Virginia, at that time, there would have been an end to all enterprise upon our part and no more reputation would have been won by us. We got there soon enough as it was. No evil consequences followed this breach of discipline. The salt works were undisturbed until a much later period.

Colonel Morgan captured nearly five hundred prisoners after he left Lexington. The railroads were destroyed, as I have related, and when he reached Gallatin, he was in a position to picket the right flank of Bragg's army, then slowly creeping around to Murfreesboro'.

When we left Hartsville the previous summer, a regiment was organizing there for Morgan's brigade, composed principally of men from Sumner county. This regiment, the Ninth Tennessee cavalry, became subsequently one of the very best in Morgan's command, and won a high reputation, but it met with many mishaps in the process of organization. It had few arms, and the enemy would come sometimes and "practice" on it. It was several times chased all over that country. When we reached Gallatin, this regiment joined the brigade; it was still in an inchoate state, but it was anxious to revenge the trouble it had been occasioned. It was organized with James Bennett as Colonel, W.W. Ward, Lieutenant Colonel, and R.A. Alston, formerly Morgan's Adjutant General, as Major. The senior captain—the famous Dick McCann—was scouting around Nashville, holding high carnival, and behaving himself much as Morgan had formerly done on the same ground.

Captain McCann had served for some time in infantry, but found it too slow for him. He accompanied our command in our first raid into Kentucky, and served with distinction as a volunteer in our advance-guard, in the operations around Gallatin, of the summer of 1862. It would be impossible to recount all of his numerous adventures. He kept himself so busy prowling around night and day, and so rarely permitted an enemy to venture beyond the fortifications of Nashville, without some token of his thoughtful attention, that, in all probability he could not remember his own history. Just before we arrived at Gallatin, however, his useful (if not innocent), existence had come very near being terminated. He had gone on a scout one night with two men, and Dr. Robert Williams (who frequently accompanied him upon those "visits," as he used to term his raids around Nashville, "to the scenes of his happy childhood)," also went with him. Not far from the city, they came upon a picket stand, and McCann sent his two men around to get between the two outpost videttes and the base, intending then to charge down on them, with the Doctor, and capture them, as he had taken many such before. The moon was shining brightly, and, as he stole closer than was prudent upon the videttes, they discovered him and fired. One ball struck him upon the brass buckle of his saber belt, which happened to be stout enough to save his life by glancing the ball, but the blow brought him from his horse and convinced him that a mortal wound was inflicted.

"Dick," said the Doctor, "are you hurt?" "Yes," groaned Dick, "killed—deader than a corpse—shot right through the bowels—Quick, Bob—pass me the bottle before I die."

Although the men had been accustomed to look forward to the time of their arrival at Gallatin, as a period when they would enjoy profound rest, they were not long left quiet after quitting there. General John C. Breckinridge had just gotten to Murfreesboro' with a small force. He was desirous of impressing the enemy at Nashville with an exaggerated idea of his strength, so that the army of Buell (or of Rosecrans it was then), might not be in any too great haste to drive him away from Murfreesboro', when it reached Nashville. General Bragg was limping on so slowly, that it was by no means certain that a swinging march would not put the enemy in possession of the whole of Middle Tennessee (with scarcely a skirmish), and shut Bragg up in East Tennessee. With the instinct, too, which he felt in common with all men who are born generals, Breckinridge wished to press upon the enemy and strike him if he discovered a vulnerable point.

He learned that a large lot of rolling-stock (of the Louisville and Nashville Railroad), had been collected in Edgefield. There were, perhaps, three hundred cars in all. If these were burned, the damage done the enemy, and the delay occasioned him, would be very great. The cars were collected at a locality commanded by the batteries on the Capitol hill, and so near the river, that all the forces in the city could be readily used to protect them. Breckinridge depended upon Morgan to burn them, but planned a diversion on the south side of the river, which he hoped would attract the enemy's attention strongly, and long enough, to enable Morgan to do his work.

The day after we arrived at Gallatin, a dispatch was received from General Breckinridge, communicating his plan. Forrest was to move on the southeastern side of Nashville, supported by the Kentucky infantry brigade, and Morgan was instructed to dash into Edgefield and burn the cars, while Forrest was making all the racket he could. There was one flaw in this plan, which no one perceived until all was over. Morgan could not hope to succeed, unless, by moving all night, he got close enough to Edgefield, to dash in early in the morning, before his presence was even suspected. If he marched in the day time, or remained after daylight in the vicinity of the place, his presence would certainly be discovered, and preparations would be made to receive him. But if he attacked at daylight, he scarcely allowed time for the troops on the other side to commence their work, or at any rate, was likely to attack simultaneously with them; when their attack, rousing every thing, would, perhaps, do more harm than good. It so turned out.

Our brigade moved all night (of the 5th), and striking through the woods came upon the northern side of Edgefield. Just as we struck the pickets, we heard Forrest's guns on the other side of the river. The Second Kentucky was in advance, and as the head of the column was struggling over a very rough place in the railroad, it was opened upon by a company of infantry pickets, who came out from behind a small house, about sixty yards off. I never saw men fight better than these fellows did. They were forty or fifty strong, and had to retreat about half a mile, to reach their lines. The timber of the ground over which they had to retreat had been cut down to leave the way clear for the play of artillery and we could not charge them. Few men beside those in the advance guard got a chance at them. They turned and fought at every step. At least eight or ten were killed, and only three captured.

I lost three of my advance guard. Conrad of the guard was riding a large gray horse, which saved his life. He rode close upon the enemy, and one of them, presenting his gun within a few feet of his breast, fired; Conrad reined his horse tightly, making him rear and receive the ball in his chest. The horse fell dead, pinning his rider to the ground. We pressed on to within a hundred yards of the railroad embankment, in the bottom near the river, and quite through Edgefield. Some little time was required to get all the regiment up, and Hutchinson and I had just formed it, and the line was advancing, when Colonel Morgan ordered us back. He had reconnoitered, and had seen a strong force of infantry behind the embankment; and the fire slackening on the other side, induced him to suppose that more infantry, which we could see double-quicking across the pontoon bridge, was the entire garrison of that side coming to oppose him. It turned out that this force coming over the bridge, was small; but the Sixteenth Illinois and part of another regiment, were stationed behind the embankment, and among the cars we wished to burn. We succeeded in burning a few—Lieutenants Drake and Quirk (who generally hunted together) superintended the work. A good deal of firing was kept up by the enemy upon the detail engaged in the work of destruction, but without effect. So little attention was paid to what Forrest was doing, that when we drew off altogether, the enemy followed us a mile or two. As the column filed off from the by-road (by which it had approached Edgefield) on the

Gallatin pike, the enemy drove back the pickets which had been sent down the pike.

The point at which we entered the pike is about a mile and a quarter from Nashville. For a while there seemed to be great danger that the enemy would take us in flank, but the column got fairly out upon the pike before the blue-coats hove in sight. A few of us remained behind after the rear guard passed to ascertain the truth of a report the pickets brought, that the enemy were moving up artillery. The head of an infantry column had made its appearance on the pike, but halted about three hundred yards from where we were, and no firing had as yet occurred on either side. They seemed disposed to reconnoiter, and we were not anxious to draw their fire.

Hutchinson soon determined to see them closer, and called to one of the advance guard, whom he had kept with him, to accompany him. This man was celebrated, not only for his cool, unflinching courage, but also as the best shot in the Second Kentucky. Every old "Morgan man" will remember, if he has not already recognized, Billy Cooper. Breckinridge and I remonstrated with Hutchinson, and urged that his action would only precipitate the enemy's attack and our retreat—that we would be driven away before we had witnessed all that we wished to see. There were only seven or eight men in our party; Gano encouraged him to go—and he declared that he would go—unless I positively ordered him to remain. He accordingly started—Cooper with him. There was a considerable depression in the pike between our position and that of the enemy. Just as our enterprising friends got down into this hollow, and about half of the distance they were going, the enemy, having completed the necessary dispositions, commenced moving forward. I shouted to Hutchinson, informing him of it, but the noise of his horse's hoofs drowned my voice; before he discovered the enemy, he was in thirty paces of their column. He fired his pistol, and Cooper, rising in his stirrups, discharged his gun killing a man; both then wheeled and spurred away at full speed. They got back into the hollow in time to save themselves, but while we were admiring their rapid retreat and particularly noticing Hutchinson, who came back in great glee, whipping his horse with his hat as was his custom when in a tight place, a volley, intended for them, came rattling into us. Two or three citizens who had collected to see the fun fled like deer, although one of them was a cripple—and, to tell the truth, we left as rapidly.

I shall never forget this occasion, because it was the first and only time that I ever saw Colonel Richard M. Gano frightened. He was sitting on his horse, complacently eyeing Hutchinson's brisk retreat, and, apparently, not even remotely supposing that the enemy were likely to fire. One ball pierced a Mexican blanket which was wrapped around him, sending the red stuff with which it was lined flying about his head. I thought, and so did he, that it was his blood. If I had been mortally wounded, I could not have helped laughing at the injured look he at once drew on; it was the look of a man who had confided, and had been deceived. "Why, Duke," he said, "they're shooting at us." Some one told Major Alston that something was going on in the rear, "that would do to go in the papers," and he joined us, as the enemy fired a second volley, just in time to get his best horse shot. Although we burned a few cars, the expedition was a failure—we went to burn all. Returning to Gallatin that night (the 6th), we found that we were not yet to be permitted rest. Our scouts soon began to bring in news of the approach of Rosecrans' army, which was marching by the Louisville and Nashville pike, and the Scottsville and Gallatin pike, to Nashville. Crittenden's corps was in advance, a portion on each road. Colonel Morgan determined to ambuscade the division marching on the Louisville and Nashville road, at a point near Tyree Springs. He selected two hundred men for the expedition. So much excitement was anticipated upon it, that all of his field officers begged to go. After a good deal of solicitation, he permitted Gano and myself to accompany him, leaving Hutchinson in command of the remainder of the brigade at Gallatin. The party detailed for this expedition, reached the neighborhood of the proposed scene of ambush late at night, and on the next morning (the 8th), at daybreak, took position.

The Federal troops had encamped at Tyree Springs the night before. First one or two sutlers' wagons passed, which were not molested, although when we saw one fellow stop, and deliberately kill and skin a sheep and throw it into his wagon, a general desire was felt to rob him in his turn. After a little while, an advance guard of cavalry came, and then the infantry rolled along in steady column, laughing and singing in the fresh morning air. As soon as the head of the column approached our position, our line arose and fired. We were within seventy-five yards of the road, on a hill, which told against our chances of doing execution, but the men had been cautioned to aim low. The column, unprepared for such an entertainment, recoiled, but soon rallied and charged the hill. Artillery was brought up and opened upon us. We did not stay long. Our loss was one man killed. I have never been able to learn satisfactorily what was the enemy's loss. Many reports were received about it, some of which must have been greatly exaggerated. Colonel Morgan immediately moved rapidly to get in the rear of this column. He accordingly struck the road again, some three miles north of Tyree Springs. Posting the bulk of his force in a woods on the side of the road, he, himself, with Lieutenant Quirk and two or three others, went some distance up the pike, and occupied themselves in picking up stragglers, which he would send back to the main body, where they would be placed under guard. In this way some forty or fifty prisoners were taken. Suddenly Stokes' regiment came up the road from toward Tyree Springs, and drove the detachment immediately upon the road, consisting of about fifty men, back to the main body, thus cutting off Colonel Morgan and his party. Couriers were immediately sent to Colonel Morgan to warn him of his danger, but they did not reach him. He was returning, however, about that time, and quickened his pace when he heard a few shots fired. He was bringing back some ten or twelve prisoners. He, Lieutenant Quirk, and one or two men, forming the head of a column, of which the prisoners composed the body. Suddenly he rode right into this Federal regiment. He was, of course, halted and questioned. He stated that he was a Federal Colonel, that his regiment was only a short distance off, and that the prisoners with him were men he had arrested for straggling. His questioners strongly doubted his story, and said that his dress was a very strange one for a Federal Colonel, that rebels often wore blue clothes, but they had never heard of their officers wearing gray. The prisoners, who knew him, and never doubted that he would be now captured in his turn, listened, grinning, to the conversation, but said nothing. He suddenly pretended to grow angry, said that he would bring his regiment to convince them who he was, and galloped away. Quirk followed him. Before an effort could be made to stop them, they leaped their horses over the fence, and struck, at full speed, across the country. In the course of an hour they rejoined the rest of us, and relieved our minds of very grave apprehensions.

It is probable that no other man than Colonel Morgan would have escaped (in such a situation) death or capture. But his presence of mind and address, in the midst of a great and imminent danger, were literally perfect. I have known many similar escapes, where the chances were not so desperate; but in each case but this, there was some circumstance to intimidate, or to contribute to mystify the enemy. On this occasion every circumstance was adverse to him. He could expect no rescue from his friends, for we had managed so badly, that the enemy had gotten between him and us. He was dressed in full Confederate uniform. The enemy knew that the Confederate forces were near by, and it was reasonable to suppose that he was attached to them. The prisoners were there to tell on him. He had nothing to depend upon but the audacity and address which never failed him, and a quality even higher than courage—I can describe it only as the faculty of subjecting every one to his will, whom he tried to influence; it was almost mesmeric. The prisoners fifty or sixty in number, were paroled in the course of the day and started back to Kentucky by a route which would enable them to avoid meeting detachments of their own army. Our party encamped that night about seven miles from Gallatin. Colonel Morgan when he started upon this expedition, knew that Wood's and Van Cleve's divisions were marching toward Gallatin, and he cautioned Hutchinson not to make a fight, if during his absence the enemy approached the town, simultaneously, upon more than two roads. He knew that Hutchinson would be vigilant, but he feared that his indisposition to avoid fighting would induce him to engage a larger force of the enemy than he could repulse. Early in the morning of the day succeeding that on which the events I have just described occurred, the enemy marched into Gallatin. They had threatened the place on three sides during the night, but Hutchinson hoping to repulse them, would not retire.

In the morning, however, they demonstrated in such strength, as to convince him that he had better not fight—and so, sending the brigade on the Lebanon road to cross the Cumberland, he retained only the advance-guard of the Second Kentucky, and the howitzers, to salute the enemy as they entered. His guns were planted upon the eminence on the Lebanon road, just outside of town, and, as the head of a column of infantry turned into that road, they were opened, causing it to recoil. Several good shots were made, but as the little pieces were limbered up to move off, a line of infantry was discovered drawn up across the road in the rear of the party—it had taken position very quietly, while they were amusing themselves cannonading the troops in town.

Hutchinson, Breckinridge, Alston, and nearly every field and staff officer of the brigade, were in the trap. They tried to escape upon another road, and found that also blockaded. Finally, sending the howitzers and the advance-guard across a pasture into the Springfield road, Hutchinson, with the numerous "officials" in his train, made the best of his way across the country, and rejoined the brigade. The advance-guard and the howitzers dashed gallantly past a large body of the enemy, but were neither checked nor injured. The retreat of the others, diverted (as was intended) attention from them to some extent, and they rattled on down the pike at a brisk canter, confident, now (that they were not surrounded), that they could whip a moderate sized brigade.

About three miles from town, they met our detachment of two hundred men; at first (thinking us a party of the enemy sent to enter the town by that road), they prepared to attack and route us, but finding out who we were, let us off with the scare. We had already learned that the enemy had entered Gallatin, and I was especially rejoiced to find the "bull pups," and my advance-guard—the flower of my regiment—all safe. Colonel Morgan learned directly from the officer in command of this party, the particulars of the affair, and was satisfied that all had gotten away. We at once turned toward the river, and marching, until we reached it, through the woods and fields, crossed at a ford, some miles lower down than that which the brigade had crossed. We reached Lebanon on the same afternoon, and found our fugitive friends there. Colonel Morgan formally congratulated Hutchinson upon his "improved method of holding a town."

This was the 9th, and the bulk of the brigade went into camp, four miles from Lebanon, on the Murfreesboro' pike. As Rosecrans' army came pouring into Nashville, the commandant there manifested a strong disposition to learn how matters stood outside. On the night of the 9th, a force of the enemy came down the Nashville and Lebanon pike to Silver Springs, seven miles from Lebanon. Scouts were sent to examine this force, and returned, reporting that it manifested no disposition to move. Almost immediately after the scouts came back to Lebanon, the enemy came, too, having moved just behind the scouts. There was no force in Lebanon to meet them, and they held the place until Hine's company, of Breckinridge's battalion, was sent to drive them out. That night Breckinridge's entire battalion was sent to the town, supported by Bennett's regiment. On the evening of the 11th, they were both driven away, by a heavy force of infantry and cavalry, but, reinforced by Gano, checked the enemy a short distance from the town. When the enemy retreated, Gano pressed them, taking one hundred and fifty-eight prisoners, and a number of guns. On the 13th or 14th, the enemy returned, and Breckinridge drove them away, following them eleven miles on the Hartsville pike. On this occasion a very handsome feat was performed by a scouting party under command of Sergeant McCormick, of Breckinridge's battalion. Billy Peyton, who had killed an officer and brought off his horse and pistol, a day or two before, went with him as "military adviser." Major Breckinridge sent this scouting party to find where the enemy halted. It went through the woods and found the enemy encamped on the river bank, fifteen miles from Lebanon. Returning by the road, the party stumbled upon a *vidette*, stationed about a half mile from the camp, and between it and a picket base, which he said was a short distance off. He also informed them that all the pickets had been notified that a scouting party would shortly leave camp, and pass through them on that road. The idea at once occurred to McCormick to represent that scouting party with his; so, carrying the prisoner with him, he rode through the pickets at the head of his men, receiving and returning their salutes. John Haps, of Company F, Second Kentucky, tightly gripping the prisoner's throat, meanwhile, to prevent inopportune disclosures. Just as the party got clear of the base, they were discovered, and one man's horse falling, he was made prisoner. On the 15th, Breckinridge and Bennett were sent to Baird's mill, eight miles from Lebanon, and eleven from Murfreesboro', where the Second Kentucky had been encamped since the 10th. During that time it had been operating in the direction of Nashville, the most successful expedition having been made by Major Bowles, who defeated a body of the enemy superior in numbers to his own detachment, killing several and taking some prisoners. About this time a large force of the enemy took position at Jefferson, seven miles from Baird's mill. This force required constant watching, and scouts were kept in sight of the encampment at all hours of the twenty-four, with instructions to fire upon the pickets as often as each detail was relieved. Spence's battery was sent from Murfreesboro' to Baird's mill, to reinforce us. On the 16th, Gano, who had remained at Lebanon, was driven away by a large force of cavalry and two brigades of infantry. One of the latter got in his rear, and gave him a good deal of trouble. After making a gallant fight, he fell back to Baird's mill; and then carried Breckinridge, Bennett, and the Second Kentucky, back to Lebanon to attack the enemy there. Colonel Morgan had been at Black's shop, four miles nearer to Murfreesboro', for several days, and I had gone to Murfreesboro' on that day, the 16th. When I returned to Baird's mill, I found every thing gone, but a few pickets, and the scouts reported indications of an advance from Jefferson. When I reached Gano, I found him just taking position to fight (he thought), and planting his battery (Spence's) to shell the camp, the fires of which we could plainly see. I dissuaded him from opening with artillery, for I did not wish to fight at Lebanon, when there seemed such an imminent prospect of an attack upon Baird's mill. Gano was not satisfied to return until an examination showed the camp deserted. The enemy had moved off, leaving their fires burning. Gano had hurried from Baird's mill, with his reinforcements, so rapidly, that he had not given his scouts time to reconnoiter. I immediately carried the brigade back to Baird's mill. The saddles were kept upon the horses all night, and the men lay down in line of battle, but the enemy did not attack. Two or three days after this, Hutchinson was sent, with a portion of the Second Kentucky, to watch the Nashville and Lebanon pike, between Stone river and Silver Springs, at which latter place a strong force of the enemy was encamped. Information had been received that foraging parties of the enemy had been habitually resorting to that particular neighborhood, and it was thought that some of them could be caught. Hutchinson missed the foragers, but captured a picket detail thirty or forty strong, at Stone river, and brought his prisoners and their horses into camp. A little later Major Steele, with a detachment from his regiment, went on an expedition to Hartsville. Just as his column had crossed the river, and ascended the bank, it was attacked by a portion of Woolford's regiment. Major Steele was forced to recross the river and return, but before doing so, beat off his first assailants. On the 23rd, Hutchinson, with Company A, of Breckinridge's battalion, and a detail from the Second Kentucky, in all, two hundred men, and the howitzers, attacked the enemy encamped at Gallatin, landing on the southern side, and drove them out of their encampment and across the river. A good many other scouts and expeditions were made, replete with personal adventures, the details of which have escaped my memory.

It was a very busy season, and a good many prisoners were taken; they were brought in from some quarter every day. Our own loss was slight. Colonel Morgan believed that, with enemies so near him, in so many quarters, he could defend himself only by assuming the offensive.

General Bragg's army did not get to Murfreesboro' until the 20th or 21st. During that time, General Breckinridge had some four thousand infantry. Rosecrans' army must have been concentrated in Nashville by the 12th. Two days' marching would have brought them to Murfreesboro'. General Breckinridge could not have repulsed it; of course it could have been subsisted for a week off of the country, or its foragers had lost their cunning. In that time General Bragg would have been forced, in all probability, to return to East Tennessee, without a chance to deliver battle with a rational hope of success. His army was footsore, weary, and could not have been readily concentrated. Buell was removed because he was thought to be "slow," and dull to perceive and seize favorable opportunities. There will always be a difference of opinion about which opportunities were the safest to seize. A very prevalent opinion obtained in "Morgan's cavalry" (who thought that they appreciated Buell), that had he been in command at Nashville, on the 12th of November, 1862, he would have marched without delay on Murfreesboro'. It is not too much to claim that Morgan's destruction of the railroads delayed, not only the concentration at Nashville, but the movement thence to Murfreesboro'. The activity of Morgan, Forrest and the other Confederate cavalry commanders, in November, and the firm attitude of Breckinridge, also contributed to prevent it.

In the latter part of November, Colonels Cluke and Chenault

rejoined the brigade. Their regiments were not improved by the trip through the mountains, and the list of absentees from each was large. Major Stoner also brought a battalion to Morgan, transferred from Marshall's brigade. About the same time, the men of the "Old Squadron," who had been captured at Lebanon, came to us. They had been exchanged a month or two previously, but had been unable to get to the brigade sooner. We were glad to welcome them back. They had been only seven months away, and they returned to find the command they had last seen as less than half a regiment, now grown to a brigade of five regiments and two battalions.

These men were organized by Colonel Morgan, into a company of scouts, to be attached to no regiment. Lieutenant Thomas Quirk was appointed to command them, and Lieutenant Owens, who had been captured and exchanged with them, was made their First Lieutenant. Lieutenant Sellers, who had been also captured at Lebanon, was assigned to one of Bennett's companies; the scouts were at once armed, equipped and mounted—the company numbered about sixty, total effective, and was a very fine one. On the 24th, the Second Kentucky, under command of Hutchinson, and Breckinridge's battalion, were sent to Fayetteville, Lincoln county, Tennessee, to rest men and horses; and the other regiments of the brigade were less severely worked than during the past two or three weeks.

Rosecrans seemed extremely anxious to shut us out from the country around Gallatin and Hartsville—perhaps on account of the supplies of meat which could be obtained there, and which the sympathy of the people enabled us to obtain, if we could readily communicate with them. Strong garrisons were established at Gallatin and Castalian Springs, about six or eight miles from Hartsville, and at the latter place. The fact that any force of Confederates marching to attack these garrisons, unless they made a wide detour eastward, would expose its flank and rear to attack from Nashville—not to consider the resistance of the garrisons themselves—seemed to insure that country from Confederate intrusion.

But it was right hard to keep Morgan out of Sumner county—he had a great affection for it. He persistently applied for permission to attack the force stationed at Hartsville, and it was at length granted him. He was allowed to select two regiments from the Kentucky infantry brigade, and to take also Cobb's battery, a very fine one, attached to that brigade. The "Kentucky brigade" was commanded by Colonel Roger W. Hanson, who had been only a short time before exchanged, with his gallant regiment, the Second Kentucky infantry, which had been captured at Donelson. One of the colonels of the brigade, was Thomas H. Hunt, a very superior officer, who, with his regiment, the Ninth Kentucky, one of the best in the Confederate service, had seen arduous and hazardous service at Shiloh, Corinth and Baton Rouge. Colonel Morgan asked that this officer (his uncle) should command the infantry regiments, which were to form part of his force for the expedition; and Colonel Hunt selected his own regiment and the Second Kentucky (infantry).

On the morning of the 7th of December, Colonel Morgan set out on this expedition. The cavalry force was placed under my command, and consisted of Gano's, Bennett's, Cluke's and Chenault's regiments, and Stoner's battalion—in all numbering about fifteen hundred men. Hanson's brigade was encamped at Baird's mill. Here the infantry detachment joined us, seven hundred strong; the full strength of neither regiment was taken. Quirk's "scouts" and other scouting parties were sent to reconnoiter in the direction of Hartsville, to watch the enemy at Castalian Springs, and the fords of the river, and to picket the Nashville and Lebanon pike. The "combined forces" left Baird's mill about 11 A.M., and passed through Lebanon about 2 P.M., taking the Lebanon and Hartsville pike. The snow lay upon the ground and the cold was intense.

The infantry had been promised that they should ride part of the way, and, accordingly, a few miles beyond Lebanon a portion of the cavalry gave up the horses to them. This, however, was an injudicious measure. The infantry had gotten their feet wet in trudging through the snow, and, after riding a short time, were nearly frozen and clamored to dismount. The cavalrymen had now gotten their feet saturated with moisture, and when they remounted, suffered greatly in their turn. There was some trouble, too, in returning the horses to the proper parties (as this last exchange was effected after dark), and the infantrymen damned the cavalry service with all the resources of a soldier's vocabulary.

The infantry and Cobb's battery reached the ferry where it was intended that they should cross, about ten o'clock at night, and were put across in two small leaky boats, a difficult and tedious job. When the cavalry reached the ford, where Colonel Morgan had directed me to cross, I found that the river had risen so much since the last reconnoisance that it was past fording at that point, and I had to seek a crossing further down. The ford (where I decided to cross) was so difficult to come at, that the operation of crossing was made very slow. The men could reach the river bank only by a narrow bridle path which admitted only one man at a time. They were then compelled to gather their horses and leap into the river, over the bluff about four feet high. Horse and man would generally be submerged by the plunge—a cold bath very unpleasant in such weather. The ascent on the other side was nearly as difficult. In a little while the passage of the horses rendered the approach to the river even more difficult. The ford was not often used, and the unbeaten path became cut up and muddy. It grew worse and worse. The cold (after the ducking in the river) affected the men horribly; those who got across first built fires, at which they partially warmed themselves while the others were crossing. Only fifteen, however, were frozen so stiff that they had to be left.

Finding, as the night wore on, that day would appear before all got across, and fearing that I would detain Colonel Morgan, I moved (with those already on the northern bank) about three o'clock, leaving a great part of my column still on the southern side of the river. I posted pickets to watch the roads by which they could be attacked, and instructed the officers to hurry on to Hartsville as soon as practicable. I had about five miles to march to rejoin Colonel Morgan, and found him at the point he had designated, some three miles from Hartsville. He decided not to wait for the remainder of the cavalry, fearing that information would be taken to Castalian Springs (where six thousand Federal troops were encamped), and he would be himself attacked. He, therefore, moved forward at once. Just at daylight the cavalry, who were marching in front, came upon a strong picket force, about half a mile from the encampment, who fired and retreated. We were thus prevented from surprising the enemy before they formed. Colonel Morgan did not, however, expect to do so, for he had no certain plan of capturing the pickets without giving the alarm.

Bennett's regiment was immediately sent around the encampment, and into the town of Hartsville. Colonel Morgan ordered me to form Cluke's and Chenault's regiments opposite the right flank of the line the enemy were establishing, and partially outflanking it. The enemy was encamped in wooded ground, slightly elevated above the surrounding fields. The left flank of the line they formed rested upon open ground near the river. Opposite their right flank and center was a large meadow, between which and the woods was a slight depression, which gradually deepened toward the southward, until from a valley it became a ravine, and when it approached the river was perhaps ten feet deep, and its banks were almost precipitous. Colonel Morgan had intended to let the infantry of his command form in this ravine and attack from it, but the enemy's line was established so near to it that this was not attempted.

When we came in sight of the enemy and saw them forming, it was at once plain that the force there was much stronger than it had been represented to be. Instead of fifteen hundred men, as Colonel Morgan had estimated it to be from the reports of his spies, it was more than twenty-five hundred strong. I said to him, "You have more work cut out for you, than you bargained for." "Yes," he answered, "you gentleman must whip and catch these fellows, and cross the river in two hours and a half, or we'll have six thousand more on our backs." Cluke's and Chenault's regiments after deducting horse-holders, numbered four hundred and fifty men, between them. I formed Cluke opposite the One Hundred and Fourth Ohio Infantry, eight hundred strong, and formed Chenault obtusely to Cluke (on the latter's left), with his (Chenault's) left flank inclining toward the enemy, and outflanking him. The infantry were shortly afterward formed opposite the center of the enemy—Cobb's battery confronted the enemy's left flank. Our entire force in the fight (Bennett having been sent to Hartsville to prevent the escape of the enemy in that direction) was twelve hundred and fifty men. I have neglected to state that Stoner's battalion had been sent, with the "Bull pups," down the Hartsville and Lebanon pike to take position opposite the enemy's encampment. Stoner was instructed to maneuver in sight of the enemy, and shell away at them briskly. Colonel Morgan knew that the little pieces could not reach the encampment, but he wished the enemy's attention attracted to that quarter.

Stoner succeeded so well that the two Parrot guns which the enemy had were engaged with him, when we took position, and we were spared the annoyance they could have inflicted while we were forming. As I have said we failed to surprise the Federal force in its camp—and the only advantage which our sudden appearance gave us, was the partial demoralization which is apt to assail all troops, when unexpectedly and promptly attacked. The enemy naturally thought that we were in overwhelming force, or that we would not have incurred such risks.

One good sign was, that, as we formed in sight of each other, our ringing shouts were answered by the feeblest of cheers. Cluke and Chenault having formed at a gallop, immediately dismounted their men and advanced. The enemy's line was about four hundred yards distant. A line of skirmishers occupied the hollow, posted behind a fence, whose fire did us some little damage. These two regiments had never been under fire before (with the exception of a slight skirmish which Cluke's had witnessed in Kentucky) and I was not at first certain that they would drive their part of the line. But they moved on with perfect steadiness, halting (after having advanced about a hundred yards) to discharge a volley which dislodged the skirmishers, and then, after reloading, pressed on at a swift run. The enemy fired by rank, each volley passing over our heads, for the men had reached the hollow. No time was given them to reload. When within sixty yards our fellows opened, Cluke pressing right upon the front, and Chenault having swept so far round, and then closed in, that the two regiments were firing almost into each other's faces.

The open cavalry formation not only enabled us with a smaller force, to cover the entire front of the enemy opposed to us, but while exposing us to less loss, made our fire more deadly. The One Hundred and Fourth Ohio backed about twenty steps, the men striving to reload their guns, and it then broke and ran in perfect disorder. Cluke and Chenault moved on, swinging around to the right, until they were formed at right angles to the original direction of their line, and the force confronting them was lapped back upon the rest of the enemy's line. This lasted about twenty minutes. By that time Colonel Hunt had formed his infantry, and he sent them in, in echelon, the Second Kentucky in advance. Cobb's battery had not been idle, and had gotten one caisson blown up by a shell from one of the enemy's Parrots.

The infantry had marched quite thirty miles, over slippery roads, and through the chilling cold, and I saw some of them stumble (as they charged), with fatigue and numbness, but the brave boys rushed in as if they were going to a frolic. The Second Kentucky dashed over the ravine, and as they emerged in some disorder, an unfortunate order was given them, to halt and "dress." There was no necessity for it—the regiment was within fifty yards of the enemy, who were recoiling and dropping before their fire. Several officers sprang to the front and countermanded the order—it was a matter of doubt who gave it—and Captain Joyes, seizing the colors, shouted to the men to follow him.

The regiment rushed on again, but in that brief halt, sustained nearly all of its loss. Just then, the Ninth Kentucky came to its support—the men yelling and gliding over the ground like panthers. The enemy gave way in confusion, and were pressed again on their right and rear by Cluke and Chenault, who were at this juncture reinforced by seventy-five men of Gano's regiment, who came up under Lieutenant Colonel Huffman, commanding the regiment in Gano's absence, and Major Steele, and at once went into the fight. A few minutes then sufficed to finish the affair. The enemy were crowded together in a narrow space, and were dropping like sheep. The white flag was hoisted in an hour after the first shot was fired. Our loss in killed and wounded was one hundred and twenty-five, of which the Second Kentucky lost sixty-five, the Ninth, eighteen; the cavalry thirty-two, and Cobb's battery, ten. Lieutenant Colonel Coleman, a gallant and accomplished officer, was seriously wounded. His regiment, the Eighth Kentucky (Cluke's), was devotedly attached to him, and could ill afford to lose his valuable services. Some fine officers were lost by the infantry regiments. A loss which was deeply regretted by Morgan's entire command, was that of little Craven Peyton. Colonel Morgan invariably selected as his orderlies bright, intelligent, gentlemanly little fellows from among the boys of his command. They were not required to perform the ordinary services of an orderly, but were treated more like staff officers, and were assigned such duties, as are usually required of an aide.

This was an excellent method of spoiling young soldiers—but Colonel Morgan permitted himself such luxuries. Of all these, Craven Peyton was the most celebrated and popular. His integrity and sense was such, that officers of the command would not hesitate to act upon an order which he bore, although unwritten, and he possessed the most remarkable daring and determination. Exposing himself in this fight with his usual recklessness, he received a wound, which disabled him so much that he could not be removed. He was made prisoner, and in a few days fretted himself to death. The enemy's loss, in killed and wounded, was over four hundred, and two thousand and four prisoners were carried off to Murfreesboro'. If there ever was a fight to which the time honored phrase, so frequent in official reports, was applicable, viz.: "That where all behaved so well," etc.,—it was this one. It would indeed be difficult to assign the palm. Every officer and man seemed inspired with the most perfect confidence and the most dauntless resolution. Every regiment and company rushed recklessly and irresistibly upon every thing confronting it, and the sudden discovery, at the beginning of the fight, that the enemy were so much stronger than we had supposed them to be, seemed only to increase their courage. They had literally made up their minds not to be beaten, and I firmly believe, that five thousand more could not have beaten them. The tents, and every thing which could not be carried off, were burned; a number of captured wagons were loaded with arms and portable stores, and hurried over the river—four or five wagons which did not cross the river, were driven into the woods and their contents secreted. Some of the most valuable captures, were in boots and shoes—for many of the men (especially of Cluke's and Chenault's regiments) had no other covering for their feet than old rags.

The prisoners were gotten across the river as rapidly as possible—

and the infantry were taken over behind the cavalrymen. Some of the prisoners were made to wade the river, as the enemy from Castalian Springs began to press upon us so closely that we could not "stand upon the order of transportation." Cluke's regiment was posted upon the Gallatin road to hold the enemy in check—Quirk's scouts having already retarded their advance. Gano's regiment was sent as soon as it got up to support Cluke. Nothing but the rapid style in which the fight had been conducted and finished saved us. We had no sooner evacuated the ground than the enemy occupied it, and our guns which opened upon them from the southern shore, were answered by their batteries.

No pursuit was attempted, and we marched leisurely back through Lebanon, regaining our camps late in the night. Two splendid pieces of artillery were among the trophies—which did good service in our hands, until they were recaptured upon the "Ohio raid." This expedition was justly esteemed the most brilliant thing that Morgan had ever done, and was referred to with pride by every man who was in it.

General Bragg in his congratulatory order issued to the army on account of it, spoke in the highest terms of the conduct of the troops—especially of the remarkable march of the infantry, and he says: "To Brigadier General Morgan and to Colonel Hunt the General tenders his thanks, and assures them of the admiration of his army. The intelligence, zeal and gallantry displayed by them will serve as an example and an incentive to still more honorable deeds. To the other brave officers and men composing the expedition the General tenders his cordial thanks and congratulations. He is proud of them and hails the success achieved by their valor as but the precursor of still greater victories. Each corps engaged in the action will in future bear upon its colors the name of the memorable field."

CHAPTER XII

The victory of Hartsville brought Colonel Morgan his long-expected and long-delayed commission of Brigadier-General. He had long been styled General by his men, and had been of late habitually so addressed in official communications from array headquarters. Many and urgent applications had been made by influential parties and officers of high rank for his promotion. General Smith had strongly urged it, General Bragg concurring, but while Brigadiers were being uttered as rapidly almost as Confederate money, he remained a simple Colonel. President Davis happened to visit Murfreesboro' a few days after the Hartsville affair, and gave him his commission, making Hanson, also, a Brigadier of even date. This promotion of my chief made me a Colonel, and Hutchinson a Lieutenant-Colonel, thus illustrating that many felicitous consequences will sometimes flow from one good act. The latter had occupied a very anomalous position; while really a Captain, he had acted us, and been styled Lieutenant-Colonel. Being a most excellent officer, who had seen a great deal of service, and acting as second in command of an unusually large regiment, he was placed frequently upon detached service, and in very responsible situations, and frequently commanded Lieutenant-Colonels of legitimate manufacture, just as Morgan, while only a General "by courtesy," commanded floating Brigadiers who came within his vortex. It proved more agreeable to men, who were really modest, to take rank by the virtue of commissions rather than by the force of impudence, and the example was better. General Hardee urged that the commission should be made out as Major-General, but Mr. Davis said, "I do not wish to give my boys all of their sugar plums at once."

At Bryantsville, in Kentucky, Colonel Joseph Wheeler had been appointed Chief of Cavalry, and Morgan, Scott, Ashby—all of the cavalry commanders had been ordered to report to him. Colonel Wheeler was a very dashing officer, and had done excellent service, but he had neither the experience nor the record of Morgan, and the latter did not fancy having to serve under him. He was with Wheeler so little, however, in Kentucky, that he found not much inconvenience from having a "Chief of cavalry" to superintend him. Morgan was, of course, perfectly independent upon his retreat out of Kentucky, and in his operations afterward in North Middle Tennessee—indeed, with the exception of having to report to General Breckinridge, while the latter was in command at Murfreesboro', and afterward to the Commander-in-chief, he was perfectly independent until a period even later than that of his promotion. But this is a subject for a later chapter. A great many injudicious friends of Morgan were inclined to attribute the delay of his promotion to prejudice upon the part of Mr. Davis, against him in particular, and Kentuckians in general.

There is no doubt but that General Morgan's free and easy way of appointing his own officers and of conducting all of his military affairs, as well as his intense aversion to subordinate positions, had excited much official disapprobation and some indignation against him at Richmond. He had been careless and dilatory, too, in making out and forwarding the muster-rolls of his regiment, an omission which was undoubtedly censurable, and unpardonable in the eyes of the *Pundits* of the War Department, with whom such papers were the gospels of military government. General Morgan paid too little attention to matters of this kind, essential to the transaction of military business, and the proper conduct of the affairs of the army, and the authorities resented a neglect that looked a good deal like contumacious disrespect. He was, however, unlucky in this respect, to some extent, for when he appreciated, which was not until after he had raised the greater portion of his brigade, the necessity and the propriety of making full, formal, and prompt returns, he met with delays and accidents in transmitting them to Richmond, which were frequent and extraordinary. The officers, who acted as his Adjutant Generals at different periods previously to his promotion, will remember and can affirm, that returns and rolls of his regiments and battalions composing his brigade, were sent into them, and forwarded by them to

Richmond. Officers were especially detailed to go to Richmond and look after these papers. And, yet, to every application made for the appointment of bonded officers (or rather for their commissions, for Morgan could manage appointments), by commanders of the oldest regiments in his brigade, the Secretary of War would politely inform the Colonel that his regiment was unknown "in the records of this office." Judging from the frequency of this reply, and the nature of some promotions that were made for that quarter, it would appear that the War Department at Richmond, and the cavalry on the western front, had no acquaintance in common. That all the evil might be cured, papers of formidable size and appearance, nearly square (I should say an acre by an arpent), were carefully made out, and forwarded to Richmond, showing the date of the organization of each regiment, the officers originally upon its rolls, all changes, and how they occurred, up to the date of the making out of the compendious document, the names of the officers serving in it at the time, and the manner in which they obtained their rank, whether by appointment, election, or promotion, and by whom appointed, when such was their status.

Notwithstanding the work expended upon the accursed things, and the perspiration, and, I regret to say, blasphemy, which they elicited from some of our officers, they did no good in the world; and after more labor and tribulation, ten to one, than an advance of the whole Federal army would have cost us, we found ourselves as much outsiders as ever. It must be distinctly understood, that nothing here written is intended as an insinuation against Mr. Davis; I will not do *that* which I would join in condemning in another man, whose antecedents are like my own. The profound respect I feel for him, prevents any attempt, upon my part, at even such criticism of his action as may seem legitimate; and unkind and carping reflections upon him are more becoming in the mouths of non-combatant rebels, than from ex-Confederate soldiers, whom self-respect should restrain from any thing of the kind. But there were certain officers at Richmond, who, if their souls had been tied up with red tape, indorsed in accordance with the latest orders, and stuffed into pigeon holes, would have preferred it to a guarantee of salvation. I honestly believe that these gentlemen thought, that when an officer made out a muster-roll, and forwarded it to them, he had done his full duty to his country, had gotten through with his part of the war, and might go to sleep without putting out pickets. It was said of a certain Confederate General, of high rank, that he would rather have from his subordinates "a neat and formal report of a defeat, than a slovenly account of a victory." It might have been said of the war office gentry, with equal propriety, that they would have preferred an army composed of Fallstaffian regiments, all duly recorded, to a magnificent soldiery unticketed at Richmond.

With this class Morgan was always unpopular; not that a stronger personal dislike was felt for him, in the official bosom, than for other men of the same stamp and style, but all such men were gravely disliked by this class. Such men were developing new ideas, not to be found in the books which the others had studied, and were in the habit of consulting. They were managing cavalry and winning fights in a thoroughly irregular and revolutionary manner; there was grave cause for apprehension that, if they were given high rank and corresponding command, they would innovate upon established infantry *tactique*, in the same unprecedented and demoralizing style. Mr. Davis did not dislike Morgan, but simply entertained no particular fancy for him, and did not believe that he was really a superior, although a successful officer; in fact, he knew very little about him.

To say Mr. Davis disliked Kentuckians, is absurd. The Kentucky vanity is as irritable, although not as radical, as the Virginian, and sees a slight in every thing short of a caress. He appointed some fifteen general officers from Kentucky, and he permitted the Kentucky loafers to secure their full share of "soft places." General Bragg, doubtless, was entirely free from any blinding affection for Kentuckians, and few of them felt a tenderness for him. Despite the terrors of his stern rule, they let few occasions escape of evincing their feeling toward him. It was said, I know not how truly, that at a later date General Bragg told Mr. Davis that "General Morgan was an officer who had few superiors, none, perhaps, in his own line, but that he was a *dangerous man*, on account of his intense desire to act independently."

When Morgan received this rank, his brigade was quite strong, and composed of seven regiments, Breckinridge's and Stoner's battalions were consolidated, and formed a regiment above the minimum strength. Breckinridge became Colonel, and Stoner Lieutenant Colonel. Shortly after the Hartsville fight, Colonel Adam R. Johnson reached Murfreesboro' with his regiment. It had been raised in Western Kentucky, and was very strong upon the rolls, but from losses by capture, and other causes, had been reduced to less than four hundred effective men. It was a fine body of men, and splendidly officered. Martin, the Lieutenant Colonel, was a man of extraordinary dash and resolution, and very shrewd in partisan warfare. Owens, the Major, was a very gallant man, and the disciplinarian of the regiment.

On the 14th of December, an event occurred which was thought by many to have materially affected General Morgan's temper, and subsequent fortunes. He was married to Miss Ready, of Murfreesboro', a lady to whom he was devotedly attached, and who certainly deserved to exercise over him the great influence which she was thought to have possessed. The marriage ceremony was performed by General Polk, by virtue of his commission as Bishop, but in full Lieutenant General's uniform. The residence of the Honorable Charles Ready, father of the bride, held a happy assembly that night—it was one of a very few scenes of happiness which that house was destined to witness, before its olden memories of joy and gayety were to give place to heavy sorrow and the harsh insolence of the invader. The bridegroom's friends and brothers-in-arms, and the Commander-in-Chief, and Generals Hardee, Cheatham and Breckinridge felt called upon to stand by him on this occasion.

Greenfell was in a high state of delight; although he had regretted

General Morgan's marriage—thinking that it would render him less enterprising—he declared, that a wedding, at which an Episcopal bishop-militant, clad in general's uniform officiated, and the chief of an army and his corps commanders were guests, certainly ought not to soften a soldier's temper. On his way home that night he sang Moorish songs, with a French accent, to English airs, and was as mild and agreeable as if some one was going to be killed.

The seven regiments which composed the brigade, represented an aggregate force of over four thousand in camp—when they were gotten together, which was about the 18th, the Second Kentucky returning then from Fayetteville. Several hundred men, however, were dismounted, and totally unarmed and unequipped. This force was so unwieldy, as one brigade, that General Morgan determined to divide it into two parts, which should be organized in all respects as two brigades, and should lack but the sanction of the General commanding (which he hoped to obtain), to be such in reality. He accordingly indicated as the commanders of the two brigades (as I shall call them for the sake of convenience), Colonel Breckinridge and myself. There was no doubt of Colonel A.R. Johnson's seniority to all the other colonels, but, for some reason, he positively declined to accept the command of either brigade, and signified his willingness to serve in a subordinate capacity.

Instances of senior officers waiving rank, and consenting to serve under their juniors, were not unfrequent at that period, and continued to occur in Morgan's command. Such conduct was generous, and prompted by the manliest and most patriotic motives; but I can not help thinking that it is an unsafe practice, and one that may lead to very great injuries to the service in which it commonly obtains. The spirit which prompted many officers (for instance, who outranked General Morgan), to serve subordinately to him, because of the influence upon the troops of his high reputation, and because of his recognized skill, was perhaps, a proper as well as a chivalric one. But, except where the talent, character and influence of the junior, are as rare as acknowledged, and as commanding as in the case of Morgan or of Forrest, it is better for the senior to assume his legal position. No bad effects ever resulted from this practice in our command, partly, because it was one which had a "genius and constitution" of its own, but, chiefly because (I do not think I am speaking too highly of my old comrades), it was officered by a class of men of remarkable intelligence, and singular directness as well as strength of character. But, supposing this custom to prevail, generally, how apparent are the results prejudicial to discipline and efficiency, which may be naturally expected to flow from it.

The senior officer who "waives his rank," may do it in perfect good faith, and believing that the junior whom he consents to serve under, is, for certain reasons, the most proper man to command—and yet, if things go wrong, he may not unnaturally complain or advise with an emphasis and a freedom that may embarrass the commander to whom it is addressed, and create the most improper feeling among other subordinates and the men.

Or if matters do not go so far as this, there may yet arise a regret, in the mind of the officer who has relinquished his right to command, when he sees, or thinks he sees, evidences of incompetency in the conduct of the other—and a corresponding jealousy may be thus awakened in the mind of the junior commanding—and that harmony which is so necessary to efficiency may become impaired. Independently of these considerations, there is the fact that this condition is abnormal and highly irregular. The men and subaltern officers will recognize it to be so, and it may become more difficult to maintain the requisite subordination and respect for rank. It is a great deal better than to follow this practice—to adopt and run almost to extremes, the system of rapid promotion for merit and distinguished conduct. The probable evils of the one practice, which have been indicated, can prevail under no system where every man fills his legitimate place. There was some discussion as to whether Cluke or Breckinridge should command one of the brigades, after Johnson declined. It was a mooted question, whether Cluke's rank as Colonel dated from the period at which he received his commission to raise a regiment, or from the period at which his regiment became filled. In the former case, he would rank Breckinridge; in the latter, he would not. None of us, then, (with the exception of Johnson), had received our commissions, although our rank was recognized.

There was no wrangle for the position, however, between these officers, as might be inferred from my language. On the contrary, each at first declined, and urged the appointment of the other. General Morgan settled the matter by appointing Breckinridge.

The first brigade (mine) was composed of the Second Kentucky, Lieut.-Colonel Hutchinson, commanding; Gano's regiment, the Third Kentucky, Lieut.-Colonel Huffman commanding (Gano was absent on furlough); Cluke's regiment, the Eighth Kentucky, Colonel Leroy S. Cluke commanding; Palmer's battery of four pieces (two twelve-pounder howitzers, and two six-pounder guns,) was attached to this brigade. The second brigade (Breckinridge's) was composed of his own regiment, the Ninth Kentucky, Lieutenant-Colonel Stoner commanding; Johnson's regiment, the Tenth Kentucky, Colonel Johnson commanding; Chenault's regiment, the Eleventh Kentucky, Colonel Chenault commanding; and Bennett's regiment, the Fourteenth Tennessee, Colonel Bennett commanding. To this brigade was attached one three-inch Parrot, commanded by Captain White, and the two mountain howitzers under Lieutenant Corbett.

On the 21st of December, the division was in camp at and around Alexandria. The first brigade was reviewed on that day, and numbered, of cavalry, eighteen hundred effective men. There were in its ranks more men than that number. The Second Kentucky mustered seven hundred and forty, and the other two regiments about six hundred each. There were in this brigade, however, nearly two hundred men unarmed but mounted. The entire strength of the brigade, of armed and unarmed men, including Palmer's battery, was very little short of two thousand and one hundred men. The second brigade was, including artillerists, about eighteen hundred strong, but it, too, had some unarmed men in its ranks. These fellows without guns were not so useless as might be imagined, for (when it was satisfactorily ascertained that it was not their own fault that they were unarmed, and that they could be trusted) they were employed as horse-holders. The division, therefore, including Quirk's "scouts," reporting to division headquarters, numbered quite three thousand and nine hundred. In General Morgan's report of the expedition undertaken into Kentucky immediately after this organization, the strength of the division is estimated at thirty-one hundred armed men. This was a mistake upon the part of his Adjutant-General, which I sought to correct at the time. The proportion of men without guns was nothing like so large. Just before the march was taken up for Kentucky from Alexandria, Colonel Greenfell, still acting as General Morgan's Adjutant-General up to that date, resigned his position and declined to accompany him upon the expedition. The cause of his dissatisfaction was the appointment of Breckinridge to the command of the second brigade. A great many believed and said that he was disappointed at not obtaining command of the brigade himself, but I am satisfied that such was not the case. It is difficult to understand how a practical man can behave as he did on that occasion, unless his own interests, or those of a friend, are involved, and there is, consequently, a general disposition to attribute such conduct to interested motives. I talked to Greenfell, and believe that he had, from some cause, conceived a violent dislike for Breckinridge, and, moreover, he had come to regard an interference in the affairs of the command as his right. At any rate when General Morgan declined to accept his suggestions upon the subject, and requested him to desist from agitating it, he became so thoroughly disgusted that he declined to act longer with the command. As he was not regularly in the Confederate service, there was nothing to be done but let him go when and where he pleased.

Captain W.M. Maginis, Acting Assistant Adjutant-General of the second brigade, was immediately appointed in his stead. This officer was very young, but had seen a great deal of arduous service. He had served in the infantry for more than a year; he had seen Belmont, Shiloh, Farmington, and Perryville, had behaved with the greatest gallantry, and had won the encomiums of his chiefs. He had been assigned to staff duty just before he came to us, and had acted in the capacity of ordnance officer, I believe, for General Walthall, an officer who, of the first class himself, would have only the same sort about him. He had been assigned upon General Morgan's application (at my urgent request) to his command, and, as has been stated, was on duty with the first brigade, when General Morgan suddenly stood in need of an Assistant Adjutant-General, and took him, intending to keep him temporarily. He was so much pleased with him that, upon his return from this expedition, he procured his commission in the Adjutant and Inspector General's Department, and his assignment to him. He remained with General Morgan until his death.

On the morning of December 22nd, the division took up its march for Kentucky. General Bragg desired that the roads which Rosecrans had repaired in rear should again be broken, and the latter's communications with Louisville destroyed. The service was an important one; it was meet that, for many reasons, the expedition, the first Confederate movement into Kentucky since Bragg's retreat, should be a brilliant one. General Morgan had under his command at that time the largest force he ever handled, previously or afterward, and he would not have permitted them to have stopped him. A writer from whom I have frequently had occasion to quote, gives a description of the commencement of the march, so spirited and so graphic, that it will serve my purpose better than any that I can write myself. He says:

"The regiments had been carefully inspected by the Surgeons and Inspectors, and every sick soldier and disabled horse had been taken from their regiments, and the stout men and serviceable horses only were permitted to accompany the expedition. The men were never in higher spirits or more joyous humor; well armed, well mounted, in good discipline, with perfect confidence in their commander, and with hearts longing for the hills and valleys, the blue-grass and woods of dear old Kentucky; they made the air vocal with their cheers and laughter and songs and sallies of wit. The division had never operated together before the brigades had first been organized, therefore every regiment was filled with the spirit of emulation, and every man was determined to make his the crack regiment of Morgan's cavalry. It was a magnificent body of men—the pick of the youth of Kentucky. No commander ever led a nobler corps—no corps was ever more nobly led. It was splendidly officered by gallant, dashing, skillful men in the flush of early manhood; for of the seven Colonels who commanded those seven regiments, five became brigade commanders—the other two gave their lives to the cause—Colonel Bennett dying early in January, 1863, of a disease contracted while in the army, and Colonel Chenault being killed on July 4, 1863, gallantly leading his men in a fruitless charge upon breastworks at Green river bridge. This December morning was a mild, beautiful fall day; clear, cloudless sky; bright sun; the camps in cedar evergreens, where the birds chirped and twittered; it felt and looked like spring. The reveille sounded before daybreak; the horses were fed, breakfast gotten. Very early came the orders from General Morgan announcing the organization of the brigades, intimating the objects of the expedition, and ordering the column to move at nine o'clock. Duke in advance. As the order was read to a regiment the utmost deathless silence of disciplined soldiers standing at attention was broken only by the clear voice of the Adjutant reading the precise but stirring words of the beloved hero-chieftain; then came the sharp word of command dismissing the parade; and the woods trembled with the wild hurrahs of the half crazy men, and regiment answered regiment, cheer re-echoed cheer, over the wide encampment. Soon came Duke, and his staff, and his column—his own old gallant regiment at the head—and slowly regiment after regiment filed out of the woods into the road, lengthening the long column.

"After some two hours march, a cheer began in the extreme rear and rapidly came forward, increasing in volume and enthusiasm, and soon General Morgan dashed by, with his hat in his hand, bowing and smiling his thanks for these flattering cheers, followed by a large and well mounted staff. Did you ever see Morgan on horseback? If not, you missed one of the most impressive figures of the war. Perhaps no General in either army surpassed him in the striking proportion and grace of his person, and the ease and grace of his horsemanship. Over six feet in hight, straight as an Indian, exquisitely proportioned, with the air and manner of a cultivated and polished gentleman, and the bearing of a soldier, always handsomely and tastefully dressed, and elegantly mounted, he was the picture of the superb cavalry officer. Just now he was in the hight of his fame and happiness; married only ten days before to an accomplished lady, made Brigadier justly but very tardily; in command of the finest cavalry division in the Southern army; beloved almost to idolatry by his men, and returning their devotion by an extravagant confidence in their valor and prowess; conscious of his own great powers, yet wearing his honors with the most admirable modesty, and just starting upon a carefully conceived but daring expedition, he was perhaps in the zenith of his fame, and though he added many a green leaf to his chaplet, many a bright page to his history, yet his future was embittered by the envy, jealously, and hatred that then were not heard."

Marching all day the column reached Sand Shoals ford on the Cumberland just before dark. The first brigade crossed, and encamped for the night on the northern bank of the river. The second brigade encamped between the Caney Fork and the Cumberland.

On the next day, moving at daylight, a march of some thirty miles was accomplished; it was impossible to march faster than this, and keep the guns up. On the 24th, the division went into camp within five miles of Glasgow. Breckinridge sent Captain Jones of Company A, Ninth Kentucky to discover if all was clear in Glasgow, and I received instructions to support him with two companies under Major Steele of the Third Kentucky who was given one of the little howitzers. Jones reached the town after dark, and just as he entered it a Michigan battalion came into it also from the other side. Captain Jones encountered this battalion in the center of the town, and in the skirmish which ensued he was mortally wounded. He was an excellent officer and as brave as steel. Poor Will Webb was also mortally wounded—only a private soldier, but a cultivated and a thorough gentleman; brave, and kindly, and genial. A truer heart never beat in a soldier's bosom, and a nobler soul was never released by a soldier's death. First Lieutenant Samuel O. Peyton was severely wounded—shot in the arm and in the thigh. He was surrounded by foes who pressed him hard, after he was wounded, to capture him. He shot one assailant, and grappling with another, brought him to the ground and cut his throat with a pocket knife. Lieutenant Peyton was by birth, education, and character a thorough gentleman. Perfectly good natured and inoffensive—except when provoked or attacked—and then—he dispatched his affair and his man in a quiet, expeditious and thorough manner. The Federal cavalry retreated from the town by the Louisville pike.

On the next morning—Christmas—the division moved by the Louisville pike. Captain Quirk, supported by Lieutenant Hays with the advance-guard of the first brigade, fifty strong, cleared the road of some Federal cavalry, which tried to contest our advance, driving it so rapidly, that the column had neither to delay its march, nor make any formation for fight. In the course of the day, Quirk charged a battalion, dismounted, and formed across the road. He went through them, and as he dashed back again, with his head bent low, he caught two balls on the top of it, which, singularly (coming from different directions), traced a neat and accurate angle upon his scalp.

Although the wounds were not serious at all, they would have stunned most men; but a head built in County Kerry, with especial reference to shillelagh practice, scorned to be affected by such trifles. Breckinridge sent Johnson's regiment during the day toward Munfordsville, to induce the belief that we were going to attack that place. Colonel Johnson executed his mission with perfect success. That night we crossed Green river. The first brigade being in advance had little trouble comparatively, although Captain Palmer had to exert energy and skill to get his battery promptly across; but the second brigade reaching the bank of the river late at night had great difficulty in getting across.

The division encamped in the latter part of the night at Hammondsville. A day before, just upon the bank of the river, the most enormous wagon, perhaps, ever seen in the State of Kentucky, was captured. It was loaded with an almost fabulous amount and variety of Christmas nicknacks; some enterprising settler had prepared it for the Glasgow market, intending to make his fortune with it. It was emptied at an earlier date, in shorter time, and by customers who proposed to themselves a much longer credit than he anticipated. There was enough in it to furnish every mess in the division something to eke out a Christmas supper with.

On the next day the column resumed its march amid the steadily pouring rain, and moved through mud which threatened to ingulf every thing, toward the Louisville and Nashville railroad. Hutchinson was sent, with several companies of the Second Kentucky, and the Third Kentucky, to destroy the bridge at Bacon creek. There was not more than one hundred men, at the most, in the stockade which protected the bridges, and he was expected to reduce the stockade with the two pieces of artillery, which he carried with him, but there was a large force at Munfordsville, only eight miles from Bacon creek, and General Morgan gave him troops enough to repulse any movement of the enemy from Munfordsville to save the bridge. A battalion of cavalry came out from Munfordsville, but was easily driven back by Companies B and D, of the Second Kentucky, under Captain Castleman. Although severely shelled, the garrison held out stubbornly, rejecting every demand for their surrender. Hutchinson became impatient, which was his only fault as an officer, and ordered the bridge to be fired at all hazards—it was within less than a hundred yards of the stockade, and commanded by the rifles of the garrison. It was partially set on fire, but the rain would extinguish it unless constantly supplied with fuel. Several were wounded in the attempt, and Captain Wolfe, of the Third Kentucky, who boldly mounted the bridge, was shot in the head, and lay unconscious for two hours, every one thinking him dead, until the beating rain reviving him, he returned to duty, suffering no further inconvenience. Some of the men got behind the abutment of the bridge, and thrust lighted pieces of wood upon it, which the men in the stockade frequently shot away. At length General Morgan arrived upon the ground, and sent a message to the garrison in his own name, offering them liberal terms if they would surrender. As soon as they were satisfied that it was indeed Morgan who confronted them, they surrendered. This was a very obstinate defense. A number of shells burst within the stockade. Some shots penetrated the walls and an old barn, which had been foolishly included within the work, was knocked to pieces, the falling timbers stunning some of the men.

The stockade at Nolin surrendered to me without a fight. The commandant agreed to surrender if I would show him a certain number of pieces of artillery. They were shown him, but when I pressed him to comply with his part of the bargain, he hesitated, and said he would return and consult his officers. I think that (as two of the pieces shown him were the little howitzers, which I happened to have temporarily) he thought he could hold out for a while, and gild his surrender with a fight. He was permitted to return, but not until, in his presence, the artillery was planted close to the work, and the riflemen posted to command, as well as possible, the loop-holes. He came to us again, in a few minutes, with a surrender. The Nolin bridge was at once destroyed, and also several culverts and cow-gaps within three or four miles of that point.

The division encamped that night within six miles of Elizabethtown. On the morning of the 27th, the division moved upon Elizabethtown. This place was held by about six hundred men, under a Lieutenant Colonel Smith. As we neared the town, a note was brought to General Morgan, from Colonel Smith, who stated that he accurately knew his (Morgan's) strength, had him surrounded, and could compel his surrender, and that he (Smith) trusted that a prompt capitulation would spare him the disagreeable necessity of using force. The missive containing this proposal—the most sublimely audacious I ever knew to emanate from a Federal officer, who, as a class, rarely trusted to audacity and bluff, but to odds and the *concours* of force—this admirable document was brought by a Dutch Corporal, who spoke very uncertain English, but was positive on the point of surrender. General Morgan admired the spirit which dictated this bold effort at bluffing, but returned for answer an assurance that he knew exactly the strength of the Federal force in the town, and that Lieutenant Colonel Smith was in error, in supposing that he (Smith) had him (Morgan) surrounded; that, on the contrary, he had the honor to state, the position of the respective forces was exactly the reverse. He concluded by demanding him to surrender. Colonel Smith replied that it was "the business of an United States officer to fight, and not to surrender." During the parley, the troops had been placed in position. Breckinridge was given the left of the road, and the first brigade the right. I dismounted Cluke's regiment, and moved it upon the town, with its left flank keeping close to the road. I threw several companies, mounted, to the extreme right of my line, and the rear of the town. Breckinridge deployed his own regiment, under Lieutenant Colonel Stoner, immediately on the left of the road, stretching mounted companies also to his left, and around the town.

The bulk of both brigades was held in reserve. The Parrot gun was placed in the pike; it was opened as soon as the last message from Colonel Smith was received; and, as suddenly as if its flash had ignited them, Palmer's four guns roared out from the hill on the left of the road, about six hundred yards from the town, where General Morgan himself was superintending their fire. Cluke moved warily, as two or three stockades were just in his front, which were thought to be occupied. When he entered the town, he had little fighting to do, and that on the extreme right. Stoner dashed in on the left with the Ninth Kentucky, at a swift run. He burst into the houses occupied by the enemy at the edge of the town, and with slight loss, compelled the inmates to surrender. The enemy had no artillery, and ours was battering the bricks about their heads in fine style. Palmer, who was a capital officer—cool and clearheaded—concentrated his fire upon the building where the flag floated, and the enemy seemed thickest, and moved his six pounders into the very edge of the town. I sent for one of the howitzers, and when it came under Lieutenant Corbett, it was posted upon the railroad embankment, where it crossed the road. Here it played like a fire engine upon the headquarters building. Breckinridge posted Company A, of his regiment, to protect the howitzer, making the men lie down behind the embankment.

The enemy could not well fire upon the gunners from the windows, on account of the situation of the piece, but after each discharge would rush out into the street and open upon them. Then the company lying behind the embankment would retaliate on the enemy in a style which took away their appetite for the game. It happened, however, that a staff officer of General Morgan, passed that way, and conceiving that this company was doing no good, ordered it, with more zeal than discretion, to charge. The men instinctively obeyed. As they ran forward, they came within fair view of the windows, and a heavy volley was opened upon them, fortunately doing little damage. Their officers, knowing that the man who gave the order, had no right to give it, called them back, and they returned in some confusion, the enemy seized the moment, and flocking out of the houses poured a sweeping fire down the street. The gunners were driven away from the howitzers, and two or three hit. Lieutenant Corbett, however, maintained his place, seated on the carriage, while the bullets were actually hopping from the reinforce of the piece. He soon called his men back, and resumed his fire.

It was as fine an exhibition of courage as I ever saw. Shortly after this, there seemed to be a commotion among the garrison, and the white flag was shown from one of the houses. Major Llewellyn, Division Quartermaster, immediately galloped into the town, reckless of the firing, waving a white handkerchief. Colonel Smith was not ready to surrender, but his men did not wait on him and poured out of the houses and threw down their arms. Among the fruits of this victory, were, six hundred fine rifles, more than enough to arm all of our men who were without guns. The entire garrison was captured. Some valuable stores were also taken. On the next day, the 28th, the command moved leisurely along the railroad, destroying it thoroughly. The principal objects of the expedition, were the great trestle works at Muldraugh's hill, only a short distance apart. The second brigade captured the garrison defending the lower trestle six hundred strong; the first brigade captured the garrison of the upper trestle two hundred strong. Both of the immense structures were destroyed and hours were required to thoroughly burn them. These trestles were, respectively, eighty or ninety feet high—and each, five hundred feet long.

Canc Run bridge, within twenty-eight miles of Louisville, was destroyed by a scouting party. Two bridges on the Lebanon branch, recently reconstructed, were also burned. Altogether, General Morgan destroyed on this expedition, two thousand two hundred and fifty feet of bridging, three depots, three water stations, and a number of culverts and cattle-guards. The impression which prevails in some quarters, that General Morgan left the road on account of the pursuit of Colonel Harlan, is entirely erroneous. With the destruction of the great trestles at Muldraugh's hill, his contract with the road expired and he prepared to return. He would have liked to have paid the region about Lexington another visit, but General Bragg had urged him not to delay his return. Harlan was moving slowly after us; but for the delay consequent upon the destruction of the road, he would never have gotten near us and, but for an accident, he would never have caught up with any portion of the column, after we had quitted work on the railroad.

On the night of the 28th, the division had encamped on the southern bank of the Rolling fork. On the morning of the 29th, it commenced crossing that stream, which was much swollen. The bulk of the troops and the artillery were crossed at a ford a mile or two above the point at which the road from Elizabethtown to Bardstown along which we had been encamped, crosses the Rolling fork. The pickets, rear-guard, and some detachments, left in the rear for various purposes, in all about three hundred men, were collected to cross at two fords—deep and difficult to approach and to emerge from. Cluke's regiment, with two pieces of artillery, had been sent under Major Bullock to burn the railroad bridge over the Rolling fork, five miles below the point where we were. A court-martial had been in session for several days, trying Lieutenant Colonel Huffman, for alleged violations of the terms granted by General Morgan to the prisoners at the surrender of the Bacon creek stockade.

Both brigade commanders, and three regimental commanders,

Cluke, Hutchinson, and Stoner, were officers or members of this court. Just after the court had finally adjourned, acquitting Colonel Huffman, and we were leaving a brick house, on the southern side of the river and about six hundred yards from its bank, where our last session had been held, the bursting of a shell a mile or two in the rear caught our ears. A few videttes had been left there until every thing should have gotten fairly across. Some of them were captured; others brought the information that the enemy was approaching. This was about eleven A.M. We knew that a force of infantry and cavalry was cautiously following us, but did not know that it was so near. It was at once decided to throw into line the men who had not yet crossed, and hold the fords, if possible, until Cluke's regiment could be brought back. If we crossed the river leaving that regiment on the southern side, and it did not succeed in crossing, or if it crossed immediately and yet the enemy pressed on vigorously after us, beating it to Bardstown—in either event it would be cut off from us, and its capture even would be probable. No one knew whether there was a ford lower down at which it could cross, and all feared that if we retreated promptly the enemy would closely follow us. I, therefore, sent a message to General Morgan, informing him of what was decided upon, and also sent a courier to Major Bullock, directing him to return with the regiment as soon as possible.

The ground on which we were posted was favorable to the kind of game we were going to play. Upon each flank were thick woods extending for more than a mile back from the river. Between these woods was a large meadow, some three hundred yards wide, and stretching from the river bank for six or eight hundred yards to a woods again in the back ground, and which almost united the other two. In this meadow and some two hundred yards from the river was a singular and sudden depression like a terrace, running straight across it. Behind this the men who were posted in the meadow were as well protected as if they had been behind an earthwork. On the left the ground was so rugged as well as so wooded that the position there was almost impregnable. There was, however, no adequate protection for the horses afforded at any point of the line except the extreme left.

The Federal force advancing upon us consisted of nearly five thousand infantry, two thousand cavalry, and several pieces of artillery. This force, which, if handled vigorously and skillfully, if its march had even been steadily kept up, would have, in spite of every effort we could have made, swept us into the turbid river at our backs, approached cautiously and very slowly. Fortunate as this was for us—indeed, it was all that saved us—the suspense yet became so sickening, as their long line tediously crept upon us and all around us, that I would almost have preferred, after an hour of it had elapsed, that Harlan had made a fierce attack.

We were not idle during this advance, but the skirmishers were keeping busy in the edges of the woods on our flanks, and the men in the meadow were showing themselves with the most careful regard to an exaggerated idea being formed of their numbers. When the enemy reached the edge of the woods which fringed the southern extremity of the meadow, and had pressed our skirmishers out of it and away from the brick-house and its out-buildings, the artillery was brought up and four or five guns were opened upon us. Just after this fire commenced, the six-pounders sent with Bullock galloped upon the ground, and a defiant yell a short distance to the right told that Cluke's regiment, "The war-dogs," were near at hand. I was disinclined to use the six-pounders after they came, because I know that they could not effectively answer the fire of the enemy's Parrots, and I wished to avoid every thing which might warm the affair up into a hot fight, feeling pretty certain that when that occurred, we would all, guns and men, "go up" together. Major Austin, Captain Logan, and Captain Pendleton, commanding respectively detachments from the Ninth, Third, and Eighth Kentucky, had conducted the operations of our line up to this time with admirable coolness and method.

The guns were sent across the meadow rapidly, purposely attracting the attention of the enemy as much as possible, to the upper ford. A road was cut through the rough ground for them, and they were crossed with all possible expedition. Cluke threw five companies of his regiment into line; the rest were sent over the river. We now wished to cross with the entire force that was on the southern side, but this was likely to prove a hazardous undertaking with an enemy so greatly out-numbering us lying just in our front. A courier arrived just about that time from General Morgan with an order to me to withdraw. In common with quite a number of others, I devoutly wished I could. The enemy's guns—the best served of any, I think, that I ever saw in action—were playing havoc with the horses (four were killed by one shell), and actually bursting shells in the lower ford with such frequency as to render the crossing at it by a column out of the question.

Our line was strengthened by Cluke's five companies to nearly eight hundred men, but when the enemy moved upon us again, his infantry deployed in a long line, strongly supported, with a skirmish line in front, all coming on with bayonets glistening, the guns redoubling their fire, and the cavalry column on the right flank (of their line) apparently ready to pounce on us too, and then the river surging at our backs, my blood, I confess, ran cold.

The final moment seemed at hand when that gallant rear-guard must give way and be driven into the stream, or be bayoneted on its banks. But not one fear or doubt seemed to trouble for a moment our splendid fellows. They welcomed the coming attack with a glad and defiant cheer and could scarcely be restrained from rushing to meet it. But we were saved by the action of the enemy.

The advancing line was withdrawn (unaccountably to us) as soon as it had come under our fire. It did not recoil—it perhaps had not lost a man. It was at once decided that a show of attack, upon our part, should be made on the center, and I ordered Captain Pendleton to charge upon our left, with three companies, and silence a battery which was annoying us very greatly; under cover of these demonstrations we had determined to withdraw. Just after this arrangement was made, I was wounded in the head by the explosion of a shell, which burst in a group of us true to its aim. The horse of my acting Aide-de-camp, Lieutenant Moreland, was killed by a fragment of it. Colonel Breckinridge at once assumed command, and energetically and skillfully effected the safe withdrawal of the entire force. Pendleton accomplished by his charge all that was expected. He killed several cannoneers and drove all from the guns, silencing them for a quarter of an hour. He, himself, was badly wounded by the fragment of a shell which burst short.

Aided by this diversion and the one made upon the front, every thing was suddenly thrown into columns and dashed across the river, leaving the army on the other side cheated of its prey which it ought to have secured. The troops were gotten across the more readily because of the discovery of a third ford in the rear of Cluke's position. It was accidentally found at the last moment. Our loss was very slight, except in horses. The enemy did not attempt pursuit. No eulogium could do justice to the conduct of the men engaged in this affair—nothing but their perfect steadiness would have enabled any skill to have rescued them from the danger. Captains Pendleton, Logan, Page, and Hines, and Major Austin, deserved the warmest praise. Cluke acted, as he did always where courage and soldierly conduct were required, in a manner that added to his reputation. Breckinridge's skill and vigor, however, were the chief themes of conversation and praise.

On that night the division encamped at Bardstown. Colonel Chenault, on the same day, destroyed the stockade at Boston, and marched on after the division at Bardstown.

Leaving that place on the 30th, the column reached Springfield at 3 P.M. "Adam Johnson had been ordered to move rapidly in advance, and attack the pickets in front of Lebanon; which he had executed with such vigor as to make Colonel Hoskins believe he intended to attack him, and he called in a regiment of cavalry stationed near New Market, thereby opening the way for us to get out without a fight."

At Springfield General Morgan learned that his situation was hazardous, and one that would elicit all of his great powers of strategy and audacity. The enemy had withdrawn the bulk of his troops from the Southern part of the State, and had concentrated them at Lebanon, only eight miles distant from his then position, and right in his path. This force was nearly eight thousand strong and well supplied with artillery. He had also received intelligence that a large force was marching from Glasgow to intercept him at Columbia, should he succeed in evading the force at Lebanon. Harlan was not so far in his rear that he could afford to dally. "In this emergency," he said, "I determined to make a detour to the right of Lebanon, and by a night march to conceal my movements from the enemy, outstrip the column moving from Glasgow to Columbia, and cross the Cumberland before it came within striking distance." Shortly before midnight, therefore, on the night of the 30th, the column moved from Springfield, turning off from the pike on to a little, rarely traveled, by-road, which passes between Lebanon and St. Mary's. Numerous fires were built in front of Lebanon, and kept up all night to induce the belief that the division was encamped there and would attack in the morning. The night was intensely dark and bitterly cold, the guides were inefficient, and the column floundered along blindly; the men worn out and half frozen, the horses stumbling at every step—nothing preserved organization and carried the column along but the will of the great Captain in the front and the unerring sagacity which guided him. It is common to hear men who served in Morgan's cavalry through all of its career of trial and hardship, refer to the night march around Lebanon as the most trying scene of their entire experience.

Morning found the column only eight miles from Springfield, and two and a half from Lebanon. At that place, however, the garrison were drawn up, confidently expecting attack from another direction. By 1 P.M., of the 31st, the column reached the top of Muldraugh's hill, on the Lebanon and Columbia road, and soon after nightfall was in Campbellsville.

Just after the column had crossed the hill, a hand-to-hand fight occurred between Captain Alexander Treble and Lieutenant George Eastin, on the one side, and Colonel Halisey, of the Federal cavalry, and one of the latter's Lieutenants, on the other. Treble and Eastin had, for some purpose, fallen behind the rear-guard and were chased by Halisey's regiment, which was following us to pick up stragglers. Being both well mounted, they easily kept ahead of their pursuers, until, looking back as they cantered down a long straight stretch in the road, they saw within three hundred yards, perhaps, of them, four men who were far in advance of the rest of the pursuers.

Treble and Eastin were both high-strung men and they did not like to continue to run from that number of enemies. So as soon as they reached a point in the road where it suddenly turned, they halted a few yards from the turn. They expected to shoot two of the enemy as soon as they came in sight and thought that they would then have little trouble with the others. But it so happened that only two, Halisey and his Lieutenant, made their appearance; the other two, for some reason, halted; and what was stranger, Treble and Eastin, although both practiced shots, missed their men. Their antagonists dashed at them and several shots were fired without effect. The combatants soon grappled, man to man, and fell from their horses. Treble forced the head of his man into a pool of water just by the side of the road and, having half drowned him, accepted his surrender. Eastin mastered Halisey and, putting his pistol to his head, bade him surrender. Halisey did so, but, still retaining his pistol, as Eastin let him arise, he fired, grazing the latter's cheek, who immediately killed him. Eastin brought off his saber, which he kept as a trophy.

In Campbellsville, luckily, there was a large supply of commissary stores, which were immediately issued to the division. Leaving early on the next morning, the 1st of January, 1863, the column reached Columbia at three P.M. All that day the roaring of artillery was distinctly heard by many men in the column. There was no cannonading going on—at least, in the volume which they declared that they heard—except at Murfreesboro', far distant, where the battle between the armies of Bragg and Rosecrans was raging; but it seems incredible that even heavy guns could have been heard at that distance.

Just before night fall, the column moved from Columbia and marched all night—a dark, bitter night and a terrible march—to Burkesville. The Cumberland was crossed on the 2nd and the danger was over. The division then moved leisurely along, through Livingston, crossing Caney Fork at Sligo Ferry, and reached Smithville on the 5th. Here it halted for several days to rest and recruit men and horses, both terribly used up by the raid.

The results of this expedition were the destruction of the railroads which has been described, the capture of eighteen hundred and seventy-seven prisoners, of a large number of stores, arms, and government property of every description. Our loss was only twenty-six in killed and wounded (only two killed), and sixty-four missing.

During our absence, the sanguinary battle of Murfreesboro' was fought, ending in the withdrawal of Bragg to Tullahoma, much, it is claimed, to the surprise of his adversary. General Bragg had sent officers to Morgan (who never reached him until it was too late) with instructions to him to hasten back, and attack the enemy in the rear. It was unfortunate that these orders were not received. To do General Bragg justice, he managed better than almost any commander of the Confederate armies to usefully employ his cavalry, both in campaigns and battles. In the battle of Murfreesboro', he made excellent use of the cavalry on the field. Wharton and Buford, under command of Wheeler, three times made the circuit of the Federal army and were splendidly efficient; at one time Wheeler was master of all between the immediate rear of Rosecrans and Nashville.

Perhaps Morgan's raid was delayed a little too long, as well as that of Forrest into Western Tennessee (undertaken about the same time, and in prisoners, captures of all sorts, and interruption of the enemy's communications, as successful as Morgan's); but these expeditions drew off and kept employed a large number of troops whose presence in the great battle would have vastly aided Rosecrans.

The Confederate Congress thought this expedition worthy of recognition and compliment, and passed a joint resolution of thanks, as follows:

"*Resolved by the Congress of the Confederate States of America*: That the thanks of Congress are due, and are hereby tendered to Gen. John H. Morgan, and the officers and men of his command, for their varied, heroic, and invaluable services in Tennessee and Kentucky, immediately preceding the battle before Murfreesboro'—services which have conferred upon their authors fame as enduring as the records of the struggle which they have so brilliantly illustrated. Approved May 17, 1863."

CHAPTER XIII

After the battle of Murfreesboro', and the retreat of the arms to Tullahoma, at which place General Bragg's headquarters were established, the infantry went into winter quarters, and General Bragg protected the front and flanks of his army with the fine cavalry corps of Van Dorn and Wheeler. The former was assigned to the left, making headquarters at Columbia, and guarding the lines far to the west, while Wheeler had the right. This latter corps was composed of the divisions of Morgan, Wharton, and Martin.

Although the armies were idle for months after this disposition was made, the cavalry was never so. General Wheeler had been placed in command of his corps by General Bragg, probably more on account of the dislike entertained by the latter to certain other officers, than because of the partiality he felt for him. The reputation of this officer, although deservedly high, hardly entitled him to command some of the men who were ordered to report to him. He became subsequently a much abler commander than he was at the time of his preferment, but he always exhibited some very high qualities. He was vigilant and energetic, thoroughly instructed in the duties of his profession, and perfectly conversant with the elaborate details of organization and military business. While he did not display the originality and the instinctive strategical sagacity which characterized Morgan and Forrest, he was perhaps better fitted than either for the duties which devolve upon the commander of large bodies of cavalry, permanently attached to the army and required to conform, in all respects, to its movements and necessities.

Thus, it was often said of him, that "he is not a good raider, but there is no better man to watch the front of the army." General Wheeler possessed in an eminent degree, all of the attributes of the gentleman. He was brave as a Paladin, just, high-toned, and exceedingly courteous. He was full of fire and enterprise, but, while thoroughly impressed with the necessity of order and discipline, was singularly unfortunate in maintaining them—perhaps, because he did not keep strict enough rule with his officers immediately next him in rank. He labored under great disadvantages, on account of the violent and unjust prejudices excited against him by General Bragg's preference for him and his rapid promotion. General Morgan said to him, when first ordered to report to him, that he (Morgan), had wished to be left free, acting independently of all orders except from the Commander-in-Chief, but that since he was to be subordinate to a corps commander, he would prefer him to any other. General Morgan always entertained this opinion, and I have reason to believe that General Wheeler reluctantly assumed command of his division.

The history of the command, for the winter of 1863, properly commences at the date of the return from the raid into Kentucky, described in the last chapter. The entire division reached Smithville upon the 4th of January, and remained in the vicinity of that little town and at Sligo ferry until the 14th. Upon the 14th, the division was marched to McMinnville, and encamped around that place—where General Morgan's headquarters were then established. The first brigade lay between McMinnville and Woodbury, at which latter point Lieutenant Colonel Hutchinson was stationed with the Second Kentucky. The weather was intensely cold, and all of the men who were unprovided with the means of adequately sheltering themselves, suffered severely. Their ingenuity was taxed to the utmost to supply the lack of cooking utensils, and it frequently happened that they had very little to cook.

Fortunately, a great many blankets had been obtained upon the last raid, and almost every man had gotten a gum cloth. These latter were stretched over the rail shanties which each mess would put up; and thus covered the sloping, shed-like structures (built of the fence rails), made very tolerable substitutes for tents, and with the help of the rousing fires, which were built at the front of them, were by no means uncomfortable. Very little system was observed in the "laying out" of the encampment—men and horses were all huddled together, for the men did not fancy any arrangement which separated them by the slightest distance from their horses, and the latter were always tied close to the lairs of their masters.

Notwithstanding the lack of method and the apparently inextricable confusion of these camps, their inmates could be gotten under arms and formed in line of battle, with a celerity that would have appeared marvelous to the uninitiated.

Colonel Chenault was ordered, in the latter part of January, to Clinton county, Kentucky, to picket against a dash of the enemy from that direction. On the 23rd of January, Colonel Breckinridge was ordered to move to Liberty, eleven miles from Smithville and about thirty from McMinnville, with three regiments—the Third Kentucky, under Lieutenant Colonel Huffman, the Ninth Kentucky, under Lieutenant Colonel Stoner, and the Ninth Tennessee, under Colonel Ward, who had come to the command of it after Colonel Bennett's death, Colonel Adam R. Johnson was already in the vicinity of that place with his regiment, the Tenth Kentucky. Captain Quirk preceded these regiments with his company, and shortly after his arrival at Liberty and before he could be supported, he, was driven away by the enemy. He returned next morning, the enemy having retreated. The three regiments, under Colonel Breckinridge, occupied the country immediately in front of Liberty, picketing all of the roads thoroughly. The enemy were in the habit of sending out strong foraging parties from Readyville toward Woodbury, and frequent skirmishes occurred between them and Hutchinson's scouts.

Upon one occasion, Hutchinson, with less than one hundred men, attacked one of these parties, defeating it with smart loss, and taking nearly two hundred prisoners and forty or fifty wagons. For this he was complimented in general orders from army headquarters. It led, however, in all probability, to disastrous consequences, by inducing the enemy to employ many more troops in that quarter than he would otherwise have sent there. This affair occurred a short time previously to the occupation of Liberty by the force under Colonel Breckinridge, and a much brisker condition of affairs began to prevail all along the line. Rosecrans was determined to make his superior numbers tell, at least, in the immediate vicinity of his army. He inaugurated a system, about this time, which resulted in the decided improvement of his cavalry. He would send out a body of cavalry, stronger than any thing it was likely to encounter, and that it might never be demoralized by a complete whipping, he would back it by an infantry force, never far in the rear, and always ready to finish the fight which the cavalry begun. This method benefited the latter greatly. On the 24th, the Second Kentucky was attacked at Woodbury by a heavy force of the enemy, and a gallant fight ensued, ending by an unhappy loss for us, in the death of Lieutenant Colonel Hutchinson.

From various causes the regiment had become much depleted, and on this day it was reduced (by the sending off of detachments for necessary duties), to less than four hundred men. The enemy advanced, over three thousand strong, principally infantry, but Hutchinson determined not to give up his position without a hard fight. He posted his men advantageously upon the brow of a hill in front of the village, sheltering a portion of his line behind a stone wall. The enemy preceded his attack with a smart fire of artillery, to which Hutchinson could make no reply, but was forced to take it patiently. But when the infantry moved up and came within range of our riflemen, the tables were (for a little while) completely turned, and they fell fast under a fire that rarely failed to do deadly execution. The unequal contest lasted more than an hour; during that time the stone wall was carried by the enemy, but was retaken by Captain Treble and Lieutenant Lea, charging at the head of their gallant companies. Much as he needed men, Hutchinson kept one of his companies idle and out of the fight, but, nevertheless, producing an effect upon the enemy. He caused Captain Cooper to show the head of his company, just upon the brow of the hill, so that the enemy could see it but could not judge correctly of its strength, and might possibly think it a strong reserve.

Constantly exposed to the fire of artillery and small arms throughout the fight, this company never flinched, nor moved from its position until it was ordered to cover the retreat. Then it filed to the left, as if moving to take the enemy in flank, and when the column had passed, wheeled into the rear, under cover of the hill. Colonel Hutchinson, at length, yielded to the conviction that he could not hold his ground against such odds. The arrival of a fresh company enabled him to retreat with greater security, and he ordered the line to retire. A portion of it was pressed hard as it did so, and he rode to the point of danger to encourage the men by his presence. He had exposed himself during the action with even more than his usual recklessness, but with impunity. Just as all seemed over, however, and he was laughing gleefully at his successful withdrawal, a ball struck him upon the temple, and he fell dead from his horse. Lieutenant Charles Allen, the gallant acting Adjutant of the regiment, and Charles Haddox (his orderly), threw his body upon his horse and carried it off under the hot fire.

Captain Castleman at once assumed command, and successfully conducted the retreat. The supply of ammunition entirely gave out just after the retreat was commenced.

Lieutenant Colonel Hutchinson was, beyond all comparison, the best field officer in Morgan's division, and indeed that I ever saw. Had he lived and been placed in situations favorable to the development of his talent, he would, I firmly believe, have become competent to any command. He had more natural military aptitude, was more instinctively the soldier; than any man I have ever known. He did not exhibit a marked partiality and gift for a particular class of military duties, so much as a capacity and fitness for all. He could make himself thorough in every thing which the service required. All that a soldier ought to know, he seemed to learn easily—all the proper feelings of a soldier seemed his natural impulses. General Morgan felt a warm and manly admiration for him, and reposed an implicit confidence in his character and ability. His brother officers loved to enhance his reputation, his men idolized him. Hutchinson had the frank generous temper, and straight forward, although shrewd, disposition which wins popularity with soldiers. While watchful and strict in his discipline, he was kind to his men, careful of their wants, and invariably shared their fare, whatever it might be. He was born to be a soldier and to rank high among soldiers. He loved the excitement of the game of war. He loved honor, as a western man loves the free air of the prairies—it was his natural element. It may seem to the general reader that I have extravagantly eulogized him, but his old-comrades will, perhaps, think that I have said too little. When killed he was barely twenty-four, but the effects of exposure and the thoughtful expression of his eye made him appear several years older. His great size and erect, soldierly bearing made him a conspicuous figure at all times, and in battle he was superb. Taller than all around him, his form, of immense muscular power, dilated with stern excitement—always in the van—he looked, as he sat upon his colossal gray charger, like some champion of an age when one man could stay the march of armies. There was some thing in his look which told his daring nature. His aquiline features, dark glittering eye, close cropped black hair, and head like a hawk's, erect and alert, indicated intense energy and invincible courage. Hutchinson's death cast a deep gloom over his regiment and (as Major Bowles, who then became Lieutenant Colonel, was absent when it occurred) an unfortunate quarrel broke out between two of the officers respecting seniority and the right to command it. This quarrel was espoused by their respective friends, and a state of feeling was induced which greatly impaired the efficiency of the regiment, until it was settled by the appointment of Captain Webber to the Majority. Webber had nothing to do with the dispute, but a committee appointed by General Morgan to investigate and decide the claims of all the Captains to seniority, pronounced him senior to both the contestants.

On the 14th of February, Colonel Cluke was sent into Eastern and Central Kentucky, for purposes which will be explained in the account which will be given of his operations. He took with him his own regiment, two companies under Major Steele—Company A, of the Second, and Companies C and I of the Third Kentucky—and about seventy men of the Ninth Kentucky under Lieutenant Colonel Stoner.

These detachments weakened the effective strength of the command at a time when it was engaged in service which tasked its energies to the utmost. That portion of "the front" which General Morgan was expected to protect, may be described as extending from Woodbury, in Tennessee, to Wayne county, in Kentucky, in an irregular curved line more than one hundred and twenty miles in length. It was exceedingly important that this entire line should be well picketed and closely watched, but it was necessary to give especial attention to that section of it in Tennessee (which was immediately confronted by formidable numbers of the enemy) and here, consequently, the greater part of the division was employed.

While it was necessary to keep strict ward at Woodbury, upon the left flank of this line, and a force adequate to the thorough picketing and scouting of that region was always kept there—the chief interest centered at Liberty, for here the efforts of the enemy to break the line and drive back the forces guarding it, were most frequently and energetically directed. This little hamlet is situated twenty-nine miles from Murfreesboro', by the turnpike, and almost due Northeast of it. A line drawn from Carthage to Woodbury would pass through Liberty, and the latter is distant some eighteen miles from each. Carthage is a little east of north, Woodbury a little west of south, from Liberty. About twenty-one or two miles from Liberty, and west of south, is Readyville—where was stationed at the time of which I write, a strong Federal force. Readyville is ten miles from Murfreesboro', and about the same distance northwest of Woodbury. Lebanon, twenty-six miles from Liberty by the turnpike which runs through Alexandria, and northwest of it, was at this time, permanently occupied by neither side, but both Federal and Confederate troops occasionally held it. Carthage, far upon the flank and virtually in the rear of the forces at Liberty, was occupied by a Federal garrison, which varied in strength, as the plans of the Federal Generals required. It could be reinforced and supplied from Nashville by the river, upon which it is situated, and it was well fortified.

A direct advance upon Liberty from Murfreesboro' promised nothing to the attacking-party but a fight in which superior numbers might enable it to dislodge the Confederates, and force them to retreat to Smithville; thence, if pressed, to McMinnville or Sparta. If such a movement were seconded by a cooperative one from Carthage, the effect would be only to hasten the retreat, for the country between Carthage and Smithville is too rugged for troops to traverse it with ease and dispatch, and they would necessarily have to march directly to Liberty, or to a point but a very short distance to the east of it. It may be stated generally that the result would be the same were an advance made upon Liberty by any or all of the routes coming in upon the front, and the enemy at Carthage was dangerous only when the Confederates exposed their rear by an imprudent advance. A rapid march through Woodbury upon McMinnville might bring the enemy at any time entirely between Liberty and the army at Tullahoma, or if he turned and marched through Mechanicsville, dash and celerity might enable him to cut off the force at Liberty entirely.

When it is remembered that about the only point of importance outside of Murfreesboro' and Nashville, and short of the line I have described (with the exception of Lebanon), whether north or south of the river, was occupied by a Federal garrison large enough to undertake the offensive, and that the country was traced in every direction by innumerable practicable roads, it will be clear that sleepless vigilance and the soundest judgment were necessary to the protection of the Confederate forces stationed in it. The three regiments encamped in the vicinity of Liberty numbered about one thousand effectives, and the other regiments under Colonel Gano, including all which were not detached in Kentucky, under Colonels Cluke and Chenault, were posted in the neighborhood of Woodbury and McMinnville, and were about the same aggregate strength.

During the latter part of January and in February and March, the entire command was kept constantly and busily employed. Scouts and expeditions of all kinds—dashes at the enemy and fights between reconnoitering parties were of almost daily occurrence, and when Colonels Gano and Breckinridge were not harassing the enemy, they were recipients of like attention from him. Perhaps no period in the history of Morgan's cavalry of equal duration can be cited, in which more exciting and arduous service was performed. I regret that my absence from it at that time, and consequent want of familiarity with these events, renders it impossible that I shall describe them with the minuteness and accuracy which belong only to the personal observer. It has been said, in allusion to this period and the action then of Morgan's command, "If all the events of that winter could be told, it would form a book of daring personal adventures, of patient endurance, of great and continued hardship, and heroic resistance against fearful odds." The narration of these scenes in the simple language of the men who were actors in them, the description by the private soldiers of what they dared then, and endured, the recital of men (unconsciously telling their own heroism) would be the proper record of these stirring and memorable months. They could tell how, worn out with days and nights of toil, the brief repose was at length welcome with so much joy. Frequently the rain and sleet would beat in their faces as they slept, and the ice would thicken in their very beds. Happy were the men who had blankets in which to wrap their limbs, other than those which protected their horses' backs from the saddle. Thrice lucky those who could find something to eat when they lay down, and another meal when they arose. It oftenest happened that before the chill, bleak winter's day had broken, the bugle aroused them from comfortless bivouacs, to mount, half frozen and shivering, upon their stiff and tired horses and, faint and hungry, ride miles to attack a foe, or contest against ten-fold odds every foot of his advance.

Some of the personal adventures, so frequent at that time, will perhaps be found interesting. An expedition undertaken by General Morgan himself, but, unlike most of those in which he personally commanded, unsuccessful, is thus related: "Upon January 29th, General Morgan, accompanied by Major Steele, Captain Cassell, and a few men, came to Liberty to execute a dangerous plan. It was to take fifty picked men, dressed in blue coats, into Nashville, burn the commissary stores there, and in the confusion of the fire, make their escape. He had an order written, purporting to be from General Rosecrans, to Captain Johnson, Fifth Kentucky cavalry, to proceed from Murfreesboro' to Lebanon, thence to Nashville, arrest all stragglers, make all discoveries, etc. I can not recollect now from what commands the fifty men were selected, but know that Steele, Cassell, and Quirk went along. The plan was frustrated by an accident. As General Morgan rode up to Stewart's ferry, over Stone river, a Captain of a Michigan regiment, with some twenty men, rode up to the other side. Morgan immediately advanced a few feet in front of his command, touched his hat, and said, "Captain, what is the news in Nashville?"

Federal Captain—"Who are you?"

"Captain Johnson, Fifth Kentucky Cavalry, just from Murfreesboro', *via* Lebanon, going to Nashville by General Rosecrans' order—what is your regiment?" "—— Michigan." Morgan then asked: "Are you going further?"—"No." "Have you any news of Morgan?" With perfect self possession Morgan answered: "His cavalry are at Liberty—none closer." He then said to Quirk: "Sergeant, carry as many men over at a load as possible, and we will swim the horses. It is too late to attempt to ferry them over."

"The Michigan Captain started to move on when Morgan asked him to wait and they would ride to Nashville together. When he consented, most of his men got down and tried to warm themselves by walking, jumping, etc. Quirk pushed across with about a dozen men, reached the bank, and started the boat back; unfortunately, as his men climbed the bank, their gray pants showed, the Michiganders became alarmed, and Quirk had to attack forthwith. The Captain and some fifteen men surrendered immediately; the remainder escaped and ran to Nashville, giving the alarm. Morgan declared that if he had succeeded in capturing them all, he would have gone immediately into Nashville. Those who knew him best, will most readily believe it." A short time after the fight at Woodbury, Lieutenant Colonel Bowles, with the greater part of the Second Kentucky, and supported by a battalion under Lieutenant Colonel Malone (Alabama), engaged a large force of the enemy at Bradyville. Attacking the advance-guard of this force (before he became aware of the strength of the main body), Colonel Bowles drove it in confusion and rout, into the town, and even forced back for some distance (so impetuous was his charge), the regiments sent to its support.

In reckless, crushing attack, Colonel Bowles had no superior among the officers of the division. His dauntless and rash bravery gave great weight to a charge, but, unluckily, he was perfectly indifferent about the strength of the enemy whom he charged. On this occasion greatly superior forces closed in on both flanks of his command, and a part of the enemy driving away Malone's battalion, gained his rear before he could disentangle himself. Quick fighting and fast running alone saved the regiment, but it was a "hard party" to capture, and it got away with a very slight loss in prisoners. Several men in the extreme rear were sabered, but, of course, not killed. One man of Company K, who had an axe strapped on his back, was collared by a Federal Captain, who struck him on the head with his saber. The "old regular" deliberately unstrapped his axe, and with one fierce blow shivered his assailant's skull.

The sloughs and mud holes were frequent and deep. Some of the men declared that they would "dive out of sight at one end of them and come up at the other." Lieutenant Colonels Huffman and Martin were especially enterprising during the early part of February, in the favorite feat of wagon catching, and each attacked with success and profit large foraging parties of the enemy. They some times ran into more difficult situations than they had bargained for, and it must be recorded that each had, on more than one occasion, to beat a hasty and not altogether orderly retreat. But these mishaps, invariably repaired by increased vigor and daring, served only to show that officers and men possessed one of the rarest of soldierly qualities, the capacity to receive a beating and suffer no demoralization from it. I have heard an incident of one of these dashes of Martin, related and vouched for by reliable men who witnessed it, which ought to be preserved. Martin had penetrated with a small force into the neighborhood of Murfreesboro', and upon his return was forced to cut his way through a body of the enemy's cavalry. He charged vigorously, and a melee ensued, in which the combatants were mixed all together. In this confused hand-to-hand fight, Captain Bennett (a dashing young officer, whose coolness, great strength and quickness had made him very successful and celebrated in such encounters), was confronted by an opponent who leveled a pistol at his head, and at the same time Bennett saw one of the men of his company just about to be shot or sabered by another one of the enemy. Bending low in his saddle to avoid the shot aimed at himself, Captain Bennett *first* shot the assailant of his follower and then killed his own foe. Upon one occasion, Captain Quirk in one of his many daring scouts got into a "tight place," which is thus briefly narrated by one familiar with the affair:

"On the same day, Captains Quirk and Davis (the latter of South Carolina), Colonel Breckinridge's aide, started for a sort of fancy trip toward Black's shop. Below Auburn they met Federal cavalry and charged; the enemy had prepared an ambuscade, which Quirk's men saw in time to avoid—but not so Quirk, Davis and Tom Murphy, who being splendidly mounted, were ahead. Into it, through it they went. Quirk unhurt—Davis wounded and captured, and Tom Murphy escaping with what he described 'a hell of a jolt,' with the butt of a musket in the stomach. Davis some how managed to escape, and reached our lines in safety, but with a severe flesh wound in the thigh." Captain Davis became afterward Assistant Adjutant General of the first brigade.

The following report of what was justly entitled "one of the most dashing and brilliant scouts of the war," will give an idea of how this force, so small and so constantly pressed, yet managed to assume the offensive, and of how far it would strike:

REPORT OF CAPTAIN T.H. HINES,

Liberty, Tennessee, March 3, 1863.

Colonel William C.P. Breckinridge, commanding 2nd Brigade, General Morgan's Division, Sir: Having been detailed with a detachment of thirteen men and one Lieutenant, J.M. Porter, of my company, to proceed to Kentucky, south of Barren river, for the purpose of destroying the Federal transports from plying between Bowlinggreen, Kentucky, and Evansville, Indiana, I have the honor of submitting my report. The detachment left this point at twelve o'clock, February 7th; on the evening of the 8th, crossed the Cumberland river at Granville, Tennessee. The night of the 11th, reached the vicinity of Bowlinggreen, but unfortunately our presence, force and design becoming known to the Federal authorities by the capture of Doctor Samuel Garvin, who had volunteered to accompany us, we were under the necessity of altering materially the plan of operations. We disbanded to meet on the night of the 20th, twelve miles south of Bowlinggreen. On the morning of the 21st, we burned the depot and three cars at South Union, on the Louisville and Memphis railroad, all stored with Federal property. At 12 o'clock, P.M., on the 25th, captured the steamer "Hettie Gilmore," in the employ of the Federal Government, and heavily laden with stores for the Army of the Cumberland, all of which we destroyed, paroling the boat. Made a circuit of forty miles, destroyed a train of twenty-one cars and an engine at Woodburn, on the Louisville and Nashville railroad, at 6 o'clock, P.M., February 26th. The whole amount of Federal property destroyed on the 21st, 25th and 26th, inclusive, can not fall short of half a million of dollars. In conclusion, Colonel, we have been twenty-one days, one hundred and fifty miles within the enemy's lines, traveled in thirty-six hours one hundred miles, injured the Federal Government half a million dollars, caused him to collect troops at points heretofore unprotected, thereby weakening his force in front of our army. After destroying the train at Woodburn, and being closely pursued by the enemy, we swam an angry little stream known as Drake's creek, in which attempt Corporal L.H. McKinney was washed from his horse and drowned. He was indeed a gallant soldier and much beloved by his comrades. Too much praise can not be given to Lieutenant Porter and the brave, true men who accompanied me on this trip, bearing all the fatigue and danger incident to such a scout without a murmur. I have the honor to be with great respect,

Your obedient servant,

T. HENRY HINES, Capt. Comd'g Scouts.

Sometime during February two fine regiments, the Fifth and Sixth Kentucky were added to the division. These regiments were commanded respectively, by Colonels D.H. Smith and Warren Grigsby. They had been recruited while General Bragg occupied Kentucky, for Buford's brigade, but upon the dissolution of that organization they were assigned at the request of their Colonels, to General Morgan's command. The material composing them was of the first order and their officers were zealous and efficient.

Sometime in the same month an order was issued from army headquarters, regularly brigading Morgan's command. The Second, Fifth, Sixth and Ninth Kentucky and Ninth Tennessee, were placed in one brigade, the first. The Third, Eighth, Eleventh and Tenth Kentucky, composed the second brigade. Colonels Smith and Grigsby were both the seniors of the other Colonels of the first brigade, but each refused to take command, on account of their recent attachment to the command, and Colonel Breckinridge was assigned to the temporary command of it. Colonel Adam Johnson was senior Colonel of the division, but was absent during the greater part of the winter, and Colonel Gano took command of the second brigade. The regiments, however, were so disposed and scattered, that the brigades were not practically organized for some time after the order was issued.

The history of the Ninth Tennessee regiment illustrates how much can be done by the efforts of an intelligent, zealous and firm officer, however discouraging may appear the prospect when he undertakes reforms. The men of this regiment, recruited principally in Sumner and Smith counties of Middle Tennessee, were capable, as the result showed, of being made excellent soldiers, but their training had commenced under the most inauspicious circumstances. They were collected together (as has been previously related) in August, 1862, in a camp at Hartsville, and their organization was partially effected in the neighborhood of a strong enemy, while they were entirely without arms or any support and protecting force. Several times during this period, they were attacked by the enemy and scattered in all directions–the fact that they always reassembled promptly demonstrating their excellent character.

When General Morgan returned from Kentucky, this regiment joined him at Gallatin. Its commander, Colonel Bennett, was deservedly popular for many genial and noble qualities. He was high minded, brave and generous, but neglected to enforce discipline among his men, and his regiment was utterly without it. Upon his death, Colonel William Ward succeeded to the command, and a marked change and improvement was at once perceptible. He instituted a far stricter discipline, and enforced it rigidly; he constantly drilled and instructed his men, and requiring a higher standard of efficiency in the officers, greatly improved them. At the same time he exercised the utmost care and industry in providing for all the wants of his regiment. In a very short time, the Ninth became, in all respects, the equal of any regiment in Morgan's division.

Colonel Ward's first exploit, with his regiment thus reformed, was to attack and completely defeat a foraging party, capturing several wagons and seventy-five prisoners. He then performed, with great ability, a very important duty, that of harassing General Crook's command, which had been stationed opposite Carthage, on the south side of the Cumberland. Colonel Ward, avoiding close battle, annoyed and skirmished with this force so constantly, that it never did any damage, and finally recrossed the river. From this time, the Ninth Tennessee did its fair share of dashing and successful service.

But some account should be given of the operations of Colonel Chenault, in Clinton and Wayne counties, Kentucky, and of Colonel Cluke, in the interior of the State. I can best describe the service of the first named of these commands by copying, *verbatim*, from the diary of a gallant field officer of the regiment. He says: "The regiment started" (January 15th) "in a pelting rain for Albany, Kentucky—we marched through mud, rain and snow for five days, swimming both Collins and Obie rivers, and reached Albany on the morning of the 22nd of January, 1863, all much exhausted, and many men dismounted. We find Albany a deserted village. It was once a flourishing village of five hundred inhabitants, and is the county seat of Clinton county. It is now tenantless and deserted, store houses, hotel, lawyers' offices, churches, dwelling houses and court house unoccupied and going to decay. Where was once joy, peace, prosperity and busy bustling trade, wicked war has left nought but desolation, ruin and solitude. We camped in the town, and were surrounded with a country teeming with good rations and abundance of forage.

"January 24th. With one hundred men I went on a scout to Monticello, distant twenty-five miles from Albany, drove a Yankee company, commanded by Captain Hare, out of Monticello and across the Cumberland river—captured two prisoners. From this date until the 15th February, we scouted and picketed the roads in every direction, and had good rations and forage, with comfortable quarters, but heavy duty, the whole regiment being on duty every two days. 'Tinker Dave' annoyed us so much that we had to establish a chain picket every night around the entire town. Colonel Jacob's Yankee regiment is at Creelsboro', twelve miles distant, and Woolford's brigade is at Burkesville, fourteen miles distant. Our little regiment is one hundred and twenty miles from support, and it is only by vigilance and activity that we can save ourselves. An order was received yesterday from the War Department forever fixing our destiny with Morgan.

"Learning from newspapers, that our Scouts brought in, that Woolford would make a speech in Burkesville on the 12th day of February, I started from Albany, with two companies, early that morning, and forming my men behind a hill, I watched from the bushes near the river the assembling of the crowd at the court house. At 1 o'clock the bell rang. A short time before that, the guard at the ferry, in four hundred yards of the court house, composed almost entirely of soldiers, and after speaking commenced I charged on foot to a school house immediately on the banks of the river, and from there drove the pickets, that had dismounted, away from their horses, and also broke up the speaking in tremendous disorder.

We killed a number of horses, and the killed and wounded among the Yankees were seven. The boys christened the school house Fort McCreary, but it did not last long, for the night after we left the Yankees crossed the river and burned it.

"February 19th. Colonel Cluke passed within a few miles of us, and sent an order from General Morgan for two companies. Companies D and E, Captains Dickens and Terrill, were sent him.

"March 4th. By order of General Morgan I moved with three companies from Albany to Monticello to-day; am camping in the town. The citizens are hospitable and polite. Woolford, with a very large force, is around Somerset. I am kept very busy picketing and scouting; it is General Morgan's object to occupy all the country this side of the Cumberland until Cluke's return from Kentucky.

"March 10th. To-day the balance of the regiment under Colonel Chenault arrived at Monticello. We have raised one company of new recruits since coming to Kentucky.

"March 20th. I crossed Cumberland river with twenty-six men last night in a horse trough, and then marched on foot two miles to capture a Yankee picket. The force at the picket base fled, but I captured two *videttes* stationed at the river. The trip was very severe. I lost one man.

"April 1st. General Pegram's brigade arrived to-day *en route* for Kentucky on a raid. The brain fever has killed seventeen of our regiment up to this date, among them Captain Sparr and Lieutenant Covington.

"April 11th. Pegram captured Somerset, and moved on to Danville, and thence commenced his retreat; was compelled to fight at Somerset and was defeated; Colonel Chenault moved our regiment to the river and helped him to cross. His forces were much scattered, and many were captured.

"April 8th. Cluke returned to-day from Kentucky; the two companies that went from this regiment were much injured. What is left reported to-day. Captain Terrill and Lieutenant Maupin both severely wounded at the Mt. Sterling fight, and left behind.

"April 29th. River being fordable, the enemy crossed in heavy force both at Mill Springs and mouth of Greasy Creek. Tucker met them on Mill Spring road, and I met them on Greasy Creek road; Chenault with part of the regiment remained at Monticello. The enemy was in large force, and we were compelled to evacuate Monticello at eleven o'clock to-night, and fell back in the direction of Travisville. Finding on the 1st day of May that the enemy was not pressing us, we returned to Monticello, and skirmished heavily with him; reinforcements to the enemy having arrived, we were compelled to fall back to the Obie River."

The "brain fever," to which the writer alluded, was a very singular disease. The patient attacked with it suffered with a terrible pain in the back of the head and along the spine; the extremities soon became cold, and the patient sank into torpor. It was generally fatal in a few hours. I recollect to have heard of no recovery from it.

As has already been mentioned, Colonel Cluke was dispatched to

Central Kentucky on the 4th of February. The force under his command, in all seven hundred and fifty effectives, was his own regiment, the Eighth Kentucky, under the immediate command of Major Robert S. Bullock, seventy-eight men of the Ninth Kentucky and two companies of the Eleventh, under command of Lieut. Colonel Robert G. Stoner—entitled the First Battalion; and two Companies C and I, of the Third Kentucky, and Company A, of the Second Kentucky, under command of Major Theophilus Steele—styled the Second Battalion. The two mountain howitzers ("Bull Pups") were also attached to his command, under charge of Lieutenant C.C. Corbett. This force was ably officered, every company having excellent commanders. Colonel Cluke was supplied also with an efficient staff, Captains C.C. and C.H. Morgan (of the General's own staff) accompanied him. Lieutenant Moreland (a staff officer of the first brigade) attended him as aide, and was eminently fitted (on account of his earnest and serious turn of mind) to act as adviser in an expedition wherein so many delicate and difficult questions might arise for solution, although his extreme gravity of temper and taciturn manner made the younger and more mercurial officers of the staff somewhat impatient of his society.

Colonel Cluke had no officer regularly detailed as A.A.A. General. Sergeant Lawrence Dickerson, clerk of the Adjutant's office of the first brigade, and thoroughly competent, performed all the duties of one.

The advance guard was commanded by Lieutenant Shuck of the Eighth Kentucky, and the scouts were commanded by Lieutenant Hopkins, of the Second, and Lieutenant S.P. Cunningham, of the Eighth. One hundred rounds of ammunition and six days' rations were issued to the men upon the morning that the command marched. The weather was inclement and intensely cold, when this expedition was commenced. A march through sleet, rain, and snow, and over terrible roads, brought Colonel Cluke to the Cumberland river on the evening of the 18th. Lieut.-Colonel Stoner and Lieutenant Hopkins crossed the river, with a few men, in a canoe, surprised and captured the Federal pickets posted to guard the ferry, at which Colonel Cluke wished to cross, and brought over flatboats and a coal barge, by means of which the entire command was crossed, the horses being made to swim. So bitter was the cold that eight horses chilled to death immediately upon emerging from the stream.

On the 19th the column reached Somerset. A strong force of the enemy had been stationed there, but fell back to Danville on learning of Colonel Cluke's approach. The greater part of the stores collected there fell into Cluke's hands. Pressing on, Cluke compelled the surrender of a detachment of Federal troops at Mt. Vernon, and did not halt until within fifteen miles of Richmond. Wretched roads and a blinding snow storm rendered this march harassing and tedious. The scouts moved to within ten miles of Richmond, and Lieutenant Hopkins halting with a portion of them, Lieutenant Cunningham went on three miles further with eight men. He found a picket post of the enemy, where four videttes were stationed. He answered their challenge by declaring himself and party friends, and, advancing to the post, persuaded the Federals that they were an advance party of Woolford's regiment, which they represented to be returning from Tennessee to Kentucky to assist in repelling an anticipated raid. Lieutenant Cunningham stated that all the various Federal forces in that region were to be immediately concentrated at Lexington, as certain information had been obtained that General Breckinridge had entered the State at the head of ten thousand infantry. The sergeant of the post then gave Lieutenant Cunningham a statement of the location and strength of all the Federal commands in the vicinity, and invited him to go to a house a short distance off, where the picket detail to which he belonged made base. Cunningham, finding this detail twenty-four strong, made an excuse to send back two of his own men and one of the Federals, thus calling Hopkins to his aid, who, in an hour or two, arrived with the other eight men of the scouts.

A skirmish immediately ensued between the parties. One Federal was killed and two wounded—the rest were made prisoners. They were completely deceived and surprised. The whole affair was as clever a piece of strategy as can be found in the annals of partisan service. Learning that two hundred and fifty of the enemy were at Richmond, Cluke broke camp at an early hour and marched rapidly in hopes to capture them. They started to Lexington, however, before he got to Richmond. The rumor (which had been industriously circulated) that Breckinridge had entered the State, was accomplishing its work. Major Steele was immediately dispatched, with three companies under his command. He overtook the rear-guard at Comb's ferry, and drove it in upon the column—a brisk skirmish and chase ensuing—Steele driving them into Lexington. He came very near being killed shortly afterward. Leaving his command halted, he rode to a picket post some distance off, with one or two men, and essayed to capture the videttes. One of them (after signifying that he would surrender) suddenly placed his rifle to the Major's breast and fired. A thick Mexican blanket wrapped tightly in many folds about his body, saved his life; yet the bullet pierced the blanket and entered his breast, breaking a rib. This wound disabled him, at a time when his services were most needed, for several days.

On the same night, Captain C.H. Morgan and Lieutenant Corbett, while reconnoitering near Lexington and seeking highly important information, were captured. Colonel Cluke moved on the night of the 22nd (crossing the Kentucky river at Boonsboro') to Winchester, reaching that place on the 23rd. He then sent detachments in various directions to excite and bewilder the enemy as thoroughly as possible. Major Bullock advancing toward Lexington, Lieutenant Colonel Stoner was sent to Mt. Sterling, and Lieutenant Cunningham was sent toward Paris. The most intense excitement prevailed and reports were rife and believed that rebels were flocking into the State from all directions. Cluke finding that he had reduced the enemy to inaction, and could do so safely, permitted men who lived in the neighboring counties to visit their homes and thus gave greater currency to these rumors. This had been one of the objects of the expedition. The other ends had in view, in undertaking it, to-wit: to obtain and keep a thorough understanding of the condition of affairs in Kentucky during the winter, and to enable the men to procure horses and clothing, were perfectly accomplished. Lieutenant Cunningham demonstrated successfully in the direction of Paris, confining the troops there to the town. Lieut. Colonel Stoner moved rapidly on Mt. Sterling and found the enemy, which had been stationed there under Colonel Wadsworth, just evacuating the town. Stoner immediately attacked and completely routed his enemy. The road by which the latter retreated, was strewn for miles with overcoats, guns, wrecked wagons, and all the debris of routed and fleeing troops. Stoner captured many prisoners and several wagons.

On the 24th, the entire command was concentrated at Mt. Sterling, and the day was spent in collecting and distributing horses, equipments, etc. The enemy at Lexington having recovered by this time from the fright given them on the 21st, by Major Steele, and learning the falsity of the rumors of a heavy Confederate advance, now came out in search of Cluke. On the morning of the 25th, a brigade dashed into Mt. Sterling. The command was much weakened, not only by the detachments which had again been sent out, but by furloughs allowed men who lived in the immediate vicinity. It was at once driven out of the town but retreated, unpursued, only a short distance. It has been said that the men came in so quickly, that the command was increased from two hundred to six hundred, before "the echoes of the enemy's artillery had died away." This brigade which had driven out Cluke, established itself at Mt. Sterling. Cluke now successfully inaugurated a strategy which has been greatly and justly admired by his comrades. Lieutenant Cunningham was sent with a few picked men to the vicinity of Lexington and directed to spy thoroughly upon the officials there. Ascertaining enough to make the project feasible, the Lieutenant sent a shrewd fellow (disguised in Federal uniform) to the headquarters of the officer commanding, upon some pretended business which enabled him to hang about the office. While there this man purloined some printed blanks and brought them out with him. One of these was filled up with an order (purporting to come from Lexington to the officer in command at Mt. Sterling), instructing him to march at once to Paris to repel a raid threatening the Kentucky Central railroad. He was directed to leave his baggage under a small garrison at Mt. Sterling. A courier properly dressed bore this order to Mt. Sterling, and dashed in with horse reeking with sweat and every indication of excited haste. He played his part so well that the order was not criticized and induced no suspicion. This courier's name was Clark Lyle—an excellent and daring scout.

As soon as the necessary preparations were made, the Federals marched to Paris and Cluke re-entered the town, capturing the garrison and stores. He remained until the 8th of March, his scouts harassing the enemy and keeping him informed of their every movement.

Another heavy advance of the enemy induced Colonel Cluke to retreat beyond Slate into the hills about Howard's mill.

Three companies were left in the vicinity of Mount Sterling, under Captain Cassell. One stationed upon the North Middletown pike, was so closely pressed by the enemy, that it was forced to cross Slate, below

Howard's mill. The other two were also hotly attacked and driven back to Colonel Cluke's encampment, sustaining, however, but slight loss. Falling back to Ficklin's tan yard, where it was posted in ambush, and failing to entice the enemy into the snare, Colonel Cluke marched to Hazelgreen, determining to await there the arrival of General Humphrey Marshall, who was reported to be approaching (from Abingdon), with three thousand men.

Captain Calvin Morgan volunteered to carry a message to Marshall, and traveled (alone), the wild country between Hazelgreen and Pound Gap, a country infested with a crowd of ferocious bushwhackers. About this time, Cluke's whole force must have been badly off, if the language of one of his officers be not exaggerated, who (in an account of the encampment at Hazelgreen) declares that, "the entire command was prostrated by a severe attack of erisipelas."

After the effects of this "attack" had somewhat worn off, Lieutenant Colonel Stoner was sent back to Montgomery, and maintained himself there for several days, with skill and gallantry. Threatening demonstrations from the enemy induced Cluke to retreat from Hazelgreen and still further into the mountains. He established himself on the middle fork of Licking, near Saliersville. On the 19th, he found himself completely surrounded. Fifteen hundred of the enemy had gained his rear, ten hundred advancing from Louisa, were on his right, and eight hundred were at Proctor, on his left. In his front was the garrison of Mt. Sterling, five hundred strong, but likely at any time to be reinforced by the forces then in Central Kentucky. The roads in all directions were so well observed that he could not hope to escape without a fight.

His command was reduced to about three hundred effectives—the rest were suffering from the erisipelas. In this emergency, Colonel Cluke conceived a determination at once bold, and exceedingly judicious. He resolved to march straight on Mount Sterling and attack it, at any hazard. He trusted that the enemy would send no more troops there, but would rather (anticipating that he would seek to escape southward), send all that could be collected to intercept him in that quarter.

A tremendous march of sixty miles in twenty-four hours, over mountains and across swollen streams, brought him to McIntyre's ferry of the Licking, thirty miles from Mt. Sterling. Crossing on the night of the 20th and morning of the 21st, Major Steele was sent with his battalion *via*, Owingsville (in Bath county), to take position on the Winchester pike, beyond Mount Sterling, that he might give timely information of the approach of reinforcements to the garrison. Colonel Cluke moved with the rest of his command through Mud Lick Spring, directly to Mount Sterling. Colonel Cluke at the head of a body of men entered the town from the east, while Lieutenant Colonel Stoner with the two companies from the Eleventh Kentucky, the men of the Ninth under Captain McCormick, and Hopkins' scouts, charged in from the northwest.

The enemy fell back and shut themselves up in the court-house. Stoner charged them, but was driven back by a terrible fire from the windows—the garrison was stronger than the force he led against them. A detachment of thirty men were then ordered to advance on the street into which the Winchester pike leads, and burn the houses in which the Federals had ensconced themselves. With torch, axe and sledge hammer these men under McCormick and Cunningham forced their way into the heart of the town. As they reached the "Old Hotel," which was occupied by a body of the Federals, and used also as a hospital, a flag of truce was displayed. McCormick, Cunningham, and six others entered, and were coolly informed by some forty or fifty soldiers that the sick had surrendered, but they (the soldier) had not, and threatened to fire upon them, from the upper rooms, if they tried to escape from the building. At the suggestion of Lieutenant Saunders, the eight Confederates forced the sick men to leave the house with them, in a mingled crowd, thus rendering it impossible for the Federals to fire without endangering the lives of their comrades. Before quitting the house, they set it on fire. In a short time the entire Federal force in the town surrendered, and victors and vanquished went to work together to extinguish the flames.

Colonel Cluke took four hundred and twenty-eight prisoners, two hundred and twenty wagons laden with valuable stores, five hundred mules, and nearly one thousand stand of arms. Captain Virgil Pendleton, a most gallant and valuable officer was killed in this affair. Captain Ferrill and Lieutenant Maupin were seriously wounded. Cluke's loss was three killed, and a few wounded. The enemy's but little greater.

The Union men of Mount Sterling were much mortified by this last capture of their town. The previous evening bets were running high that Cluke would be made prisoner. Cluke immediately evacuated the town, and was attacked some five miles to the eastward of it, by a force of Federal cavalry, preceding a body of infantry which were approaching to relieve the place. An insignificant skirmish resulted, and Cluke marched to Owingsville unpursued. On the next day he encamped at McIntyre's ferry, and collected his entire command, now convalescent. Marshall marching from Pound Gap, about this time, dispersed the forces which had gone to capture Cluke at Saliersville. On the 25th, Major Steele was sent across the Kentucky river to join General Pegram, who had advanced with a brigade of Confederate cavalry to Danville. Major Steele reached him much further south. As he was retreating from the State, General Pegram halted near Somerset to fight a strong force of the enemy which was following him and was defeated. Major Steele's battalion was highly complimented for the part it took in the action, and in covering the subsequent retreat. On the 26th, Colonel Cluke again advanced, and encamped in the vicinity of Mount Sterling. He received orders soon after from General Morgan to return, and marched southward accordingly. Colonel Cluke had good right to be proud of this expedition. He had penetrated into the heart of Kentucky, and maintained himself, for more than a month, with inferior forces—always fighting and never defeated, the enemy at last did not drive him out. He recrossed the Cumberland at the same point, and was stationed with Colonel Chenault, in the vicinity of Albany. Colonel Cluke's command was stronger by eighteen men when he returned than when he set out upon his raid.

In order to trace properly the history of the division, during this period, it is necessary that I disregard chronological arrangement, and return to the winter in Tennessee. In the latter part of February a new regiment was formed of Major Hamilton's battalion and some loose companies which had long been unattached, and some which had recently been recruited for General Morgan. Colonel R.C. Morgan (brother of the General), was assigned to the command of this regiment, and Major Hamilton became Lieutenant Colonel. A month or two later, a valuable addition was made to it in Quirk's scouts. Colonel Morgan was an excellent officer and had acted as Assistant Adjutant General to Lieutenant General A.P. Hill through all the stern battles and glorious campaigns, in which his chief had figured so conspicuously. Becoming tired of staff duty, and anxious to exchange the infantry service for the less monotonous life in the cavalry, he naturally chose his brother's command, and obtained a transfer to it. He became a dashing cavalry officer, and as an essential preliminary relaxed the rigidity of some of his military notions acquired while serving on the staff. He soon gave in to the prevalent cavalry opinion that horses were, or at least ought to be, "common carriers." During this winter, more prisoners were taken than there were effective men in the division, or men actively at work. The loss in killed and wounded which it inflicted was also severe, and the captures of stores, munitions, etc., were valuable and heavy.

The exertions made to equip and supply the command, by the division Quartermaster and Commissary of Subsistence, Majors Llewellyn and Elliott, ought to be mentioned, if for no other reason than the injustice which has been done them and the unmerited censures which have been showered upon them. Even now, there are, doubtless, few officers or men of the former Confederate army who can so far overcome the prejudice deeply rooted against men who served in those departments, that they can speak with any sort of commendation of Quartermasters and Commissaries. It has rarely happened that even the most industrious, efficient and honest of these officers have escaped the severest denunciation. I can testify that both of these gentlemen strove hard to provide for the wants of the division, although the tender attention they paid to their own, prevented them getting credit for it. They might have done better it is true, and the same can be said of all of us—but they certainly did a great deal. Major Elliott was never himself except when encompassed by difficulties—when there was really some excuse for failure, when supplies were really hard to obtain, then he became great. The avalanche of curses which invariably descend upon a Commissary, at all times, never disturbed his equanimity, except when he was in a barren country—then he would display Napoleonic resources.

Once a large lot of meat stored at Smithville took fire. He issued cooked hams to the troops, and the loss was scarcely felt. Once he lost all of his papers, accounts, receipts; vouchers, memoranda all went down on abstract, L., as the Quartermaster said of himself, who was picked off by a sharpshooter. The loss did not disturb him for a moment. He declared he could supply every paper from memory, and produced an entirely new set, which he claimed to be identical in substance with the originals. Of course every one laughed at him, but in the course of time, the old papers turned up, and, sure enough, there was not a dollar's difference between them and the new.

The great lack of supplies necessary to the comfort of troops, required to do constant and severe duty in such weather, told injuriously upon the discipline of the command. It was impossible to obtain clothing, shoes, etc., in quantities at all adequate to the demand and the greatest efforts of energy and enterprise upon the part of the subaltern officers, never make up for the deficiency in the regular supply of these articles from the proper sources.

Pay was something the men scarcely expected, and it benefited them very little when they received it. If the Confederate Government could have made some provision, by which its soldiers would have been regularly paid, the men would have been far better satisfied, for there is something gratifying to human nature in the receipt of money even when it is smartly depreciated. Certainly, if comfortable clothing and good serviceable boots and shoes had been issued, as they were needed, and the rations had been occasionally improved by the issue of coffee, or something which would have been esteemed a delicacy, the discipline and efficiency of all the troops would have been vastly promoted. It is hard to maintain discipline, when men are required to perform the most arduous and harassing duties without being clothed, shod, paid or fed. If they work and fight they will have little time to provide for themselves. But they certainly will not starve, and they object, decidedly, to doing without clothing if by any means and exertions they can obtain it. Then the converse of the proposition becomes equally true, and if they provide for themselves, they will have little time to work and fight. With cavalry, for instance, the trouble of keeping men in camp who were hungry and half frozen, and who felt that they had done good service, was very great. The infantryman, even if equally destitute, could not well straggle, but the cavalry soldier had his horse to take him, although the distance was great and the road was rough.

When men once commenced running about, they became incorrigible in the habit. Hunger might draw them out at first, but whisky would then become an allurement, and a multitude of seductive inducements would cause them to persist in the practice. In nine cases out of ten, when a man became an inveterate straggler, he was no loss if he were shot. These seem truisms, too palpable to need mention, but for three years they were dinned into the ears of certain officials, and not the slightest impression was made. These gentlemen preferred to attribute all evils, of the peculiar class which have just been mentioned, to the inherent and wicked antipathy to discipline, which the cavalry (they declared) entertained. They declared, moreover, that these articles could not be procured. This excuse passed current until the latter part of the war, when

Federal raids and dashes disclosed the fact (by destroying or cutting them off from our use) unknown to all but the officials and employees, that hoarded and stored them away, at the very time that the Confederate armies were melting away for the lack of them.

It is no answer to the charge of incompetency or malfeasance upon the part of men charged with their distribution to say, that there was not enough to supply the demand. They should have been made to go as far as they would. It is difficult for one unfamiliar with the workings of these departments and the obstacles in the way of procuring supplies, to suggest a remedy for these shortcomings, but it is certain that the Confederacy owned cotton and tobacco and could have gotten more; that blockade running was active and could have been stimulated. An abstinence from certain luxurious but costly experiments might have enabled the Confederacy to buy more clothing, shoes, and meat. The opinion is hazarded with diffidence, and is that of one who was naturally prone to attach more importance to the sustenance of the military than of the naval power of the Confederacy, but would it not have been better to have expended upon the army the money paid for the construction of those fine and high-priced iron-clads, which steamed sportively about for a day or two after they left the stocks, and were then inevitably scuttled?

The winter wore away, and the condition of affairs in Tennessee, as described in the first part of this chapter, continued unchanged. Three times the enemy advanced in heavy force (cavalry, infantry, and artillery) to Liberty. Upon each occasion, the regiments stationed there under Colonel Breckinridge, after skillfully and courageously contesting his advance for many miles to the front of Liberty, fell back to Snow's Hill, three miles to the east of it, and returned to press hard upon the enemy's rear when he retired. At length, upon the 19th of March, when Colonel Ward was absent with his regiment reconnoitering in the direction of Carthage, and the force at Liberty was weakened by other detachments, until it was scarcely more than six hundred strong, information was received that the enemy were advancing and were near Milton, a small village about eighteen miles from Liberty. General Morgan had, the day before, notified Colonel Breckinridge of his intention to be at Liberty on the 19th. Colonel Breckinridge, when it became clear that the enemy was certainly pressing, posted his command in a good position upon the Murfreesboro' pike, and sent a courier to Gano with a request that the latter would promptly join him with his entire effective force. Colonel Breckinridge says of this disposition of his command: "To delay the enemy and give Gano time to come up, the pickets were strengthened and thrown forward. The enemy, being infantry, came on slowly but gradually drove our pickets nearly in. The peculiar formation of the ground gave the brigade great advantage, and admirably concealed its weakness. The enemy made demonstrations, but made no attack, and before nightfall bivouacked in line in sight of our skirmishers. Just at dark Morgan rode upon the ground, and was received with deafening cheers; and soon afterward Colonel Gano came up. Under cover of night the enemy withdrew to Auburn."

General Morgan, in his official report of the fight which ensued on the next day at Milton, says: "On the evening of the 19th inst. I reached Liberty, Tenn., and learned that the Federals were moving upon that place from Murfreesboro', their numbers being variously reported at from two thousand to four thousand infantry, and two hundred cavalry, with one section of artillery. At the time I reached my videttes on the Milton road, the enemy was within five miles of Liberty; it being near night, they fell back to Auburn, and encamped. Determining to attack them next morning, I ordered Colonels Breckinridge and Gano, who were in command of brigades, to move within four miles of the enemy, and hold themselves in readiness to move at any moment. In the meantime, I sent the 'scouts' to watch the movements of the enemy and to report, and to see if any reinforcements came up; also, to send me information when the enemy moved, for I was determined not to make the attack at Auburn, as they held a very strong position, and I was desirous they should move beyond a gorge in the mountains before the attack was commenced; for, if they had been permitted to take position there, it would have been impossible to dislodge them. After daylight, one of the scouts returned, bringing intelligence that the enemy was moving. Captain Quirk was ordered to move forward with his company, and attack the enemy's rear when they passed the mountain, and retard their progress until the main column arrived. When within a mile of Milton, Captain Quirk came up with their rear guard and commenced a vigorous attack upon them. The enemy immediately halted, deploying their skirmishers to the rear, and, bringing their pieces into position, commenced shelling Captain Quirk's men and the road upon which they had advanced. In a short time I arrived upon the ground. Finding that the main column of the enemy was still falling back, and their artillery was unsupported by any troops (with the exception of their skirmishers) I determined, if possible, to capture it. I, therefore, ordered Lieutenant Colonel Martin to move to the left with his regiment, and Colonel Breckinridge to send one to the right—to go forward rapidly and when within striking distance, to move in and cut off the pieces. Having two pieces of artillery, I ordered them to go forward on the road, supported by Colonel Ward's regiment, dismounted, and the remainder of the command to move in column in supporting distance.

"Just before the two regiments which had moved to the right and left reached the proper place to move upon the artillery, the enemy's skirmishers and artillery fell back rapidly upon their main column, which occupied a steep hill covered with cedars. They placed their battery on a line, with their column on the road immediately upon their right. To reach this position we would have to pass through a cedar brake, the ground being very rough and broken. A few of the enemy's skirmishers were thrown forward to that point. I ordered my two pieces of artillery to move upon the left of the road until they reached a point within four hundred yards of the enemy's artillery and then to silence their guns.

"They went forward gallantly, supported by a part of Ward's regiment. Lieutenant Colonel Martin who still occupied his position on the left was ordered forward to threaten the right of the enemy. At the same time, I ordered the command under Colonel Gano to move up, dismount and attack the enemy, vigorously, immediately in the front. Colonel Breckinridge was ordered to move to the right with his command and attack their extreme left. Captain Quirk, in the meantime, had been ordered to get upon the pike, immediately in the rear of the enemy, which he did in a most satisfactory manner, capturing fifteen or twenty prisoners.

"He remained in the rear of the enemy until reinforcements came to them from Murfreesboro' (being only thirteen miles distant), when he was driven back. When our artillery opened, the whole command moved forward. Colonel Martin charged up in most gallant style, and had a number of his horses killed with canister, as the guns of the enemy were turned upon him. The remainder of the command was moved up to within one hundred yards of the main column of the Federals and dismounted. Moving rapidly to the front, they drove in the enemy's skirmishers, and pushed forward in the most gallant manner upon the hill occupied by the enemy, which was about sixty yards from the cedar brake alluded to. Colonel Breckinridge who commanded our extreme right, had his men dismounted, and went boldly up, the enemy's artillery being at this time moved from the pike to a position upon the top of the hill immediately in their center; but this was not accomplished until it came near being captured by Colonel Grigsby, who was within fifty yards of it and moving rapidly upon it, when his ammunition giving completely out, he was forced to halt, and the battery was saved. It was near this point that Colonel Napier was severely wounded while cheering and leading his men up. Colonel Grigsby was also wounded while in front of his command and encouraging his men. At the same time the firing from the center of the line nearly ceased; a few scattering shots, now and then, gave evidence that nearly all of the ammunition was exhausted. Two more rounds would have made our victory complete, and two thousand Federals would have been the result of the day's fighting."

Finding his ammunition completely gone, General Morgan ordered a withdrawal, and his forces fell back to Milton, the enemy neither firing upon nor pursuing them. Here he found an ordnance train and four pieces of artillery which had been sent from McMinnville. He was encouraged to renew the attack, hoping to capture the entire opposing force. "Martin was placed in the same position which he had previously occupied, and Gano, whose entire command had by this time arrived, was sent to the right.

The artillery took position in about eight hundred yards of the enemy's battery, and commenced a rapid and severe fire upon them. They had again taken position upon the pike, from which they were soon driven by Lieutenant Lawrence, who was in command of my battery. Our pieces were served with the greatest precision and coolness, and the men stood by their guns like veterans. Although they had but few men in the fight, the casualties were two killed and eighteen wounded, showing the determination with which they held their position. Too much praise can not be awarded to Lieutenant Lawrence. Three times the enemy had to change the position of their battery, and were silenced until reinforced by additional guns. While this artillery duel was progressing, my men were moving to the front and were about dismounting, when Captain Quirk was driven from the rear by a large force of the enemy which had just arrived in time to save the force in our front. I immediately ordered my entire command to fall back to Milton, and from thence to Liberty. The enemy did not follow."

General Morgan expressed his perfect satisfaction with the conduct of the officers and men in this fight, and complimented his brigade commanders and his personal staff.

One reason of the want of success in the first onset was the fatigue of men and horses by the long and rapid ride to Auburn, and thence to the position taken by the enemy. In the stretching gallop down the road, which General Morgan ordered in his impatience to overtake the enemy, and apprehensive lest they should get away, the column necessarily became prolonged, the men scattered, and many (their horses falling) dropped out entirely. But few men, consequently, were available when the attack commenced. As the detached portions of regiments, divided by this speedy march, came up, there was, necessarily, some confusion, and some difficulty in putting them, at once, promptly and smoothly into the fight.

For these reasons, and on account of the usual details for horse holders, perhaps not more than one thousand men were engaged on our side, and these (as has been just explained) could not be handled as effectively as was necessary to force a strong position, held by superior numbers. Colonel Ward's regiment is frequently alluded to in General Morgan's report, but it should be stated that the bulk of that regiment was absent, only sixty men (one of its companies), under Captain Cates, were present. The scanty supply of ammunition, however, and its failure at the critical moment, was the principal cause of the repulse, or rather withdrawal of our troops. All who have given any account of this battle concur in praising the conduct of the combatants. It was fought with the utmost determination, and with no flinching on either side.

One incident is thus described by an eye-witness:

"Just here Martin performed one of those acts of heroic, but useless courage, too common among our officers. When his regiment wavered and commenced to fall back, he halted until he was left alone; then at a slow walk, rode to the pike, and with his hat off rode slowly out of fire. He was splendidly mounted, wore in his hat a long black plume, was himself a large and striking figure, and I have often thought that it was the handsomest picture of cool and desperate courage I saw in the war."

Our loss in this fight was very heavy, especially in officers. The list of wounded officers was large. Captains Sale, Marr, Cooper and Cossett, and a number of other officers, were killed. Captain Sale was the third Captain of Company E, Second Kentucky, who was killed. Captain Cossett, of the Ninth Tennessee, was under arrest at the time, for charges of which he was acquitted after death. He was killed, fighting with his musket, as a volunteer. General Morgan's clothing was torn with balls.

About this time an impression prevailed at General Bragg's Headquarters, that the enemy was about to evacuate Murfreesboro' and, perhaps, Nashville. General Morgan had come to Liberty on the 19th, in order to reconnoiter with reference to ascertaining the truth of this rumor.

Upon the day before, Colonel Breckinridge had been ordered to move to Lebanon with his brigade, and a section of Byrne's battery, and was informed that he would be supported by Gano. In the order he was told: "The object of these demonstrations is to discover, if possible, whether the rumored evacuation of Murfreesboro' by the Federals is true, and if so, to what point they are moving their forces. In the event that they are falling back to Nashville, the command will move from Lebanon, cross the river and attack and harass them. At Lebanon, or within twenty-four hours after your arrival at that point, certain information can be obtained as to what is taking place on the enemy's lines. In the event your pickets or scouts report an advance from Readyville or Murfreesboro', you will not leave your present position."

Upon the 19th the following dispatch came from General Bragg's Headquarters to Wheeler:

"To Major General James Wheeler, McMinnville, Tennessee:

"Ascertain what direction the enemy takes after leaving Gallatin.

[Signed] "GEO. WM. BRENT, *A.A. Gen'l.*"

This proved conclusively that General Bragg believed that Nashville and the whole of Middle Tennessee was about to be evacuated by the Federal army.

General Morgan did not believe so, nor did Colonel Breckinridge, who was charged with the scouting of all the extreme right flank. The latter officer says: "It is true, that, at this time, General Rosecrans ordered back his sick, his surplus baggage, camp followers, increased his guard at every station in his rear, displayed greater vigilance at his pickets, vailed his movements in greater secrecy, and became stringent in his rules about passes to and from his camps and lines. All our scouts reported these movements, and our Generals concluded he meant a retreat. Morgan believed otherwise," etc.

General Morgan, in reality, believed that these were all the indications of an advance rather than of retreat, and he confidently anticipated the former in the early part of April. On the 3rd of April there *was* an advance, which, although not of the entire Federal army, yet comprehended so large a part of it, as to completely rid the country, in which our command had been wintering, of their presence for a short time.

This force approached Liberty on the 2nd of April, causing the concentration there of both brigades, with the exception of the detachments necessarily sent to observe different important points.

The entire command, after some skirmishing, took position near Liberty, but to the east of it, and encamped in line of battle, on the night of the 2nd.

The enemy retreated about a mile and bivouacked. Scouts were sent through his camp that night and discovered that behind the cavalry, was a heavy infantry force. Other scouts also reported that Hazen was advancing from Readyville and Crook from Carthage. Colonel Ward was sent to watch the Carthage roads, and all the rest were disposed to resist the advance of the enemy directly in front. Colonel Gano was senior officer and leaving Breckinridge to conduct the retreat to "Snow's hill," he took charge of the preparations for defense there.

"Snow's hill" was regarded by the majority of the officers (who had served about Liberty) as a very strong position, but, I believe, that they all agreed subsequently that the opinion was a mistaken one. As a defensive position against attack from an enemy who came through Liberty, it possessed no strong features at all—in reality the advantages were all on the side of the attacking party if he possessed a numerical strength which would enable him to occupy all the approaches to the position and maintain a connected line. It is a long slope, or rather collection of sloping ridges, which, beginning at the table land eastward of the valley in which Liberty is situated, point due westward.

The road from Liberty to Smithville runs through the center of the position upon Snow's hill, which was selected for defense, but bends and curves according to the necessities of the grade. The ridges all point toward Liberty and are parallel to the general direction of the road. They can not be called rugged and inaccessible, for although their northern and southern sides are somewhat precipitous, the back-bone of each is comparatively smooth and the ascent is by no means abrupt or difficult from the points where they subside into the valley to their summit at the eastern ends. The ravines between these ridges can be readily traversed by troops and the bluffs at the eastern extremity of each, or where they "head," can be easily climbed. It is true, that the conformation of the ground presents at one side, a serious obstacle to an attacking force. The base of these ridges, which have been described, or the parent hill, of which they seem to be offshoots, is separated from the level ground to the eastward by a singular and deep gulf, some two or three hundred yards wide and I know not how long. This abyss (it may be called) is crossed by a sort of natural wall, or what would be termed in railroad parlance, "fill," the sides of which are very abrupt and steep. It is not more than thirty or forty feet wide, and the road runs along it. To the southward of this deep, long chasm, is a gap in the hill through which ran a road by which the rear of the entire position could be gained. If this gap had been occupied and the narrow road across the wide, deep chasm had been adequately commanded by earthworks which could protect the defenders from artillery planted on the tops of the hills, the position would have been impregnable, perhaps, from attack against its front, and the enemy could have carried it only by marching far around upon one or the other flank.

But the position always selected by our forces, stationed there, for fight, was about half way down the ridges toward Liberty. Here the enemy's artillery had full play at them, his infantry marching up the ravines and ridges had an equal chance with them, for there was no cover and all were equally exposed; the regiments defending the position were necessarily separated from each other and could not act in concert, their horses embarrassed them, unless carried a long distance to the rear, and their every movement was completely apparent to the enemy. The left flank was, also, always in danger, and if turned by cavalry, the retreat would be necessarily compromised.

During the night of the 2nd, the Sixth Kentucky and Quirk's scouts were posted to watch the enemy, and the rest of the command was withdrawn to the eastward of Liberty and took position upon the hill. Two guns of Byrne's battery were planted, to sweep the road, a few hundred yards from the town. At daylight the enemy's cavalry charged the force in front of the town and drove it back. Major Bullitt, commanding Sixth Kentucky, held them back for a while, but their numbers and the dash with which they came told, and they forced him to rapid retreat. Soon their close pursuit brought the enemy within the range of the guns, and their fire made them call a halt, and Bullitt and Quirk charged in their turn. The Confederates, however, were borne steadily backward.

To the eastward of Liberty the enemy met with another check at the long covered bridge over Dry creek about a mile from the town. The guns were planted to command the bridge and masked; when the enemy had crowded it full, Byrnes opened and burst his shells right in their midst. In a short time answering artillery drove the Confederates away.

Established on Snow's hilt, the line was not able to remain long in position under the heavy fire of artillery and the attack of the infantry. A long column of cavalry moved up Dry creek, and turning upon the left flank, came through the gap which has been mentioned. Lieutenant Colonel Huffman was sent with the Third Kentucky, to check them, but, unluckily, did not reach the gap in time. He prevented, however, their further advance until the troops under Colonel Breckinridge (which about the same time began to retreat) had passed the point where this force could have cut them off.

I came up to the rear, about this time, in company with Colonel Smith—we had ridden from McMinnville together and had heard cannonading, and learned that there was a fight going on. We saw nothing of it, however, but it's effects upon the stragglers and "bummers," who seemed to have unaccountably increased. I had been absent from the command for more than two months, but knew of the gallant service it had done, and took for granted that its *morale* was unimpaired. Colonel Smith, who had left Liberty only two or three days before, was more surprised than myself at the stream of stragglers which we met. The moral condition of the men was the most singular I ever witnessed. There was no panic, no running, jostling, wild fear. They rode along quietly, talked rationally, seemed utterly free from any lively and immediate apprehension, but "just couldn't be made to fight," and yet quiet and "serene" as seemed to be their timidity, it made some of them go clear off, swim unfordable streams, and stay away for days. We were unprovided with a guard, and although we could stop these fellows, until the road was packed and jammed with them, it was utterly impossible to make them turn back. At length, in disgust, we gave up the attempt, and rode on to see what was the condition of affairs nearer the scene of actual fighting. Colonel Smith hastened to his regiment, and I went in quest of Colonels Gano and Breckinridge, and kept a watch for the Second Kentucky.

I met the column of Colonel Breckinridge retreating, but in excellent order; the ranks were depleted by the stragglers, but the men who were left were as firm and cool as ever. The same was true of that portion of Colonel Gano's brigade which I saw. The men were occasionally cheering, and seemed perfectly ready to return, if necessary, to fight. When Lieutenant Colonel Huffman, in accordance with orders sent him by Colonel Gano, undertook to withdraw from his position upon the left, his men became crowded and confused, on account of the peculiar conformation of the ground. The enemy, taking advantage of this confusion, charged him. The Fourth Regulars came vigorously upon his rear, and did smart damage. The regiment recoiled in disorder for some distance. At length, Gano, with some thirty or forty men, charged the Fourth Regulars, and checked them. Quirk dashed to his assistance with about the same number of men, and the enemy was driven completely away. No further pursuit was attempted, and the column retreated toward Smithville. On the way Lieutenant Colonel Martin was sent with a few men to watch the roads leading from the ground in possession of the enemy, to the Smithville and McMinnville road, in order to prevent any effort of the enemy to surprise us upon that road. The wagon train had been previously ordered to move through Smithville to McMinnville by this same road. Some of Martin's men (dressed in blue overcoats) came out upon the road, suddenly, in front of the train. The teamsters took them to be Yankees, and the wildest stampede ensued. The teamsters and wagon attachees ran in every direction, crazy with fright. Some turned their teams and put back to Smithville, others floundered off of the road and tried to drive through thickets that a child's toy cart could scarcely have been hauled through. Many wagons were, consequently, smashed up before the panic could be abated.

That night we encamped some fourteen miles from McMinnville. At this date Colonel Gano's connection with the command ceased, and we lost the benefit of his character as an officer and man. No officer had won more and better merited distinction, and his popularity was justly very great. Functional disease of the heart, brought about by exposure, hard work and intense excitement, compelled him to withdraw, for a time, from active service, and when he returned, with re-established health, to the field, it was to win new laurels and accomplish brilliant work in the Trans-Mississippi.

The division received more injury from this affair than I would have supposed a hard fight and serious defeat would have done it. Nearly two weeks were required to collect the fugitives.

General Morgan, on his way to join us on the night of the 3rd, met a straggler, wandering loosely about, and demanded sternly why he was absent from his regiment, "Well, General," answered the fellow, ingenuously, "I'm scattered."

CHAPTER XIV

On the 5th, the command under General Morgan, in person, moved to Liberty, which the enemy had by this time evacuated. Scouts and pickets were thrown out, but although the enemy were reported to be still at Alexandria in large force, there was no collision even with his videttes. After remaining at Liberty a few hours, General Morgan withdrew, moving about ten o'clock at night, to Smithville again. He had no desire to attack the enemy, if in any such force as he was represented to be, nor was he willing to await an attack in the then condition of his command. A report, too, had reached him, which turned out to be unfounded, that McMinnville had been taken, that afternoon, by another expedition from Murfreesboro'.

We remained at Smithville until the 7th, and then returned to Liberty, in accordance with orders from General Wheeler, who had reached Alexandria on the same evening, with Wharton's division. Two or three days subsequently, General Wheeler proceeded to Lebanon with all of the troops at his disposal, and sending, thence, five hundred men to La Vergne, under Lieutenant Colonel Ferril, of the Eighth Texas, to intercept and capture railroad trains, he moved with the remainder of his forces to the "Hermitage," on the Nashville and Lebanon pike, twelve miles from Nashville. Here he left all of his command, except one regiment, to repel any advance from Nashville—and proceeded with that regiment and two or three pieces of artillery to the river—distant about four miles—and fired across it with artillery at a train of cars, knocking the engine off the track. No movement was made by the enemy from Nashville, and on the same evening General Wheeler returned to Lebanon. The next day, the party sent to La Vergne returned also. Colonel Ferril had captured a train, taking a number of prisoners, released some men of our division captured at Snow's hill and on their way to Nashville, and he had gotten, besides, nearly forty thousand dollars in greenbacks—Quartermaster's funds. This money, General Wheeler appropriated to buying fresh horses for the men who had captured it.

General Wheeler remained at Lebanon three days. During that time, the enemy advanced once from Murfreesboro', but retreated before reaching our pickets. Upon our return from Lebanon, a portion of the forces, only, were sent to Alexandria; more than half, under command of General Wheeler, passed through Rome, to the immediate vicinity of Carthage. Remaining here during the night, General Wheeler, just at daylight, fell back toward Alexandria, reaching that place about 1 or 2 P.M. Wharton's division was again encamped here, and Morgan's division, under my command, was sent to Liberty, except Smith's regiment which was stationed near Alexandria.

General Morgan on the night of the 5th, had returned to McMinnville, and had not since rejoined us. Two or three days after this, the enemy moved out from Carthage, so far as New Middleton, ten miles from Alexandria, where General Wheeler attacked them and drove them back to Carthage. On the 19th or 20th, the enemy advanced upon McMinnville with a strong force of infantry, cavalry and artillery. There was no cavalry force at the place at all, except General Morgan's escort (forty or fifty strong), but there was some ninety infantry, under command of Major Wickliffe of the Ninth Kentucky infantry, stationed there. After a good deal of preliminary reconnoitering and some skirmishing with the men of the escort, the enemy's cavalry dashed into the town, eight abreast, driving out General Morgan and several officers, who happened to be collected at McMinnville upon sick leave, or on special duty of some sort. Among them were Colonel Cluke, Lieutenant Colonel Martin, and Major McCann. Exchanging a few shots with the cavalry, this party retreated upon the Sparta road—McCann's horse was shot in the melee and fell, bringing him to the ground. He sprang to his feet and standing in front of the charging column, shouted "You have got the old chief at last," seeking to produce the impression that he was General Morgan and so favor the latter's escape. He was ridden over, severely sabered, and captured; but having been placed in an old stable, and allowed a canteen of apple brandy, he got the guard drunk and dug out under the logs, during the night, effecting his escape. Lieutenant Colonel Martin received a bad wound through the lungs, but sat on his horse and escaped. All of the others escaped uninjured. The infantry retreated, in perfect order, to the mountains two or three miles distant. The enemy pursued, but were driven back by the volleys given them whenever they pressed closely.

When the news of this affair reached General Wheeler's headquarters, General Wharton urged that the entire force should be withdrawn from Alexandria and Liberty, and concentrated at Smithville. He believed that the enemy, in withdrawing from McMinnville, would come by Liberty—the infantry moving through Mechanicsville, and the cavalry through Smithville. This route, they might calculate, would remove them from all danger of molestation by any infantry force sent after them from our army, and would bring them right upon the flank of our cavalry, which could annoy their rear if they retreated through Woodbury, but would, perhaps, be driven off by the movement upon Liberty. Then, a good pike conducted them to Murfreesboro', and their cavalry, coming on from Smithville, protected their rear.

A concentration of our whole force at Smithville, would not only make us secure, but would enable us to punish the cavalry severely, if the movement was made as Wharton anticipated. We remained, however, in the same positions, picketing and scouting vigilantly. The enemy moved exactly as Wharton had foreseen that they would do, and the troops at Liberty fell back to Alexandria, whence, both divisions retreated across Caney Fork, to Buffalo valley.

The road by which we moved was a rough and bad one, and the ford at which we crossed, execrable, making it a tedious affair. A demonstration was made, on the same day, from Carthage, but too late to interfere with our retreat. Morgan's division, during these operations, on account of heavy detachments having been made from it, and pretty heavy straggling, was very much reduced.

During a week or ten days' stay in Buffalo valley, the stragglers were collected and the regiments were gotten into pretty good order again. Cluke's, Chenault's, and Morgan's regiments were still stationed upon the Cumberland, in Wayne, Clinton and Cumberland counties. The latter regiment was driven away from Celina, some time in the early part of May; it had been posted there to protect the collection of commissary stores for Wheeler's corps. After taking the town of Celina, the Federal forces burned it and took position along the Cumberland, on the northern side, confronting our forces on the southern. Pegram's brigade was also stationed at Monticello, in Wayne county, Kentucky. It was attacked and driven away on the 28th of May. General Morgan after these affairs occurred, was ordered to move with his division to Wayne county, and drive the enemy from the region south of the Cumberland; or if he found him too strong to be driven, and he manifested an intention (which was somewhat feared) of pressing into East Tennessee, to at least retard his advance.

When General Morgan reached Monticello, which the enemy had evacuated shortly after the affair with Pegram, he found Cluke, with his own regiment and Chenault's, lying in front of a superior Federal force in Horseshoe bottom on Greasy creek, in the western end of Wayne county. Cluke had been skirmishing with them for two or three days. General Morgan sent couriers to hasten the march of his other regiments—the Second, Third, Fifth and Sixth Kentucky, and Ninth Tennessee, and of his artillery.

Notwithstanding that the utmost expedition was used, we did not arrive upon the ground until after 3 P.M., although the order arrived at 9 or 10 A.M. During the day, Cluke and Chenault were fighting with the enemy, at intervals, neither losing nor gaining ground. When we arrived, these regiments had almost entirely expended their ammunition, and averaged but two cartridges per man. The rough road over which we had marched, and the rapidity with which the march was made, had not only caused the Artillery to be left far in the rear, but had told severely on the column. Several horses dropped dead. Many gave out so completely that they had to be left. The strength of the five regiments was reduced to eight hundred men, when they arrived upon the field.

One instance of uncommon gallantry, upon the part of a private soldier—Theodore Bybee of Company C, Second Kentucky—ought to be related. His horse fell dead beneath him, and he caught the stirrup of a comrade, and ran thus eight or ten miles to the scene of the fighting. As soon as we arrived, General Morgan ordered us to form for attack. No one in the command was familiar with the ground, and the disposition of the line was made with reference only to what could be seen.

On the left of our position, was a deep ravine, with which the road ran parallel, and about one hundred yards distant. The whole ground was covered, in every direction, with thick timber, except for perhaps ten or fifteen acres directly in front of the line formed by Cluke's and Chenault's regiments. In this open space, which was an old field and orchard, and nearly square, was situated a small house. Just on the other side of it, and in the edge of the woods, the enemy were posted. The road ran through the center of it, and, immediately after entering the woods at the northern extremity, turned to the left, crossing the ravine.

The mistake General Morgan made in supposing that the road continued to run straight, and thus inducing him to make no inflection of his line on the right of the road, toward the enemy's left flank, prevented his capturing a good many prisoners, and perhaps the enemy's artillery. Cluke's and Chenault's regiments were, together, not more than three hundred and fifty strong, upon the field. The Fifth Kentucky, and Ninth Tennessee were formed about one hundred yards in the rear of Cluke and Chenault, and were placed under command of Colonel Smith. The Third and Sixth Kentucky, were formed about two hundred yards in the rear of Colonel Smith's line and a little further to the right. The Second Kentucky, and Colonel Morgan's regiment, which had also arrived, were held in reserve, the former on foot, the latter mounted. All of the horses were placed on the left of the road. Just as these dispositions were completed, the enemy opened upon us with two pieces of artillery, which did no damage, except to the horses, several of which were killed. As no artillery had been used previously, General Morgan thought that its appearance upon the field betokened the arrival of reinforcements to the enemy, perhaps in considerable numbers, and he thought, for a moment, of withdrawing his troops. In this view, every officer about him at the time, concurred, except Colonel Morgan.

A few seconds of time elapsing, it was demonstrated that before we could retreat, we would be forced to repulse the enemy. At the roar of the guns, they came charging across the open ground, yelling like devils, or rebels. The crash of musketry, for a minute, in the limited space, was quite heavy. Cluke's line quickly discharged all of its ammunition, and then gave back before the enemy's determined rush, without, however, losing its formation, or any of the men turning their faces from the enemy. These two regiments were exceedingly reliable in battle.

After this line had *backed* some twenty-five paces, Smith's line came to its support, and the men in the latter, passing through the intervals between the files of the former, poured into the faces of the Federals, at that time almost mingled with the men of Cluke's and Chenault's regiments, a volley which amazed and sent them back. As our line pressed after them across the open ground, the artillery, only a short distance off, told severely on it and continued its fire until our foremost were close upon the guns.

The enemy made a stand at the point where the road crosses the ravine, to enable the guns to escape, but the Third and Sixth Kentucky coming up, they were again driven. So dense was the woods, that pursuit was almost impossible. Colonel Morgan dashed down the road, but secured only a few prisoners. The enemy conducted the retreat with the most perfect coolness. About three hundred yards from the point where the last stand was made, one company halted and picketed the road, while all the rest (as we afterward ascertained) continued to rapidly retreat to the river. Our loss in this skirmish, which lasted about half an hour, was, in the first brigade, ten killed and sixteen wounded, and in the second five or six killed and wounded. The enemy lost, I believe, twenty-one killed, and a smaller number of wounded. His loss was in all, as nearly as I remember, thirty-one or two. Very few prisoners were taken. General Morgan, despairing of being able to surround or rush over the enemy, in the rugged, wooded country, sent a flag of truce, proposing a surrender. Captain Davis, Assistant Adjutant General of the first brigade (who bore the flag), was detained until communication could be had with Colonel Jacobs, who commanded all the United States forces in that immediate region. Colonel Jacobs was some distance off, on the other side of the river, and it was growing dark. General Morgan sent another message, demanding the release of Captain Davis, and declaring his intention of advancing as soon as that was done. Immediately upon the return of Captain Davis, the column was moved forward. The pickets saluted the advance guard with a volley, and gracefully fell back, and although we pressed on close to the river, we saw nothing more of them. As late as the close of the war, no answer had been received from Colonel Jacobs, although that officer was distinguished for his courtesy as well as gallantry.

The division remained on the line of the Cumberland, picketing from Stagall's ferry to Celina for nearly three weeks. The headquarters of the first brigade was at Albany, county seat of Clinton county, that of the second at Monticello, county seat of Wayne. In that time the ranks filled up again, nearly all absentees, with or without leave, returning. The horses were grazed on the rich grass and carefully attended to, and got in excellent condition again. Several scouting expeditions were undertaken, during this period, against the enemy on the north side of the river, the most successful of which were under command of Captain Davis and Captain Thomas Franks, of the Second Kentucky. Each of these officers, with two companies, penetrated far into the enemy's lines, and attacking and routing the forces that they met, with small loss to themselves, brought off prisoners, horses, and captured property of various kinds. These expeditions were not only of essential use in annoying the enemy, but were absolutely necessary to the maintenance of a proper spirit and energy among our men, whose *morale* and discipline were, invariably, sensibly impaired by an indolent and monotonous life.

This period of the history of Morgan's cavalry has been generally esteemed one of entire inaction, upon the part of both leader and men. It is true that nothing was done in all this period, which would at all compare with the dashing, enterprising career of the previous year. But a great deal of useful, if not brilliant service, was performed, and a vast deal of hard work was cheerfully gone through with. The public had become so accustomed to expect "raids" and "dashes" from Morgan, that they thought his command idle and useless, when engaged in the performance of regular routine duty. It should be remembered that, at the very time when Morgan's division was thought to be so inactive, it was constantly occupied with exactly the kind of service at which the other cavalry, except Forrest's, were always engaged.

During the winter and spring of 1863, and until nearly the middle of the summer, our command was guarding and picketing a long front, and scouting thoroughly a great extent of country besides. For six months the country about Liberty, Alexandria and Lebanon, and that about Monticello and Albany, was in a great measure committed to Morgan's care. This gave him a front of quite one hundred and fifty miles to watch and guard, and at least half of the time he had to do it single-handed. Then there was a great portion of Middle Tennessee, and of Southern, Central and Eastern Kentucky, which his scouts constantly traversed. It is fair to say that from January to July 1863, inclusive, the period of the supposed inaction, during which time Morgan made no "raid," nor achieved any very brilliant success, that in all that time, our division was as constantly serving, fought and won as many skirmishes, guarded and scouted as great an extent of country, captured as many prisoners, and gave the Confederate Government as little trouble on the subject of supplies, as any other cavalry division in the Confederate army.

But, in this year, the glory and the *prestige* began to pass away from the Southern cavalry. It was not that their opponents became their superiors in soldiership, any more than in individual prowess. Although the Federal cavalry had greatly improved, had become formidable for its enterprise and fighting capacity, it can yet be said that the Confederate cavalry, when in proper condition, still asserted its superiority upon every field where there was an equality of forces. But it was daily becoming more and more difficult to keep the Confederate cavalry in good condition. An impression prevailed, no doubt a correct one, that as for the great efforts of war, the infantry was so much more useful and necessary, a far greater care ought to be taken of it than of the cavalry; and, then, an idea obtained that, inasmuch as our cavalry supplied itself so often, and occasionally so well, by its own captures, it ought to do so all the time. A corollary resulted from these two propositions, which played the wild with the cavalry, viz: that it was highly improper to issue anything which the Government had to furnish to that arm of the service. So it happened that, while to the cavalry were entrusted the most responsible and important duties, scarcely any encouragement or assistance was afforded it; and, on the contrary, a tone and conduct were adopted toward it apparently expressly intended to disgust it. I speak in reference to Western cavalry and Western affairs altogether, for I served at no time with the Army of Northern Virginia, and know nothing of it but the bare outline of its glorious and unequaled record. Cavalry officers, after long and arduous service, and a thorough initiation into all the mysteries of their craft, were rewarded and encouraged by having some staff officer, or officer educated to shoot heavy artillery, run steamships, or mix chemical preparations, promoted over their heads; and were expected to be delighted with him, although he might not practically know whether a horse-shoe was put on with nails or with hooks and eyes, and whether pickets were posted to look out for an enemy, or to show Brigadier-Generals the way to their headquarters when they were lost.

Cavalry which was expected to be constantly engaging the enemy, and upon whose efficiency and success a vast deal depended, were grudgingly provided with or altogether denied arms and ammunition, unless they could be captured from the enemy. Hard and constant as was the service the cavalryman performed, exposed as he was to the severity of all sorts of climate, without shelter, and often without the means of building the fire which stood him in stead of tent, and sometimes had to furnish him the strength and cheer of the food he lacked, he was yet snubbed mercilessly, and Generals commanding stared aghast if he presumed to ask for anything. The infantryman, lying snug and idle in camp, was given his blanket and his tent, good clothing (if it could possibly be had) and stout shoes (I speak, of course, in a Confederate sense); all was done for him to get him in condition for the day of battle; they fattened him for the sacrifice. But the cavalryman, had it not been for his own exertions, and the energy with which he indemnified himself for his Government's neglect of him, would not have been worth killing. When I reflect upon the privations I have seen the men endure, and remember that they well knew that there was no escape from them, except by taking what they wanted wherever they found it; and remember, further, the chances that were offered, I am lost in astonishment at their honesty and forbearance. I am aware that our "distant brethren" of the North, or those, rather, who will be our brethren, it is inferred, when an amendment to the Constitution decides who and what we are—it is a matter perfectly well understood that they will concede no such honesty to us, and naturally enough. It is a stale, but all the more certain-on-that-account fact, that they have discovered that "the earth belongs to the saints," and that they "are the saints." Therefore, to take anything (upon this continent, at least), in any manner, is to rob the "saints;" and, while a man may pardon a fellow who robs his neighbor, it is not in reason that he should forgive the rogue who robs him.

One special cause of the degeneracy of the Southern cavalry, in the latter part of the war, was the great scarcity of horses and the great difficulty of obtaining forage within the Confederate lines, and consequently, of keeping the horses which we had in good condition. Morgan's men had the reputation, and not unjustly, of procuring horses with great facility and economy. Adepts as we were, in the art of "horse-pressing," there was this fact nevertheless to be said in favor of the system which we adopted: while making very free with the horse-flesh of the country into which we would raid, there was never any wanton waste of the article. We did not kill our tired stock, as did the Federal commanders on their "raids," when we got fresh ones. The men of our command were not permitted to impress horses in a friendly country. It is true that horses were sometimes stolen from people who were most devoted to our cause, and who lived within our lines, but such thefts did not often occur, and the perpetrators were severely punished. The witty editors of Yankee-land would doubtless have explained our rebuke of this practice, by an application of the old saying that "there is honor among thieves," which would have been very just and apposite. The difference between our thieves and those on the other side was, that the latter were entirely destitute of every sort of honor. General Morgan took fresh horses to enable his command to make the tremendous marches which ensured so much of his success, and to prevent his men from falling into the hands of the enemy, but he hedged around the practice with limitations which somewhat protected the citizen. He required that, in every instance where a man desired to exchange his tired horse for a fresh one, he should have his horse inspected by his company commander, who should certify to the condition of the horse and the necessity of the exchange. If the company commander certified that his horse was unfit for service, the man obtained from his regimental commander permission to obtain a fresh one, which had also, before it was valid, to be approved by the brigade commander. Whenever it was practicable, the exchange was required to be made in the presence of a commissioned officer, and, in every case, a horse, if the soldier had it, was ordered to be left in the place of the one impressed. When a man was without a horse, altogether, his company commander could impress one for him. No doubt, this seems to the unmilitary reader, only systematic robbery—but is not *that* going on all the time, all over the world? Is it not, too, a great comfort to the citizen, to know that (when he is robbed), there are laws and the "proper papers" for it!

When men or officers were detected with led horses, they were punished, and the horses were taken away from them, unless they could prove that they were entitled to them. Morgan's men were habitually styled "horse-thieves" by their enemies, and they did not disclaim the title—I should like to see a statistical report showing the number of horses stolen in Kentucky by the respective belligerents—we would lose some laurels. The Confederate Government could not, and did not attempt to supply the cavalry of its armies with horses. The cavalry soldier furnished his own horse, and (if he lost him), had to make the best shift he could for another. The cavalryman was not subjected to the rigid discipline of the infantryman, for the reason that he was harder to catch. It is more difficult to regulate six legs than two. For the very reason that it was outside of the pale of regular discipline and the highest military civilization, it was more necessary to give to the cavalry officers who practically understood that sort of service, as well as were men of controlling character. Such men could make of the cavalryman, a soldier—with an inferior officer or one who was awkward at cavalry business over him, he became an Ishmael.

There existed among the infantry, not exactly a prejudice against cavalry (for they all wanted to join it), but that sort of feeling against it, which is perhaps natural upon the part of the man who walks against the man who rides. When the "web-feet" called us "buttermilk rangers," we did not get angry with them, for we knew that they were gallant fellows and that much walking tries the temper—but we did not admire the official prejudice against us, and thought an affected contempt of our arm in very bad taste, upon the part of Generals who not only never won battles but who never tried to win them.

In the spring and summer of 1863, supplies could be obtained for neither men nor horses of the cavalry of Bragg's army, without the greatest difficulty and great oppression of the citizens. It was not the custom to issue (out of army supplies), rations to the men, or forage to the horses of the cavalry commands—they were required to provide for themselves in these respects. It was impracticable, too, to supply them from the stores collected for army use. Certain regions, therefore, in which, for the proper protection of the lines, it was absolutely necessary to keep large bodies of cavalry—sections of country not fertile and at no time abounding in supplies—were literally stripped of meat, grain and every thing edible. All that would feed man or horse disappeared, as if a cloud of Titanic and omniverous locusts had settled upon the land—and after the citizens were reduced to the extremity of destitution and distress, the soldiers and their horses suffered, also, with slow famine.

One instance of the kind will serve to show how destructive of the efficiency of cavalry was service under such circumstances. When the division was ordered to Wayne and Clinton counties, Kentucky, the Ninth Kentucky, one of the best regiments in the cavalry of the West, was sent to Woodbury to picket that immediate section of country. For many miles around this little place, the country had been exhausted of provisions and forage by the constant requisition upon it during the winter and spring. The men of the Ninth Kentucky suffered severely for want of rations, but they esteemed their own sufferings lightly, compared with those of their horses. Long forage (oats, fodder, etc.) could not be procured at all; and corn had to be hauled a distance of over thirty miles, from a region whence other cavalry commands were also drawing supplies of forage, or else it could only be gotten from Tullahoma out of the forage stored there for army consumption. Consequently, corn was rare at that time at Woodbury; two or three ears per day to each horse was the usual issue. Upon some days none was issued. Every blade of grass in the vicinity of the camp was eaten, and the trees were barked by the poor animals as high as they could reach.

The men stood picket on foot; all of the stock was rendered utterly unserviceable, and one fourth of it died. By such usage (necessary, however,) this regiment was made unfit for active and efficient service for months, and its discipline and morale were seriously, although only temporarily, impaired. More than half—at any rate, a large proportion of the cavalry of General Bragg's army were suffering, at that time, precisely as this regiment was. In this condition of things is to be found the explanation of the apparent degeneracy of the Confederate cavalry, in the latter part of the war.

Another fact, too, should not be lost sight of. In common with every other arm of the service, our cavalry became very greatly reduced in numbers as the war wore on. We could not fill up our regiments as easily as the Federals could fill their wasted organizations. Those who wonder why well known Confederate regiments, brigades, and divisions did not accomplish as much in the latter as in the early part of the war, do not know, or do not reflect, that it was because they were reduced to a fourth or a fifth of their original strength. This, however, was not the case at the period of which I write. It was, too, in the summer of 1863 that serious doubt of the successful establishment of Southern independence began to gain ground among the masses of the Southern people; and a lukewarmness first, and next a feeling almost of disaffection to the Confederate Government and cause widely prevailed. This indifference was very unlike the strange absence of anxiety and solicitude about the result of the war, which characterized its early stages. The latter feeling proceeded from a blind and overweening confidence, and those who entertained it were not the less intensely patriotic and devoted to the cause. Nor was this species of disaffection, which began to influence so many, characterized by the slightest tendency toward treachery or renegadeism. Hundreds of citizens, who were fiercely opposed to the administration, and cordially disliked Mr. Davis, who had even lost much of their interest in the Confederate army and its fortunes, nevertheless hated the Northern people, the Federal Government, and the invading army, with a hatred immeasureably more thorough, rabid, and ineradicable, than at the beginning of the war, ere they knew practically what invasion was like. With a strange inconsistency, these men would have done any thing to have injured the enemy, even when averse to making further sacrifices for the benefit of the Confederacy. So far from renegading and pandering to Federal rule and success, the large majority of this class would have pawned their souls for power to crush the Federal arms. This is why the Southern renegade is regarded by the Southern people with loathing, scorn, and hatred, burning and inextinguishable. Although destitution and suffering were not general, at this time, in the South, they had prevailed, and to a fearful extent, in many sections; and everywhere a solemn and well-founded apprehension was felt upon the subject. Still it took two years more of disaster—of an invasion which probed every nook and corner of the South, and a condition of almost famine, to finally break the spirit of the Southern people, and make them, in the abjectness of their agony, actually welcome a peace which heralded subjugation as a relief from the horrors of war. It was the submission of the people which took the steel out of the army.

It is the fashion, with a certain class of Southern writers, to denounce Mr. Davis as the author of this condition of things, and to revile the Southern people because of their ultimate despair and surrender. Many and great blunders were committed in the conduct of the civil and military affairs of the Confederacy, and doubtless Mr. Davis was responsible for some of them.

In an affair of such magnitude, as was the Southern movement and the consequent war, errors would have characterized, in all probability, the administration of the most practiced and skillful military and political chiefs—how then could the administration of men, unschooled in the practical arts of managing revolutions and wars, be free from them? The wonder is, not that blunders were made, but that the bad effect of so many was partially repaired. The faults, which marred our fortunes, were the natural concomitants of a state of prolonged and constant warfare, and the latter weakening of our people was the inevitable result of a struggle against adverse circumstances and superior numbers and resources. The only way to have lessened the number of the former, and to have prevented the latter, would have been to fight, not a waiting, but a quick war.

On the 26th, the division was ordered back to Liberty and Alexandria. That country had been occupied and picketed, just before our return from Albany and Monticello, by a brigade of Wharton's division, commanded by Colonel (afterward Brigadier General) Harrison, of the Eighth Texas, a gallant and highly esteemed officer. Breckinridge's regiment (the Ninth Kentucky) was still kept at Woodbury. About this time Colonel A.R. Johnson returned from Texas, and was immediately assigned, by General Morgan, to the command of the second brigade—his rank entitled him to be second in command. This brigade had been ably commanded, since Gano's absence, by Cluke. Colonel Johnson retained none of the former brigade staff, except Lieutenant Sidney Cunningham, a brave and efficient officer, who was afterward Lieutenant Colonel of the Fifteenth Kentucky. The effective strength of the division, at this time, was twenty-eight hundred men. The horses were in better condition, and the men were better provided for in every respect, than at any period since the "December raid." New and excellent clothing had been issued them while on the Cumberland—a thing unprecedented in the history of the command—and their general equipment was much superior to what it had been at the close of the winter. All were well armed, and with the kind of guns which were always preferred in Morgan's cavalry. The Second Kentucky had managed to get rid of a great many guns, during the latter part of the winter and early part of the spring. The men of this regiment were styled by General Morgan his "Regulars," on account of their veteranship and proficiency in drill, etc., and, yet, notwithstanding its excellent reputation, this unsoldierly practice of losing and throwing away guns, had prevailed to such an extent in the regiment, that, at one time, nearly one half of its members were unarmed. The men did not seem to do it, to escape duty, or going into battle, for they all remained in camp and answered to the bugle—it seemed to be a fashion which they had suddenly adopted. This practice is one of the few, for which officers, inclined to be lenient in most particulars, may well be willing to have their men shot. Except that I have seen it prevail, at times, among troops of unquestionable bravery and fidelity, I would say that the most cowardly and treacherous spirit induces it. The Second Kentucky was a regiment which never had its superior—it possessed, not only courage and steadiness, but the highest "dash" and inflexible constancy, and yet, at one period, the practice which has been mentioned, prevailed in it to an extraordinary extent. Major Webber, commanding it at the time, made every man lacking a gun, after punishment in other ways, carry a heavy fence rail upon his shoulder, until he procured an Enfield or Springfield rifle. The facility with which the men found the required arms at the country houses, induced a suspicion that many of them had previously deposited the same guns where they subsequently got them. They were also threatened with being left behind on the next expedition to Kentucky, and with being sent to the infantry, if they did not speedily arm themselves, both of which intimations had an excellent effect.

The first brigade made headquarters at Alexandria. The regiments composing it, and Morgan's regiment (ordered to temporarily report to it) were encamped on the Lebanon pike, and the roads to Carthage and Statesville. The second brigade, with its headquarters at Auburn, was disposed upon the road to Murfreesboro', and between Auburn and Statesville. One regiment was posted at Statesville, which little place was nearly equi-distant from Auburn and Alexandria. The country around was picketed and scouted thoroughly in every direction, and the disposition of the regiments gave us such command of all the roads, that we could have concentrated without difficulty, and as the exigency might require, at Auburn, Alexandria, or Liberty. The period that we remained here was passed in assiduous and diligent instruction of the troops. Drills, dress-parades, inspections, etc., were constantly had—we had never before had so much time for those duties, when the division was so nearly concentrated. The strictest vigilance was maintained in our camps, to prevent the passage through them of Federal spies, who, at this period and at this quarter of our lines, were unusually numerous, cunning, and audacious. The strict guard and watch maintained to frustrate and detect these parties, operated favorably upon our own men, who were necessarily restricted, by the unusual precautions adopted, of much of the liberty they had previously enjoyed. The division was, perhaps, never in as high and salutary a state of discipline as at this time.

The enemy came near us but once during this, our last sojourn in this country. Colonel Morgan had been sent to Baird's mill, and returning, halted all night at Lebanon. The enemy advanced upon him at Lebanon, and as he fell back slowly toward Alexandria, followed him. I reinforced him with the Second Kentucky, and believing that it was a large force, formed my brigade in front of Alexandria, and requested Colonel Johnson to reinforce me with his brigade. He immediately set out to do so, leaving pickets to watch the Murfreesboro' pike. While we were awaiting his arrival, Colonel Morgan, Major Brent, (whom I should have stated was with him, in command of a small detachment of the Fifth Kentucky), and a portion of the Second Kentucky under Captain Franks, were skirmishing with the enemy, who continued slowly but steadily to advance, until reaching a locality called Watertown, he halted. Nothing had been learned definitely of his strength, but we believed it to be large, simply because every force previously sent against us, in this quarter, had greatly outnumbered us. When Colonel Johnson arrived (about 1 P.M.,) we at once moved forward to attack, but had proceeded only a short distance, when Colonel Morgan reported that the enemy were again in motion, pressing briskly upon him, and apparently determined to fight. This information induced me to return to the position I had just left—an admirable one, both to receive and return an attack—it was about three quarters of a mile to the rear of the head of the column, which had not yet gotten clear of it. This was a mistake greatly to be regretted, and prevented the fight. The enemy came within a mile of the position, maneuvered a little while, and fell back. By this time it was getting late. We followed him with two companies and two pieces of artillery, skirmished with and shelled him.

That night, while we still doubted their strength and intentions—they went off entirely. I learned, then, that they were not more than eighteen hundred strong, while we were at least twenty-five hundred. This affair would not be worth mentioning, except that it illustrated how a lack of enterprise, and a too great fancy for "good positions" will sometimes prevent excellent opportunities from being improved. If I had attacked, promptly, the whole force, in all likelihood, would have been captured. The enemy for some reason conceived a very exaggerated idea of our strength. Shortly after this, it was reported in Murfreesboro', if the papers we captured spoke truth, that Wheeler's entire corps and some infantry were stationed at Alexandria and Liberty, harvesting the magnificent wheat crop, with which the adjacent country teemed.

On the 10th of June, General Morgan arrived at Alexandria, and orders were at once issued to prepare the division to march on the next day. It soon became known to all the officers at least, that he was about to undertake an expedition which he had long contemplated, and which he had often solicited permission to make. This was the greatest of all his "raids," the one known as the "Ohio raid." Although it resulted disastrously to his own command, it had a great influence upon the pending campaign between Bragg and Rosecrans, and greatly assisted the former. It was beyond all comparison the grandest enterprise he ever planned, and the one which did most honor to his genius.

The military situation in Tennessee, at that time, may be briefly described:

General Bragg's army lay around Tullahoma, his cavalry covering his front and stretching far out upon both wings. General Buckner was in East Tennessee, with a force entirely inadequate to the defense of that important region. General Bragg, confronted by Rosecrans with a vastly superior force, dared not detach troops to strengthen Buckner. The latter could not still further weaken his small force by sending aid to General

Bragg—if the latter should need it. General Burnside was preparing (in Kentucky), a force, variously estimated, at from fifteen to more than thirty thousand men, for the invasion of East Tennessee. With this force he could easily drive out Buckner. It was estimated that at various points in Southern Kentucky, Bowlinggreen, Glasgow, and along the Cumberland river—and at Carthage in Tennessee, and other points in that vicinity, there were from eight to twelve thousand Federal troops—the greater part of them under the command of a General Judah, whose headquarters were at Glasgow. Of these forces, some five thousand were excellent cavalry. General Judah's official papers (captured on the Ohio raid), gave the exact strength of his forces, but I have forgotten it.

There was perfect unanimity of opinion (among the Confederate officers), about the plan and method of the anticipated Federal movement. Rosecrans (all believed), would press hard upon General Bragg—Burnside, simultaneously, or as soon afterward as was practicable, would move against Buckner. Judah's force could be used to keep open direct communication between these two armies, and also as a reserve. When the advance was fairly inaugurated, Judah, who in the meantime might guard against the raids of our cavalry, could be concentrated and moved through Burkesville, Livingston and Sparta—turning then, if General Bragg staid to fight, upon the right flank of the army at Tallahoma—or, if General Bragg retreated, pressing down through the Sequatchie valley to Chattanooga. A junction of all these forces, it was thought, would be made, and the Confederate army would then confront a host too formidable to be beaten.

This was the belief which prevailed in our army regarding the intentions of the enemy. It may have been incorrect—the feature, which we of Morgan's cavalry especially dwelt upon, to-wit, the part, in the supposed programme, to be played by Judah, may have been altogether uncontemplated—perhaps he was not a man capable of having executed it. But whatever may have been the Federal plan of the campaign, it is certain that terrible dangers menaced the army of General Bragg, and all the salient points of his department.

General Bragg regarded the peril with just apprehension—he took in its full proportions. He decided and (as was conceded by all who understood the situation), with good and sufficient reasons, to retreat beyond the Tennessee river, and then somewhere near Chattanooga, turning upon his foes, fight the battle which had to be delivered for the protection of his department. But that retreat would be very hazardous. He was right in the path of the avalanche, and the least movement upon his part might precipitate it upon him. The difficulty and danger of crossing the Tennessee, with Rosecrans hard upon his rear, would be greatly augmented, if these other Federal forces were poured down upon his flank.

General Bragg, it may be repeated, knew how to use, and invariably used, his cavalry to good purpose, and in this emergency he resolved to employ some of it to divert from his own hazardous movement, and fasten upon some other quarter, the attention of a portion of the opposing forces. He hoped, not only to give them enough to do, to prevent them from annoying and endangering his retreat, but, also, to draw off a part of their forces from the great battle which he expected to fight. He selected Morgan as the officer who should accomplish this design.

In the conference between them, General Morgan expressed a perfect confidence in his ability to effect all that was desired of him, but dissented from General Bragg in one important particular. The latter wished him to confine himself to Kentucky—giving him *carte blanche* to go wherever he pleased in that State, and urging him to attempt the capture of Louisville. General Morgan declared, that, while he could by a dash into Kentucky and a march through that State, protect General Bragg's withdrawal from the position his army then held, he could not thus accomplish the other equally important feature of the plan, and draw off troops which would otherwise strengthen Rosecrans for the decisive battle.

A raid into Kentucky would keep Judah busy, and hold Burnside fast until it was decided, but, he contended it would be decided very soon, and he would be driven out or cut to pieces in a few days, leaving the Federal forces so disposed that they could readily commence their previously determined operations. A raid into Indiana and Ohio, on the contrary, he contended, would draw all the troops in Kentucky after him, and keep them employed for weeks. Although there might be sound military reasons why Judah and Burnside should not follow him, but should stick to what the Confederate officers deemed the original programme of Rosecrans, General Morgan urged, that the scare and the clamor in the States he proposed to invade, would be so great, that the military leaders and the administration would be compelled to furnish the troops that would be called for. He thought that, even if he lost his command, he could greatly benefit General Bragg by crossing the Ohio river and only in that way.

General Bragg refused him permission to make the raid as he desired to make it and ordered him to confine himself to Kentucky. I was not present at the interview between them, but General Morgan told me that General Bragg had ordered him to operate in Kentucky, and further stated that he intended, notwithstanding his orders, to cross the Ohio. I do not mean to justify his disobedience of orders, but simply to narrate the facts as I learned them, and to explain General Morgan's ideas regarding the movement, which were definite and fixed. This expedition into the Northwestern States had long been a favorite idea with him and was but the practical development of his theory of the proper way to make war, to-wit: by going deep into the country of the enemy. He had for several weeks foreseen the necessity of some such diversion in General Bragg's behalf, and believed that the period for the accomplishment of his great desire was at hand.

He had ordered me, three weeks previously, to send intelligent men to examine the fords of the upper Ohio—that at Buffington among them—and it is a fact, of which others, as well as myself, are cognizant, that he intended—long before he crossed the Ohio—to make no effort to recross it, except at some of these fords, unless he found it more expedient, when he reached that region, to join General Lee, if the latter should still be in Pennsylvania.

Never had I been so impressed with General Morgan's remarkable genius—his wonderful faculty of anticipating the exact effect his action would have upon all other men and of calculating their action—his singular power of arriving at a correct estimate of the nature and capacities of a country, which he knew only by maps and the most general description—and the perfect accuracy with which he could foretell the main incidents of a march and campaign—as when he would briefly sketch his plan of that raid. All who heard him felt that he was right in the main, and although some of us were filled with a grave apprehension, from the first, we felt an inconsistent confidence when listening to him. He did not disguise from himself the great dangers he encountered, but was sanguine of success. As it turned out, only the unprecedented rise in the Ohio caused his capture—he had avoided or had cut his way through all other dangers.

On the 11th of June, the division marched from Alexandria to the Cumberland and crossed the river not far from the little town of Rome. General Morgan desired to attack the Federal force stationed at Carthage, and strongly fortified. General Bragg had authorized him to do so.

The division encamped two or three miles from the northern bank of the river, and not far from the turnpike which runs from Carthage to Hartsville. Information had been received that the mail passed on this road twice or three times a week, guarded by a small escort, and that comfortably lined sutlers' wagons sometimes accompanied the cavalcade for the benefit of the protection the escort afforded. Colonel Ward was sent, with two or three companies of his regiment, to a point on the pike some eight miles from Carthage, and two or three from our encampment. He reached it just before sundown, and shortly afterward the mail train, accompanied by several sutlers' wagons, and under charge of an escort eighty or a hundred strong, came by, no one apparently suspecting the slightest danger, and all keeping careless watch. When the procession came opposite to where Colonel Ward had posted his men (some seventy yards from the road), the Colonel gave the order to fire in a loud voice. At the unexpected command, which so suddenly indicated danger, mail-carriers, sutlers, and guard halted in amazement, and when the answering volley broke upon them, they went in every direction in the wildest confusion. Not a shot was fired in return, but the escort manifested plainly that it felt a very inferior degree of interest in the integrity of postal affairs.

Few prisoners were taken, but the mail and the wagons were secured. In one of the latter, a corpulent sutler was found, wedged in a corner, and much alarmed. He was past speaking when drawn out, but faintly signed that a bottle he had in his pocket should be placed to his lips.

That evening a staff officer arrived from General Bragg with orders to General Morgan. He was instructed to make no attack upon Carthage, but to march as rapidly as possible to Monticello, and strive to intercept a Federal raiding party which had broken into East Tennessee, under Brigadier General Saunders, and was threatening Knoxville. Upon the next morning, consequently, we recrossed the Cumberland and marched in the direction ordered. After passing through Gainesboro', we got into a very rugged country and upon the very worst roads. At Livingston we were overtaken by a tremendous rain, which lasted for two or three days, and rendered the road almost impassable for artillery. This retarded our march very greatly, and we arrived at Albany three days later than we would otherwise have done, to learn that the enemy had already passed out of East Tennessee by way of Jamestown.

The second brigade was encamped in Turkey-neck Bend of the Cumberland river, some fifteen miles in direct line from Burkesville. The first brigade was encamped along the river, from a point opposite Burkesville to Irish Bottom. The division remained here for three or four days, awaiting the return of General Morgan, who had left us at the recrossing of the Cumberland to go to McMinnville and hurry forward some supplies and ammunition. These stores were hauled to our camp in six wagons, which had nearly not gotten to us at all. The heavy rains which had so retarded the march of the division to Albany, had made the roads which these wagons had traveled perfect quagmires. When they reached the Obie and Wolf rivers, which are six miles apart at the points where the road from Sparta to Monticello crosses them, they met with a very discouraging sight. These little rushing mountain streams were much swollen and too deep for any kind of fording. General Morgan instructed his Acting Inspector, Captain D.R. Williams, an officer of great energy, to have the wagons taken to pieces, and stowed, with their contents, in canoes, and so ferried across. In this manner, all were crossed in a single night. The mules were made to swim.

On the 2nd of July, the crossing of the Cumberland began, the first brigade crossing at Burkesville and Scott's ferry, two miles above, and the second crossing at Turkey-neck Bend. The river was out of its banks, and running like a mill-race. The first brigade had, with which to cross the men and their accouterments, and artillery, only two crazy little flats, that seemed ready to sink under the weight of a single man, and two or three canoes. Colonel Johnson was not even so well provided. The horses were made to swim.

Just twelve miles distant upon the other side, at Marrowbone, lay Judah's cavalry, which had moved to that point from Glasgow, in anticipation of some such movement upon Morgan's part as he was now making. Our entire strength was twenty-four hundred and sixty effective men—the first brigade numbering fourteen hundred and sixty, the second one thousand. This, however, was exclusive of artillery, of which we had four pieces—a section of three-inch Parrots attached to the first brigade, and a section of twelve-pound howitzers attached to the second. Videttes, posted at intervals along the river bank, would have given General Judah timely information of this bold crossing, and he would have been enabled to strike and crush or capture the whole force. But he depended on the swollen river to deter Morgan, forgetting that Morgan invariably did that which was least expected of him. As soon as the latter learned of the strange supineness and lack of vigilance of his foe, he commenced and hastened the work of crossing the river. About two or three P.M., the enemy began to threaten both brigades, but did not advance with determination. The Sixth Kentucky and Ninth Tennessee had all been gotten across at Burkesville by this time, and portions of the other regiments were also across, as well as two pieces of artillery. General Morgan formed this entire force, and led it to attack the enemy threatening Burkesville. He placed a portion of it in ambush at a point about a mile from the town, and, when the head of the enemy's column approached, fired such a volley into it as made it at once recoil. Then charging, he drove the enemy back in confusion and at full speed, never letting them halt until they reached the encampment at Marrowbone. He pursued the force which he had routed into the camp, but was repulsed in an attack upon the latter by the artillery and reserve forces there.

The effect of this bold dash, was to draw back the force threatening Johnson, also, and allow him to cross without molestation. Our loss was very slight—among other gallant fellows who were hurt, Captain Quirk was so severely wounded in the arm that he could go no further upon the expedition. Several prisoners were taken. The enemy, after this hint not to interfere, remained shut up in his encampment until we were no longer in any danger.

The division encamped that night about ten miles from the river, on the road to Columbia. A large party of Commissaries of Subsistence were with us, sent by General Bragg to collect supplies north of the Cumberland and bring them to Tullahoma, escorted by one of Morgan's regiments. A variety of causes conspired to prevent these gentlemen from returning at the time, and in the manner contemplated by General Bragg. In the first place, we learned, immediately after we had crossed the Cumberland, by men who came from the rear, that General Bragg had already commenced his retreat—this would considerably lengthen the distance which the Commissaries would have to drive their cattle. Secondly, General Morgan came to the conclusion that he had use for all of his troops, and that he would not detach the regiment which was to have guarded the cattle. This resolution not only prevented the cattle from being driven to General Bragg, but also decided the Commissaries not to return immediately. The country through which they would have had to pass, was infested by a set of bushwhackers, in comparison with whose relentless ferocity, that of Bluebeard and the Welch giants sinks into insignificance. Chief among them was "Tinker Dave Beattie," the great opponent of Champ Ferguson. This patriarchal old man lived in a cove, or valley surrounded by high hills, at the back of which was a narrow path leading to the mountain. Here, surrounded by his clan, he led a pastoral, simple life, which must have been very fascinating, for many who ventured into the cove never came away again. Sometimes Champ Ferguson, with his band, would enter the cove, harry old Dave's stock and goods, and drive him to his retreat in the mountain, to which no man ever followed him. Then, again, when he was strong enough, he would lead his henchmen against Champ, and slay all who did not escape. But it must not be understood that he confined his hostility to Captain Ferguson and the latter's men: on the contrary, he could have had, had he so chosen, as many scalps drying in his cabin as ever rattled in the lodge of a Camanche war-chief, and taken with promiscuous impartiality. There were not related of Beattie so many stories, illustrative of his personal strength and bull-dog courage, as of Champ Ferguson. I have heard of the latter having gone, on one occasion, into a room where two of his bitter enemies lay before the fire, both strong men and armed, and, throwing himself upon them, he killed both (after a hard struggle) with his knife. But Beattie possessed a cunning and subtlety which the other, in great measure, lacked. Perhaps he was more nearly civilized. Both of these men were known to have spared life on some rare occasions, and perhaps none were so much astonished, thereat, as themselves. On one occasion, Ferguson was called upon to express an opinion regarding the character of a man who had been arrested near a spot where bushwhackers had just fired upon the party he (Ferguson) was with, and, from several suspicious indications, this man was thought to be one of them. By way of giving him a chance, it was decided that Ferguson, who knew every man in that country, should declare his doom, influenced by his previous knowledge of him. Ferguson, somewhat to the astonishment of the tribunal, begged that he should be released, saying, that he knew he was a Union man, but did not believe that he was a bushwhacker. The man was released. Subsequently, Ferguson said, after a long fit of silence, "I have a great notion to go back and hunt that man. I am afraid I have done wrong, for he is the best shot in this part of the State, and, if he does turn bushwhacker, he will kill a man at every shot." Such extreme nicety of conscience was not attributed to Beattie, nor was he said to be as faithful to his friends as was Ferguson.

Such were the kind of men whom our friends, of the Subsistence Department, would have had to encounter, if they had gone back. There were, at the time, no Confederate troops in that country, and Champ Ferguson was resting in inglorious ease at Sparta. Dave Beattie had broken out of his cove, and was ready to hold "bloody assizes" as soon as he secured his victims. Our friends were not accustomed to "raiding" and to cavalry habits, but, after thorough reflection, they resolved, with a heroism that would have done honor to the heavy artillery service, not to return, but to face all the hardships and dangers of the expedition. They were gallant men, and endured the tremendous fatigue, and shared the hardships as cheerfully as if they had come legitimately by them.

The chief of this party, Major Highley (from Mobile), was as full of dash and as fond of adventure, as a man could be. He sought the front on all occasions, and soon became a thorough cavalryman in all respects. General Morgan placed him upon his staff and he proved a very efficient officer, and seemed much gratified that his commissaries had been cut off.

There was one case of almost abduction, however, which excited universal regret and commiseration:

An old gentleman, from Sparta, had come with the division to

Burkesville to get a barrel of salt—as there was none to be had at Sparta. His benevolent virtues had endeared him to all who knew him, and, so, when it became apparent that he must go back, leaving behind him his purchase, and at the risk of fearful dangers, or follow us through the whole raid, he received much and unaffected condolence. He perfectly realized his situation. He knew that, if he fell into "Tinker Dave's" hands, he would be pickled without salt, and he had not the slightest idea of trying it on. And yet he felt a natural sorrow at going so far away from home. Some two weeks later, when we were in Ohio, and being peppered by the militia, he said to an officer of the first brigade with tears in his eyes, and a touching pathos in his voice: "Captain, I would give my farm in White county, Tennessee, and all the salt in Kentucky (if I had it), to stand once more—safe and sound—on the banks of the Calf-killer creek."

On the morning of the 3rd, the division resumed its march, pushing on to Columbia. Colonel Morgan's regiment, although included in the field return of the first brigade, was detached and used as an advance-guard for the column. In the afternoon, as we neared Columbia, this regiment came upon the enemy moving out from the town. In the skirmish which ensued, Colonel Morgan lost a few wounded—among the number Captain J.T. Cassell, who was shot in the thigh as he was charging with his accustomed gallantry. He was placed in an ambulance and went, in that way, through the raid, and escaped capture. Captain Cassell had been ordered to report to Colonel Morgan with his Company, a few weeks previously, and was acting as second in command of the advance-guard. Captain Franks of the Second Kentucky was ordered to report to Colonel Morgan, to fill the position left vacant by the disabling of Captain Cassell. After this skirmish had lasted a short time, the Second Kentucky was ordered up to support Colonel Morgan. Major Webber dismounted his men and attacked with great vigor. The enemy did not stand a moment—were driven back into the town, fought a short time from the houses, and were soon dislodged and driven pell-mell out of the town. Major Webber lost two men killed. The enemy's loss was also slight. It was a detachment of Woolford's regiment, and retreated toward Jimtown. Some disgraceful scenes occurred in Columbia as the troops were passing through. One or two stores were broken into and plundered. General Morgan immediately went to the spot, arrested the marauders, punished them, and compelled the restitution of the goods.

On that evening the division encamped six or eight miles from Columbia. A regiment of Federal infantry was stationed at Green river bridge, where the road from Columbia to Campbellsville and Lebanon crosses the Green river. General Morgan sent Captain Franks to watch them, who reported that, during the entire night, he heard the ringing of axes and the crash of falling timber. The next morning we learned what it meant. Early on the 4th the column was put in motion, and the second brigade (marching in front), soon came upon the enemy. Colonel Moore, the officer commanding the Federal force (a Michigan regiment), had selected the strongest natural position, I ever saw, and had fortified it with a skill equal to his judgment in the selection. The Green river makes here a tremendous and sweeping bend, not unlike in its shape to the bowl of an immense spoon. The bridge is located at the tip of the bowl, and about a mile and a half to the southward, where the river returns so nearly to itself that the peninsula (at this point) is not more than one hundred yards wide—at what, in short, may be termed the insertion of the handle—Colonel Moore had constructed an earthwork, crossing the narrow neck of land, and protected in front by an abattis. The road upon which we were advancing, runs through this position. The peninsula widens again, abruptly, to the southward of this extremely narrow neck, and just in front of the skirt of woods, in which the work and abattis was situated, is an open glade, about two hundred yards in extent in every direction. Just in front of, or south of this plateau of cleared ground, runs a ravine deep and rugged, rendering access to it difficult, except by the road. The road runs not directly through, but to the left of this cleared place. All around it are thick woods, and upon the east and west the river banks are as steep and impassable as precipices. At the southern extremity of the open ground, and facing and commanding the road, a rifle-pit had been dug, about one hundred and twenty feet long—capable of containing fifty or sixty men, and about that number were posted in it. When Colonel Johnson's brigade neared the enemy, he sent Cluke with his own regiment and the Tenth Kentucky, then greatly reduced in numbers, to cross the river at a ford upon the left of the road, and take position on the northern side of the river, and commanding the bridge.

This was intended to prevent the retreat of the enemy and keep off reinforcements that might approach from the northward. A flag of truce was then sent to Colonel Moore, demanding the surrender of his command. He answered, "It is a bad day for surrenders, and I would rather not." Captain Byrnes had planted one of the Parrots, about six hundred yards from the rifle-pit, and skirmishers had been thrown out in front of it. As soon as the bearer of the flag returned, Byrnes opened with the gun. He fired a round shot into the parapet thrown up in front of the trench, knocking the fence rails, with which it was riveted, into splinters, and probing the work. One man in the trench was killed, by this shot, and the rest ran (just as our skirmishers dashed forward) and retreated across the open ground to the work in the woods beyond. Now the serious business commenced. Artillery could not be used to dislodge them from the position which was meant to be defended in earnest. This open ground, between the points where were constructed the rifle-pit (which was only a blind) and the strong work where Moore intended to fight, is the flat summit (for crest, properly speaking, it has none) of a hill, or rather swell of land, which slopes gently away on both the northern and southern sides. Guns planted anywhere, except upon this plateau, and near its center, could not have borne upon the enemy's position at all—and, if they had been planted there, every cannoneer would have been killed before a shot could have been fired. The only way to take the work was by a straight forward attack upon it, and Colonel Johnson moved against it his brigade, or rather the two regiments of it, left on the southern side of the river. The men, gallantly led, dashed across the open ground and plunged into the woods beyond.

The Federal force, some four hundred strong, was disposed behind the work and abattis, holding a line not much more than a hundred yards long. The first rush carried the men close to the work, but they were stopped by the fallen timber, and dropped fast under the close fire of the enemy. Colonel Chenault was killed in the midst of the abattis—his brains blown out as he was firing his pistol into the earthwork and calling on his men to follow. The second brigade had started with an inadequate supply of ammunition, and the fire of the attacking party soon slackened on that account. General Morgan ordered me to send a regiment to Colonel Johnson's assistance, and I sent the Fifth Kentucky. Colonel Smith led his men at a double-quick to the abattis, where they were stopped as the others had been, and suffered severely. The rush through a hundred yards of undergrowth, succeeded by a jam and crowding of a regiment into the narrow neck, and confronted by the tangled mass of prostrate timber and the guns of the hidden foe—was more than the men could stand. They would give way, rally in the thick woods, try it again, but unsuccessfully. The fire did not seem, to those of us who were not immediately engaged, to be heavy. There were no sustained volleys. It was a common remark that the shots could almost be counted—but almost every shot must have taken effect.

Our loss in less than half an hour's fighting, and with not over six hundred men engaged, for only portions of the regiments, sent into the fight, were engaged, was thirty-six killed, and forty-five or six wounded. Twenty, or more of the wounded were able to ride, and in a few days returned to duty. The loss of the enemy (according to the most authoritative account) was nine killed, and twenty-six wounded.

Many fine officers were included in our list of casualties. Colonel Chenault, whose death has been described—an officer who had no superior in bravery and devotion to the cause he fought for—was a noble gentleman. Major Brent, of the Fifth Kentucky, was killed. He was an officer who was rapidly taking—in reputation and popularity—the place among the field officers of the division which Hutchinson had held. He was recklessly brave, and possessed a natural military aptitude, and a resolution in exacting duty from his subordinate officers and men, which made him invaluable to his regiment. Captain Treble, who a short time previously had been transferred from the Second to the Eleventh Kentucky (Chenault's regiment) was also killed. He displayed, in this his last battle, the same high courage which ever animated him. Lieutenant Cowan, of the Third Kentucky, and Lieutenants Holloway and Ferguson, of the Fifth Kentucky—all very fine officers were also among the killed. Among the wounded officers, of the Fifth Kentucky, was the gallant and efficient Adjutant, Lieutenant Joseph Bowmar.

When General Morgan learned that the men were falling fast, and that no impression was being made upon the enemy, he ordered their withdrawal. He had not been fully aware, when the attack commenced, of the exceeding strength of the position, although he knew it to be formidable, and he thought it probable that the garrison would surrender to a bold attack. It was his practice to attack and seek to capture all, but the strongest, of the forces which opposed his advance upon his raids, and this was the only instance in which he ever failed of success in this policy. He believed that the position could have been eventually carried, but (as the defenders were resolute) at a cost of time and life which he could not afford. Colonel Moore ought to have been able to defend his position, against direct attacks, had an army been hurled against him. But this does not detract from the credit of his defense. His selection of ground showed admirable judgment; and, in a brief time, he fortified it with singular skill. He deliberately quitted a strong stockade, near the bridge (in which other officers would, probably have staid) and which our artillery would have battered about his ears directly, to assume the far better position; and his resolute defense, showed he appreciated and meant to hold it to the last. We expected to hear of his promotion—men had been promoted for beatings received from Morgan.

Crossing the river at the same ford at which Cluke had previously crossed, the division marched toward Campbellsville. Our wounded and dead were left under the charge of Surgeons and Chaplains, who received every assistance, that he could furnish, from Colonel Moore, who proved himself as humane as he was skillful and gallant. We passed through Campbellsville without halting. On that evening a horrible affair occurred. A certain Captain Murphy took a watch from a citizen who was being held, for a short time, under guard, to prevent his giving information of our approach and strength to the garrison at Lebanon. Captain Magenis, Assistant Adjutant General of the division, discovered that this theft had been perpetrated, and reported it to General Morgan, who ordered Murphy to be arrested. Murphy learned that Magenis had caused his arrest, and persuaded the guard (who had not disarmed him) to permit him to approach Magenis. When near him, Murphy drew and cocked a pistol, and denounced the other furiously, at the same time striking him. Captain Magenis attempted to draw his saber, and Murphy fired, severing the carotid artery and producing almost instant death. Murphy made his escape on the night that General Morgan had ordered a court-martial to try him—the night before we crossed the Ohio. The wretch ought to have been butchered in his tracks, immediately after the murder had been committed. There was no officer in the entire Confederate army, perhaps, so young as he was, who had evinced more intelligence, aptitude and zeal, than had Captain Magenis. Certainly, there was not among them all a more true-hearted, gallant, honorable gentleman. General Morgan deeply regretted him. His successor, Captain Hart Gibson, was in every way qualified to discharge, with ability and success, the duties of the position, doubly difficult in such a command and under such circumstances.

On the night of the 4th, the division encamped five miles from Lebanon, upon the ground whence we drove the enemy's pickets. Lebanon was garrisoned by Colonel Hanson's regiment, the Twentieth Kentucky, and not far off, on the road to Harrodsburg, two Michigan regiments were stationed. On the morning of the 5th, the division approached the town, and a demand for its surrender was made, which was declined. The first brigade was formed on the right of the road, with two regiments in reserve. The second was assigned the left of the road. The artillery was planted in the center, and at once opened upon the slight works which were thrown up, south of the town. As the regiments in the front line advanced, the enemy retreated into the town. Both brigades lost slightly in effecting this, and succeeded, immediately afterward, in dislodging the enemy from the houses in the edge of the town, both on the left and on the right. The enemy, then, mainly concentrated in the large depot building upon the railroad; a few sought shelter in other houses. Grigsby's and Ward's regiments, of the first brigade, held the right of the town and the houses looking upon the depot in that quarter. From these houses they kept up a constant fire upon the windows of the depot. Cluke's and Chenault's regiments, the latter under command of Lieutenant Colonel Tucker, were as effectively located and employed upon the left. Our artillery, although under able officers, proved of little use to us in this affair. On account of the situation of the depot in low ground, the shots took effect in the upper part of the building (when they struck at all), doing the occupants little damage. Lieutenant Lawrence, however, at length posted one of his guns—the Parrots—on a hill immediately overlooking the building, and, greatly depressing it, prepared to fire into it at an angle which threatened mischief. But the sharpshooters prevented his men from working the guns effectively. This state of affairs lasted for two or three hours. The Michigan regiments, before mentioned, drew near and threatened interference, and General Morgan, who had sought to reduce the garrison without storming their stronghold, in order to save his own men, at length ordered it to be carried by assault. Smith's regiment, at first held in reserve in the first brigade, had, previously to this determination upon the part of the General, been engaged, but the Second Kentucky was still in reserve. Major Webber was now ordered to bring that regiment forward, enter the town and storm the buildings occupied by the enemy. The Second Kentucky had tried that sort of work before, and advanced with serious mien, but boldly and confidently. Major Webber skillfully aligned it and moved it forward. The heavy volley it poured into the windows of the depot, drove the defenders away from them before the regiment reached the building, and Colonel Hanson surrendered. The other houses occupied by the enemy were surrendered shortly afterward.

At the last moment of the fight, a sad loss befell us. Lieutenant Thomas Morgan, younger brother of the General, was killed just before the enemy surrendered. He was first Lieutenant of Company I, of the Second Kentucky, but was serving at the time of his death upon my staff. He habitually sought and exposed himself to danger, seeming to delight in the excitement it afforded him. He had repeatedly been remonstrated with on that day, regarding his reckless exposure of his person, and General

Morgan had once ordered him to leave the front. He was stricken by the fate which his friends feared for him. When the Second Kentucky advanced, he rushed in front of it, and, while firing his pistol at the windows of the depot, was shot through the heart. He exclaimed to his brother Calvin, that he was killed, and fell (a corpse) into the latter's arms. He was but nineteen when killed, but was a veteran in service and experience. The first of six brothers to join the Confederate army, he had displayed his devotion to the cause he had espoused in the field and the prison. I have never known a boy of so much genius, and of so bright and winning a temper. His handsome, joyous face and gallant, courteous bearing made him very popular. He was the pet and idol of the Second Kentucky. General Morgan (whose love for the members of his family was of the most devoted character) was compelled to forego the indulgence of his own grief to restrain the Second Kentucky, furious at the death of their favorite. When his death became generally known, there was not a dry eye in the command.

Although our loss in killed and wounded was not heavy in numbers, it included some valuable officers and some of our best men. We lost eight or nine killed, and twenty-five or thirty wounded. In the early part of the fight, Captain Franks led a party of the advance guard to the southern end of the depot, and set it on fire. He was severely wounded in doing this, making the third officer, occupying the position of second in command of the advance guard, wounded in four days. The loss in the guard fell principally upon members of the "Old Squadron." Of these were killed Lieutenant Gardner and private Worsham; and Sergeant William Jones and privates Logwood and Hawkins were badly wounded, all very brave men and excellent soldiers. A gallant deed was performed, on that day, by private Walter Ferguson, one of the bravest men I ever knew; poor fellow, he was hung by Burbridge afterward. His friend and messmate Logwood lay helpless not far from the depot, and Ferguson approached him under the galling fire from the windows, lifted and bore him off. Several men were lost out of the Second Kentucky; among them Sergeant Franklin, formerly Captain of a Mississippi company in the Army of Northern Virginia.

A large quantity of ammunition, many fine rifles, an abundant supply of medicines, and a field full of ambulances and wagons were the fruits of this victory. The prisoners were double-quicked to Springfield, eight miles distant, for the dilatory Michiganders had at length began to move, and there was no reason for fighting, although we could have whipped them. At Springfield the prisoners were paroled. Company H, of the Second Kentucky, was detached here, and a company of the Sixth Kentucky went off without leave or orders. Company H was sent to Harrodsburg to occupy the attention of Burnside's cavalry. The division marched all night, reaching Bardstown at 4 o'clock on the morning of the 6th. During the night Lieut.-Colonel Alston (acting chief of staff to General Morgan) lay down to sleep in the porch of a house, and awakened to find himself in the hands of the enemy.

At Bardstown, Captain Sheldon, of Company C, Second Kentucky, detached at Muldraugh's hill to reconnoiter toward Louisville, and rejoin us at Bardstown, was patiently watching a party of twenty Federal soldiers, whom he had penned up in a stable. The tramp of the column marching through the town alarmed them, and they surrendered. Leaving Bardstown at ten A.M. on the 6th, the division marched steadily all day. Just at dark the train from Nashville was captured at a point some thirty miles from Louisville. A little of Ellsworth's art applied here discovered for us the fact that Morgan was expected at Louisville, confidently and anxiously, but that an impression prevailed that he would meet with a warm reception. He had no idea of going to receive it.

We marched during the entire night, and on the next morning, after crossing the bridge over Salt river, halted for two or three hours. Captains Taylor and Merriwether, of the Tenth Kentucky, were sent forward to capture boats to enable us to cross the Ohio, and went about their errand in good earnest. On the afternoon of that day, Captain Davis, A.A. General of the first brigade, was selected by General Morgan to undertake a service very important to the success of the expedition. He was directed to proceed, with Company D of the Second Kentucky, and Company A, of Cluke's regiment, to cross the river at Twelve Mile Island, seize boats and cross the river, keep the militia of lower Indiana employed in watching their own "firesides," chicken coops, and stables, so that the column might be comparatively free from molestation, in at least one direction, and to rejoin the division at Salem, Indiana. These two companies, the two detached at Springfield—or rather one detached there; the other marched off without leave—and Captain Salter's company detached near Columbia, to attract Burnside's attention to the country around Crab Orchard, Stanford, etc., (whither he at once hastened and did splendid service, keeping the enemy as busily employed as an ordinary-sized brigade might have done), these companies made five, in all, which were permanently detached from the division.

On the afternoon of the 7th, the column halted at Garnettsville, in Hardin county, and went into camp. It has been frequently surmised, in the North, that Morgan crossed the Ohio river to escape from Hobson. Of all the many wildly and utterly absurd ideas which have prevailed regarding the late war, this is, perhaps, the most preposterous. It is difficult to understand how, even the people whose ideas of military operations are derived from a vague rendition of the newspaper phrases of "bagging" armies, "dispositions made to capture," "deriving material advantages," when the derivers were running like scared deer, it is hard to comprehend how even such people, if they ever look upon maps, or reflect for a moment upon what they read, can receive, as correct, such assertions as the one under consideration. Hobson was from twenty-four to thirty-six hours behind us. He was pursuing us, it should be stated, with the cavalry of Judah's corps—he was, at any rate, a good fifty miles in our rear, and could learn our track only by following it closely. General Morgan, if anxious to escape Hobson, and actuated by no other motive, would have turned at Bardstown, and gone out of Kentucky through the western part of the State, where he would have encountered no hostile force that he could not have easily repulsed. It was not too late to pursue the same general route when we were at Garnettsville. Roads, traversable by artillery and excellent for cavalry, ran thence in every direction. Hobson would have had as little chance to intercept us, as a single hunter has to corner a wild horse in an open prairie. To rush across the Ohio river, as a means of escape, would have been the choice of an idiot, and yet such conduct has been ascribed to the shrewdest, most wide-awake, most far-seeing Captain (in his own chosen method of warfare), the greatest master of "cavalry strategy," that ever lived. That military men in the North should have entertained this opinion, proves, only, that in armies so vast, as that which the United States put into the field, there must necessarily be many men of very small capacity. General Morgan certainly believed that he could, with energy and care, preserve his command from capture after crossing the Ohio, but he no more believed that it would be safer, after having gained the Northern side of the river, than he believed that it was safer in Kentucky than south of the Cumberland.

The division marched from Garnettsville, shortly after midnight, and by 9 or 10 A.M. we were in Brandenburg, upon the banks of the river. Here we found Captains Samuel Taylor and Clay Merriwether, awaiting our arrival. They had succeeded in capturing two fine steamers; one had been taken at the wharf, and, manning her strongly, they cruised about the river until they found and caught the other. We were rejoined here by another officer, whose course had been somewhat eccentric, and his adventure very romantic. This was Captain Thomas Hines, of the Ninth Kentucky, then enjoying a high reputation in our command for skill, shrewdness, and exceeding gallantry, but destined to become much more widely celebrated. While the division was lying along the Cumberland in May, Captain Hines had been sent to Clinton county, with the men of the Ninth Kentucky, whose horses were especially unserviceable, to place them where, with good feeding, rest and attention, the stock might be recruited—to establish, in other words, what was technically known as a "convalescent camp," and in regimental "slang," a "dead horse camp." Captain Hines established his camp and put it into successful operation, but then sought permission to undertake more active and exciting work. He was not exactly the style of man to stay quiet at a "convalescent camp;" it would have been as difficult to keep him there, as to confine Napoleon to Elba, or force the "Wandering Jew" to remain on a cobbler's bench. He obtained from General Morgan an order to take such of his men as were best mounted, and scout "north of the Cumberland." He, therefore, selected thirty or forty of his "convalescents," whose horses were able to hobble, and crossed the river with them. Immediately exchanging his crippled horses for good, sound ones, he commenced a very pleasant and adventurous career, which lasted for some weeks. He attacked and harassed the marching columns of the enemy, and kept the smaller garrisons constantly in fear, and moved about with such celerity that there was no getting at him, occasionally interluding his other occupations by catching and burning a railroad train. He once came very near being entirely destroyed. The enemy succeeded, on one occasion, in eluding his vigilance and surprising him. While he and his men were peacefully bathing in a creek, molesting no one, they were suddenly attacked. Several were captured and the rest were dispersed, but Hines collected them, again, in a day or two.

After a while, finding Kentucky grow warm for him, and not wishing to return to the command to be remanded to the "convalescent camp," he determined to cross over into Indiana and try and stir up the "copperheads." He thought that (according to the tenor of his instructions), he had the right to do so. The order did not specify when he should return from his scout, and Indiana was certainly "north of the Cumberland." He accordingly crossed into Indiana—made his presence known to the people of the State in various ways—and penetrated as far into the interior of the State, as Seymour, at the junction of the Ohio and Mississippi and Cincinnati and Indianapolis Railroads. He here effected a junction with a greatly more numerous body of militia, which induced him to retrace his steps rapidly to the Ohio (which he recrossed), and arrived at Brandenburg on the very day that we got there. We found him leaning against the side of the wharf-boat, with sleepy, melancholy look—apparently the most listless, inoffensive youth that was ever imposed upon. I do not know what explanation he made General Morgan (of the lively manner in which he had acted under his order), but it seemed to be perfectly satisfactory, and he was ordered to report to Colonel Morgan to assume the position left vacant by the wounding of Captain Franks.

Just before the crossing of the river was commenced, an unexpected fusillade was delivered, from the Indiana shore, upon the men who showed themselves in the little town and upon the boats, which was soon followed by the sharp report of a rifled-cannon. The river at this point is some eight hundred or a thousand yards wide—and the musketry produced no effect. The shell, however, from the piece of artillery pitched into a group on the river bank, scattering it, and wounding Captain Wilson, Quartermaster of the First Brigade. The mist, hanging thick over the river, had prevented us from seeing the parties who directed this firing, take position. Soon the mist lifted or was dispersed by the bright sun, and disclosed a squad of combatants posted behind one or two small houses, a clump of hay stacks, and along the brink of the river on the other side. Apparently, from the mixture of uniforms and plain clothes, which could be discovered by the glass, this force was composed of militia and some regular troops. Several shots were fired from the gun while we were getting our pieces in readiness to reply—but as soon as Lawrence opened upon them with his Parrots, a manifest disposition to retire was seen among our friends who had shown themselves so anxious to give us a warm and early welcome. They attempted to carry the piece of artillery off with them, but were induced by Lawrence to relinquish it. It was mounted upon the wheels of a wagon from which the body had been removed, and, as they moved it by hand, its transportation was difficult and tedious and very disagreeable under fire.

Leaving the piece, they fell back to a wooded ridge five or six hundred yards from the river bank and parallel with it. The Second Kentucky and Ninth Tennessee were immediately put across the river, leaving their horses on the Kentucky shore, and were formed under the bluff bank. As they ascended the bank they were greeted by a volley from the enemy which did no damage, and Colonel Ward and Major Webber at once pressed them on toward the ridge. Scarcely had the boats returned, and while yet the two regiments on the other side were moving across the open fields between the river and the ridge, when a small boat which had for some minutes been in sight, steaming rapidly down the river, began to take a part in the affair. We had watched her with great interest, and were inclined to think, from her bold unhesitating advance, that she was a river gunboat, and when she came within a mile of the town all doubts upon the subject were dispelled. Suddenly checking her way, she tossed her snub nose defiantly, like an angry beauty of the coal-pits, sidled a little toward the town, and commenced to scold. A bluish-white, funnel-shaped cloud spouted out from her left-hand bow and a shot flew at the town, and then changing front forward, she snapped a shell at the men on the other side. The ridge was soon gained by the regiments, however, the enemy not remaining to contest it, and they were sheltered by it from the gunboat's fire. I wish I were sufficiently master of nautical phraseology to do justice to this little vixen's style of fighting, but she was so unlike a horse, or a piece of light artillery, even, that I can not venture to attempt it. She was boarded up tightly with tiers of heavy oak planking, in which embrasures were cut for the guns, of which she carried three bronze twelve-pounder howitzers, apparently. Captain Byrnes transferred the two Parrots to an eminence just upon the river and above the town, and answered her fire. His solid shot skipped about her, in close proximity, and his shells burst close to her, but none seemed to touch her—although it was occasionally hard to tell whether she was hit or not. This duel was watched with the most breathless interest by the whole division; the men crowded in intense excitement upon the bluffs, near the town, to witness it, and General Morgan exhibited an emotion he rarely permitted to be seen.

Two of his best regiments were separated from him by the broad river, and were dismounted, a condition which always appeals to a cavalryman's strongest sympathies; they might at any moment, he feared, be attacked by overwhelming forces, for he did not know what was upon the other side, or how large a swarm Hines had stirred up in the hornet's nest. He himself might be attacked, if delayed too long, by the enemy that he well knew must be following his track. Independently of all considerations of immediate danger, he was impatient at delay and anxious to try his fortune in the new field he had selected. There were many with him who could appreciate his feelings. Behind us two broad States separated us from our friends—a multitude of foes, although we thought little of them, were gathering in our rear.

On the other side of the great river were our comrades needing our aid, perhaps never to be received. When we, too, were across, we would stand face to face with the hostile and angry North—an immense and infuriated population, and a soldiery out-numbering us twenty to one, would confront us. Telegraph lines, tracing the country in every direction, would tell constantly of our movements; railways would bring assailants against us from every quarter, and we would have to run this gauntlet, night and day, without rest or one moment of safety, for six hundred miles. As we looked on the river, rolling before us, we felt that it divided us from a momentous future, and we were eager to learn our fate. After an hour perhaps had elapsed, but which seemed a dozen, the gunboat backed out and steamed up the river. Her shells had nearly all burst short, doing no damage. The boats were put to work again without a moment's delay, to ferry the command over. First, the horses of the men on the other side were carried to them, affording them exquisite gratification. Although no time was lost, and the boats were of good capacity, it was nearly dark before the first brigade was all across. The gunboat returned about five P.M., accompanied by a consort, but a few shots from the Parrots, which had been kept in position, drove them away without any intermission having occurred in the ferriage. The second brigade and the artillery were gotten across by midnight. One of the boats, which was in Government employ, was burned; the other was released.

The first brigade encamped that night about six miles from the river. "A great fear" had fallen upon the inhabitants of that part of the State of Indiana. They had left their houses, with open doors and unlocked larders, and had fled to the thickets and "caves of the hills." At the houses at which I stopped, every thing was just in the condition in which the fugitive owners had left it, an hour or two before. A bright fire was blazing upon the kitchen hearth, bread half made up was in the tray, and many indications convinced us that we had interrupted preparations for supper. The chickens were strolling before the door with a confidence that was touching, but misplaced. General Morgan rode by soon afterward, and was induced to "stop all night." We completed the preparations, so suddenly abandoned, and made the best show for Indiana hospitality that was possible under the disturbing circumstances.

On the next day, the 9th, the division marched at an early hour, the second brigade in advance. At the little town of Corydon, Colonel Morgan's advance guard found a body of militia posted behind rail barricades. He charged them, but they resolutely defended their rail piles, killing and wounding several men, among the latter Lieutenant Thorpe, of Company A, Second Kentucky, Colonel Morgan's acting Adjutant, and a very fine young officer. A demonstration was made upon the flank of the enemy, by one regiment of the second brigade, and Colonel Morgan again advanced upon their front, when, not understanding such a fashion of fighting upon two or three sides at once, the militia broke and ran, with great rapidity, into the town, their progress accelerated (as they got fairly into the streets) by a shot dropped among them from one of the pieces.

Passing through Corydon, we took the Salem road, and encamped some sixteen or eighteen miles from the latter place. On the morning of the 10th, we set out for Salem. Major Webber was ordered to take the advance, and let nothing stop him. He accordingly put his regiment at the head of the column, and struck out briskly. Lieutenant Welsh, of Company K, had the extreme advance with twelve men. As he neared Salem, he saw the enemy forming to receive him, and, without hesitation, dashed in among them. The party he attacked was about one hundred and fifty strong, but badly armed and perfectly raw, and he quickly routed them. He pursued as they fled, and soon, supported by Captain W.J. Jones' company, drove them pell-mell into the town. Here some two or three hundred were collected, but, as the Second Kentucky came pouring upon them, they fled in haste, scattering their guns in the streets. A small swivel, used by the younger population of Salem to celebrate Christmas and the Fourth of July, had been planted to receive us: about eighteen inches long, it was loaded to the muzzle, and mounted in the public square by being propped against a stick of fire wood. It was not fired, however, for the man deputed to perform that important duty, somewhat astounded by the sudden dash into the town, dropped the coal of fire with which he should have touched it off, and before he could get another the rebels captured the piece. The shuddering imagination refuses to contemplate the consequences had that swivel been touched off. Major Webber might have had some trouble with this force, which was being rapidly augmented, but for the promptness and vigor of his attack. He made favorable mention of Captain Cooper, of Company K, and Lieutenant West, of Company I, for gallant and judicious conduct.

A short halt was made in Salem to feed men and horses, and during that time several railroad bridges were burned. The Provost guard had great difficulty in restraining the men from pillaging, and was unsuccessful in some instances, Major Steele, of the Third Kentucky, had been appointed Provost Marshal of the division, and was assisted by picked officers and men from each of the brigades. Major Steele was a most resolute, vigilant, energetic officer, and yet he found it impossible to stop a practice which neither company nor regimental officers were able to aid him in suppressing. This disposition for wholesale plunder exceeded any thing that any of us had ever seen before. The men seemed actuated by a desire to "pay off" in the "enemy's country" all scores that the Federal army had chalked up in the South. The great cause for apprehension, which our situation might have inspired, seemed only to make them reckless. Calico was the staple article of appropriation—each man (who could get one) tied a bolt of it to his saddle, only to throw it away and get a fresh one at the first opportunity. They did not pillage with any sort of method or reason—it seemed to be a mania, senseless and purposeless. One man carried a bird-cage, with three canaries in it, for two days. Another rode with a chafing-dish, which looked like a small metallic coffin, on the pummel of his saddle, until an officer forced him to throw it away. Although the weather was intensely warm, another, still, slung seven pairs of skates around his neck, and chuckled over his acquisition. I saw very few articles of real value taken—they pillaged like boys robbing an orchard. I would not have believed that such a passion could have been developed, so ludicrously, among any body of civilized men. At Piketon, Ohio, some days later, one man broke through the guard posted at a store, rushed in (trembling with excitement and avarice), and filled his pockets with horn buttons. They would (with few exceptions) throw away their plunder after awhile, like children tired of their toys.

Leaving Salem at one or two o'clock, we marched rapidly and steadily. At nightfall we reached Vienna, on the Indianapolis and Jeffersonville railroad. General Morgan placed Ellsworth in the telegraph office here, the operator having been captured before he could give the alarm. Ellsworth soon learned all the news to be had from Louisville and Indianapolis, some of it valuable to us. General Morgan ascertained also that orders had been issued to the militia to fell timber and blockade all of the roads we would be likely to travel—our rapid marching had, hitherto, saved us this annoyance. That night we went into camp near Lexington, a little place six or seven miles from Vienna. General Morgan slept in the town with a small escort, and during the night a party of Federal cavalry entered the town and advanced as far as the house in which he slept, but retired as suddenly as they came. We moved at an early hour on the road to Paris—Colonel Smith was detached to feint against Madison, in order to hold there troops who might prove troublesome if they came out. The division moved quietly through Paris, and in the afternoon arrived in sight of Vernon. Here Colonel Smith rejoined us. A strong force was posted in Vernon, which General Morgan did not care to attack. Fortunately, there were men in the command who knew the country, and the General was enabled to carry the division around the place to the Dupont road. Skirmishers were thrown out on the road, leading into the town which we had left, and also upon the other road, while this movement was being executed. General Morgan sent a demand for the surrender of the place, which was declined, but the officer commanding asked two hours to remove the non-combatants, which reasonable request General Morgan granted. Humane considerations are never inopportune. By the time that the non-combatants were safely removed, the column had become straightened out on the new road, and the skirmishers, after they had burned a bridge or two, were withdrawn.

We encamped that night at 12 P.M., and moved next morning at 3. The fatigue of the marches, from the date of the crossing of the Ohio to the period of the close of the raid, was tremendous. We had marched hard in Kentucky, but we now averaged twenty-one hours in the saddle. Passing through Dupont a little after daylight, a new feature in the practice of appropriation was developed. A large meat packing establishment was in this town, and each man had a ham slung at his saddle. There was no difficulty at any time in supplying men and horses, in either Indiana or Ohio—forage and provisions were to be had in abundance, stop where we would. There is a custom prevailing in those States, which is of admirable assistance to soldiery, and should be encouraged—a practice of baking bread once a week in large quantities. Every house is full of it. The people were still laboring under vast apprehensions regarding us, and it was a rare thing to see an entire family remaining at home. The men met us oftener in their capacity of militia than at their houses, and the "Copperheads" and "Vallandighammers" fought harder than the others. Wherever we passed, bridges and depots, water-tanks, etc., were burned and the railroads torn up, but I knew of but one private dwelling being burned upon the entire raid, and we were fired upon from that one. The country, for the most part, was in a high state of cultivation, and magnificent crops of wheat, especially, attracted our notice on all sides.

What was peculiarly noticeable, however, to men who were fighting against these people, and just from thinned out "Dixie," was the dense population, apparently untouched by the demands of the war. The country was full, the towns were full, and the ranks of the militia were full. I am satisfied that we saw often as many as ten thousand militia in one day, posted at different points. They would frequently fight, if attacked in strong position, but could be dispersed by maneuvering. Had they come upon us as the fierce Kentucky Home-guards would have done, if collected in such numbers, we could not have forced our way through them.

In this immediate country had been recruited the regiment which burned the homes of Company F, the Mississippi company of the Second Kentucky. Colonel Grigsby was detached with his regiment to press on and burn the bridges near Versailles. He dashed into the town, where several hundred militia were collected devising the best means of defending the place, and broke up the council. He captured a large number of horses, rather better stock than had hitherto been procured in Indiana. Marching on steadily all day and the greater part of the next night, we reached a point on the Ohio and Mississippi road, twenty-five miles from Harrison, called Summansville. Here twenty-five hundred militia lay loaded into box cars. We halted to rest, and, unconscious of our presence, although we were close upon them, they moved off in the morning toward Cincinnati. Moving at 5 A.M., we reached Harrison by one o'clock of the 13th. Here General Morgan began to maneuver for the benefit of the commanding officer, at Cincinnati. He took it for granted (for it was utterly impossible moving as rapidly as we were forced to do, and in the midst of a strange and hostile population, to get positive information regarding any matter), that there was a strong force of regular troops in Cincinnati. Burnside had them not far off, and General Morgan supposed that they would, of course, be brought there. If we could get past Cincinnati safely, the danger of the expedition, he thought, would be more than half over. Here he expected to be confronted by the concentrated forces of Judah and Burnside, and he anticipated great difficulty in eluding or cutting his way through them. Once safely through this peril, his escape would be certain, unless the river remained so high that the transports could carry troops to intercept him at the upper crossings. The cavalry following in his rear could not overtake him as long as he kept in motion, and the infantry could not be transported so rapidly by rail to the eastern part of the State that it could be concentrated in sufficient strength to stop him. His object, therefore, entertaining these views and believing that the great effort to capture him would be made as he crossed the Hamilton and Dayton railroad, was to deceive the enemy as to the exact point where he would cross this road, and denude that point as much as possible of troops. He sent detachments in various directions, seeking, however, to create the impression that he was marching to Hamilton.

After two or three hours' halt at Harrison, the division moved directly toward Cincinnati, the detachment coming in in the course of that afternoon. Hoping that his previous demonstrations would induce the sending of the bulk of the troops up the road, and that if any were left at Cincinnati his subsequent threatening movements would cause them to draw into the city, remain on the defensive, and permit him to pass around it without attacking him, he sought to approach the city as nearly as possible without actually entering it and involving his command in a fight with any garrison which might be there. He has been sometimes accused of a lack of enterprise in not capturing Cincinnati. It must be remembered that Cincinnati was not the objective point of this raid; it was not undertaken to capture that city. General Morgan knew nothing, and, in the nature of things, could know nothing of the condition of affairs in the city, or whether it was weakly or strongly garrisoned.

Starting that morning from a point fifty miles distant from Cincinnati, and reaching the vicinity of the city after nightfall, he must have possessed more than human means of obtaining information, had he known these things then, and he did not have a rapping medium on his staff. Moreover, of the twenty-four hundred and sixty effectives with which he had started, he had not two thousand left. He could get fights enough to employ this force handsomely, without running into a labyrinth of streets, and among houses (each one of which might be made a fortification), with the hope that the town might be unoccupied with troops, or that it might be surrendered. Our "Copperhead friends," who could have given us the necessary information, were too loyal, or too busy dodging Burnside's Dutch corporals to come out.

The men in our ranks were worn down and demoralized with the tremendous fatigue, which no man can realize or form the faintest conception of until he has experienced it. It is as different from the fatigue of an ordinary long march, followed by some rest, as the pain given by an hour's deprivation of water is unlike the burning, rabid thirst of fever. Had the city been given up to us, and had the least delay occurred in getting boats with which to cross the river, the men would have scattered to all quarters of the city, and twenty-four hours might have been required to collect them. In that time the net would have been drawn around us. But it must be borne in mind (independently of all these considerations) that General Morgan had given himself a particular work to accomplish. He determined, as has been stated, to traverse Ohio.

To have recrossed the river at Cincinnati, would have shortened the raid by many days, have released the troops pursuing us, and have abandoned the principal benefits expected to be derived from the expedition.

In this night march around Cincinnati, we met with the greatest difficulty in keeping the column together. The guides were all in front with General Morgan, who rode at the head of the second brigade then marching in advance. This brigade had no trouble consequently. But the first brigade was embarrassed beyond measure. Cluke's regiment was marching in the rear of the second brigade, and if it had kept closed up, we would have had no trouble, for the entire column would have been directed by the guides. But this regiment, although composed of superb material, and unsurpassed in fighting qualities, had, from the period of its organization, been under lax and careless discipline, and the effect of it was now observable. The rear companies straggled, halted, delayed the first brigade, for it was impossible to ascertain immediately, whether the halt was that of the brigade in advance, or only of these stragglers, and when forced to move on, they would go off at a gallop. A great gap would be thus opened between the rear of one brigade and the advance of the other, and we who were behind were forced to grope our way as we best could. When we would come to one of the many junctions of roads which occur in the suburbs of a large city, we would be compelled to consult all sorts of indications in order to hit upon the right road. The night was intensely dark, and we would set on fire large bundles of paper, or splinters of wood to afford a light. The horses' tracks (on roads so much traveled), would give us no clue to the route which the other brigade had taken, at such points, but we could trace it by noticing the direction in which the dust "settled," or floated. When the night is calm, the dust kicked up by the passage of a large number of horses will remain suspended in the air for a considerable length of time, and it will also move slowly in the same direction that the horses which have disturbed it have traveled. We could also trace the column by the slaver dropped from the horses' mouths. It was a terrible, trying march. Strong men fell out of their saddles, and at every halt the officers were compelled to move continually about in their respective companies and pull and haul the men who would drop asleep in the road—it was the only way to keep them awake. Quite a number crept off into the fields and slept until they were awakened by the enemy. The rear of the first brigade was prevented from going to pieces, principally by the energetic exertions of Colonel Grigsby. Major Steele was sent in the extreme advance to drive pickets, scouts, and all parties of the enemy which might be abroad from the road. He was given a picked body of men, and executed the mission in fine style.

At length day appeared, just as we reached the last point where we had to anticipate danger. We had passed through Glendale and across all of the principal suburban roads, and were near the Little Miami Railroad. Those who have marched much at night, will remember that the fresh air of morning almost invariably has a cheering effect upon the tired and drowsy, and awakens and invigorates them. It had this effect upon our men on this occasion, and relieved us also from the necessity of groping our way.

We crossed the railroad without meeting with opposition, and halted to feed the horses in sight of Camp Dennison. After a short rest here, and a picket skirmish, we resumed our march, burning in this neighborhood a park of Government wagons. That evening at 4 P.M. we were at Williamsburg, twenty-eight miles east of Cincinnati, having marched, since leaving Summansville, in Indiana, in a period of about thirty-five hours, more than ninety miles—the greatest march that even Morgan had ever made.

Feeling comparatively safe here, General Morgan permitted the division to go into camp and remain during the night. One great drawback upon our marches, was the inferiority of the Indiana and Ohio horses for such service. After parting with our Kentucky stock, the men were compelled to exchange constantly. Sometimes three or four times in twenty four hours. The horses obtained were, not only unable to endure the hard riding for a reasonable length of time, but they were also unshod and grew lame directly. After leaving Williamsburg, we marched through Piketon (Colonel Morgan was sent with his regiment by way of Georgetown), Jackson, Vinton and Berlin (at which latter place we had a skirmish with the militia), and several towns whose names I have forgotten, as well as the order in which they came. In the skirmish at Berlin, Tom Murphy, popularly known as the "Wild Irishman," and technically described by his officers as the "goingest man" (in the advance-guard), was severely wounded. Small fights with the militia were of daily occurrence. They hung around the column, wounding two or three men every day and sometimes killing one. We captured hundreds of them daily, but could only turn them loose again after destroying their guns.

On one occasion a very gallant fellow of the Second Kentucky, Charlie Haddox, came upon five of them, who had made some of the command prisoners. He captured them, in turn, and brought them in. The prisoners who could be taken by such men hardly deserved to be released. Two men distinguished themselves very much as advance videttes, privates Carneal Warfield and Burks. The latter frequently caused the capture of parties of militia, without blood-shed on either side, by boldly riding up to them, representing himself as one of the advance guard of a body of Federal cavalry, and detaining them in conversation until the column arrived. But it is impossible to recount the one tenth part of the incidents of this nature which occurred. At Wilkesville we halted again before nightfall, and remained until 3 o'clock next morning. The militia, about this time, turned their attention seriously to felling trees, tearing up bridges, and impeding our progress in every conceivable way. The advance guard was forced to carry axes to cut away the frequent blockades. In passing near Pomeroy, on the 18th, there was one continual fight, but, now, not with the militia only, for some regular troops made their appearance and took part in the programme. The road we were traveling runs for several miles at no great distance from the town of Pomeroy, which is situated on the Ohio river. Many by-roads run from the main one into the town, and at the mouths of these roads we always found the enemy. The road runs, also, for nearly five miles through a ravine, and steep hills upon each side of it. These hills were occupied, at various points, by the enemy, and we had to run the gauntlet. Colonel Grigsby took the lead with the Sixth Kentucky, and dashed through at a gallop, halting when fired on, dismounting his men and dislodging the enemy, and again resuming his rapid march. Major Webber brought up the rear of the division and held back the enemy, who closed eagerly upon our track.

About 1 o'clock of that day we reached Chester and halted, for an hour and a half, to enable the column to close up, to breathe the horses, and also to obtain a guide, if possible (General Morgan declaring that he would no longer march without one). That halt proved disastrous—it brought us to Buffington ford after night had fallen, and delayed our attempt at crossing until the next morning.

Before quitting Ohio, it is but just to acknowledge the kind hospitality of these last two days. At every house that we approached, the dwellers thereof, themselves absent, perhaps unable to endure a meeting that would have been painful, had left warm pies, freshly baked, upon the tables. This touching attention to our tastes was appreciated. Some individuals were indelicate enough to hint that the pies were intended to propitiate us and prevent the plunder of the houses.

We reached Portland, a little village upon the bank of the river, and a short distance above Buffington Island, about 8 P.M., and the night was one of solid darkness. General Morgan consulted one or two of his officers upon the propriety of at once attacking an earthwork, thrown up to guard the ford. From all the information he could gather, this work was manned with about three hundred infantry—regular troops—and two heavy guns were mounted in it. Our arrival at this place after dark had involved us in a dilemma. If we did not cross the river that night, there was every chance of our being attacked on the next day by heavy odds. The troops we had seen at Pomeroy were, we at once and correctly conjectured, a portion of the infantry which had been sent after us from Kentucky, and they had been brought by the river, which had risen several feet in the previous week, to intercept us. If transports could pass Pomeroy, the General knew that they could also run up to the bar at Buffington Island. The transports would certainly be accompanied by gunboats, and our crossing could have been prevented by the latter alone, because our artillery ammunition was nearly exhausted—there was not more than three cartridges to the piece, and we could not have driven off gunboats with small arms. Moreover, if it was necessary, the troops could march from Pomeroy to Buffington by an excellent road, and reach the latter place in the morning. This they did. General Morgan fully appreciated these reasons for getting across the river that night, as did those with whom he advised, but there were, also, very strong reasons against attacking the work at night; and without the capture of the work, which commanded the ford, it would be impossible to cross. The night, as I have stated, was thoroughly dark. Attacks in the dark are always hazardous experiments—in this case it would have been doubly so. We knew nothing of the ground, and could not procure guides. Our choice of the direction in which to move to the attack would have been purely guess work. The defenders of the work had only to lie still and fire with artillery and musketry directly to their front, but the assailants would have had a line to preserve, and would have had to exercise great care lest they should fall foul of each other in the obscurity. If this is a difficult business at all times, how much is the danger and trouble increased when it is attempted with broken-down and partially demoralized men?

General Morgan feared, too, that if the attacking party was repulsed, it would come back in such disorder and panic that the whole division would be seriously and injuriously affected. He determined, therefore, to take the work at early dawn and instantly commence the crossing, trusting that it would be effected rapidly and before the enemy arrived. By abandoning the long train of wagons which had been collected, the wounded men, and the artillery, a crossing might have been made, with little difficulty, higher up the river at deeper fords, which wc could have reached by a rapid march before the enemy came near them. But General Morgan was determined (after having already hazarded so much) to save all if possible, at the risk of losing all. He ordered me to place two regiments of my brigade in position, as near the earthwork as I thought proper, and attack it at daybreak. I accordingly selected the Fifth and Sixth Kentucky, and formed them about four hundred yards from the work, or from the point where I judged it to be located. Lieutenant Lawrence was also directed to place his Parrots upon a tongue of land projecting northward from a range of hills running parallel with the river. It was intended that he should assist the attacking party, if, for any reason, artillery should be needed. Many efforts were made, during the night, to find other fords, but unsuccessfully.

As soon as the day dawned, the Fifth and Sixth Kentucky were moved against the work, but found it unoccupied. It had been evacuated during the night. Had our scouts, posted to observe it, been vigilant, and had this evacuation, which occurred about two P.M., been discovered and reported, we could have gotten almost the entire division across before the troops coming from Pomeroy arrived. The guns in the work had been dismounted and rolled over the bluff. I immediately sent Gen. Morgan information of the evacuation of the work, and instructed Colonel Smith to take command of the two regiments and move some four or five hundred yards further on the Pomeroy road, by which I supposed that the garrison had retreated. In a few minutes I heard the rattle of musketry in the direction that the regiments had moved, and riding forward to ascertain what occasioned it, found that Colonel Smith had unexpectedly come upon a Federal force advancing upon this road. He attacked and dispersed it, taking forty or fifty prisoners and a piece of artillery, and killing and wounding several. This force turned out to be General Judah's advance guard, and his command was reported to be eight or ten thousand strong, and not far off. Among the wounded was one of his staff, and his Adjutant-General was captured. I instructed Colonel Smith to bring the men back to the ground where they had been formed to attack the work, and rode myself to consult General Morgan and receive his orders. He instructed me to hold the enemy in check, and call for such troops as I might need for that purpose. This valley which we had entered the night before, and had bivouacked in, was about a mile long, and perhaps eight hundred yards wide at the southern extremity (the river runs here nearly due north and south), and gradually narrows toward the other end, until the ridge, which is its western boundary, runs to the water's edge. This ridge is parallel with the river at the southern end of the valley, but a few hundred yards further to the northward both river and ridge incline toward each other. About half way of the valley (equi-distant from either end) the road, by which we had marched from Chester, comes in.

Colonel Smith had posted his men, in accordance with directions given him, at the southern extremity of the valley, with the ridge upon his right flank. At this point the ridge, I should also state, bends almost at right angles to the westward. As I returned from consultation with General Morgan, I found both of the regiments under Colonel Smith in full retreat. When the main body of the enemy (which was now close upon us) appeared, an order had been issued by some one to "rally to horses." While doing this, the line was charged by the enemy's cavalry, of which they had three regiments, two of them, the Seventh and Eighth Michigan, were very fine ones. A detachment of the Fifth Indiana (led by a very gallant officer, Lieutenant O'Neil) headed this charge. The men rallied and turned, as soon as called on to do so, and had no difficulty in driving back the cavalry, but a portion of the Fifth Kentucky was cut off by this charge, and did not take part in the fight which succeeded. These two regiments were not more than two hundred and fifty strong each, and they were dismounted again, and formed across the valley. The Parrot guns had been captured, and, although our line was formed close to them, they were not again in our possession. I sent several couriers to General Morgan, asking for the Second Kentucky, a portion of which I wished to post upon the ridge, and I desired to strengthen the thin, weak line with the remainder. Colonel's Johnson's rear videttes (still kept during the night upon the Chester road) had a short time previously been driven in, and he had formed his brigade to receive the enemy coming from that direction. Colonel Johnson offered me a detachment of his own brigade with which to occupy the part of the ridge immediately upon my right—the necessity of holding it was immediately apparent to him. Believing that the Second Kentucky would soon arrive, I declined his offer.

The force advancing upon the Chester road was General Hobson's, which our late delays had permitted to overtake us. Neither Judah nor Hobson was aware of the other's vicinity, until apprised of it by the sound of their respective guns. We could not have defeated either alone, for Judah was several thousand strong, and Hobson three thousand. We were scarcely nineteen hundred strong, and our ammunition was nearly exhausted—either shot away or worn out in the pouches or cartridge-boxes. The men, had on an average, not more than five rounds in their boxes. If, however, either Judah or Hobson had attacked us singly, we could have made good our retreat, in order, and with little loss.

The attack commenced from both directions, almost simultaneously, and at the same time the gunboats steamed up and commented shelling us without fear or favor. I heartily wished that *their* fierce ardor, the result of a feeling of perfect security, could have been subjected to the test of two or three shots through their hulls. They were working, as well as I could judge, five or six guns, Hobson two, and Judah five or six. The shells coming thus from three different directions, seemed to fill the air with their fragments. Colonel Johnson's line, confronting Hobson, was formed at right angles to mine, and upon the level and unsheltered surface of the valley, each was equally exposed to shots aimed at the other. In addition to the infantry deployed in front of my line, the ridge upon the right of it was soon occupied by one of the Michigan regiments, dismounted and deployed as skirmishers. The peculiar formation we were forced to adopt, exposed our entire force engaged to a severe cross fire of musketry. The Second Kentucky and Ninth Tennessee, of the first brigade, were not engaged at all—nor the Eight and Eleventh Kentucky, of the second brigade. These regiments, however, were as completely under fire, in the commencement of the action, as were the others which were protecting the retreat.

The scene in the rear of the lines engaged, was one of indescribable confusion. While the bulk of the regiments, which General Morgan was drawing off, were moving from the field in perfect order, there were many stragglers from each, who were circling about the valley in a delirium of fright, clinging instinctively, in all their terror, to bolts of calico and holding on to led horses, but changing the direction in which they galloped, with every shell which whizzed or burst near them. The long train of wagons and ambulances dashed wildly in the only direction which promised escape, and becoming locked and entangled with each other in their flight, many were upset, and terrified horses broke lose from them and plunged wildly through the mass. Some of them in striving to make their way out of the valley, at the northern end, ran foul of the section of howitzers attached to the second brigade, and guns and wagons were rolled headlong into the steep ravine. Occasionally a solid shot or shell would strike one and bowl it over like a tumbled ten-pin. All this shelling did little damage, and only some twenty-odd men were killed by the musketry—the enemy lost quite as many—but the display of force against us, the cross fire, and our lack of ammunition, seriously disheartened the men, already partially demoralized by the great and unremitted fatigue.

The left flank of my line, between which and the river there was an interval of at least three hundred yards, was completely turned, and the Sixth Kentucky was almost surrounded. This regiment (under the command of Major William Bullitt, an officer of the calmest and most perfect bravery), behaved nobly. It stood the heavy attack of the enemy like a bastion. At length seeing that General Morgan had gotten out of the valley with the rest of the division, Colonel Johnson and myself, upon consultation, determined to withdraw simultaneously. We had checked this superior force for more than half an hour—which, as much as our assailants boasted of their victory, was quite as good as an equal number of the best of them could have done against such odds.

The men were remounted without confusion, and retreated in column of fours from right of companies, and for quite a mile in perfect order. The Sixth Kentucky formed to the "rear into line" three times, and with empty guns, kept the pursuing cavalry at bay. But when we neared the other end of the valley and saw that there were but two avenues of escape from it—the men broke ranks and rushed for them. In a moment, each was blocked. The gunboats sought to rake these roads with grape—and although they aimed too high to inflict much injury, the hiss of the dreaded missiles increased the panic. The Seventh Michigan soon came up and dashed pell-mell into the crowd of fugitives. Colonel Smith, Captain Campbell, Captain Thorpe, and myself, and some fifty other officers and men, were forced by the charge of this regiment into a ravine on the left of the road and soon afterward captured. Captain Thorpe saved me from capture at an earlier date, only to ultimately share my fate. He had acted as Adjutant General of the First Brigade, since the detachment of Captain Davis, and had performed all of his duties with untiring assiduity and perfect efficiency. On this day, there was allowed opportunity for the display of courage only, and for that he was ever distinguished.

About seven hundred prisoners were taken from us in this fight. Among the officers captured were Colonels Ward and Morgan, Lieutenant Colonel Huffman, who was also severely wounded, and Majors Bullock and Bullitt.

On the next day, the 20th, we were marched down the river bank some ten miles to the transport which was to take us to Cincinnati, and she steamed off as soon as we were aboard of her. A portion of the Ninth Tennessee had been put across the river, in a small flat, before the fight fairly commenced, and these men, under command of Captain Kirkpatrick, pressed horses and made their escape. Colonel Grigsby and Captain Byrnes also crossed the river here, and succeeded in escaping. Between eleven and twelve hundred men retreated with General Morgan, closely pursued by Hobson's cavalry—the indefatigable Woolford, as usual, in the lead. Some three hundred of the command crossed the river at a point about twenty miles above Buffington. Colonel Johnson and his staff swam the river here and got safely ashore, with the exception of two or three of the latter, who were drowned in the attempt.

The arrival of the gun boats prevented the entire force from crossing. General Morgan had gained the middle of the river, and, having a strong horse, could have gained the other shore without difficulty, but seeing that the bulk of his command would be forced to remain on the Ohio side, he returned to it. At this point, a negro boy named Box, a great favorite in the Second Kentucky, thorough rebel and deeply impressed with a sense of his own importance, entered the river and started across; General Morgan called to him to return, fearing that he would be drowned. "Marse John," said Box, "If dey catches you, dey may parole you, but if dis nigger is cotched in a free State he ain't a gwine to git away while de war lasts." He swam the river safely although nearly run down by a gun boat. From this time, for six days, it was a continual race and scramble. That men could have endured it, after the previous exhausting marches, is almost incredible.

The brigades were reorganized. Colonel Cluke was placed in command of the second, Major Webber of the first, each was a little more than four hundred strong. "The bold Cluke" had need of all of his audacity and vigor during these six days of trial. It is impossible for the reader to appreciate the true condition in which these brave men were placed. Worn down by tremendous and long sustained exertion, encompassed by a multitude of foes, and fresh ones springing up in their path at every mile, allowed no rest, but driven on night and day; attacked, harassed, intercepted at every moment, disheartened by the disasters already suffered—how magnificent was the nerve, energy and resolution which enabled them to bear up against all this and struggle so gallantly to the very last against capture. Major Webber had long been suffering from a painful and exhausting disease, and when he started upon the raid he could not climb into his saddle without assistance. But he could not endure the thought of being absent from such an expedition. He was one of the very best officers in the Confederate cavalry, and his ideas of duty were almost fanatical. All through the long march to Buffington, he rode at the head of the "old regulars," without a murmur escaping his lips to tell of the pain which paled his brave, manly face, but could not bend his erect form. Of his conduct after the Buffington disaster, General Morgan, and his comrades spoke in enthusiastic praise—one officer in describing his unflinching steadiness called him the "Iron man." No description could do justice to these six days, and I will not attempt one. One incident will serve to show how constantly the enemy pressed the command. Once, when there seemed leisure for it, General Morgan called a council of his officers. While it was in session, the enemy were skirmishing with the advance and rear-guards of the column, and were upon both flanks. A bullet struck within two inches of the General's head, while he was courteously listening to an opinion. When the council was closed, General Morgan moved the column back toward "Blennerhassett's Island," where he had previously attempted to cross the river. Clouds of dust marked his march (although he quitted the main road) and also the track of his enemies, and in that way the exact position of all the columns was known to each. That night he halted with a bold mountain upon one side of him and the enemy on the other three. His pursuers evidently thought that the morning would witness his surrender, for they made no effort to force him to yield that evening. But when night had fairly fallen and the camp fires of his foes were burning brightly, he formed his men, partially ascended the mountain, stole noiselessly and in single file along its rough slope and by midnight was out of the trap, and again working hard for safety.

Here is a description from Major Webber's diary, of how General Morgan eluded the enemy posted to ensnare him when he should cross the Muskingum. He had been compelled to drive off a strong force in order to obtain a crossing; after he had crossed he found himself thus situated. "The enemy had fallen back on all of the roads—guarding each one with a force in ambush much larger than ours—and to make our way through seemed utterly impossible; while Hobson had made his appearance with a large force on the opposite bank of the Muskingham so that to retrace our steps would be ruin. Finding every road strongly guarded, and every hill covered with troops, it would have been impossible for any one except Morgan to have led a column out of such a place, and he did it by what the citizens tell us, is the only place which a horse can go; and that down a narrow pass leading up a narrow spring branch hundreds of feet below the tops of the hills, the perpendicular sides of which pressed closely on our horses as we passed in single file. And then we went up another hill, or rather mountain side, up which nobody but a Morgan man could have carried a horse. Up that hill, for at least one thousand feet, we led our tired horses, where it seemed that a goat couldn't climb, until we reached the plain, and were soon in the rear of the enemy and on our road again. Colonel Cluke who was in the rear lost two men killed.

In looking around for a place to carry the column, Adjutant S.F. McKee and two of our men ran into an ambuscade, and were fired on, about thirty yards distant, by three hundred men, without striking either of them or their horses." But all this brave, persistent effort, was unavailing. General Morgan maintained his high spirit to the last, and seemed untouched by the weariness which bore down every one else, but he was forced at last to turn at bay, and a fresh disaster on the 26th, reducing his command to two hundred and fifty men, and a fresh swarm of enemies gathering around this remnant, left him no alternative (in justice to his men) but surrender. I may be permitted to mention (with natural pride), that the last charge made upon this expedition, was made by Company C, of my old regiment, the Second Kentucky, the "Regulars." This company had maintained its organization and discipline without any deterioration, although greatly reduced in numbers. In this last fight, it was ordered to charge a body of Federal cavalry, who were dismounted and lay behind a worm fence, firing upon the column with their Spencer rifles. Led by its gallant Captain, Ralph Sheldon, one of the best of our *best*, officers, this company dashed down upon the enemy. The tired horses breasted the fence, without being able to clear it, knocking off the top rails. But with their deadly revolvers our boys soon accomplished the mission upon which they were sent.

General Morgan surrendered in a very peculiar manner. He had, many days before, heard of the retreat of General Lee, after Gettysburg, from Pennsylvania, and of the fall of Vicksburg. In at least twenty towns through which we had passed, in Indiana and Ohio, we had witnessed the evidences of the illuminations in honor of these events. He feared that, in consequence of the great excess of prisoners thus coming in Federal possession, the cartel (providing for the exchange of prisoners and the paroling of the excess upon either side, within a short period after their capture) would be broken. He was anxious, therefore, to surrender "upon terms." Aware that he was not likely to get such terms as he wished, from any officer of the regular troops that were pursuing him, unless he might happen to hit upon Woolford, who was as noted for generosity to prisoners (if he respected their prowess) as for vigor and gallantry in the field, he looked around for some militia officer who might serve his turn. In the extreme eastern part of Ohio (where he now was), he came into the "district" of a Captain Burbeck, who had his militia under arms. General Morgan sent a message to Captain Burbeck, under flag of truce, requesting an interview with him. Burbeck consented to meet him, and, after a short conference, General Morgan concluded a treaty with him, by which he (Morgan) engaged to take and disturb nothing, and do no sort of damage in Burbeck's district, and Burbeck, on his part, covenanted to guide and escort Morgan to the Pennsylvania line. After riding a few miles, side by side, with his host, General Morgan, espying a long cloud of dust rolling rapidly upon a course parallel with his own (about a mile distant), and gaining his front, thought it was time to act. So he interrupted a pleasant conversation, by suddenly asking Burbeck how he would like to receive his (Morgan's) surrender. Burbeck answered that it would afford him inexpressible satisfaction to do so. "But," said Morgan, "perhaps you would not give me such terms as I wish." "General Morgan," replied Burbeck, "you might write your own terms, and I would grant them." "Very well, then," said Morgan; "it is a bargain. I will surrender to you." He, accordingly, formally surrendered to Captain Burbeck, of the Ohio militia, upon condition that officers and men were to be paroled, the latter retaining their horses, and the former horses and side-arms. When General Shackleford (Hobson's second in command, and the officer who was conducting the pursuit in that immediate region) arrived, he at once disapproved this arrangement, and took measures to prevent its being carried into effect. Some officers who had once been Morgan's prisoners, were anxious that it should be observed, and Woolford generously interested himself to have it done. The terms of this surrender were not carried out. The cartel (as Morgan had anticipated) had been repudiated, and the terms for which he had stipulated, under that apprehension, were repudiated also.

Although this expedition resulted disastrously, it was, even as a failure, incomparably the most brilliant raid of the entire war. The purposes sought to be achieved by it were grander and more important, the conception of the plan which should regulate it, was more masterly, and the skill with which it was conducted is unparalleled in the history of such affairs. It was no ride across a country stripped of troops, with a force larger than any it should chance to encounter.

It was not an expedition started from a point impregnably

garrisoned, to dash by a well marked path to another point occupied by a friendly army. It differed from even the boldest of Confederate raids, not only in that it was vastly more extended, but also in the nerve with which the great natural obstacles were placed between the little band with which it was undertaken and home, and the unshrinking audacity with which that slight force penetrated into a populous and intensely hostile territory, and confidently exposed itself to such tremendous odds, and such overwhelming disadvantages. Over one hundred thousand men were in arms to catch Morgan (although not all employed at one time and place), and every advantage in the way of transporting troops, obtaining information, and disposing forces to intercept or oppose him, was possessed by his enemy, and yet his wily strategy enabled him to make his way to the river, at the very point where he had contemplated recrossing it when he started from, Tennessee; and he was prevented from recrossing and effecting his escape (which would then have been certain) only by the river having risen at a season at which it had not risen for more than twenty years before.

The objects of the raid were accomplished. General Bragg's retreat was unmolested by any flanking forces of the enemy, and I think that military men, who will review all the facts, will pronounce that this expedition delayed for weeks the fall of East Tennessee, and prevented the timely reinforcement of Rosecrans by troops that would otherwise have participated in the battle of Chickamauga. It destroyed Morgan's division, however, and left but a remnant of the Morgan cavalry. The companies in Kentucky became disintegrated—the men were either captured or so dispersed that few were ever again available. Captain Davis crossed into Indiana, with the two companies assigned him, but failed to rejoin the division, and was surrounded by overwhelming numbers, and himself and the greater part of his command captured. Some of the men in those companies escaped—the majority of them returned to the South, others remained in Kentucky to "guerrilla." Two fine companies of the Ninth Tennessee, under Captains Kirkpatrick and Sisson, crossed the river at Buffington; two companies of the Second Kentucky, under Captains Lea and Cooper, effected a crossing a day or two later. Besides these organized bodies of men, there were stragglers from all the regiments to the number of three or four hundred, who escaped. These men were collected by Colonels Johnson and Grigsby, and marched through Western Virginia to Morristown, in East Tennessee, where all that was left of Morgan's command was rendezvoused.

Although the consequences were so disastrous, although upon the greater part of those who followed Morgan in this raid was visited a long, cruel, wearisome imprisonment, there are few, I imagine, among them who ever regretted it. It was a sad infliction upon a soldier, especially upon one accustomed to the life the "Morgan men" had led, to eat his heart in the tedious, dreary prison existence, while the fight which he should have shared was daily growing deadlier. But to have, in our turn, been invaders, to have carried the war north of the Ohio, to have taught the people, who for long months had been pouring invading hosts into the South, something of the agony and terror of invasion—to have made them fly in fear from their homes, although they returned to find those homes not laid in ashes; to have scared them with the sound of hostile bugles, although no signals were sounded for flames and destruction—these luxuries were cheap at almost any price. It would have been an inexpiable shame if, in all the Confederate army, there had been no body of men found to carry the war, however briefly, across the Ohio, and Morgan by this raid saved us, at least, that disgrace.

One of the many articles which filled the Northern papers, upon the disastrous termination of this expedition, prophetically declared the true misfortune which would result to Morgan himself from his ill-success to-wit: the loss of his unexampled prestige—hitherto of itself a power adequate to ensure him victories, but never to be recovered. This writer more sagacious, as well as more fair than others of his class, said:

"The raid through Indiana and Ohio has proved an unfortunate business to him and his command. His career, hitherto has been dashing and brilliant, and but few rebel commanders had won a higher reputation throughout the South. He had been glorified by rebels in arms everywhere, but this last reckless adventure will doubtless rob his name of half its potency. The prestige of success is all powerful, while a failure is death to military reputation. It would now be a difficult matter to rally to his standard as many enthusiastic and promising young men, who infatuated and misguided, joined him during the period of his success. Many of them blindly seemed to entertain the opinion that no reverse could befall him, and all he had to do was to march along, and victory after victory would perch upon his banner. They couldn't even dream of a disaster or an end to his triumphs. Many of them have already sadly and dearly paid for their infatuation, while others are doomed to a similar fate. This remarkable raid, certainly the most daring of the war, is about at an end. Morgan is trapped at last and his forces scattered, and if he escapes himself it will only be as a fugitive. The race he has run since crossing the Cumberland river, eluding the thousands of troops which have been put upon his track, proved him a leader of extraordinary ability. The object of the raid is yet a mystery. Time alone will develop the plan, if plan there was. Moving on with such a force, far from all support—at the very time, too, that Bragg's army was falling back and scattering—makes the affair look like one of simple bravado, as if the leader was willing to be captured, provided he could end his career in a blaze of excitement created by his dash and daring. But it is useless to speculate now. Broken into squads, some few of his men will doubtless escape across the river, and make their way singly to the Confederacy, to tell the story of their long ride through Indiana and Ohio; but the power of the noted partisan chieftain and his bold riders is a thing of the past."

CHAPTER XV

The prisoners taken at Buffington were carried to Cincinnati as rapidly as the low stage of water, and the speed of the little boat, upon which we were placed, would permit. We were some three days in making the trip. Fortunately for us, the officers and men appointed to guard us, were disposed to ameliorate our condition as much as possible. Our private soldiers, crowded on the hurricane decks, were, of course, subjected to inconvenience, but the wish of the guards was evidently to remedy it as much as possible. This crowding enabled a number of them to make their escape by leaping into the river at night, as the sentries could not possibly detect or prevent their efforts at escape. Captain Day, General Judah's inspector, who was in immediate charge of us, while he was rigidly careful to guard against escape, showed us the most manly and soldierly courtesy. As the only acknowledgment we could make him, the officers united in requesting him to accept a letter which we severally signed, declaring our appreciation of his kindness. We trusted that, if he should ever be so unfortunate as to become a prisoner himself, this evidence of his consideration for our situation would benefit him.

It was habitually remarked that, in the first two years of the war at least, there was a prevalent disposition among the men of both armies who served in "the front," to show courtesy to prisoners. The soldiers who guarded us from Buffington to Cincinnati were characterized by this spirit in an unusual degree, and carried out this practice, which even those who neglect it, approve, more thoroughly, I must say, than any troops I had ever seen. We met with treatment so different, afterward, that we had occasion to remember and compare. For my own part, I was more than once compelled, during my long and chequered imprisonment, to express my sense of courteous and considerate treatment; and, as I believe, that a gentleman ought not to say, at any time or in any event, that which he can not unhesitatingly confirm, however changed may be the circumstances (every legitimate *ruse-de-guerre*, being, of course, an exception), I shall take great pains, in the course of this chapter, to specify wherein and by whom such treatment was accorded me, or my comrades. I am aware that this is not customary, and the contrary habit, may have become an established canon of this sort of literature, the violation of which will occasion grave criticism. But my own people will appreciate my explanation. I should have accepted no kindness at the hands of my captors; I ought to have repelled every courtesy offered me, if clearly prompted by a generous and manly spirit; if I were capable of altogether omitting mention of such acts, in a description, purporting to be truthful and accurate, of my prison experience.

In all else, my readers may rest assured that the rule shall be observed. He would be a poor-spirited prisoner, who would not tell all the mean things he knows about his jailors, and since Wirtz was hung, at any rate, such gentry have become fair game.

When we arrived at Cincinnati, we met with a grand ovation. The fact that none of the citizens had come out to meet us, when we marched around the city, had caused us to conceive a very erroneous impression regarding them. They pressed closely upon the guard of soldiers who were drawn up around us, as we were marched through the streets to the city prison, and attempted many demonstrations of their feeling toward us. There seemed to be little sympathy between the soldiers and the populace. The former muttered pretty strong expressions of disgust for the previous tameness and present boldness of the latter, and once or twice when jostled, plied their bayonets. The privates were immediately sent to camps Morton and Douglass. The officers were kept at the city prison in Cincinnati for three days. During that time, we were reinforced by a good many others, taken in the two or three days which, succeeded Buffington fight.

On the last day of our sojourn here, we learned of General Morgan's capture. We had hoped and almost felt confident, that he would escape.

We were removed from this prison on the second of July (or within a day or two of that date), and taken to Johnson's Island. At every station on the railroad, from Cincinnati to Sandusky, large and enthusiastic crowds assembled to greet us. The enthusiasm, however, was scarcely of a nature to excite agreeable emotions in our bosoms. There seemed to be "universal suffrage" for our instant and collective execution, and its propriety was promulgated with much heat and emphasis. A change seemed to have come over the people of Ohio in the past two weeks. In our progress through the State, before our capture, the people left their homes—apparently from a modest disinclination to see us. But, now, they crowded to stare at us.

When we reached Sandusky, we were transferred to a small steam tug, and, in twenty minutes, were put across the arm of the lake which separates Johnson's Island from the main land. We were marched, as soon as landed, to the adjutant's office, and after roll-call, and a preliminary scrutiny to ascertain if we had money or weapons upon our persons, although it was, perhaps, the strict rule to search—the word of each man in our party was taken—we were introduced into the prison inclosure. It was the custom, in those days, in the various prisons for the older inmates to collect about the gates of the "Bull-pen" when "Fresh fish," as every lot of prisoners just arrived were termed, were brought in, and inspect them. We, consequently, met a large crowd of unfortunate rebels, when we entered, in which were not a few acquaintances, and some of our own immediate comrades. The first man I saw, or, at least, the first one to whom my attention was attracted, was First Lieutenant Charles Donegan, of the Second Kentucky. He had been a private in the heroic Fourth Alabama, and, when his term of service had expired in that regiment, he "joined Morgan," becoming a private in Company A, of the "old squadron." When the Second Kentucky was organized, he was made a non-commissioned officer, and was shortly afterward promoted to First Lieutenant for gallantry, excellent conduct, and strict attention to duty. In the prison he met with his old comrades of the Army of Northern Virginia, and was prompt to welcome all of the "Morgan men" who "happened in," and to initiate them in the art of making life in a prison endurable. A few months before, I had visited his father, one of the most hospitable men in Huntsville, famed for that virtue, and he charged me with a message to "Charlie," which I delivered in the barracks at Johnson's Island. Lieutenant Donegan remained in prison more than twenty months—one of those men whose patient heroism will never be justly appreciated.

It is only by citing personal instances of this kind, that the history of the Southern soldiery can be written so that it will be understood.

The Gettysburg prisoners had arrived, only a few days before, and from them we heard the first intelligible account of the great battle. Not a whit was the courage and fire of these gallant representatives of the army of heroes abated. They seemed to have perfect faith in the invincibility of their comrades, and they looked for the millenium to arrive, much sooner, than for serious discomfiture to befall "Uncle Robert."

Johnson's Island was the most agreeable prison I ever saw—which is much as if a man were to allude to the pleasantest dose of castor oil he ever swallowed. However, there is little doubt but that it *would* have been pleasant (for a short time), if it had not been a prison. The climate in the summer is delightful, and the prospect highly gratifying—except to a man who would like to escape and can not swim. The winters, there, are said to have been very severe—but then the barracks were open and airy. We, who were shortly afterward transferred to the Ohio Penitentiary, thought and spoke of Johnson's Island as (under the circumstances), a very "desirable location." The rations were good, and we were permitted to purchase any thing we wished from the sutler. As we were there only four days, however, it is possible that some others who remained nearly two years, may be right in contending that the regime (in process of time), underwent some change.

It was not uncommon to hear men say, that they would rather be sent to that locality which is conceded by all sects to be exceedingly uncomfortable, than go again to Johnson's Island—but a shuddering recollection of the bitter winter weather, evidently induced the preference. After remaining at Johnson's Island four days, some forty of us were called for one morning, and bidden to prepare for departure—whither we were not informed. But our worst fears were realized, when we were taken off of the cars at Columbus and marched to the penitentiary. The State of Ohio claimed Morgan and his officers, as her peculiar property—because we had been captured on her soil by Michiganders, Kentuckians, etc., and demanded us, that we might be subjected to the same treatment which she inflicted upon her felons. It was rumored, also, that Colonel Streight, an Ohio officer, captured by Forrest, had been placed in the penitentiary in Georgia, and we were told that we were being penitentiaried in retaliation. It turned out subsequently that Colonel Streight was treated precisely as the other prisoners in the South, but the Governor of Ohio having gotten hold of a batch of Confederate soldiers, captured for him by troops from other States, was disposed to make the most of them, and would not consent to let them out of his hands.

Two men figured in the "Ohio raid" and the subsequent treatment of the raiders, with a peculiar eclat. The Commander-in-Chief of the department, who prepared to flee from the city where his headquarters were established, upon the approach of two thousand wearied men, whom with an army of fine troops he could not stop—was one of them. The other was the Governor of a State he could not defend; but who could torture if he could not fight. Burnside turned us over to Todd—but instructed that, "these men shall be subjected to the usual prison discipline." He could part with his prisoners and enjoin, in doing so, that they be treated as convicted felons. But his name would blister the tongue of a brave man, and I should apologize for writing it.

When we entered this gloomy mansion of "crime and woe," it was with misery in our hearts, although an affected gaiety of manner. We could not escape the conviction, struggle against it as we would, that we were placed there to remain while the war lasted, and most of as believed that the war would outlast the generation. We were told, when we went in, that we "were there to stay," and there was something infernal in the gloom and the massive strength of the place, which seemed to bid us "leave all hope behind." While we were waiting in the hall, to which we were assigned, before being placed in our cells, a convict, as I supposed, spoke to me in a low voice from the grated door of one of the cells already occupied. I made some remark about the familiarity of our new friends on short acquaintance, when by the speaker's peculiar laugh I recognized General Morgan. He was so shaven and shorn, that his voice alone was recognizable, for I could not readily distinguish his figure. We were soon placed in our respective cells and the iron barred doors locked. Some of the officers declared subsequently, that when left alone, and the eyes of the keepers were taken off of them, they came near swooning. It was not the apprehension of hardship or harsh treatment that was so horrible; it was the stifling sense of close cramped confinement. The dead weight of the huge stone prison seemed resting on our breasts. On the next day we were taken out to undergo some of the "usual prison discipline," and were subjected to a sort of dress-parade. We were first placed man by man, in big hogsheads filled with water (of which there were two), and solemnly scrubbed by a couple of negro convicts. This they said was done for sanitary reasons. The baths in the lake at Johnson's Island were much pleasanter, and the twentieth man who was ordered into either tub, looked ruefully at the water, as if he thought it had already done enough for health. Then we were seated in barber chairs, our beards were taken off, and the officiating artists were ordered to give each man's hair "a decent cut." We found that according to the penitentiary code, the decent way of wearing the hair was to cut it all off—if the same rule had been adopted with regard to clothing, the Digger Indians would have been superfluously clad in comparison with (what would have been), our disheveled condition. Some young men lost beards and moustaches on this occasion, which they had assiduously cultivated with scanty returns, for years. Colonel Smith had a magnificent beard sweeping down to his waist, patriarchal in all save color—it gave him a leonine aspect that might have awed even a barber. He was placed in the chair, and in less time, perhaps, than Absalom staid on his mule after his hair brought him to grief, he was reduced to ordinary humanity. He felt his loss keenly. I ventured to compliment him on features which I had never seen till then, and he answered, with asperity, that it was "no jesting matter."

When we returned to the hall, we met General Morgan, Colonel Cluke, Calvin Morgan, Captain Gibson, and some twenty-six others—our party numbered sixty-eight in all. General Morgan and most of the officers who surrendered with him, had been taken to Cincinnati and lodged in the city prison (as we had been), with the difference, that we had been placed in the upper apartments (which were clean), and he and his party were confined in the lower rooms, in comparison with which the stalls of the Augean stables were boudoirs. After great efforts, General Morgan obtained an interview with Burnside, and urged that the terms upon which he had surrendered should be observed, but with no avail. He and the officers with him, were taken directly from Cincinnati to the Ohio Penitentiary, and had been there several days when we (who came from Johnson's Island), arrived. It is a difficult thing to describe, so that it will be clearly understood, the interior conformation of any large building, and I will have to trust that my readers will either catch a just idea of the subject from a very partial and inadequate description, or that they will regard it as a matter of little importance whether or no they shall understand the internal plan and structure of the Ohio State Prison. For my purpose, it is only necessary that the architecture of one part of it shall be understood. Let the reader imagine a large room (or rather wing of a building), four hundred feet in length, forty-odd in width, and with a ceiling forty-odd feet in hight. One half of this wing, although separated from the other by no traverse wall, is called the "East Hall."

In the walls of this hall are cut great windows, looking out upon one of the prison yards. If the reader will further imagine a building erected in the interior of this hall and reaching to the ceiling, upon each side of which, and between its walls and the walls of the hall, are alleys eleven feet wide and running the entire length of the hall, and at either extremity of this building, spaces twenty feet in width—he will have conceived a just idea of that part of the prison in which General Morgan and his officers were confined. In the interior building the cells are constructed—each about three feet and a half wide and seven feet long. The doors of the cells—a certain number of which are constructed in each side of this building—open upon the alleys which have been described. At the back of each, and of course separating the ranges of cells upon the opposite sides of the building, is a hollow space reaching from the floor to the ceiling, running the whole length of the building, and three or four feet wide. This space is left for the purpose of obtaining more thorough ventillation, and the back wall of every cell is perforated with a hole, three or four inches in diameter, to admit the air from this passage.

We were placed in the cells constructed in that face of the building which looks toward the town. No convicts were quartered in the cells on that side, except on the extreme upper tiers, but the cells on the other side of the building were all occupied by them. The cells are some seven feet in hight, and are built in ranges, or tiers, one above the other. They are numbered, range first, second, third, and so on—commencing at the lower one. The doors are grates of iron—the bars of which are about an inch and a quarter wide, and half an inch thick, and are, perhaps, two inches apart, leaving, as they are placed upright and athwart, open spaces of two inches square between them. In front of each range of cells were balconies three feet wide, and ladders led from each one of these to the other just above it.

We were permitted to exercise, during the day, in the alley in front of our cells, although prohibited from looking out of the windows. Twice a day we were taken to meals, crossing (when we went to breakfast) a portion of the yard, before mentioned, and passing through the kitchen into the large dining-hall of the institution. Here, seated at tables about two feet wide and the same distance apart, a great many prisoners could be fed at the same time. We were not allowed to breakfast and dine with the convicts, or they were not allowed to eat with us—I could never learn exactly how it was. We crossed the yard, on the way to breakfast, for the purpose of washing our faces, which was permitted by the prison regulations, but a certain method of doing it was prescribed. Two long troughs were erected and filled with water. The inhabitants of the First Range washed in one trough, and those of the Second Range used the other. We soon obtained permission to buy and keep our own towels. In returning from breakfast, and in going to and returning from dinner, we never quitted the prison building, but marched through a wing of the dining-room back to the long wing, in one end of which was our hall.

At seven P.M. in summer (earlier afterward), we were required to go to our respective cells at the tap of the turnkey's key on the stove, and he passed along the ranges and locked us in for the night. In a little while, then, we would hear the steady, rolling tramp of the convicts, who slept in the hall at the other end of the wing, as they marched in with military step and precision, changing after awhile from the sharp clatter of many feet simultaneously striking the stone floor to the hurried, muffled rattle of their ascent (in a trot) of the stairways. Then when each had gained his cell, and the locking-in commenced, the most infernal clash and clang, as huge bolts were fastened, would be heard that ever startled the ear of a sane man. When Satan receives a fresh lot of prisoners, he certainly must torture each half by compelling it to hear the other locked into cells with iron doors.

The rations furnished us for the first ten days were inferior to those subsequently issued. The food allowed us, although exceedingly coarse, was always sufficiently abundant. After about ten days the restriction, previously imposed, preventing us from purchasing or receiving from our friends articles edible, or of any other description, was repealed, and we were allowed to receive every thing sent us. Our Kentucky friends had been awaiting this opportunity, and for fear that the privilege would be soon withdrawn, hastened to send cargoes of all sorts of food and all kinds of dainties. For a few days we were almost surfeited with good things, and then the trap fell. When piles of delicacies were stacked up in his office, the Warden of the prison, Captain Merion, confiscated all to his own use, forbade our receiving any thing more, and rather than the provisions should be wasted, furnished his own table with them.

For several weeks one or two soldiers were habitually kept in the hall with us, during the day. The turnkey, who was the presiding imp in that wing—the ghoul of our part of the catacombs—was rarely absent, but passed back and forth, prying and suspicious. Scott (familiarly Scotty) was the name of the interesting creature who officiated as our immediate keeper, for the first four months of our confinement in this place. He was on duty only during the day. At night a special guard went the rounds. The gas-burners, with which each cell was furnished, were put into use as soon as we were locked up, and we were allowed (for a time) to burn candles for an hour after the hour for which the gas was turned on had expired. We were permitted to buy books and keep them in our cells, and for some weeks were not restricted in the number of letters which we might write. Indeed for a period of nearly three months our condition was uncomfortable only on account of the constant confinement within the walls of the prison—the lack of exercise, and sun-light, and free air, and the penning up at night in the close cells. To a man who has never been placed in such a situation, no words can convey the slightest idea of its irksomeness. There was not one of us who would not have eagerly exchanged for the most comfortless of all the prisons, where he could have spent the days in the open air, and some part of the time have felt that the eyes of the gaolers were not upon him. Every conceivable method of killing time, and every practical recreation was resorted to. Marbles were held in high estimation for many days, and the games were played first, and discussed subsequently with keen interest. A long ladder, which had been left in the hall, leaning against the wall, was a perfect treasure to those who most craved active exercise. They practiced all sorts of gymnastics on this ladder, and cooled the fever in their blood with fatigue. Chess finally became the standard amusement, and those who did not understand the game watched it nevertheless with as much apparent relish as if they understood it. Chess books were bought and studied as carefully as any work on tactics had ever been by the same men, and groups would spend hours in discussing this gambit and that, and an admiring audience could always be collected at one end of the hall to hear how Cicero Coleman had just checkmated an antagonist at the other, by a judicious flank movement with his "knight," or some other active and effective piece.

In spite, however, of every effort to sustain health and spirits, both suffered. The most robust could not endure the life to which we were condemned, without injury. I am satisfied that hard labor—furnishing at once occupation and exercise—alone prevents the inmates of these prisons (sentenced to remain so many years, as some of them are) from dying early. The effect of this confinement is strange, and will doubtless appear inconsistent. It affected every man of our party with (at the same time) a lethargy and a nervousness. While we were physically and mentally impaired by it—and every faculty was dulled, and all energy was sapped—every man was restless without aim or purpose, and irritable without cause or reason. These effects of imprisonment became far more apparent and difficult to repress, after a few months had elapsed.

The method adopted in the Ohio Penitentiary, for punishing the refractory and disobedient, was to confine them in cells called the "dungeons"—and dungeons indeed they were. Captain Foster Cheatham was the first man, of our party, who explored their recesses. His private negotiations, with one of the military guard, for liquids of stimulating properties (which he thought would benefit his health) were not only unsuccessful, but were discovered by the "Head-devil," and the Captain was dragged to a "loathsome dungeon." He remained twenty-four hours and came out wiser, on the subject of prison discipline, and infinitely sadder than when he went in. The next victim was Major Higley. One of the keepers was rough to him, and Higley used strong language in return. Disrespectful language to, or about, officials was not tolerated in the institution, and Higley "came to grief." He also remained in the dungeon for the space of a solar day. He was a man of lean habit and excitable temperament, when in his best state of health—and he returned from the place of punishment, looking like a ghost of dissipated habits and shattered nervous system. Pale and shaking—he gave us a spirited and humorous account of his interview with the superior gaolers, and his experience in the dark stifling cell.

It was claimed that while punishment was invariably inflicted for violation of the rules, those rules were clearly defined. That no man need infringe the regulations—that every one could (if he chose) avoid punishment. An incident happened which did not strongly corroborate this beautiful theory. Shortly after Major Higley's misfortune, Captain Cheatham was again honored with an invitation to inspect the dungeons, and take up his quarters in one of them. He, with great modesty, protested that he had done nothing to deserve such a distinction, but his scruples were overruled and he was induced to go. The offense charged was this: An anonymous letter had been picked up in the hall—in which the prison officials were ridiculed. Merion fancied that the handwriting of this letter resembled Cheatham's—there was no other evidence. So far as the proof went, there was as much right to attribute it to one of the prison corps as to one of the prisoners, and to any other one of the prisoners as to Cheatham. After he was placed in the dungeon, where he remained forty-eight hours, and it became known upon what charge, and that he denied it, General Morgan first, and soon many others, demanded that, if another prisoner had written the letter, he should own it and suffer for it. There was not a man in the sixty-eight of our party (with four exceptions) who would have permitted a comrade to be punished for an offense committed by himself.

It was never known who wrote the letter. Captain Cheatham always denied having done so. So justice was not always so impartially administered in the sacrificial temple of the Ohio law, and the governed had it not always in their power to escape punishment.

After we had been in the penitentiary some three or four weeks, Colonel Cluke and another officer were taken out and sent to McLean barracks, to be tried by court-martial upon the charge of having violated some oath, taken before they entered the Confederate service. They were acquitted and Colonel Cluke was sent to Johnson's Island, where during the ensuing winter he died of diphtheria. He was exceedingly popular in the division, and was a man of the most frank, generous and high-toned nature. But he possessed some high soldierly qualities. In the field, he was extremely bold and tenacious—and when threatened by a dangerous opponent, no one was more vigilant and wary. He displayed great vigor and judgment on many occasions, both as a regimental and brigade commander. The news of his death excited universal sorrow among his comrades.

Shortly before Colonel Cluke's removal, Major Webber and Captains Sheldon and McCann had been brought to the penitentiary from Camp Chase. They, of course, declined the tonsorial ceremonies and were remanded to Camp Chase. In the course of two or three weeks Captains Bennett and Merriwether, of the Tenth Kentucky, were sent from Camp Chase to the penitentiary, for having attempted to make their escape, and with them came Captain Sheldon again, for the same offense. This time no questions were asked, but hair and beards came off.

Somewhat later, Major Webber was sent back also. He was placed in solitary confinement, in a cell in a remote part of the prison, and permitted to hold no intercourse with the rest of us. The reason of his receiving this treatment, was that he had written a letter in which occurred the following passage: "I can't say how long I will be a prisoner. Until the end of time; yes, until eternity has run its last round, rather than that our Government shall acknowledge the doctrine of negro equality, by an exchange of negro soldiers. I wish that all negroes, and their officers captured with them, will be hung, I am willing to risk the consequences." Webber unhesitatingly confirmed this language, stating that he had, from the commencement of the war, entertained such sentiments, and that he felt his right to express them as a prisoner of war, as well as in any other condition. He claimed that the very fact that the letters of all prisoners were examined, and suppressed if disapproved by the officer appointed to examine them, gave the prisoners a right to use such language as they chose. If the language was thought improper, the letter could be burned, and no one but the examiner would be any the wiser. This would seem to be the correct and manly view to take of the matter. If a prisoner were detected in clandestine correspondence, it was, perhaps, right and fair that he should be punished, but I do not believe that in any army whose officers are, for the most part gentlemen, a man would be countenanced, who would cause prisoners to send letters to his office for perusal, with the understanding that they should be suppressed if disapproved, and would then punish the prisoner who wrote sentiments which did not accord with his own.

There were officers in position at Camp Chase, when I was sent there some months afterward, who, I believe, could have been induced by no combination of influences to do such a thing, or to tolerate the man who would do it.

Major Webber's description of his initiation into prison usages is very graphic, and as many of my readers know him, it will be highly amusing to them, although any thing but amusing to the Major. He says: "In the office of the penitentiary, I was stripped of my clothing and closely searched. Everything in the way of papers, knife, money, toothpick, and even an old buckeye, which I had carried in my pocket all through the war, at the request of a friend, were taken from me. I was then marched to the wash-room, stripped again, and placed in a tub of warm water, about waist deep, where a convict scrubbed me with a large, rough, horse brush and soap; while a hang-dog looking scoundrel, and the deputy-warden Dean, urged the convict to 'scrub the d—d horse-thief,' and indulged in various demoniacal grins and gesticulations of exultation at my sufferings and embarrassment." The Major describes "his feelings," in the strong language of which he never lacked command; but it is unnecessary to quote from him farther—there is no man, so devoid of imagination, that he can not divine what the patients' feeling must have been under such treatment.

When two or three months had elapsed, General Morgan's impatience of the galling confinement and perpetual espionage amounted almost to frenzy. He restrained all exhibition of his feelings remarkably, but it was apparent to his fellow prisoners that he was chafing terribly under the restraint, more irksome to him than to any one of the others.

The difficulty of getting letters from our families and friends in the South, was one of the worst evils of this imprisonment; and if a letter came containing anything in the least objectionable, it was, as likely as not, destroyed, and the envelope only was delivered to the man to whom it was written. Generally, the portion of its contents, which incurred Merion's censure, having been erased, it was graciously delivered, but more than once a letter which would have been valued beyond all price, was altogether withheld, and the prisoner anxiously expecting it, was mocked, as I have stated, with being given the envelope in which it came, as evidence that he was robbed of it. The reader can imagine the feelings of a man, whose wife and children were in far off "Dixie," while he lay in prison tortured with anxiety to hear from them, and who, when the letter which told of them at last came, should be deprived of it because it contained some womanly outburst of feeling, and should be tantalized with the evidence of his loss.

The introduction of newspapers was strictly forbidden, except when Merion, as a great favor, would send in some outrageously abusive sheet, in which was published some particularly offensive lie. If the newspapers, which the convicts who occasionally passed through our hall in the transaction of their duties, some times smuggled into us, were discovered in any man's hands or cell, woe be unto him—a first class sinner could be easier prayed out of purgatory, than he could avoid the dungeon.

Captain Calvin Morgan was once reading a newspaper, that had "run the blockade," in his cell at night, and had become deeply interested in it, when the "night guard," stealing along with noiseless step, detected him.

The customary taps (by the occupants of the other cells who discovered his approach and thus telegraphed it along the range) had been (this time) neglected. "What paper is that," said the guard. "Come in and see," said Morgan. "No," said the guard, "you must pass it to me through the bars." "I'll do nothing of the kind," was the answer. "If you think that I have a paper which was smuggled into me, why unlock the door, come in, and get it." The fellow apparently did not like to trust himself in the cell with Captain Morgan, who was much the more powerful man of the two, and he hastened off for reinforcements. During his absence Morgan rolled the paper up into a small compass, and, baring his arm, thrust it far up into the ventillator at the back part of the cell. Fortunately there was in the cell a newspaper given him that day by one of the sub-wardens named Hevay—a very kind old man. Morgan unfolded this paper and was seated in the same attitude (as when first discovered) reading it, when the guard returned. The latter brought Scott with him and unlocked the door. "Now give me that paper," he said. "There it is," said Morgan handing it to him, "Old man Hevay gave it to me to-day." The guard inspected it closely and seemed satisfied. "Why did you not give it to me before," he asked. "Because," returned Captain Morgan, "I thought you had no right to ask it, and I had, moreover no assurance that you would return it." With a parting injunction to do so no more, or the dungeon would reveal him its secrets, the guard after a thorough search to find another paper (if there should have been a deception practiced upon him) left the cell. He examined the ventillator, but Morgan's arm being the longer the paper was beyond his reach. Captain Morgan's literary pursuits were suspended, however, for that night.

When the news of the battle of Chickamauga was coming in, and we were half wild with excitement and eagerness to learn the true aversion of the reports that prevailed—for every thing told us by the prison officials was garbled—we by good luck got in two or three newspapers containing full accounts of the battle. I shall never forget listening to them read, in General Morgan's cell, while four or five pickets (regularly relieved) were posted to guard against surprise. These papers were read to the whole party in detachments—while one listened, the succeeding one awaited its turn in nervous impatience. As I have said, General Morgan grew more restless under his imprisonment, every day, and finally resolved to effect his escape, at any hazard, or labor.

Several plans were resolved and abandoned, and at length one devised by Captain Hines was adopted. This was to "tunnel" out of the prison—as the mode of escape by digging a trench, to lead from the interior to the outside of the prisons, was technically called. But to "tunnel" through the stone pavement and immense walls of the penitentiary—concealing the tremendous work as it progressed—it required a bold imagination to conceive such an idea. Hines had heard, in some way, a hint of an air chamber, constructed under the lower range of cells—that range immediately upon the ground floor. He thought it probable that there was such a chamber, for he could account in no other way for the dryness of the cells in that range. At the first opportunity he entered into conversation with Old Hevay, the deputy-warden mentioned before. This old man was very kind-hearted, and was also an enthusiast upon the subject of the architectural grandeur of that penitentiary. Hines led the conversation into that channel, and finally learned that his surmise was correct. If, then, he could cut through the floor of his cell and reach this air chamber, without detection, he would have, he saw, an excellent base for future operations. He communicated his plan to General Morgan, who at once approved it. Five other men were selected (whose cells were on the first range) as assistants.

The work was commenced with knives abstracted from the table. These knives—square at the end of the blade instead of pointed—made excellent chisels, and were the very best tools for the inauguration of the labor. Putting out pickets to prevent surprise, they pecked and chiseled away at the hard floor, which was eighteen inches thick of stone cement and brick—concealing the rubbish in their handkerchiefs and then throwing part of it into the stoves, and hiding the rest in their beds. They soon dug a hole in the floor large enough to permit the body of a man to pass. The iron bedsteads, which stood in each cell, could be lifted up or let down at pleasure. Hines would prop his up, each morning, sweep out his cell (in which the aperture had been cut) and throw a carpet sack carelessly over the mouth of the shaft he had sunk, and when the guard would come and look in, every thing would appear so neat and innocent, that he would not examine further. One kick given that hypocritical carpet bag (with its careless appearance) would have disclosed the plot, at any time from the date of the inception of the work to its close. After the air chamber was reached, a good many others were taken into the secret, in order that the work might go constantly on.

The method adopted, then, was for two or three to descend and go to work, while the others kept watch; in an hour or two a fresh relief would be put on, and the work would be kept up in this way throughout the day, until the hour of locking up arrived, except at dinner time, when every man who was absent from the table had to give a reason for his absence. The work, conducted underground, was tedious and difficult, but all labored with a will. The candles which had been purchased and hoarded away, now did good service. Without them it would have been almost impossible to finish the task. A code of signals was invented to meet every possible contingency. By pounding a bar of wood upon the stone floor, those above communicated to those underneath information of every danger which threatened, and called on them to come forth, if necessary. The walls of the air chamber were two or three feet thick, and built of huge stones. Two or three of these stones were removed, and a tunnel was run straight to the outer wall of the hall. Fortune favored the workmen, at this juncture, and threw in their way an adequate tool with which to accomplish this part of their work. Some one had discovered lying in the yard through which we passed on our way to breakfast, an old rusty spade with a broken handle. It was at once determined that the said spade must be secured. Accordingly men were detailed and instructed in their proper parts, and at the first opportunity the spade was transferred to the air chamber, and put to work in digging the tunnel. This is the manner in which that valuable, that priceless, old, rusty, broken spade was gotten: One man was selected to secrete the spade about his person—him I will call No. 1. He wore, for the occasion, a long, loose sack coat. Six or seven other men were his accomplices. It was a usual occurrence for those who were awaiting their turns at the washing troughs, to romp and scuffle with each other in the yard. The conspirators were, this morning, exceedingly frolicsome. At length No. 1 fell, apparently by an accident, upon the spade, his accomplices tumbled in a heap upon him. No. 1 dexterously slipped the spade under his coat, and buttoned it up. He went into breakfast with it, and sat wonderfully straight, and carried it safely into the hall and down into the air chamber.

When the main wall of the hall was reached, the heavy stones of its foundation were removed in sufficient number to admit of the passage of a man. But it was then discovered that the tunnel led right under an immense coal pile. It was necessary that this difficulty should be remedied; but how? Without a view of the ground just outside of the wall, no one could calculate how far, or in what direction to run the tunnel, so that when it was conducted to the surface, all obstructions might be avoided. In this emergency, General Morgan engaged Scott in conversation about the remarkable escape of some convicts, which had occurred a year or two previously, and which Scott was very fond of describing. These convicts had climbed by the balconies, in front of the ranges of cells, to the ceiling, and had passed out through the skylight to the roof of the prison. Scott declared his belief that there were no two other men on the continent who could perform the feat of ascending by the balconies.

"Why," says General Morgan, "Captain Sam. Taylor, small as he is, can do it."

Thereupon a discussion ensued, ending by Scott's giving Taylor permission to attempt it. Taylor, who, although very small, was as active as a squirrel, immediately commenced the ascent, and sprang from one to the other of the balconies, until he reached the top one. He was one of the men who had been selected to escape with General Morgan, and comprehended immediately the latter's object in having him attempt this feat. It would afford him a chance to glance out of the windows at the ground just beyond the wall. As he leisurely swung himself down, he studied "the position" carefully, and his observations enabled them to direct the tunnel aright.

Once during the tunneling, while Captain Hockersmith (another of the projectors of the plan) was at work underground, Scott called for him and seemed anxious to find him at once. General Morgan's presence of mind prevented a discovery, or, at least, a strong suspicion of the plot from at once resulting from Hockersmith's absence. The General said to Scott, "Hockersmith is lying down in my cell; he is sick," and he requested Scott to examine and give his opinion upon a memorial which he (the General) held in his hand, and which he proposed forwarding to Washington. It was something regarding our removal to a military prison. Scott (highly flattered by this tribute to his judgment) took the memorial, looked at it attentively for some minutes, and returned it, saying, "I think it will do first rate." It *did do*. In the mean time, Hockersmith had been signaled, and had "come up," and he made his appearance complaining of a serious indisposition.

While the work was going on, General Morgan and those who were to escape with him habitually slept with their faces covered and their hands concealed. This was done to accustom the night guard to take their presence in the cells for granted, by the appearance of the bulk upon the beds, without actually seeing them. This guard went the rounds at the expiration of every two hours during the night, and he would place his lantern close to each cell door, in order that the light should fill the cell and show the occupant. General Morgan used to say that a peculiar shuddering and creeping of the flesh would assail him whenever this man approached. He would frequently creep about with list slippers on his feet, and he moved then without the slightest noise. He used to remind me of a sly, cruel, bloated, auspicious, night-prowling spider.

When the tunneling approached its completion, all the other necessary preparations were made. The prison yard, into which they would emerge from the tunnel, was surrounded by a wall twenty-five feet high, and means for scaling that had to be provided. There was an inner wall running from the corner of the "East Hall" to a smaller building, in which some of the female convicts were imprisoned, but it was comparatively low, and they anticipated little difficulty in getting over it. The coverlids of several beds were torn into strips, and the strips were plaited into a strong rope nearly thirty feet in length. A strong iron rod, used for stirring the fires in the stoves, was converted into a hook, and the rope was attached to it. Rope and hook were taken down into the air-chamber, where all the "valuables" were stored.

General Morgan had managed to get a suit of citizen's clothing, and the six men who were going to escape with him, were similarly provided. The Warden had prohibited the introduction into the prison of uniform clothing, but occasionally allowed plain suits to be received. The General had also gotten a card of the schedule time on the Little Miami Railroad, and knew when the train left Columbus, and when it arrived in Cincinnati—for this he paid fifteen dollars, the only money used in effecting his escape.

Despite the strict search instituted, when we first entered

the penitentiary, several of the party had managed to secrete money so that it was not found. This was now divided among the seven who were to escape. These were, besides General Morgan, Captains Thomas H. Hines, Ralph Sheldon, Sam Taylor, Jacob Bennett, James Hockersmith, and Gustavus McGee. It is plain that, as each man was locked in a separate cell, and could not get out of it by the door, without an interview with the night-guard, it was necessary to cut an opening into the air-chamber, through the floor of each cell, from which each one of the seven would escape. If these apertures were cut from the top of the floors of the cells, the risk of detection would be proportionally increased; so an accurate measurement of the distance between the cells was taken, and with Hines' cell as a point of departure, it was easy to calculate where to commence cutting from *underneath*, in order that the floors of all these particular cells should be perforated. A thin crust, only, of the cement was left, but to all outward appearance, the floor was as sound as ever.

By means of an arrangement which had been perfected for obtaining all absolutely necessary articles, each one of the party about to escape had procured a stout, sharp knife—very effective weapons in case of surprise and an attempt to stop their escape. When every thing was ready, they waited several nights for rain—trusting to elude the vigilance of the guards more easily in the obscurity of such a night—and taking the chance, also, that the dogs which were turned loose every night in the yard, would be driven by the rain into their kennels, which were situated on the other side of the yard from that where they would emerge. Two or three days before the effort was made, General Morgan received a letter from an Irishwoman in Kentucky, warning him not to attempt to make his escape, from which, she predicted, great evils to him would result. She alluded to his kindness to the poor in Lexington, and claimed that she was informed of the future in some supernatural manner.

On the 26th of November, General Morgan learned that there had been a change of military commandants at Columbus. Well knowing that this would be followed by an inspection of the prison and a discovery of the plot, he determined that the effort should be made that very night. His own cell was in the second range, from which it was impossible to reach the air-chamber and tunnel, but the cell of his brother, Colonel Richard Morgan, had been prepared for him, and when Scott tapped, as usual, on the stove, as a signal for each man to retire to his cell, the exchange was effected. There was a sufficient resemblance between them to deceive a man who would not look closely—especially when they were seated with their faces turned away from the door.

At any rate, Scott and the night-guard, were both deceived, and efforts were made by the occupants of the cells near to both of those, where close inspection would have been dangerous, to attract to themselves the attention of the guard when he went the rounds. As it was especially necessary, on this occasion, to know certainly when the night-guard approached, small bits of coal had been sprinkled, just before the hour for locking up on the floor of the first range, so that (tread as lightly as he would), the slinking cur could not help making loud noise.

It had been arranged that, just after the twelve o'clock visit from the guard, Captain Taylor should descend into the air-chamber and give the signal underneath the floor of each cell. Fortunately, the only man who was vile enough to have betrayed the plan, was absent in the hospital. Six hours elapsed after the locking-in; regularly during that time the night-guard went his rounds, making an awful crackling as he passed along the lower range. Sixty-odd men lay awake, silent and excited—with hearts beating louder and blood rushing faster through their veins than the approach of battle had ever occasioned. Perhaps the coolest of all that number, were the seven who were about to incur the risk.

Twelve o'clock struck, and the clang of the bell seemed to be in the hall itself—the guard passed with his lantern—a few minutes elapsed (while the adventurers lay still lest he should slip back), and then at the signal they sprang from their beds; hastily stuffed flannel shirts with material prepared beforehand, and made up bundles to lie in their beds and represent them. Then stamping upon the floor above the excavations, the thin crust of each gave way and they descended into the air-chamber. They passed one by one along the tunnel, until the foremost man reached the terminus, and with his knife cut away the sod which had of course been left untouched. Then they emerged into the open air and inner yard.

The early part of the night had been bright and clear, but now it was cloudy, and rain was falling. They climbed the low wall and descended into the large yard. The rain had caused the sentries to seek shelter, and had driven the dogs to their kennels. They moved cautiously across the yard—if detected, their knives must have saved or avenged them. Discovery would have been hard upon them, but it would have, also, been unhealthy for the discoverer. They were resolved to be free—they were powerful and desperate men—and if they failed, they were determined that others, besides themselves, should have cause for sorrow. But they reached and climbed the outer wall in safety. There was a coping upon it which they grappled with the hook, and they climbed, hand over hand, to the top. When all had ascended, the hook was grappled upon the inner shelf of the coping, and they let themselves down. When they were all on the ground, they strove to shake the hook loose, but it held fast and they were forced to leave the rope hanging. That circumstance caused the detection of their escape two hours sooner than it would otherwise have happened, for the rope was discovered at day light, and the alarm was given. But time enough had been allowed the fugitives to make good their escape. They at once broke into couples.

General Morgan and Hines went straight to the depot. Hines bought tickets to Cincinnati, and when the train came they got on it.

General Morgan was apprehensive that they would be asked for passes or permits to travel, and arrested for not having them. He saw an officer of field rank, seated in the car which he entered, and it occurred to him that if he were seen in familiar conversation with this officer, he would not, perhaps, be asked for a pass. He spoke to Hines and they seated themselves near this officer and courteously addressed him—he replied as suavely. After a short conversation, General Morgan produced a liquor flask, they were very generally carried then, and invited the officer to take a drink of brandy, which invitation was gracefully accepted. Just then the train moved past the penitentiary. "That is the hotel at which Morgan stops I believe," said the officer. "Yes," answered the General, "and *will stop*, it is to be hoped. He has given us his fair share of trouble, and he will not be released. I will drink to him. May he ever be as closely kept as he is now."

This officer was a pleasant and well informed gentleman, and General Morgan passed the night in an agreeable and instructive conversation with him—asking many questions and receiving satisfactory replies.

When the suburbs of Cincinnati were reached, a little after daylight, it was time to get off. General Morgan pulled the bell rope and moved to one platform; Hines went to the other, and they put the brakes down with all their strength. The speed of the train slackened and they sprang off.

Two or three soldiers were sitting on a pile of lumber, near where General Morgan alighted. "What in the h—ll are you jumping off the train for?" asked one of them. "What in the d—l is the use of a man going on to town when he lives out here?" responded the General. "Besides what matter is it to you?" "Oh nothing," said the soldier, and paid him no further attention. Reaching the river, which runs close to this point, they gave a little boy two dollars to put them across in a skiff.

In Newport, Kentucky, they found friends to aid them, and before the telegraph had given to Cincinnati the information of his escape, he was well on his way to Boone county—sure asylum for such fugitives. In Boone fresh horses, guides, and all that was necessary were quickly obtained. He felt no longer any apprehension; he could travel from Boone to Harrison, or Scott counties, thence through Anderson to Nelson, and thence to the Tennessee line; and, during all that time, no one need know of his whereabouts but his devoted friends, who would have died to shield him from harm.

A writer who described his progress through Kentucky, shortly after it occurred, says, truly: "Everybody vied with each other as to who should show him the most attention—even to the negroes; and young ladies of refinement begged the honor of cooking his meals." He assumed more than one disguise, and played many parts in his passage through Kentucky—now passing as a Government contractor buying cattle, and again as a quartermaster or inspector.

When he reached the Little Tennessee river, his serious difficulties began; in passing through a portion of Tennessee, he had met friends as truly devoted to him as any of those who had assisted him in Kentucky.

In portions of Middle Tennessee, he was so constantly recognized, that it was well for him that he was so universally popular there. One day he passed a number of citizens, and one woman commenced clapping her hands and called out, "Oh I know who it is," then suddenly catching herself, turned away. The region in which he struck the Little Tennessee river, was strongly Union, and the people would have betrayed him to a certainty, if they had discovered who he was. The river was guarded at every point, and there was no boat or raft upon it, which was not in possession of the enemy. He was, in this vicinity, joined by some thirty nomadic Confederates, and they set to work and constructed a raft for him to cross upon.

When it was finished, they insisted that he and Hines should cross first—the horses were made to swim. While General Morgan was walking his horse about, with a blanket thrown over him, to recover him from the chill occasioned by immersion in the cold water—he suddenly (he subsequently declared) was seized with the conviction that the enemy were coming upon them, and instantly commenced to saddle his horse, bidding Hines do the same. Scarcely had they done so, when the enemy dashed up in strong force on the other side and dispersed the poor fellows who were preparing to cross in their turn. He and Hines went straight up the mountain at the foot of which they had landed. It grew dark and commenced to rain—hc knew that if he remained all night on the mountain, his capture would be a certain thing in the morning, and he determined to run the gauntlet of the pickets, at the base of the mountain, on the opposite side, before the line was strengthened. As he descended, leading his horse, he came immediately upon one of the pickets. As he prepared to shoot him, he discovered that the fellow slept, and stole by without injuring or awakening him.

At the house of a Union man not far from the base of the mountain, the two tired and hunted wanderers found shelter and supper, and General Morgan, representing himself as a Federal Quartermaster, induced the host, by a promise of a liberal supply of sugar and coffee, to guide them to Athens. Every mile of his route through this country was marked by some adventure. Finally Hines became separated from him. The General sent him, one evening, to a house, to inquire the way to a certain place, while he himself remained a short distance off upon the road. In a few minutes he heard shots and the tramp of several horses galloping in the opposite direction, and he knew at once that Hines was cut off from him. That night he narrowly escaped being shot—that fate befell a man mistaken for him. At length, after hazard and toil beyond all description, he reached the Confederate lines. Hines was captured by the party who pursued him from the house, and he was confined in a little log hut that night, in which his captors also slept. He made himself very agreeable—told a great many pleasant stories, with immense effect. At length the sentry, posted at the door, drew near the fire, at the other end of the room, to hear the conclusion of a very funny anecdote. Hines seized the opportunity and sprang through the door—bade the party good night, and darted into the bushes. He effected his escape and reached Dixie in safety.

When the escape of General Morgan, and the others, was discovered on the morning after it was effected—there was an extraordinary degree of emotion manifested by the penitentiary officials. The rope, hanging upon the wall, was seen by some one at day light; it was apparent that some body had escaped, the alarm was given to the warden, and his suspicion at once turned toward the prisoners of war.

About 6 A.M., a detachment of guards and turnkeys poured into the hall and began running about, unlocking doors and calling on various men by name, in the wildest and most frantic manner. For some time they were puzzled to determine who had escaped. Colonel Morgan was still taken for the General, and the "dummies" in the cells, which had been vacated, for a while, deceived them into the belief that those cells were still occupied. But at length, a more careful and calm examination revealed the fact and the method of the escape, and then the hubbub broke out afresh. In the midst of it Captain Bennett called out, "Well gentlemen, I like a moderate stir, but you are going it too brash," an expression of opinion which, to judge from the unanimous shout of approval from the prisoners and the laughter they could no longer restrain, met with their cordial indorsement.

It was generally feared that Colonel Morgan would be severely dealt with, and he expected a long term of service in the dungeon; but to the surprise and gratification of all of us, it was announced that he was thought no more guilty than the rest, and should be punished no more harshly. The first step taken was to remove all of the first range men to the third range. Then a general and thorough search was instituted. Every cell was carefully examined, every man was stripped and inspected, every effort was made, after the bird was flown, to make the cage secure.

It was the desire of every prisoner, to secure General Morgan's escape—that was of paramount importance. We were willing to trust to his efforts to effect our release. We were now constantly locked up in our cells, night and day, except when we were marched to our meals and straight back. The cells were, I have already said, very small, and the bed took up half of each. The only method we had of exercising, was to step sideways from one end of the cells to the other. The weather was intensely cold, and when the stone flooring of the hall was removed and a deep trench cut, in order that the damage done by the tunneling might be repaired, the chill arising from the damp earth was terrible.

Every thing which we had been allowed in the way of luxuries was now forbidden, except books. We were forbidden to speak while at the table, to speak aloud in our cells after the gas was lit at night, to address one of the convicts, even those who frequented the hall in which we were confined, no matter what the necessity might be. It would be difficult to enumerate the restrictions which were now imposed upon us, confinement in the dungeon being the inevitable penalty attached to the violation of any of these rules. These dungeons were really very unpleasant places in which to spend even the hours of a penitentiary life—hours which (without the proper experience) might have appeared unsusceptible of additional embitterment. I saw the inside of one of them during my stay in the "Institution," and speak advisedly when I say that the pious stock company which proposed "to build a hell by subscription" for the especially heretical, could have found no better model for their work than it. These cells were rather smaller than the cells in which we were habitually confined, and the doors were half a foot thick, with sheet-iron nailed on the outside, and so contrived that (extending beyond the edges of the door) it excluded every ray of air and light. In all seasons, the air within them was stagnant, foul, and stifling, and would produce violent nausea and headache. In summer, these places were said to be like heated ovens, and in winter they were the coldest localities between the South Pole and Labrador. The rations allowed the inmates of them were a piece of bread about the size of the back of a pocket account book (and perhaps with as much flavor) and half a tin-cup full of water, repeated twice a day. If a man's stomach revolted at the offer of food (after the foul reek of the dungeon) the crop-eared whelp of a she-wolf (who was boss-inquisitor) would pronounce him sulky and double his term of stay.

Merion, the Warden, would about realize the Northern ideal of a Southern overseer. He was an obstinate man, and his cruelty was low, vulgar, and brutal like his mind. He would have been hypocritical, but that his character was too coarse-grained to be pliant enough for successful dissimulation. The members of the Board of Directors (with one or two exceptions) were men of much the same stamp as the Warden—with rather more cultivation perhaps, and less force. He entirely controlled them all. He knew enough of medicine to pronounce quinine "a luxury," but he directed the treatment of the sick, as he did all else.

After some three weeks of close confinement, we were permitted to exercise in the hall for four hours during the day, and were locked in for the rest of the time. The nervous irritability induced by this long and close confinement, sometimes showed itself in a manner which would have amused a man whose mind was in a healthy condition. Just as soon as we were permitted to leave our cells in the morning and meet in the hall, the most animated discussions, upon all sorts of topics, would begin. These would occasionally degenerate into clamorous and angry debates. The disputants would become as earnest and excited over subjects in which perhaps they had never felt the least interest before, as if they had been considering matters of vital and immediate importance. A most heated, and finally acrimonious dispute once arose regarding General Joseph E. Johnston's hight. One party asserted positively that his stature was just five feet nine inches and a quarter. The other affirmed, with a constancy that nothing could shake, that he was no taller than five feet eight inches and a half. Numerous assertions were made by as many men, that they had frequently stood near him, and that he was about their hight. If these declarations were all as true as they were dogmatic, the General's stature must have varied in a remarkable manner, and his tailor could have had little peace of mind. Warm friendships, of long standing, were interrupted by this issue for entire days, until happily a new question was sprung, and parties were reorganized. A grave and radical difference of opinion arose as to whether Selma was on the east or the west bank of the Alabama river. Two intimate friends got into an argument regarding the relative excellence of the ancients and moderns in material civilization and the mechanical arts. The discussion lasted three weeks; during its continuance each alluded (in support of his position) to architectural and engineering triumphs, which the most learned encyclopedist might in vain consult his books or torture his memory to verify. It was at last dropped, unsettled. But for months the most casual reference by either to the Egyptian Pyramids, or the bridge over the Menai Straits, would produce a coolness between them. The battle of Waterloo was an inexhaustible theme of contention. Wellington did not wish for night on the day itself half as cordially as he would have wished for it, if he had been a prisoner at the penitentiary and condemned to listen to the conflicting opinions about his strategy.

Exchange and escape, however, were the topics of most earnest and constant thought. One or the other was the first thought which came into our minds in the morning, and the last that occupied them at night. Victor Hugo has, in his wonderful book, "Les Miserables," daguerreotyped the thoughts and the feelings of a prisoner. That book was a great favorite with the inmates of our hall and the admiration it excited was so general and honest, that (it is a literal fact) there was not more than one or two disputes about it. Two of the officers who escaped with General Morgan, Captains Sheldon and Taylor, were recaptured, and brought back to the penitentiary. They ventured into Louisville, where they were well known, were recognized, and arrested.

After General Morgan's escape, the treatment we received was not only more rigorous, but the sneaking, spying instincts of the keepers seemed stimulated. It was, of course, to be expected that they would be suspicious (especially after the lesson they had received), but these creatures evinced suspicion, not as I had been accustomed to see men show it—they stole and pried about, eaves-dropping, creeping upon and glaring at us (when they thought they could do so undetected) like cellar-bred, yellow-eyed, garbage-fed curs. Their manner gave one an impression of cold cruelty and slinking treachery that is indescribable, it was snakish.

A military guard was placed at the prison immediately after the General's escape, and for some time sentinels (with bayonets fixed) paced the hall. None of us had imagined that we could welcome the presence of Federal soldiers with so much satisfaction. The difference in the tone and manner of the soldiers from that of the convict-drivers, made it a relief to have any thing to say to the former. They were evidently disgusted with their associate goalers. There was a sergeant with this guard (named Lowe, I think,) who, while he rigidly discharged his duty, seemed desirous to avoid all harshness.

In February I was removed, at the solicitation of friends, to Camp Chase. Having made no application for this removal, nor having heard that one had been made in my behalf, I was surprised when the order for it came, and still more surprised when I learned at Camp Chase that I was to be paroled. I was permitted to go freely where I pleased within the limits of the camp, excellent quarters were assigned me, and my condition was, in all respects, as comfortable as that of the officers on duty there. Colonel Richardson, the commandant, was a veteran of the army of the Potomac, and had accepted the charge of the prison after he had been disabled by wounds. If the treatment which I received at his hands, was a fair sample of his conduct toward prisoners generally, it is certain that none had a right to complain of him, and it would have been a fortunate thing if just such men had been selected (upon both sides) to be placed over those whose condition depended so entirely upon the will and disposition of the officers in charge of them. Finding that my parole was not likely to result in my exchange, and that there was no other Confederate officer similarly indulged, I applied to be sent back to the penitentiary. Enough had reached my ears to convince me that others would be granted paroles in order to tempt them to take the oath, and I did not care to be caught in such company.

When I left Camp Chase, where every one had been uniformly polite and respectful in demeanor, and I had enjoyed privileges which amounted almost to liberty, the gloom of the penitentiary and the surly, ban-dog manner of the keepers wcrc doubly distasteful, and the feeling was as if I were being buried alive. I found that, during my absence, the prisoners had been removed from the hall, which they had all the time previously occupied, to another in which the negro convicts had formerly slept, and this latter was a highly-scented dormitory. The cause of the removal was that (desperate at their long confinement and the treatment they were receiving) a plan had been concocted for obtaining knives and breaking out of the prison by force. A thorough knowledge of the topography of the entire building was by this time possessed by the leaders in this movement. They had intended to secure Merion, and as many as possible of the underlings, by enticing them into the hall upon some pretext, and then gagging, binding, and locking them up in the cells. Then giving the signal for the opening of the doors, they expected to obtain possession of the office and room where the guns were kept. One of the party was to have been dressed in convict garb, to give the necessary signal, in order that all suspicion might have been avoided. It is barely possible that, with better luck, the plan might have succeeded, but it was frustrated by the basest treachery.

Among the sixty-eight prisoners of war confined in the penitentiary, there were four whose nerves gave way and they took the oath of allegiance to the United States in other words, they deserted. One of this four betrayed the plan to the warden. Men were sometimes induced "to take the oath" by a lack of pride and fortitude, and absence of manly stamina, who would have done nothing else prejudicial to the cause which they abandoned, or that would have compromised their former comrades. Their were men, however, who added treachery to apostacy, and this man was one of that infamous class. The four were so fearful of exciting the suspicion of the other prisoners, and so well aware of the bitter scorn and resentment which their conduct would raise against them, that they carefully concealed their design to the last moment. It was not until our release from prison, that the proofs of the utter and base treachery of the spying and informing villain were obtained.

There is a reason why the name of this wretch should not be given here. Enough know of his crime to damn him forever in the estimation of all honorable men, and gallant and devoted men, than whom no truer gentlemen and braver soldiers served under the Confederate banner, bear the same name. His relatives (who fought throughout the war and quit with records upon which there are no stains), must not see the name (which they made honorable), associated with his shame.

Search was at once made for the knives which the prisoners had obtained and for other evidence which might corroborate the informer's report. Fifteen knives had been introduced into the hall, and were in the hands of as many prisoners. The search was inaugurated secretly and conducted as quietly as possible, during the time that the prisoners were locked in the cells, but information was gotten along the ranges that it was going on, and only seven knives were discovered. The remaining eight were hidden, so ingeniously, that, notwithstanding the strict hunt after every thing of the kind, they were not found. Merion's fury at the idea of any danger threatening him was like that of some great cowardly beast which smells blood and is driven mad with fear. All of the party were at once closely confined again, and the seven who were detected with the knives, were sent to the dungeons, where they were kept seven days, until the surgeon declared that a longer stay would kill them.

They passed the period of their confinement in almost constant motion (such as the limits of the cell would permit), and said that they had no recollection of having slept during the whole time. When they came out they were almost blind and could scarcely drag themselves along.

One of the party, Captain Barton, was so affected, that the blood streamed from under his finger nails. When I returned (after a month passed at Camp Chase), I was startled by the appearance of those, even, who had not been subjected to punishment in the dungeon. They had the wild, squalid look and feverish eager impression of eye which lunatics have after long confinement.

At last, in March 1864, all were removed to Fort Delaware, and the change was as if living men, long buried in subterranean vaults, had been restored to upper earth. About the same time one hundred and ten officers of Morgan's division, who had been confined in the Pennsylvania Penitentiary, were transferred to Point Lookout. These officers described the treatment which they received as having been much better than that adopted toward us, yet one of their number had become insane. All that I have attempted to describe, however, must have been ease and luxury compared with the hardship, hunger and harsh cruelty inflicted upon the Confederate private soldiers imprisoned at Camps Morton and Douglass and at Rock Island. These men would often actually pick up and devour the scraps thrown out of the scavenger carts. Some of them froze to death—insufficient fuel was furnished, when it was furnished at all, and the clothing sent them by friends was rarely given them. The men of my regiment told me of treatment, inflicted upon them at Camp Douglass, which if properly described and illustrated with engravings, and if attributed to Confederate instead of Federal officials, would throw the whole North into convulsions. Many of these men, of this regiment, had escaped in the first two or three months of their imprisonment, and a bitter hatred was then excited against the less fortunate. They were, in some instances, tied up and beaten with the belts of the guards, until the print of the brass buckles were left on the flesh; others were made to sit naked on snow and ice, until palsied with cold; others, again were made to "ride Morgan's mule" (as a scantling frame, of ten or twelve feet in hight, was called), the peculiar and beautiful feature of this method of torture, was the very sharp back of "the mule." Sometimes, heavy blocks, humorously styled spurs, were attached to the feet of the rider. As for the shooting of men for crossing the "dead line" (upon which, so much stress has been laid in accounts of Andersonville), that was so well understood, that it was scarcely thought worthy of mention. But an elaborate description of life in the Federal prisons is unnecessary.

The eighty thousand Confederate prisoners of 1864 and 1865, or rather the survivors of that host, have already told it far better than I can, in their Southern homes, and we have had sufficient experience of the value of sympathy away from home, to make no effort for it. Moreover, a contest with the Yankee journalists is too unequal—they really write so well, and are so liberal in their ideas regarding the difference between fact and falsehood, have so little prejudice for, or against either, that they possess, and employ, a tremendous advantage. And then the pictorials—a special artist has only to catch a conception, in a Philadelphia or New York hospital, and straightway he works off an "Andersonville prisoner," which carries conviction to those who can not read the essay, upon the same subject, by his co-laborers with the pen. What chance has a Southern writer against men who possess such resources? At Fort Delaware, General Schoeff, the commandant, placed some eighteen or twenty of us in the rooms built in the casemates of the fort, and allowed us, for some time, the privilege of walking about the island, upon our giving him our paroles not to attempt escape.

General M. Jeff. Thompson, of Missouri, was the only Confederate officer at that prison, before our party arrived, but many others from Camp Chase, came about the same time. General Thompson's military career, is well known to his countrymen, but only his prison companions know how kind and manly he can be under circumstances which severely try the temper. His unfailing flow of spirits kept every one else, in his vicinity cheerful and his hopefulness was contagious. He possessed, also, an amazing poetical genius. He wrote with surprising fluency, and his finest compositions cost him neither trouble nor thought. Shut him up in a room with plenty of stationery, and in twenty-four hours, he would write himself up to the chin in verse. His muse was singularly prolific and her progeny various. He roamed recklessly through the realm of poesy. Every style seemed his—blank verse and rhyme, ode and epic, lyrical and tragical, satiric and elegiac, sacred and profane, sublime and ridiculous, he was equally good at all. His poetry might not perhaps have stood a very strict classification, but he produced a fair, marketable sample, which deserved (his friends thought) to be quoted at as liberal figures as some about which much more was said. General Thompson would doubtless have been more successful as a poet, if he had been a less honest and practical business man. He persisted in having some meaning in all that he wrote, and only a first class poet can afford to do that.

The cunning New England method is also the safest in the long run—when a versifier suspects that he lacks the true inspiration, he had better try the confidence game, and induce the public to admire by writing that which no one can understand. It would seem, too, that writing poetry and playing on the fiddle have this much in common, that a true genius at either is fit for nothing else. The amateurs can take care of themselves, but the born-masters display an amiable worthlessness for every thing but their art. Now General Thompson was thoroughly wide-awake and competent in all practical matters.

At Fort Delaware the prevailing topic of conversation was exchange; men who were destined to many another weary month of imprisonment, sustained themselves with the hope that it would soon come. At last a piece of good fortune befell some of us. It was announced that General Jones, the officer in command at Charleston, had placed fifty Federal officers in a part of the city where they would be exposed to danger from the batteries of the besiegers. An order was issued that fifty Confederate officers, of corresponding rank, should be selected for retaliation. Five general and forty-five field officers were accordingly chosen from the different prisons, Fort Delaware furnishing a large delegation for that purpose. The general officers selected were Major General Frank Gardner, the gallant and skillful commander of Port Hudson; Major-General Edward Johnson, one of the fighting Generals of the army of Northern Virginia (which is to say one of the bravest of the very brave), and a true man, whose sterling worth, intelligence and force of character would win him respect and influence wherever those qualities were valued; Brigadier-General Stewart, of the Maryland brigade, another officer who had won promotion in that heroic army of Northern Virginia, and had identified his name with its deathless fame. There was still another of these fortunate men—fortunate in having helped to win fields where Confederate soldiers had immortalized the title—Brigadier-General Archer was the fourth general officer. A favorite officer of General A.P. Hill, he was in every respect worthy of a hero's friendship and confidence. The fifth was Brigadier-General M. Jeff. Thompson. Among the field officers who went were seven of the penitentiary prisoners—Colonels Ward, Morgan, and Tucker, Majors Webber, Steele, and Higley and myself.

We left our comrades with a regret, felt for their bad fortune, for we felt assured that our apparent ill-luck would terminate in an exchange. Colonel Coleman, who had been confined in the Fort with the party of which so many were sent on this "expedition," was bitterly disappointed at being left behind, and we regretted it equally as much. Three of our companions through so many vicissitudes, we never saw again—three of the worthiest—Captains Griffin, Mullins, and Wardour died shortly afterward.

On the 26th of June, we were put on board of a steamer, and puffed away down the Delaware river. It was confidently affirmed that we were going to be placed on Morris Island, where the Charleston batteries would have fair play at us, so that our friends (blissfully unconscious of how disagreeable they were making themselves) might speedily finish us. The prospect was not absolutely inviting, but after the matter was talked over, and General Gardner, especially, consulted (as he had most experience in heavy artillery), we felt more easy. General Thompson, who had fought that way a good deal, said that "a man's chance to be struck by lightning was better than to be hit by a siege gun." This consoled me very little, for I had all my life been nervously afraid of lightning. However, we at last settled it unanimously that, while we would perhaps be badly frightened by the large bombs, there was little likelihood of many being hurt, and, at any rate, the risk was very slight compared with the brilliant hope of its resulting in exchange.

After we got fairly to sea, very little thought was wasted on other matters. The captain of the vessel, said that there was "no sea on," or some such gibberish, and talked as if we were becalmed, at the very time that his tipsy old boat was bobbing about like a green rider on a trotting horse. It is a matter of indifference, what sort of metal encased the hearts of those who first tempted the fury of the seas, but they must have had stomachs lined with mahogany. It is difficult to believe men, when they unblushingly declare that they go to sea for pleasure. There has been a great deal of pretentious declamation about the poetry and beauty of the ocean.

Some people go off into raptures about a "vast expanse" of dirty salt water, which must, in the nature of things, be associated in every one's mind with sick stomachs and lost dinners. The same people get so tired of their interminable view of *poetry*, that they will nearly crowd each other overboard, to get sight of a stray flying fish, or porpoise, or the back fin of a shark sticking out of the water. This trip to Hilton Head came near taking the poetry out of General Thompson.

Ten of us were lodged in a cabin on the upper deck, where we did very well, except that for one half of the time we were too sick to eat any thing, and for the other half we were rolling and tumbling about in such a manner that we could think of nothing but keeping off of the cabin's roof. The others were stowed away "amidships," or in some other place, down stairs, and as all the ports and air-holes were shut up, when the steamer began to wallow about, they were nearly smothered, and their nausea was greatly increased. They were compelled to bear it, for they could not force their way on deck and they had nothing with which to scuttle the ship. One western officer declared to me afterward, that he seriously thought, at one time, that he had thrown up his boot heels.

When we reached Hilton Head, we were transferred to the brig

"Dragoon" (a small vessel lying in the harbor), and she was then anchored under the guns of the frigate Wabash. Here we remained five weeks. The weather was intensely hot. During the day we were allowed to go on deck, in reliefs of twenty-five each, and stay alternate hours, but at night we were forced to remain below decks. A large stove (in full blast until after nightfall), at one end of the hold in which we were confined, did not make the temperature any more agreeable. The ports were kept shut up, for fear that some of the party would jump out and swim eight miles to the South Carolina shore. As there were fifty soldiers guarding us and three ship's boats (full of men), moored to the vessel, there was little reason to apprehend any thing of the kind.

The sharks would have been sufficient to have deterred any of us from attempting to escape in that way. There was a difference of opinion regarding their appetite for human flesh, but no man was willing to personally experiment in the matter. A constant negotiation was going on during these five weeks, between the authorities at Hilton Head and Charleston, which seemed once or twice on the point of being broken off, but fortunately managed each time to survive.

We were never taken to Morris' Island, although our chances for that situation, seemed more than once, extremely good. Subsequently a party of six hundred Confederate officers were taken there, and quartered where they would have the full benefit of the batteries. None, however, were injured by the shells, but three fourths of them were reduced to a condition (almost as bad as death), by scurvy and other diseases, brought about by exposure and bad food. At last, on the 1st of August, it was authoritatively announced that we were to be taken on the next day to Charleston to be exchanged. Only those who have themselves been prisoners, can understand what our feelings then were—when the hope that had become as necessary to our lives as the breath we drew, was at length about to be realized. That night there was little sleep among the fifty—but they passed it in alternate raptures of congratulation at their good luck, or shivering apprehension lest, after all, something might occur to prevent it.

But when the next day came and we were all transferred to a steamer, and her head was turned for Charleston, we began to master all doubts and fears. We reached Charleston harbor very early on the morning of the 3rd, lay at anchor for two or three hours, and then steamed slowly in toward the city, until we passed the last monitor, and halted again. In a short time, a small boat came out from Charleston, with the fifty Federal prisoners on board and officers of General Jones' staff, authorized to conclude the exchange. When she came alongside, the final arrangements were effected, but not until a mooted point had threatened to break off the negotiation altogether. Happily for us, we knew nothing of this difficulty until it was all over, but we were made very nervous by the delay. When all the details were settled, we were transferred to the Confederate boat, and the Federal officers were brought on board of the steamer which we left;

then touching hats to the crew we parted from, we bade our captivity farewell.

Twelve months of imprisonment, of absence from all we loved, was over at last. No man of that party could describe his feelings intelligibly—a faint recollection of circumstances is all that can be recalled in such a tumult of joy. As we passed down the bay, the gallant defenders of those works around Charleston, the names of which have become immortal, stood upon the parapets and cheered to us, and we answered like men who were hailing for life. The huge guns, which lay like so many grim watch dogs around the city, thundered a welcome, the people of the heroic city crowded to the wharves to receive us. If anything could repay us for the wretchedness of long imprisonment and our forced separation from families and friends, we found it in the unalloyed happiness of that day.

General Jones had then (and has now), the profound gratitude of fifty of his comrades. Ever doing his duty bravely and unflinchingly, he had, now, ransomed from the enemy, men who would have consented to undergo any ordeal for that boon. The citizens of Charleston hastened to offer us the traditional hospitality of their city. General Jones had informed them of the names of our party, and they had settled among themselves where each man was to be taken care of. If that party of "ransomed sinners" shall ever become "praying members" the Charlestonians will have a large share in their petitions.

But the recollection of our gallant comrades left behind would intrude itself and make us sad, ever in the midst of our good fortune. Some of them were not released until the summer after the close of the war.

No men deserve more praise for constancy than the Confederate prisoners, *especially* the private soldiers, who in the trials to which they were subjected steadfastly resisted every inducement to violate the faith they had pledged to the cause.

A statistical item may not come amiss, in concluding this chapter. There were, in all during the war, 261,000 Northern prisoners in Southern prisons, and 200,000 Confederate prisoners in Northern prisons; 22,576 Northern prisoners died, and 22,535 Confederate prisoners died; or two Federals died out of every twenty-three, and two Confederates died out of every fifteen.

CHAPTER XVI

The men who made their escape from Ohio, after the disastrous fight at Buffington, marched for many a weary mile through the mountains of Virginia. At last, worn down and half famished, they gained the Confederate lines, and first found rest at the beautiful village of Wytheville, in Southwestern Virginia.

Thence they passed leisurely down the fair valley, not then scarred by the cruel ravages of war, to the vicinity of Knoxville. Colonel Adam R.

Johnson then endeavored to collect and organize them all. "On the—of August, 1863," says an officer who was a valuable assistant in this work, "Colonel Johnson issued orders, under instructions from General Buckner, Department Commander, for all men belonging to Morgan's command to report to him (Colonel J.) at Morristown, in East Tennessee. These orders were published in the Knoxville papers, and upon it becoming known that there was a place of rendezvous, every man who had been left behind when General Morgan started on the Ohio raid now pushed forward eagerly to the point designated. When that expedition was undertaken, many had been sent back from Albany as guards for returning trains, and because their horses were unserviceable. Many, too, had to be left on account of sickness or disability from wounds. In a week or ten days, Colonel Johnson had collected between four and five hundred men (including those who made their escape from Ohio) in his camp at Morristown. These men were organized into two battalions—one commanded by Captain Kirkpatrick, representing the first brigade of the division, and the other commanded by Captain Dortch, representing the second brigade.

"The camp was well selected, with wood and water in abundance, and plenty of forage in the neighborhood. Colonel J. was making great efforts to have the men paid off, and properly armed, clothed, etc., when the enemy moved upon Knoxville. The evacuation of that place by our troops made it necessary for us to leave our comfortable resting place. We immediately broke camp at Morristown, and joined General Buckner, who was moving to reinforce General Bragg in front of Chattanooga. * * * * * At Calhoun, the men were paid off, and received a scanty supply of clothing. Many of them had not been paid before for fourteen months. From Calhoun we were ordered to Lafayette, from Lafayette to Dalton, thence to Tunnel Hill. On the morning of the 18th of September, the whole army moved out for battle. Our small force, was ordered to report to General Forrest, and did so about ten A.M. on the field. We were immediately deployed as skirmishers, mounted, in front of Hood's division, of Longstreet's Corps, just come from Virginia. As the men galloped by Forrest, he called to them in language which inspired them with still higher enthusiasm. He urged them to do their whole duty in the battle. He spoke of their chief, who had been insulted with a felon's treatment, and was then lying in the cell of a penitentiary. He gave them 'Morgan' for a battle-cry, and bade them maintain their old reputation.

"The infantry objected to having 'the d—d cavalry' placed in front of them in a fight. But they did not easily catch up with 'the d—d cavalry.' After moving briskly forward for perhaps half a mile, through the tangled undergrowth of pine, the clear crack of rifles told that the enemy was on the alert. Driving in their pickets, we pushed on and found a regiment of cavalry in line to receive us. This fled upon the receipt of the first volley. The undergrowth was too thick for maneuvering on horseback, and we were dismounted and advanced at double-quick. Our boys were anxious to drive the enemy and keep them going without letting the infantry overtake us. The enemy first engaged fell back upon a supporting regiment. We soon drove both back upon a third. By this time our small 'Lay out' found the fighting rather interesting. Engaging three time our number, and attacking every position the enemy chose, was very glorious excitement, but rather more of it than our mouths watered for. Yet no man faltered—all rushed on as reckless of the opposing array of danger as of their own alignment.

"The enemy had formed in the edge of a woods, in front of which was an open field. This field was fought over again and again, each side charging alternately, and forced back. At last a charge upon our part, led by Lieutenant Colonel Martin, was successful. The enemy fell back still further. We now saw clearly from many indications, and were told by prisoners, that the Federal line of battle, the main force, was not far off. We, therefore, moved more cautiously. Just about sundown, we found the enemy's cavalry drawn up directly in front of the infantry, but they made little resistance. After one or two volleys, they fell back behind the protecting 'Web-feet.' Night falling stopped all further operations for that day. We camped in line of battle, and picketed in front. On the morning of the 19th, we were ordered to report to Colonel Scott, and found him engaging the enemy on our extreme right, at thc 'Red House.' Colonel Scott gave us position, dismounted, and put us in. The fighting continued at intervals throughout the day.

"Late in the evening Scott made a vigorous charge and drove the enemy handsomely. We learned from prisoners that we had been fighting a select body of infantry commanded by General Whitaker of Kentucky, which had been detailed to guard the ford, here, across the Chickamauga. The fighting ceased at nightfall and we were again camped in line of battle. The fighting of the next day was very similar to that of the previous ones—the enemy falling back slowly with his face toward us. But late in the evening the retreat became a rout. The army made no attack on the 21st. In the afternoon Colonel Scott was sent with his brigade over Missionary ridge into the valley, and engaged a few scattered cavalry and an Illinois regiment of infantry—capturing nearly all of the latter before they could reach the works around Chattanooga. Forming his brigade Colonel Scott sent a portion of our command, on foot, to reconnoiter the enemy's position. The reconnoitering party drove in the pickets, took the outside rifle pits, and forced the enemy to their breastworks and forts.

"This closed the battle of Chickamauga—Morgan's men firing the *first* and *last* shot in that terrible struggle.

"General Forrest and Colonel Scott, both complimented our little command more than once during the battle. Immediately after the battle, the entire cavalry of the Army of Tennessee was actively employed. The two battalions of our command were separated. Dortch going with Forrest up the Chattanooga and Knoxville railroad. Kirkpatrick went with Wheeler on his raid through Middle Tennessee. Dortch was in the fight (against Woolford) at Philadelphia—in the skirmishes at Loudon and Marysville, and was at the siege of Knoxville. Kirkpatrick's battalion was at the fights at McMinnville, Murfreesboro', Shelbyville and Sugar creek. In the latter fight, Wheeler's whole force fell back rapidly, and Kirkpatrick was kept in the rear until we reached the Tennessee river. When we returned to the army, Kirkpatrick's battalion was placed on severe picket duty—its line extending from the mouth of the Chickamauga up the Tennessee some three miles, where it connected with the line of the First Kentucky cavalry.

"This duty was exceedingly heavy. The pickets stood in squads of three every four hundred yards, with mounted patrols to ride the length of the whole line. One would suppose that men who had ridden through the States of Tennessee, Kentucky, Ohio, Indiana, Virginia and Georgia, and been in as many as twenty-five or thirty engagements, in the space of three months, would be completely worn out, discouraged, and disheartened. Not so, however, the few left were willing and anxious to thoroughly do soldier's duty."

The writer goes on to narrate how after all these trials, came the order to dismount Morgan's men—generous reward for their toil and sacrifices. He speaks of Forrest's gallant stand against it—preventing the execution of the order, but costing the high-souled chief his own command, forcing him to seek other fields of enterprise, and with an organization of conscripts and absentees win fights that a romancer would not dare to imagine. He speaks, too, of unhappy dissensions among officers which added to the discouraging condition of the little command.

But the brave fellows patiently endured all—watching and hoping fondly for the return of the imprisoned leader. The two battalions were at length placed in a brigade commanded by Colonel Grigsby; in which were the Ninth and First Kentucky.

The writer describes the dreary days and long cold nights of that winter. The arduous duty—men shivering through the dark, dragging hours, with eyes fixed on the enemy's signal lights burning on Waldron's ridge and Lookout mountain. Then the Federal battalions pouring, one night, across the river—the bright blaze and quick crash of rifles, suddenly breaking out along the picket line. The hurried saddling and rapid reinforcement, but the steady Federal advance driving the cavalry back. Even amid the snarl of musketry and roar of cannon, could be heard the splash of the boats plying from shore to shore. Couriers were sent to army headquarters, with the information, but, losing their way in the pitch darkness, did not report until day light. Next day came the grand Federal attack and the terrible and unaccountable "stampede" of the entire Confederate army from Missionary ridge—that army which a few weeks before had won the great victory of Chickamauga.

When General Bragg halted at Dalton, this brigade was again posted on the front and suffered, hungry, half clad (many barefooted), through that awful winter.

But a great joy awaited them—before the spring came it brought them relief. General Morgan made his way safely (after his escape) to the Confederate lines. All along his route through South Carolina and Georgia, he was met by a series of heart-felt ovations. Crowds flocked to congratulate him. All the people united in greeting him. The officials in all the towns he visited, prepared his reception. The highest and lowest in the land were alike eager to do him honor. The recollection of his former career and the romantic incidents of his escape combined to create a wonderful interest in him. Perhaps no man ever received such a welcome from the people of his choice. At Richmond, the interest manifested in him knew no bounds. He was the guest of the city for weeks—but none others felt the true and earnest satisfaction at his deliverance and return, which repaid the devoted band of his followers who had so anxiously looked for him. The Morgan men felt, in the knowledge that their idolized leader was safe, a consolation for all that they had endured.

General Morgan's first care, upon arriving at Richmond, was to strongly urge measures which he thought would conduce, if not to the release, at least to a mitigation of the rigorous treatment of his officers and men in prison. He repeatedly brought the subject to the notice of the Confederate authorities, but perfect indifference was manifested regarding it. The officials found nothing in their soft berths at Richmond which could enable them to realize the discomforts of a prison, and the chances of their own captivity appeared so remote that they really could not sympathize with those who had the ill-luck to be captured. Just before leaving Richmond, General Morgan addressed a letter to President Davis, dated the 24th of March, in which he declared that, while imperatively summoned by a sense of duty to place himself at the head of the remnant of his old division, which was still in the field, he desired to earnestly press the claims of those who were captive to the best offices of their Government. No men, he said, better deserved than his own "the proud title of Confederate soldiers," and none had a better right to expect that every effort would be made by their countrymen in their behalf. He stated that in his entire service, "not one act of cruelty was ever committed by men of my command, but prisoners of war met with uniform good treatment at our hands." In response to all this, Commissioner Ould made a public protest against the treatment of the officers confined in the penitentiaries, and was assured that their condition was good enough and would not be bettered.

General Morgan was naturally desirous of having all of the men of his old command assigned him, but in this he was grievously disappointed. Breckinridge's regiment, the Ninth Kentucky, was positively refused him; nor was he permitted to have Dortch's battalion, although it was composed of men from more than one regiment of his old division, the bulk of which was in prison. Kirkpatrick's battalion petitioned to be assigned to him, immediately that the news of his arrival within the Confederate lines was known. General Morgan was, in this respect, the victim of an utterly absurd policy regarding organization and discipline, which was prevalent about this time among the military sages at Richmond. Some other equally insane idea having just gone out of date, this one was seized on with all the enthusiasm with which theorists adopt fancies costing them nothing but the exercise of a crazy imagination. It is hard to combat a fantasy. Three years of warfare had elapsed, and the red-tape and closet warriors suddenly discovered and gravely declared a reform which was to produce a military millenium. All officers were to be removed from the commands with which they had served during these three years, and placed elsewhere. This *reform* was to pervade the army. This separation of officers and men who had learned mutual trust in each other, was intended to produce a perfect and harmonious discipline. A commander who had acquired the confidence and love of his men, was, in the opinion of the Richmond gentry, a dangerous man—such a feeling between troops and officers was highly irregular and injurious. They thought that the best way to improve the morale of the army was to destroy all that (in common opinion) goes to make it.

They said that this policy would make the army "a machine," and it would be difficult to conceive of a more utterly worthless machine than it would have then been. It is highly probable that, under certain conditions, the Southern boys can be disciplined. If a few of them were caught up at a time, and were penned up in barracks for five or six years, so that a fair chance could be had at them, they might perhaps be made automatons, as solemn and amenable as the Dutch of the "old army." But it was absolutely impossible to so discipline the thousands of volunteers who were suddenly organized and initiated at once into campaigns and the most arduous duties of the field. In the lack of this discipline, it was imperatively necessary to cherish between officers and men the most cordial relations, and to leave always in command those officers whose characters and services had inspired love, confidence, and respect.

In the spring of 1864, General Morgan was sent to take command of the Department of Southwestern Virginia, and which included also a portion of East Tennessee.

The forces at his disposal were two Kentucky cavalry brigades and the militia, or "reserves," of that region. One of these brigades of cavalry had been previously commanded by General George B. Hodge, and was subsequently commanded by General Cosby. The other was commanded by Colonel Giltner. Both were composed of fine material, and were together some two thousand or twenty-five hundred strong.

Kirkpatrick's battalion had passed the latter part of the winter and early part of spring at Decatur, Georgia, a small village near Atlanta. Here it enjoyed comparative rest and comfort. The men recovered from the effects of previous hardships, and the effective strength of the command was more than doubled by men who escaped from prison, or who, having been absent upon various pretexts, hurried back as soon as they learned of General Morgan's return.

Leaving Decatur in April, the battalion marched leisurely through Georgia and South and North Carolina—receiving everywhere the greatest kindness at the hands of the citizens—and reported, in early May, to General Morgan at Saltville in Western Virginia. Almost immediately after its arrival, it was called upon to again confront the enemy.

Upon the 8th or 9th of May, the intelligence was received of the advance of strong columns of the enemy; the department was threatened, simultaneously, by a raid upon the salt works, and the approach of a heavy force of infantry and cavalry to Dublin depot, not far from New river bridge. The cavalry column advancing upon Saltville was commanded by General Averill, and the other by General Crook. It was of the utmost importance to repulse both. The former, if successful, would capture the salt works, and the lead mines near Wytheville, and the loss of either would have been a great and irreparable disaster; the latter, if established at New river, or that vicinity, would entirely cut off communication with Richmond, prevent the transmission of supplies, from all the region westward, to General Lee's army and might do incalculable damages besides. It was necessary then that battle should be given to both, and that they should be crippled to some extent, if too strong to be defeated.

The dismounted cavalry of the department–most of which were men of Morgan's old division–about four hundred strong, were sent to reinforce the troops under General Jenkins. The latter had fallen back before Crook to Dublin depot. General Morgan prepared with Giltner's brigade, and the mounted men of his old command, now formed into two battalions commanded by Captains Kirkpatrick and Cassell, and about six hundred strong in all, to fight Avcrill. The two battalions of Kirkpatrick and Cassell, or the "Morgan brigade," as the organization was then called, were placed under the command of Lieutenant Colonel Alston.

On the 9th, General Morgan became convinced, from reports of his scouts, that Averill did not intend to attack Saltville but that he was about to march on Wytheville. Leaving Saltville on the 10th, General Morgan followed upon the track of the enemy to the junction of the Jeffersonville and Wytheville and Jeffersonville and Crab Orchard roads. Here Averill had taken the Crab Orchard road, designing, General Morgan believed, to induce a close pursuit.

Had General Morgan followed upon his track, Averill, by the judicious employment of a comparatively small force, could have held him in check in the mountains, and could himself have turned upon Wytheville, captured the provost-guard there, destroyed the military stores, the lead mines, and torn up the railroad, rendering it useless for weeks.

General Morgan therefore moved directly through Burk's garden to Wytheville, thus (taking the shorter road) anticipating his wily adversary. Reaching Wytheville some hours in advance of his command. General Morgan placed a small detachment of General Jones' brigade of cavalry, which he found there, under Colonel George Crittenden and ordered that officer to occupy a small pass in the mountain between "Crocket's Cave" and Wytheville, through which the enemy would have to advance upon the town, or else be forced to make a wide detour.

On the afternoon of the 11th, the command reached Wytheville and were received by the terrified citizens with the heartiest greetings. The little town had been once captured by the Federals and a portion of it burned. The ladies clapped their hands and waved their handkerchiefs joyfully in response to the assurances of the men that the enemy should not come in sight of the town. Fortunately, while the men were resting near Wytheville, their attention was attracted by the efforts of a squad of citizens to handle an old six-pounder which "belonged to the town." A good deal of laughter was occasioned by their impromptu method.

General Morgan, having no artillery, at once took charge of it and called for volunteers to man it. Edgar Davis and Jerome Clark of Captain Cantrill's company and practical artillerists came forward and were placed in command of the piece.

About 3½ P.M., the enemy engaged Colonel Crittenden at the gap. The column was immediately put in motion and marched briskly in the direction of the firing. When near the gap, it filed to the left, and moving around the mountain and through the skirting woods, was soon in line, upon the right flank and threatening the rear of the enemy. Alston's brigade was formed on the right, occupying an open field, extending from Giltner's left to the mountain. The enemy at the first intimation of this movement had withdrawn from the mouth of the gap and was advantageously posted upon a commanding ridge. Both brigades were dismounted, under a smart fire from sharpshooters, and advanced rapidly, driving in the skirmishers and coming down upon the enemy (before his formation was entirely completed), they dislodged him from his position.

Falling back about five hundred yards, he took position again around the dwelling and buildings upon Mr. Crockett's farm, and maintained it obstinately for some time. The piece of artillery, well served by the gallant volunteers, did excellent service here.

General Morgan, himself, assisted to handle it. The enemy were dislodged from this position also. The fight continued until after nightfall, and was a succession of charges upon the one side and retreats upon the other. The Federal troops were well trained and their officers behaved with great gallantry.

General Morgan's loss in this engagement, in killed and wounded, was about fifty. The enemy's loss was more severe. Nearly one hundred prisoners were taken and more than that number of horses.

General Morgan was cordial in his praise of the alacrity, courage and endurance of officers and men.

It was, indeed, a very important affair and a defeat would have been exceedingly disastrous.

The dismounted men who had been sent under Colonel Smith to reinforce General Jenkins, were engaged at the hotly contested action at Dublin depot, and behaved in a manner which gained them high commendation.

Colonel Smith reached Dublin about 10 A.M. on the 10th, and learned that the forces under the command of General Jenkins were being hard pressed by the enemy and that the gallant General was severely wounded.

Colonel Smith immediately marched with his command, about four hundred strong, toward the scene of the action. After proceeding a short distance, he found the Confederate forces in full retreat and some disorder. He pressed on toward the front, through the retreating mass.

Reporting to Colonel McCausland (who assumed command upon

the fall of General Jenkins), and who was bravely struggling with a rear-guard to check the enemy's pursuit, Colonel Smith was instructed to form his command in the woods upon the left of the road and endeavor to cover the retreat.

This was promptly done, and in a few minutes Colonel Smith received the pursuing enemy with a heavy and unexpected volley.

Driving back the foremost assailants, Colonel Smith advanced in turn and pressed his success for an hour. Then the entire hostile force coming up, he was forced back slowly and in good order to Dublin, which had already been evacuated by the troops of Colonel McCausland.

Colonel Smith followed thence after Colonel McCausland to New River bridge, crossing the river just before sunset, and encamping on the opposite bank.

After some skirmishing on the next morning, the Confederates retreated, giving up the position. The fight on the 10th was a most gallant one—highly creditable to the commanding officer, subordinates and men.

Among the killed was C.S. Cleburne (brother of General Pat Cleburne), one of the most promising young officers in the army. General Morgan had made him a captain, a short time previously, for unusual gallantry.

In the latter part of May, General Morgan undertook the expedition known as the "last" or "June raid" into Kentucky. He had many reasons for undertaking this expedition. He was impatient to retrieve, in some manner, the losses of the Ohio raid, by another campaign of daring conception, and, he hoped, successful execution. He wished to recruit his thinned ranks with Kentuckians, and to procure horses for the men who had none. Moreover, there were excellent military reasons for this movement.

Averill and Cook were not far off, and could pounce down at any moment, but were supposed to be awaiting reinforcements, without which they would not return.

These reinforcements were coming from Kentucky under Burbridge and Hobson, and consisted of all or nearly all the troops in Kentucky, available for active service.

General Morgan despaired of successfully resisting all these forces if they united and bore down on the department. But he believed that, if he could move into Kentucky, and gain the rear of the forces coming thence before the junction with the other Federal forces was affected, he could defeat the plan. The Kentucky troops would turn and pursue him, and the attack upon the department would not be made. In short, he hoped to avoid invasion and attack by assuming the offensive—to keep the enemy out of Southwestern Virginia by making an irruption into Kentucky.

He wrote on the 31st of May to General S. Cooper, Adjutant General, detailing his plan and the information upon which it was based.

In this letter, he said: "While General Buckner was in command of this department, he instructed me to strike a blow at the enemy in Kentucky.

"As I was on the eve of executing this order, the rapid movement of the enemy from the Kanawha valley, in the direction of the Tennessee and Virginia Railroad, made it necessary that I should remain to co-operate with the other forces for the defense of this section. Since the repulse of the enemy, I have obtained the consent of General Jones to carry out the original plan agreed on between General Buckner and myself."

"I have just received information that General Hobson left Mt. Sterling on the 23rd inst., with six regiments of cavalry (about three thousand strong), for Louisa, on the Sandy. This force he has collected from all the garrisons in Middle and Southeastern Kentucky. At Louisa there is another force of about two thousand five hundred cavalry, under a colonel of a Michigan regiment, recently sent to that vicinity. It is the reported design of General Hobson to unite with this latter force, and co-operate with Generals Averill and Crook in another movement upon the salt works and lead mines of Southwestern Virginia." "This information has determined me to move at once into Kentucky, and thus distract the plans of the enemy by initiating a movement within his lines. My force will be about two thousand two hundred men. I expect to be pursued by the force at Louisa, which I will endeavor to avoid. There will be nothing in the State to retard my progress but a few scattered provost-guards."

In the latter part of May, General Morgan commenced the movement indicated in this letter.

His division consisted of three brigades. The first under command of Colonel Giltner, was between ten and eleven hundred strong, and was a magnificent body of hardy, dashing young men, drawn chiefly from the middle and eastern counties of Kentucky. The second brigade was composed of the mounted men of the old Morgan division. It consisted of three small battalions, commanded respectively by Lieutenant Colonel Bowles and Majors Cassell and Kirkpatrick. It was between five and six hundred strong and was commanded by Lieutenant Colonel Alston. The third brigade was composed of the dismounted men of both the other commands, the greater number, however, being from the second brigade. It was organized into two battalions, commanded respectively by Lieutenant Colonel Martin and Major Geo. R. Diamond, a brave and exceedingly competent officer of Giltner's brigade. The third brigade was about eight hundred strong and was commanded by Colonel D. Howard Smith. No artillery was taken—it could not have been transported over the roads which General Morgan expected to travel. The column reached Pound Gap on the 2nd of June and found it occupied by a force of the enemy. Colonel Smith was ordered to clear the path, and pushing his brigade forward, he soon did it. Several horses were captured, which was accepted as a happy omen.

Sending a scouting party to observe the direction taken by the retreating enemy, and to ascertain if they joined a larger force and turned again, General Morgan pressed on, hoping to reach Mt. Sterling—the general Federal depot of supplies and most important post in that portion of Kentucky—before General Burbridge could return from the extreme eastern part of the State. As Burbridge was incumbered with artillery and would be two or three days in getting the news, General Morgan confidently believed that he could reach Mt. Sterling first. The mountainous country of Southeastern Kentucky, so rugged, steep and inhospitable, as to seem almost impossible of access, had to be traversed for this purpose. More than one hundred and fifty miles of this region was marched over in seven days. The dismounted men behaved heroically. Straining up the steep mountain sides, making their toilsome way through gloomy and deep ravines, over tremendous rocks and every formidable obstacle which nature collects in such regions against the intrusion of man, footsore, bleeding, panting, they yet never faltered or complained, and richly won the enthusiastic eulogy of their commander. They marched from twenty-two to twenty-seven miles each day. This march was terribly severe upon the mounted commands also. The fatigue and lack of forage caused many horses to break down—and the dismounted brigade was largely augmented. Colonel Giltner stated that he lost more than two hundred horses in his brigade.

On the 6th of June, Colonel Smith was transferred to the command of the second brigade. Lieutenant Colonel Martin was then assigned to command of the third. On the 7th, finding that he would succeed in anticipating Burbridge at Mt. Sterling and that he would not require his whole force to take the place, General Morgan dispatched Captain Jenkins with fifty men to destroy the bridges upon the Frankfort and Louisville Railroad to prevent troops arriving from Indiana for the defense of Lexington and Central Kentucky. He sent Major Chenoweth to destroy bridges on the Kentucky Central Railroad to prevent the importation of troops from Cincinnati, and he sent Captain Peter Everett with one hundred men to capture Maysville. General Morgan instructed these officers to accomplish their respective commissions thoroughly but promptly, to create as much excitement as possible, occasion the concentration of forces already in the State at points widely apart, to magnify his strength and circulate reports which would bewilder and baffle any attempt to calculate his movements and to meet him within three or four days at Lexington.

When the command emerged from the sterile country of the mountains into the fair lands of Central Kentucky, the change had a perceptible and happy effect upon the spirits of the men. Night had closed around them, on the evening of the 7th, while they were still struggling through the ghastly defiles or up the difficult paths of the "Rebel trace," still environed by the bleak mountain scenery. During the night, they arrived at the confines of the beautiful "Blue Grass country," and when the sun arose, clear and brilliant, a lovely and smiling landscape had replaced the lowering, stony, dungeon like region whence they had at last escaped. The contrast seemed magical—the song, jest and laugh burst forth again and the men drew new life and courage from the scene.

In the early part of the day, the 8th, the column reached the vicinity of Mt. Sterling, and preparations were made for an immediate attack upon the place. On the previous day, Captain Lawrence Jones, commanding the advance-guard, had been sent with his guard to take position upon the main road between Mt. Sterling and Lexington, and Captain Jackson was sent with one company to take position between Mt. Sterling and Paris. These officers were instructed to prevent communication, by either telegraph or courier, between Mt. Sterling and the other two places. The enemy were simultaneously attacked by detachments from the first and second brigades and soon forced to surrender with little loss on either side. Major Holliday, of the first brigade, made a gallant charge upon the encampment which drove them in confusion into the town. Three hundred and eighty prisoners were taken, a large quantity of stores and a number of wagons and teams.

Leaving Colonel Giltner to destroy the stores, and provide for the remounting upon the captured horses of a portion of the dismounted men, General Morgan marched immediately for Lexington with the second brigade. Burbridge making a wonderful march—moving nearly ninety miles in the last thirty hours—reached Mt. Sterling before daybreak on the 9th. Then occurred a great disaster to General Morgan's plans and it fell upon the brave boys who had so patiently endured, on foot, the long, painful march. Some of these men had marched from Hyter's Gap in Virginia, to Mt. Sterling, a distance of two hundred and thirty miles in ten days. Their shoes were worn to tatters and their feet raw and bleeding, yet on the last day they pressed on twenty-seven miles. Encamping not far from the town but to the east of it, Colonel Martin directed Lieutenant Colonel Brent, who had been left with him in command of some forty or fifty men to act as rear-guard, to establish his guard at least one mile from the encampment and picket the road whence the danger might come. Lieutenant Colonel Brent had been assigned to General Morgan's command a short time previously to this expedition and was not one of his old officers. Information which had been received a day or two before had induced the belief that Burbridge was not near. Scouts sent by General Morgan to observe his movements had returned, reporting that he had moved on toward Virginia. This information convinced General Morgan that he would not arrive at Mt. Sterling for two or three days after the 8th—although satisfied that he would come.

Colonel Giltner's command was encamped some distance from Martin's and upon a different road, and was not in a position to afford the latter any protection. Brent, neglecting the precaution enjoined by Martin, posted his guard only one or two hundred yards from the encampment of the dismounted men and extended his pickets but a short distance further.

On the next morning, about three o'clock, the enemy dashed into the camp, the pickets giving no warning, and shot and rode over the men as they lay around their fires. Many were killed before they arose from their blankets. Notwithstanding the disadvantage of the surprise, the men stood to their arms and fighting resolutely, although without concert, soon drove the assailants out of the camp. Being then formed by their officers, they presented a formidable front to the enemy who returned, in greater strength as fresh numbers arrived to the attack. The fight was close and determined upon both sides. Colonel Martin's headquarters were at a house near by. He was awakened by the rattling shots and springing upon his horse, rode toward the camp to find the enemy between himself and his men. Without hesitation he rode at full speed through the hostile throng, braving the volleys of both lines, and rejoined his command. The enemy brought up a piece of artillery, which was taken by a desperate effort, but was soon recaptured. The poor fellows undaunted by weariness, the sudden attack upon them, and their desperate situation fought with unflinching courage for more than an hour.

At length Colonel Martin fell back, cutting his way through Mt. Sterling which was occupied by the enemy. Two miles from the town he met Colonel Giltner, and proposed to the latter that, with their combined forces, the fight should be renewed. Giltner acceding, it was arranged that he should attack in front, while Martin, moving around to the other side of the town again, should take the enemy in the rear. This being done, the fight was pressed again with energy, until Martin's ammunition failing he was compelled to withdraw. The enemy was too much crippled to pursue.

In this affair, although inflicting severe loss on the enemy, Martin's command lost heavily. Fourteen commissioned officers were killed and forty privates. Eighty were so severely wounded that they could not be removed, one hundred were captured and more than that number cut off and dispersed. Colonel Martin was twice wounded.

On the morning of the 10th, General Morgan entered Lexington after a slight skirmish. He burned the government depot and stables and captured a sufficient number of horses to mount all of the dismounted men, who were then returned to their respective companies in the first and second brigades.

Moving thence to Georgetown, General Morgan sent Captain Cooper with one company to demonstrate toward Frankfort. Captain Cooper ably executed his orders, alarming and confining to the fortification around the town a much superior force of the enemy.

From Georgetown, General Morgan directed his march to Cynthiana, reaching that place on the morning of the 11th. After a sharp fight the garrison, four hundred strong, was captured. Unfortunately, a portion of the town was burned in the engagement, the enemy having occupied the houses. While the fight was going on in town, Colonel Giltner engaged a body of the enemy, fifteen hundred strong, under General Hobson. General Morgan, after the surrender of the garrison, took Cassell's battalion and, gaining Hobson's rear, compelled him also to surrender.

A large quantity of stores were captured and destroyed at Cynthiana. General Hobson was paroled and sent, under escort of Captain C.C. Morgan and two other officers, to Cincinnati, to effect, if possible, the exchange of himself and officers for certain of General Morgan's officers then in prison and, failing in that, to report as prisoner within the

Confederate lines. He was not permitted to negotiate the exchange and his escort were detained for some weeks.

On the 12th, the command numbering, after all losses, and deducting details to guard prisoners and wagon train and to destroy the track and bridges for some miles of the Kentucky Central railroad, some twelve hundred men, was attacked by a force of infantry, cavalry and artillery under General Burbridge which General Morgan estimated at five thousand two hundred strong. Giltner's command had been encamped on the Paris road and was first engaged by the enemy. This brigade was almost entirely out of ammunition. The cartridges captured the day before did not fit the guns with which it was armed. General Morgan had directed Colonel Giltner to take, also, the captured guns for which this ammunition was available, but he was unwilling to abandon his better rifles and provided his brigade with neither captured guns nor cartridges. Giltner soon became hotly engaged with the advancing enemy and although the second brigade moved to his support, their united strength could oppose no effectual resistance.

General Morgan ordered the entire command to retreat upon the Augusta road and charged with the mounted reserve to cover the withdrawal. The action was very disastrous. Colonel Giltner, cut off from the Augusta, was forced to retreat upon the Leesburg road. Colonel Smith, at first, doubtful of the condition of affairs, did not immediately take part in the fight. His gallant and efficient Adjutant, Lieutenant Arthur Andrews, rode to the scene of the fight, and returning, declared that Colonel Giltner required his prompt support. Colonel Smith instantly put his brigade in motion and was soon in front of the enemy.

He says: "My brigade, gallantly led by its battalion commander, attacked the enemy with great spirit and drove him back along its entire length. The first battalion moved with more rapidity than the third, doubtless on account of the better nature of the ground it had to traverse, until it swung around almost at right angles with the line of the third battalion. Hastening to correct this defect, I rode to Colonel Bowles, but before he could obey my instructions a heavy force was massed upon him, and after a desperate contest he was forced back. I directed him to reform his command behind a stone fence on the Ruddle's Mill road, which he did promptly and checked the enemy with heavy loss. At this juncture I looked for Kirkpatrick, who had been holding his line with his usual energy and determination. I found that his battalion had been separated—two companies, commanded respectively by Captain Cantrill and Lieutenant Gardner, had been fighting hard on his left, while the other two were acting with the first battalion. Captain Kirkpatrick, severely wounded, was forced to quit the field. About the same time, gallant Bowles was driven from his second position, strong as it was, by overpowering numbers. Colonel Smith now retreated through Cynthiana, seeking to rejoin General Morgan on the Augusta road. He suddenly found himself intercepted and surrounded on three sides by the enemy, while upon the other side was the Licking river. Seeing the condition of affairs, the men became unmanageable and dashed across the river. Having been reformed on the other side, they charged a body of cavalry which then confronted them and made good their retreat, although scattered and in confusion.

Collecting all the men, who could be gathered together upon the Augusta road, General Morgan paroled his prisoners and rapidly retreated. His loss in this action was very heavy, and he was compelled to march instantly back to Virginia. Moving through Flemingsburg and West Liberty, he passed on over the mountains and reached Abingdon on the 20th of June. On this raid, great and inexcusable excesses were committed, but, except in two or three flagrant instances, they were committed by men who had never before served with General Morgan. The men of his old division and Giltner's fine brigade were rarely guilty. General Morgan had accomplished the result he had predicted, in averting the invasion of Southwestern Virginia, but at heavy cost to himself.

CHAPTER XVII

Upon his return to Southwestern Virginia, General Morgan applied himself assiduously to collect all of his men, however detached or separated from him, and correct the organization and discipline of his command. It was a far less easy task then than ever before. Not only was a conviction stealing upon the Confederate soldiery (and impairing the efficiency of the most manly and patriotic) that the fiat had gone forth against us, and that no exercise of courage and fortitude could avert the doom, but the demoralizing effects of a long war, and habitude to its scenes and passions had rendered even the best men callous and reckless, and to a certain extent intractable to influences which had formerly been all potent with them as soldiers. Imagine the situation in which the Confederate soldier was placed: Almost destitute of hope that the cause for which he fought would triumph and fighting on from instinctive obstinate pride, no longer receiving from the people—themselves hopeless and impoverished almost to famine by the draining demands of the war—the sympathy, hospitality and hearty encouragement once accorded to him; almost compelled (for comfort if not for existence) to practice oppression and wrong upon his own countrymen, is it surprising that he became wild and lawless, that he adopted a rude creed in which strict conformity to military regulations and a nice obedience to general orders held not very prominent places? This condition obtained in a far greater degree with the cavalry employed in the "outpost" departments than with the infantry or the soldiery of the large armies. It is an unhappy condition, and destructive of military efficiency and any sort of discipline, but under certain circumstances it is hard to prevent or correct. There is little temptation and no necessity or excuse for it among troops that are well fed, regularly paid in good money and provided with comfortable clothing, blankets and shoes in the cold winter; but troops whose rations are few and scanty, who flutter with rags and wear ventillating shoes which suck in the cold air, who sleep at night under a blanket which keeps the saddle from a sore-backed horse in the day time, who are paid (if paid at all) with waste paper, who have become hardened to the licentious practices of a cruel warfare—such troops will be frequently tempted to violate the moral code. Many Confederate cavalrymen so situated left their commands altogether and became guerrillas, salving their consciences with the thought that the desertion was not to the enemy. These men, leading a comparatively luxurious life and receiving, from some people, a mistaken and foolish admiration, attracted to the same career young men who (but for the example and the sympathy accorded the guerrilla and denied the faithful, brave and suffering soldier) would never had quitted their colors and their duty. Kentucky was at one time, just before the close of the war, teeming with these guerrillas. It was of no use to threaten them with punishment—they had no idea of being caught. Besides, Burbridge shot all that he could lay hands on, and (for their sins) many prisoners (guilty of no offense), selected at random, or by lot, from the pens where he kept them for the purpose, were butchered, by this insensate blood-hound. Not only did General Morgan have to contend with difficulties thus arising, but now, for the first time, he suffered from envy, secret animosity and detraction within his own command. Many faithful friends still surrounded him, many more lay in prison, but he began to meet with open enmity in his own camp. It had happened in the old times that some of his warmest and surest adherents had occasionally urged strenuous remonstrances against his wishes, but they were dictated by devotion to his interests; now officers, recently connected with him, inaugurated a jealous and systematic opposition to him in all matters, and were joined in it, with ungrateful alacrity, by some men whom he had thought his fastest friends. Reports of excesses committed by some of the troops in Kentucky had reached Richmond and created much feeling. General Morgan had instructed his Inspector General, Captain Bryant H. Allen, to investigate the accusations against the various parties suspected of guilt and to prefer charges against those who should appear to be implicated. Captain Allen was charged with negligence and lack of industry in pursuing the investigation and complaints were made that General Morgan was seeking to screen the offenders. All sorts of communications, the most informal, irregular and some of them, improper, were forwarded to Richmond by General Morgan's subordinates, often unknown to him because not passing through his office, and they were received by the Secretary of War, Mr. Seddon, without questioning and with avidity. It was at length announced that a commission would be appointed to sit at Abingdon and inquire into these charges, and also into the charge that General Morgan had undertaken the raid into Kentucky without orders.

While in daily expectation of the arrival of these commissioners, the sudden irruption of the enemy into that part of the country which was occupied by his command, caused General Morgan to proceed to the threatened points. Colonels Smith and Giltner, and a portion of General

Vaughn's brigade which was stationed in East Tennessee, under Colonel Bradford, were driven back to Carter's Station, on the Wetauga river, some thirty-five miles from Abingdon. When General Morgan reached that place, and took command of the troops assembled there, the enemy were retreating. He followed as closely as possible until he had reoccupied the territory whence the Confederates had been driven. While at Granville, a small town upon the Tennessee and Virginia Railroad, seventy-two miles from Abingdon, and eighteen from Bull's Gap, where a portion of his troops was stationed, he had occasion to revoke the parole, granted a few days previously, to a wounded Federal officer, assistant adjutant general to General Gillem, who was staying at the house of a Mrs. Williams, where General Morgan had made his headquarters. The daughter-in-law of this lady, Mrs. Lucy Williams, a Union woman and bitterly opposed to the Confederate cause and troops, was detected with a letter written by this officer, accurately detailing the number, condition and position of General Morgan's forces, which letter she was to have sent to Colonel Gillem. Dr. Cameron, General Morgan's chaplain, discovered the letter in a prayer book, where it had been deposited by the lady.

This being a clear violation of his parole, General Morgan sent the officer to Lynchburg, to be placed in prison. The younger Mrs. Williams (his friend) resented this treatment very much, declaring that in his condition, it might prove fatal to him.

This incident is related because it has been thought to have had a direct influence in causing General Morgan's death. When General Morgan returned to Abingdon, he found an excitement still prevailing regarding the investigation, but the members of the commission had not yet arrived.

I met him, then, for the first time since he had made his escape, or I had been exchanged. He was greatly changed. His face wore a weary, care-worn expression, and his manner was totally destitute of its former ardor and enthusiasm. He spoke bitterly, but with no impatience, of the clamor against him, and seemed saddest about the condition of his command. He declared that if he had been successful in the last day's fight at Cynthiana, he would have been enabled to hold Kentucky for months; that every organized Federal force which could be promptly collected to attack him, could have then been disposed of, and that he had assurance of obtaining a great number of recruits. He spoke with something of his old sanguine energy, only when proclaiming his confidence that he could have achieved successes unparalleled in his entire career, if fortune had favored him in that fight. But no word of censure upon any one escaped him. It had never been his habit to charge the blame of failure upon his subordinates—his native magnanimity forbade it; and tried so sorely as he was at this time, by malignant calumny, he was too proud to utter a single reproach. A letter which he intended to forward to the Secretary of War, but the transmission of which his death prevented, shows his sense of the treatment he had received. This letter was written just after the conversation, above mentioned, occurred, while he was again confronting the enemy, and immediately before he was killed. I can not better introduce it than by first giving the letter of the officer who forwarded it to me (I had believed it lost), and who was for more than a year Adjutant General of the Department of Southwestern Virginia and East Tennessee, and served for some months on General Morgan's staff. He is well known to the ex-Confederates of Kentucky, as having been an exceedingly intelligent, competent, and gallant officer, and a gentleman of the highest honor.

"COVINGTON, December —, ——.

"*Dear General*: In looking over some old papers (relics of the late war), a few days ago, I discovered one which, until then, I did not know was in my possession. It is the last letter written by General Morgan, and, in a measure, may be considered his dying declaration. I can not recollect how it came into my possession, but believe it to have been among a bundle of papers that were taken from his body after he was killed, and forwarded to Department Headquarters; the letter of Captain Gwynn, which I will also inclose you, leaves hardly a doubt upon that point.

I have noticed through the press, that you were engaged in writing a history of "Morgan's command," and under the impression that this paper will be of service to you, I herewith forward it. I am familiar with the embarrassments that surrounded the General for some time previously to his death, and in reading this last appeal to the powers that had dealt with him so unjustly, the remembrance of them still awakens in my bosom many emotions of regret. If the General acted adversely to his own interests, in endeavoring to adjust quietly the unfortunate affairs that he refers to, those who understood his motives for so doing would excuse this error of his judgment when they realized the feelings that prompted it. He saw his error when it was too late to correct it, and died before opportunity was given to vindicate his character. I remember distinctly the last conversation I had with him, only a few days before his death, and the earnest manner in which he spoke of this trouble, would have removed from my mind all doubt of the perfect rectitude of his intentions, if any had ever existed. I remember, too, my visit to Richmond during the month of August, 1864, on which occasion, at the General's request, I called upon the Secretary of War to lay before him some papers entrusted to my care, and also to make some verbal explanations regarding them. The excited, I may say the exasperated manner in which the Honorable Secretary commented upon the documents, left but one impression upon my mind, and that was, that the War Department had made up its mind that the party was guilty and that its conviction should not be offended by any evidence to the contrary. The determination to pursue and break the General down was apparent to every one, and the Kentucky expedition was to be the means to accomplish this end (the reasons for a great deal of this enmity are, of course, familiar to you). I endeavored to explain to Mr. Seddon the injustice of the charge that General Morgan had made this expedition without proper authority (I felt this particularly to be my duty as I was the only person then living who could bear witness upon that point), but being unable to obtain a quiet hearing, I left his office disappointed and disgusted.

With the hope that you may succeed in the work you have undertaken, believe me,

Very truly, your friend,

J.L. SANDFORD."

"HEADQUARTERS CAV. DEP'T, EAST TENNESSEE,} *Jonesboro', Sept. 1, 1864.*}

"SIR: I have the honor to ask your early and careful consideration of the statements herein submitted, and, although I am aware that the representations which have been made you, concerning the matters to which these statements relate, have so decided your opinion that you do not hesitate to give it free expression, I yet feel that it is due to myself to declare how false and injurious such representations have been and to protest against the injustice which condemns me unheard.

You will understand that I allude to the alleged robbery of the Bank of Mt. Sterling, Kentucky, and other outrages which my command is charged with having committed during the late expedition into that State. I will not, myself, countenance a course of procedure against which I feel that I can justly protest, by citing testimony or waging my own affirmation in disproof of the accusations which have been filed against me at your office—but I will demand a prompt and thorough investigation of them all, and will respectfully urge the propriety of yourself instituting it.

If, as has been asserted, I have obstructed all examination into the truth of these imputations, a proper regard for the interests of the service, as well as the ends of justice requires that some higher authority shall compel an exposure. Until, very recently, I was ignorant how the rumors which had already poisoned the public mind, had been received and listened to in official circles, and I can not forbear indignant complaint of the injury done my reputation and usefulness by the encouragement thus given them.

Allegations, directly implicating me in the excesses above referred to, that I had connived at, if I did not incite them, and that I have striven to shield the perpetrators from discovery and punishment—allegations, the most vague and yet all tending to impeach my character, have obtained hearing and credence at the department.

I have not been called on, indeed I may say I have not been permitted one word in my defense. Permit me to say that an officer's reputation may suffer from such causes, in official and public opinion, and that he may find it difficult, if not impossible, to vindicate it, unless his superiors assist him by inviting inquiry. I am informed that communications and documents of various kinds, relating to the alleged criminal transactions in Kentucky, have been addressed you by certain of my subordinates, and I have been profoundly ignorant of their existence, until after their receipt, and the intended impression had been produced. I have but little acquaintance with the forms and regulations of your office, and I would respectfully ask if communications so furnished are not altogether irregular and prejudicial to good order and proper discipline? If these parties believe my conduct culpable, is it not their plain duty to prefer charges against me and bring me before a court martial? And if failing to adopt measures suggested alike by law, justice and propriety, they pursue a course which tends to weaken my authority, impair my reputation and embarrass my conduct, have I not the right to expect that their action shall be condemned and themselves reprimanded? Indeed, sir, discipline and subordination have been impaired to such an extent in my command by proceedings, such as I have described, that an officer of high rank quitted a responsible post, without leave and in direct disobedience to my orders, and repaired to Richmond to urge in person his application for assignment to duty more consonant with his inclinations. It is, with all due respect, that I express my regret that his application was successful.

Permit me again, sir, to urge earnestly, that the investigation, which can alone remove the difficulties which I now experience, shall be immediately ordered.

I have the honor to be, very respectfully,

Your obedient servant,

JOHN H. MORGAN.

TO HON. JAMES A. SEDDON, *Secretary of War.*

On the 28th or 29th of August, General Morgan left Abingdon, and taking command of the troops at Jonesboro' on the 31st, immediately prepared to move against the enemy. Our forces had again been driven away from their positions at Bull's Gap and Rogersville, and had fallen back to Jonesboro'. After two or three days delay for refitment, etc., General Morgan marched from Jonesboro' with the intention of attacking the enemy at Bull's Gap. If he could drive them from that position, by a sudden and rapidly executed movement, he would, in all probability, cut off that force at Rogersville and either force it to surrender or compel it to retreat into Kentucky. In the latter event, the enemy's strength would be so much reduced, that all of East Tennessee, as far down as Knoxville, would be for some time, in possession of the Confederates. General Morgan's strength, including the portions of General Vaughan's brigade, was about sixteen hundred and two pieces of artillery. The men were badly armed and equipped and had been much discouraged by their late reverses, but reanimated by the presence of their leader, whom they loved all the more as misfortunes befell them, they were anxious for battle.

A small frame house upon the left side of the road leading from Jonesboro' to Greenville, was often pointed out to me subsequently, as the spot where General Morgan received (as he rode past the column), the last cheer ever given him by his men. Reaching Greenville about 4 P.M. on the 3rd of September, he determined to encamp there for the night and move on Bull's Gap the next day. The troops were stationed on all sides of the place, and he made his headquarters in town, at the house of Mrs. Williams. The younger Mrs. Williams left Greenville, riding in the direction of Bull's Gap at the first rumors of the approach of our forces, to give, we have always believed, the alarm to the enemy.

The Tennesseeans of Vaughan's brigade (under Colonel Bradford), were encamped on the Bull's Gap road, and were instructed to picket that road and the roads to the left. Clark's battalion of Colonel Smith's brigade and the artillery were encamped on the Jonesboro' road, about five hundred yards from the town. The remainder of Colonel Smith's brigade was encamped on the Rogersville road. Colonel Giltner's command was also stationed in this quarter, and the two picketed all the roads to the front and right flank. The town, had all instructions been obeyed and the pickets judiciously placed, would have been perfectly protected. It has been stated, I know not how correctly, that the enemy gained admittance to the town, unchallenged, through an unaccountable error in the picketing of the roads on the left. According to this account, the enemy, who left Bull's Gap before midnight, quitted the main road at Blue Springs, equi-distant from Greenville and Bull's Gap, and marched by the Warrensburg road, until within one mile and a half of the town.

At this point, a by-road leads from the Warrensburg to the Newport road. The pickets on the Warrensburg road were not stationed in sight of this point, while on the Newport road the base of the pickets was beyond the point where the by-road enters, and there were no rear videttes between the base and town. The enemy (it is stated), took this little by-road, and turning off in front of one picket, came in behind the other. At any rate, about daylight, a body perhaps of one hundred cavalry dashed into Greenville and were followed in a short time by Gillem's whole force. It was the party that came first which killed General Morgan. His fate, however, is still involved in mystery. Major Gassett, of his staff, states that they left the house together and sought to escape, but found every street guarded. They took refuge once in the open cellar of a house, expecting that some change in the disposition of the Federal forces would leave an avenue for escape, or that they would be rescued by a charge from some of the troops at the camps. They were discovered and pointed out by a Union woman. Gassett succeeded in effecting his escape. General Morgan made his way back to the garden of Mrs. Williams house. Lieutenant X. Hawkins, a fearless young officer, charged into the town with fifteen men and strove to reach the point where he supposed the General to be, but he was forced back. General Morgan was killed in the garden—shot through the heart. It is not known whether he surrendered or was offering resistance.

His friends have always believed that he was murdered after his surrender. Certain representations by the parties who killed him, their ruffianly character, and the brutality with which they treated his body, induced the belief; and it was notorious that his death, if again captured, had been sworn. His slayers broke down the paling around the garden, dragged him through, and, while he was tossing his arms in his dying agonies, threw him across a mule, and paraded his body about the town, shouting and screaming in savage exultation. No effort was made by any one except Lieutenant Hawkins to accomplish his rescue. The three commands demoralized by General Morgan's death, became separated and were easily driven away. The men of his old command declared their desire to fight and avenge him on the spot, but a retreat was insisted upon.

Thus, on the 4th of September, 1864, in this little village of East Tennessee, fell the greatest partisan leader the world ever saw, unless it were the Irishman, Sarsfield. But not only was the light of genius extinguished then, and a heroic spirit lost to earth—as kindly and as noble a heart as was ever warmed by the constant presence of generous emotions was stilled by a ruffian's bullet.

As the event is described, the feelings it excited come back almost as fresh and poignant as at the time. How hard it was to realize that his time, too, had come—that so much life had been quenched. Every trait of the man we almost worshiped, recollections of incidents which showed his superb nature, crowd now, as they crowded then, upon the mind.

When he died, the glory and chivalry seemed gone from the struggle, and it became a tedious routine, enjoined by duty, and sustained only by sentiments of pride and hatred. Surely men never grieved for a leader as Morgan's men sorrowed for him. The tears which scalded the cheeks of hardy and rugged veterans, who had witnessed all the terrible scenes of four years of war, attested it, and the sad faces told of the aching hearts within.

His body was taken from the hands which defiled it, by General Gillem, as soon as that officer arrived at Greenville, and sent to our lines, under flag of truce. It was buried first at Abingdon, then removed to the cemetery at Richmond, where it lies now, surrounded by kindred heroic ashes, awaiting the time when it can be brought to his own beloved Kentucky—the hour when there is no longer fear that the storm, which living rebels are sworn to repress, shall burst out with the presence of the dead chieftain.

The troops again returned to Jonesboro', the enemy returning after a short pursuit to Bull's Gap. Immediately upon learning of General Morgan's death, General Echols, then commanding the department, ordered me to take command of the brigade composed of his old soldiers—the remnant of the old division. I found this brigade reduced to two hundred and seventy-three effective men, and armed in a manner that made it a matter of wonder how they could fight at all. There were scarcely fifty serviceable guns in the brigade, and the variety of calibers rendered it almost a matter of impossibility to keep on hand a supply of available ammunition. They were equipped similarly in all other respects. Every effort was at once instituted to collect and procure guns, and to provide suitable equipments. General Echols kindly rendered all the assistance in his power, and manifested a special interest in us, for which we were deeply grateful. Our friends at Richmond and throughout the Confederacy, seemed to experience fresh sympathy for us after General Morgan's death.

In this connection it is fitting to speak of a gentleman to whom we were especially indebted, Mr. E.M. Bruce, one of the Kentucky members of the Confederate Congress. It would, indeed, be unjust as well as ungrateful, to omit mention of his name and his generous, consistent friendship. Not only were we, of Morgan's old command, the recipients of constant and the kindest services from him, but his generosity was as wide as his charity, which seemed boundless. His position at Richmond was such as to enable him to be of great assistance to the soldiers and people from his state, and he was assiduous and untiring in their behalf. The immense wealth which his skill and nerve in commercial speculations procured him, was lavished in friendly ministrations and charitable enterprises. An intelligent and useful member of the Congress, a safe and valuable adviser of the administration in all matters within the province of his advice, he was especially known and esteemed as the *friend* of the soldiery, the patron of all who stood in need of aid and indulgence. At one time he maintained not only a hospital in Richmond for the sick and indigent, but a sort of hotel, kept up at his own expense, where the Kentucky soldiers returning from prison were accommodated. It is safe to say that he did more toward furnishing the Kentucky troops with clothing, etc., than all of the supply department put together. The sums he gave away in Confederate money would sound fabulous; and, after the last surrender, he gave thousands of dollars in gold to the Kentucky troops, who lacked means to take them home. His name will ever be held by them in grateful and affectionate remembrance.

My command remained encamped near Jonesboro' for nearly two weeks. The commands of Vaughan, Cosby (that formerly commanded by General George B. Hodge) and Giltner were also stationed in the same vicinity, all under command of General John C. Vaughan.

Upon the 15th of September, I received my commission as Brigadier General and accepted it—as it has turned out—an *unpardonable* error. During the time that we remained near Jonesboro', the brigade improved very much. Fortunately several of the best officers of the old command, who had escaped capture, were with it at the time that I took command, Captains Cantrill, Lea and Messick, and Lieutenants Welsh, Cunningham, Hunt, Hawkins, Hopkins, Skillman, Roody, Piper, Moore, Lucas, Skinner, Crump and several others equally as gallant and good, and there were some excellent officers who had joined the command just after General Morgan's return from prison. The staff department was ably filled by the acting adjutants, Lieutenants George W. Hunt, Arthur Andrews, James Hines and Daniels. These were all officers of especial merit.

Colonels Ward, Morgan and Tucker, and Majors Webber and Steele had been exchanged at Charleston, and their valuable services were secured at a time when greatly needed. The gallant Mississippi company, of my old regiment, was there, all, at least, that was left of it, and Cooper's company, under Welsh, as staunch and resolute as ever, although greatly reduced in numbers. All the old regiments were represented.

Daily drills and inspections soon brought the brigade into a high state of efficiency and the men longed to return to the debatable ground and try conclusions, fairly, with the enemy which had boasted of recent triumphs at their expense. An opportunity soon occurred. In the latter part of September, General Vaughan moved with all of these commands stationed about Jonesboro', in the direction of Greenville. One object of the movement was to attempt, if co-operation with General John S. Williams, who was known to be approaching from toward Knoxville, could be secured, the capture of the Federal forces at Bull's gap. General Williams had been cut off, in Middle Tennessee, from General Wheeler who had raided into that country. His command consisted of three brigades. One under command of Colonel William Breckinridge was the brigade of Kentucky cavalry which had won so much reputation in the retreat from Dalton and the operations around Atlanta. In this brigade were Colonel Breckinridge's own regiment, the Ninth Kentucky and Dortch's battalion. Another of these brigades was a very fine one of Tennessee troops, under General Debrell, an excellent officer. The third commanded by General Robertson, a young and very dashing officer, was composed of "Confederate" battalions—troops enlisted under no particular State organization. General Vaughan learning of General Williams' approach dispatched him a courier offering to co-operate with him and advising that General Williams should attack the rear, while he, Vaughan would attack it in front.

Passing through Greenville at early dawn upon the second day after we left Jonesboro', the column marched rapidly toward the gap. My brigade was marching in advance. It was at this time three hundred and twenty-two strong and was organized into two battalions, the first commanded by Colonel Ward and the second by Colonel Morgan. About four miles from Greenville, Captain Messick, whose Company A, of the second battalion, was acting as advance-guard, encountered a scouting party of the enemy fifty or sixty strong. Messick immediately attacked, routed the party and chased it for several miles, taking eight or ten prisoners. Pressing on again in advance, when the column had overtaken him, he discovered the enemy in stronger force than before, advantageously posted upon the further side of a little stream about two miles from Lick creek. Halting his command here, Captain Messick, accompanied by Lieutenant Hopkins, galloped across the bridge and toward the enemy to reconnoiter. Approaching, despite the shots fired at them, to within forty or fifty yards of the enemy, they were then saluted by a volley from nearly two hundred rifles. Thinking it impossible, or impolitic, to procure "further information" they rapidly galloped back. Upon the approach of the column this party of the enemy fell back to Lick creek, where it met or was reinforced by some two or three hundred more. Lick creek is some three miles from Bull's gap. There were no fords in the vicinity of the road and it was too deep for wading except at one or two points. A narrow bridge spanned it at the point where it crossed the road. On the side that we were approaching there is a wide open space like a prairie, perhaps half a mile square. Thick woods border this opening in the direction that we were coming and wooded hills upon the left—running down to the edge of the creek.

Perceiving the enemy show signs of a disposition to contest our crossing, my brigade was at once deployed to force a passage. A portion of the second battalion was double-quicked, dismounted, across the open to the thickets near the bank of the creek. Although exposed for the entire distance to the fire of the enemy, this detachment suffered no loss. One company of the second battalion was also sent to the right, and took position near the creek in that quarter. The greater part of the first battalion was sent, on foot, to the left, and, concealed by the thickets upon the hills, got near enough the creek without attracting the attention of the enemy. Lieutenant Conrad was ordered to charge across the bridge with two mounted companies. As he approached it at a trot, a battalion of the enemy galloped down on the other side (close to the bridge) to dispute his passage. The dismounted skirmishers, who had taken position near the creek, prevented Conrad's column from receiving annoyance from the remainder of the Federal force.

When within so short a distance of the bridge that the features of the Federal soldiers at the other extremity were plainly discernible, Conrad suddenly halted, threw one company into line, keeping the other in column behind it, and opened fire upon it, which was returned with interest. Just then Lieutenant Welsh carried his company across the creek on the extreme left, followed by Lea (the water coming up to the men's shoulders) and attacked the enemy in flank and rear. This shook their line. General Vaughan, at the same time, brought up a piece of artillery and opened fire over the heads of our own men. Conrad seized the moment of confusion and darted across the bridge with the company which was in column, the other following. It was then a helter-skelter chase until the enemy took refuge in the gap.

General Vaughn marched on, but hearing nothing of General Williams, and knowing the strength of the position, did not attack. He had a brass band with him, which he made play "Dixie," in the hope that it would lure the enemy out; but this strategical banter was treated with profound indifference. General Williams had marched on the north side of the Holston river to Rogersville, and thence to Greenville, where we met him upon our return next day. His command was about two thousand strong, but a part of it badly armed, and his ammunition was exhausted. It turned out that his advent in our department was most opportune and fortunate.

We remained at Greenville several days, and then marched to Carter's Station. This withdrawal was occasioned by the unformation of the approach of Burbridge, from Kentucky, with a heavy force. His destination was supposed to be the Salt-works, and General Echols judged it expedient to effect a timely concentration of all the forces in the department. The system of procuring information from Kentucky, the most dangerous quarter to the Department, was so well organized that it was nearly two weeks after the first intimation of danger before Burbridge entered Virginia. Giltner's brigade had been moved very early to Laurel Gap, or some position in that vicinity, between the Salt-works and the approaching enemy. Leaving General Vaughan with his own brigade at Carter's Station,

General Echols ordered General Cosby and myself to Bristol. General Williams, who, with great exertion, had rearmed his command, moved a few days subsequently to the Salt-works, where the "reserves" of militia were now, also, collecting. Simultaneously with Burbridge's advance, the enemy approached from Knoxville (under Generals Gillem and Ammon), marching over the same ground which we had traversed shortly before.

General Vaughan was attacked, and was compelled to divide his brigade, the greater part remaining at Carter's Station, and a part being sent, under Colonel Carter, to Duvault's ford, five miles below on the Wetauga, where the enemy sought to effect a passage. Upon the night after the first demonstration against General Vaughan, General Cosby and I were sent to reinforce him, and, marching all night, reached the position assigned early the next morning. General Cosby was posted where he could support most speedily whichever point needed it, and I was instructed to proceed directly to Duvault's ford. Upon arriving there, I found Colonel Carter making all the preparations within his power to repel the attack which he anticipated. About nine A.M., the enemy recommenced the fight at Carter's Station, and toward one or two P.M. made his appearance again upon the other side of the river, opposite our position. The firing by this time had become so heavy at Carter's Station that I feared that General Vaughan would not be able to prevent the enemy from crossing the river there, and became anxious to create a diversion in his favor. I thought that if the force confronting us could be driven off and made to retreat on Jonesboro', that confronting General Vaughan would also fall back, fearing a flank attack, or it would, at least, slacken its efforts. The steep and difficult bank just in our front forbade all thought of attack in that way, but there was a ford about a mile and a half below, from which a good road led through level ground to the rear of the enemy's position. I instructed Captain Messick to take fifty picked men, cross at this ford, and take the enemy in the rear, and requested Colonel Carter to cause one of his battalions to dash down to the brink of the river, as soon as the firing commenced, and cross and attack if the enemy showed signs of being shaken by Messick's movement.

Captain Messick had crossed the river and gotten two or three hundred yards upon the other side, when he met a battalion of Federal cavalry approaching, doubtless to try a flank movement on us. They were marching with drawn sabers, but foolishly halted at sight of our men. Messick immediately ordered the charge and dashed into them. The impetus with which his column drove against them made the Federals recoil, and in a little while entirely give way. Stephen Sharp, of Cluke's regiment, rode at the color-guard, and shooting the color-bearer through the head, seized the flag. While he was waving it in triumph, the guard fired upon him, two bullets taking effect, one in the left arm, the other through the lungs. Dropping the colors across his saddle, he clubbed his rifle and struck two of his assailants from their horses, and Captain Messick killed a third for him. Twelve prisoners were taken, and ten or fifteen of the enemy killed and wounded. Messick, pressing the rout, whirled around upon the rear of the position. Colonel Carter ordered the Sixteenth Georgia to charge the position in front, when he saw the confusion produced by this dash, and the whole force went off in rapid retreat, pursued by the detachment of Captain Messick and the Georgia battalion for four or five miles.

Shortly afterward the demonstration against Carter's Station ceased. Lieutenant Roody, a brave and excellent young officer, lost a leg in this charge. Stephen Sharp, whose name has just now been mentioned, was perhaps the hero of more personal adventures than any man in Morgan's command. He had once before captured a standard by an act of equal courage. He had made his escape from prison by an exercise of almost incredible daring. With a companion, named Hecker, he deliberately scaled the wall of the prison yard, and forced his way through a guard assembled to oppose them. Sharp was shot and bayoneted in this attempt, but his wounds were not serious, and both he and his companion got away. When, subsequently, they were making their way to Virginia through the mountains of Kentucky, they were attacked by six or seven bushwhackers. Hecker was shot from his horse. Sharp shot four of his assailants and escaped. His exploits are too numerous for mention. Although the wounds he received at Duvault's were serious, he survived them, to marry the lady who nursed him.

On the next day, we received orders from General Echols to march at once to Saltville, as Burbridge was drawing near the place. In a very short time the energy and administrative skill of General Echols had placed the department in an excellent condition for defense. But it was the opportune arrival of General Williams which enabled us to beat back all assailants. When we reached Abingdon, we learned that General Breckinridge had arrived and had assumed command. After a short halt, we pressed on and reached Saltville at nightfall to learn that the enemy had been repulsed that day in a desperate attack. His loss had been heavy.

General Williams had made a splendid fight—one worthy of his very high reputation for skill and resolute courage. His dispositions were admirable. It is also positively stated that, as he stood on a superior eminence midway of his line of battle, his voice could be distinctly heard above the din of battle, as he shouted orders to all parts of the line at once. The Virginia reserves, under General Jackson and Colonel Robert Preston, behaved with distinguished gallantry. Upon the arrival of our three fresh brigades it was determined to assume the offensive in the morning. But that night the enemy retreated. General Cosby and I were ordered to follow him. We overtook his column beyond Hyter's Gap, but owing to mistakes in reconnoisance, etc., allowed it to escape us. General Williams coming up with a part of his command, we pressed the rear but did little damage. After this, my brigade was stationed for a few days at Wytheville.

In the middle of October, I was directed to go with two hundred men to Floyd and Franklin counties, where the deserters from our various armies in Virginia had congregated and had become very troublesome. In Floyd county they had organized what they called the "New State" and had elected a provisional Governor and Lieutenant Governor. I caught the latter—he was a very nice gentleman, and presented the man who captured him with a horse. After a little discipline the gang broke up, and some two hundred came in and surrendered.

Captain Cantrill, of my brigade, was sent with some forty men to Grayson county, about the same time. In this county the deserters and bushwhackers had been committing terrible outrages. Upon Cantrill's approach they retreated just across the line into North Carolina, into the mountains and bantered him to follow. He immediately did so. His force was increased by the reinforcement of a company of militia to about eighty men. He came upon the deserters (mustering about one hundred and twenty-five strong), posted upon the side of a mountain, and attacked them. Turning his horses loose, after finding that it was difficult to ascend mounted—he pushed his men forward on foot. The horses galloping back, induced the enemy to believe that he was retreating. They were quickly undeceived. Letting them come close to a belt of brush in which his men were resting, Captain Cantrill poured in a very destructive fire. The leader of the gang was killed by the first volley and his men soon dispersed and fled.

Twenty-one men were killed in this affair, and the others were phased away from the country. They gave no further trouble. Captain Cantrill's action justified the high esteem in which his courage and ability were held by his superiors. Almost immediately after the return of these detachments, the brigade was ordered back to East Tennessee again.

General Vaughan, supported by Colonel Palmer's brigade of North Carolina reserves, had been attacked at Russellville, six miles below Bull's Gap, and defeated with the loss of four or five pieces of artillery. General Breckinridge, immediately upon hearing of this disaster, prepared to retrieve it. The appointment of General Breckinridge to the command of the department, was a measure admirably calculated to reform and infuse fresh vitality into its affairs. He possessed the confidence of both the people and the soldiery. His military record was a brilliant one, and his sagacity and firmness were recognized by all. With the Kentucky troops, who were extravagantly proud of him, his popularity was of course unbounded. Although this unfortunate department was worse handled by the enemy after he commanded it than ever before, he came out of the ordeal, fatal to most other generals, with enhanced reputation. His great energy and indomitable resolution were fairly tried and fully proven. He could personally endure immense exertions and exposure. If, however, when heavy duty and labor were demanded, he got hold of officers and men who would not complain, he worked them without compunction, giving them no rest, and leaving the reluctant in clover. He could always elicit the affection inspired by manly daring and high soldierly qualities, and which the brave always feel for the bravest.

Leaving Wytheville on the night of the 19th of October, the brigade marched nearly to Marion, twenty-one miles distant. A blinding snow was driving in our faces, and about midnight it became necessary to halt and allow the half frozen men to build fires. Marching on through Abingdon and Bristol, we reached Carter's station on the 22nd. Here General Vaughn's brigade was encamped, and on the same day trains arrived from Wytheville bringing dismounted men of my brigade and of Cosby's and Giltner's. The bulk of these two latter brigades were in the Shenandoah valley, with General Early. There were also two companies of engineers. The dismounted men numbered in all between three and four hundred. They were commanded by Lieutenant Colonel Alston, who was assisted by Major Chenoweth, Captain Jenkins and other able officers. Six pieces of artillery also arrived, commanded by Major Page. On the 23rd, the entire force was marched to Jonesboro'. From Jonesboro' two roads run to Greenville, or rather to within three miles of Greenville, when they join. These roads are at no point more than three miles apart. My brigade was ordered to march upon the right hand, or Rheatown, road and General Vaughan took the other. The dismounted men marched along the railroad, which runs between them. A short distance beyond Rheatown, Captain Messick, who was some ten miles in front of the column with the advance-guard of twenty men, came upon an encampment of the enemy. He immediately attacked and drove in the pickets. Privates Hi Rogers, Pat Gilroy, Porter White, and another brave fellow of Ward's battalion, followed them into the encampment and came back unhurt. Messick halted his guard about four hundred yards from the encampment and awaited the movements of the enemy. His men were all picked for their daring and steadiness and could be depended on. In a little while the enemy came out, but continued, for a while, to fire at long range. Fearing that arrangements were being made to surround him, Messick began to retreat. The enemy then pursued him, and a battalion continued the pursuit for ten miles. Although closely pressed, this gallant little squad repeatedly turned and fought, sometimes dismounting to fire more accurately, and repeatedly checked their pursuers. Every round of their ammunition was exhausted and they were at no time disordered or forced into flight. Captain Messick lost not a single man captured and only one wounded.

When the column at length came up, the enemy had abandoned the chase and returned. That evening we marched through their deserted camp. Passing through Greenville the next morning, which the enemy had evacuated the night before, we reached Lick creek about 4 P.M. The enemy showed themselves on the further side, but did not contest our passage. A mile or a mile and a half in front of the gap we came upon them again, about twelve hundred strong. General Breckinridge ordered me to attack. I did so and in a short time drove them into the gap. They came out twice and were as often driven back. General Vaughan had been sent to demonstrate in the rear of the gap, and the dismounted men had not gotten up. After the third trial outside of the works, the enemy contented himself with shelling us. I witnessed, then, a singular incident. One man was literally set on fire by a shell. I saw what seemed a ball of fire fall from a shell just exploded and alight upon this poor fellow. He was at once in flames. We tore his clothing from him and he was scorched and seared from head to foot.

All that night we stood in line upon the ground we occupied when it fell. The enemy's pickets were a short distance in our front and fired at every movement. During the night the artillery arrived and was posted upon a commanding position protected by my line. The dismounted men also arrived during the night.

On the next morning, at day light, the dismounted men and one hundred and fifty of my brigade, in all some five hundred men, were moved to the extreme right to assault the gap from that quarter. General Vaughan was instructed to attack it in the rear, and Colonel George Crittenden was posted to support the artillery, with one hundred and eighty men, and to demonstrate in front. The right was the real point of attack. General Breckinridge hoped to carry the works there, and the other movements were intended as diversions. The enemy's force, as shown by captured field returns, was about twenty-five hundred men.

Climbing up the steep mountain side, the party sent to the right gained the ridge a little after daybreak. The position to be assaulted was exceedingly strong. Two spurs of the hill (on which the fortifications were erected) run out and connect with the mountain upon which we were formed. Between them is an immense ravine, wide and deep. The summits of these spurs are not more than forty yards wide, and their sides are rugged and steep. Across each, and right in the path of our advance, earthworks were erected, not very formidable themselves, but commanded by the forts. A direct and cross fire of artillery swept every inch of the approach. About the time that we reached the top of the mountain, Major Page opened with his pieces upon the plain beneath, and we immediately commenced the attack. Colonel Ward crossed the ravine with the greater part of our column, and I moved upon the left-hand spur with eighty or a hundred men of my brigade. A good many men of the hastily organized companies, of the dismounted command, hung back in the ravine as Colonel Ward advanced, and did no service in the fight.

General Breckinridge personally commanded the assault. Colonel Ward pressed on vigorously, and despite the hot fire which met him, carried the line of works upon the right, but was driven out by the fire from the fort, which he could not take. He returned repeatedly to the assault, and could not be driven far from the works. Upon the left we advanced rapidly, driving in the enemy's skirmishers, until, when within thirty yards of the earthwork, the men were staggered by the fire, halted, and could not be made to advance. Both ridges were completely swept by the enfilading fire, which each now poured upon us. The enemy once sprang over the work upon the left and advanced upon us, but was forced back. The men were much galled by the fire at this point.

Major Webber had but one company of his battalion present. It was twenty-eight strong, and lost fourteen. After failing to carry the works, we remained close to them, upon both the ridges, for more than an hour, replying as effectively as we could to the enemy's fire. Several instances of great gallantry occurred. Sergeant James Cardwell, of my old regiment, finding that the men could not be brought up again to the attack, walked deliberately toward the enemy, declaring that he would show them what a soldier's duty was. He fell before he had taken a dozen steps, his gallant breast riddled with balls. Gordon Vorhees, a brave young soldier, scarcely out of his boyhood, was mortally wounded when Colonel Ward carried the works upon the right. His comrades strove to remove him, but he refused to permit them to do so, saying that it was their part to fight and not to look after dying men.

Colonel Crittenden had pressed his slight line and Page's guns close to the front of the gap, during our attack, and did splendid service. But the attack in the rear was not made in time, and almost the entire Federal force was concentrated on the right, and this, and the strength of the position, was some excuse for our failure to take it. General Breckinridge exposed himself in a manner that called forth the almost indignant remonstrance of the men, and it is a matter of wonder that he escaped unhurt. He spoke in high terms of the conduct of the men who pressed the attack, although much disappointed at its failure, and especially commended Colonel Ward's cool, unflinching, and determined bravery. The latter officer was wounded, and when we withdrew was cut off from the command, but found his way back safely. Our loss was heavy.

After our retreat, which was not pressed by the enemy, Col. Crittenden was in a critical situation. It was necessary that he should also withdraw, and as he did so, he was exposed for more than half a mile to the Federal artillery. Six guns were opened upon him. The chief aim seemed to be to blow up Page's caissons, but, although the shelling was hot, they were all brought off safely.

That afternoon Colonel Palmer arrived from Ashville, North Carolina, with four or five hundred infantry. General Breckinridge decided to make no further attack upon the position, but to march through Taylor's Gap, three miles to the west, and get in the rear of the Federals and upon their line of retreat and communication with Knoxville. Accordingly, we broke camp and marched about ten o'clock that night. Vaughan, who had returned, moved in advance. Palmer's infantry, the dismounted men, and the artillery, were in the rear.

As we passed through Taylor's Gap, information was received that the enemy were evacuating Bull's Gap, and that an opportunity would be afforded us to take him in flank. General Breckinridge at once ordered Vaughan to post a strong detachment at Russellville, in their front, and to attack with his whole command immediately upon the detachments becoming engaged. I was ordered to turn to the left before reaching Russellville, go around the place and cut the enemy off upon the main road, a mile or two below, or, failing to do this, take him in flank.

The enemy broke through the detachment stationed in his front, but was immediately attacked by Vaughan. "Fight, d—n you!" yelled a Federal officer to his men, as the firing commenced; "it's only a scout." "No, I'll be d—d if it is," shouted one of Vaughan's men; "*we're all here.*" The greater part of Gillem's column and his artillery escaped here, but one regiment was cut off and driven away to the right. Moving very rapidly, my brigade managed to strike the main body again at Cheek's Cross Roads, about two miles from the town, and drove another slice from the road and into the fields and woods. While the column was scattered and prolonged by the rapid chase, we came suddenly upon the enemy halted in the edge of a wood, and were received with a smart fire, which checked us. Captain Gus Magee, one of the best and most dashing officers of the brigade, commanding the advance guard, charged in among them. As, followed by a few men, he leaped the fence behind which the enemy were posted, he was shot from his horse. He surrendered, and gave his name, and was immediately shot and sabered. He lived a short time in great agony. One of his men, Sergeant Sam Curd, avenged his death that night. Curd saved himself when Magee was killed, by slipping into the Federal line, and in the darkness, he escaped unnoticed. Some twenty minutes afterward, the murderer of Magee was captured, and Curd, recognizing his voice, asked him if he were not the man. He at once sprang upon Curd, and tried to disarm him. The latter broke loose from his grasp and killed him. Vaughan, after we moved on, kept the road, and I moved upon the left flank, endeavoring to gain the enemy's rear, and intercept his retreat. Colonel Napier, who kept in the advance with a small detachment, succeeded in this object.

Three or four miles from Morristown, the enemy halted, and, for half an hour, offered resistance. We, who were moving to take them in flank and rear, then saw a beautiful sight. The night was cloudless, and the moon at its full and shedding a brilliant light. The dark lines of troops could be seen almost as clearly as by day. Their positions were distinctly marked, however, by the flashes from the rifles, coming thick and fast, making them look, as they moved along, bending and oscillating, like rolling waves of flame, throwing off fiery spray. When my brigade had moved far around upon the left, and had taken position, obliquing toward the enemy's rear, it suddenly opened. The Federal line recoiled, and closed from both flanks toward the road, in one dense mass, which looked before the fighting ceased and the rout fairly commenced, like a huge Catherine wheel spouting streams of fire.

The enemy retreated rapidly and in confusion from this position, pursued closely by Vaughan's foremost battalions. At Morristown a regiment, just arrived upon the cars, and a piece of artillery, checked the pursuit for a short time, and enabled the enemy to reform. They were again driven, and making another and a last stand a short distance beyond the town, abandoned all further resistance when that failed to stop us.

Then the spoils began to be gathered, and were strewn so thickly along the road that the pursuit was effectually retarded. Major Day, of Vaughan's brigade, followed, however, beyond New Market, more than twenty-five miles from the point where the affair commenced, and the rest of us halted when day had fairly broken. More than one hundred ambulances and wagons were captured, loaded with baggage; six pieces of artillery, with caissons and horses, and many prisoners. The rout and disintegration of Gillem's command was complete.

On the next day we moved to New Market, and, when all the troops had gotten up, proceeded to Strawberry Plains, seven miles beyond. Here the enemy, posted in strong fortifications, were prepared to contest our further advance. We remained here three or four days.

Shelling and sharpshooting was kept up during the day, and a picket line, which required our entire strength, was maintained at night. The Holston river, deep and swollen, was between us, the enemy held the bridge and neither of the combatants ventured an attack. Vaughan was sent across the river at an upper ford and had another brush with Gillem, who came out from Knoxville with a few of his men whom he had collected and reorganized. He was easily driven back. General Breckinridge was called away to Wytheville by rumors of an advance of the enemy in another quarter, and we fell back to New Market and shortly afterward to Mossy creek, eleven miles from Strawberry plains.

Some ten days after our withdrawal from the latter place, reports reached us that a large force was being collected at Beau's Station, upon the north side of the Holston. These reports were shortly confirmed. We withdrew to Russellville, and subsequently to Greenville. To have remained further down would have exposed the rest of the department entirely. Having the short route to Bristol, the enemy could have outflanked and outmarched us, and getting first to the important points of the department, which they would have found unguarded, they could have captured and destroyed all that was worth protecting, without opposition. General Vaughan took position at Greenville, and my brigade was stationed, under command of Colonel Morgan, at Rogersville.

Five or six days after these dispositions were made, the enemy advanced upon Rogersville in heavy force, drove Colonel Morgan away and followed him closely. He retreated without loss, although constantly skirmishing to Kingsport, twenty-five miles from Rogersville, and crossing Clinch river at nightfall, prepared to dispute the passage of the enemy. He believed that he could do so successfully, but his force was too small to guard all of the fords, and the next morning the enemy got across, attacked and defeated him, capturing him, more than eighty men, and all of our wagons. Colonel Napier took command and retreated to Bristol. I met the brigade there, and found it reduced to less than three hundred men.

General Vaughan was hurrying on to Bristol, at this time, but had to march further than the enemy, who also had the start of him, would be required to march in order to reach it. On the night of the 13th, the enemy entered Bristol at 3 or 4 P.M. Vaughan was not closer than twelve or fifteen miles, and so he was completely separated from the forces east of Bristol. We now had tolerably accurate information of the enemy's strength. Burbridge's Kentucky troops composed the greater part of his force, and Gillem was present with all of his former command, whom he had succeeded in catching, and one fine regiment, the Tenth Michigan. General

Stoneman commanded. His column numbered in all, as well as we could judge, between six and seven thousand men.

After the enemy occupied Bristol, I fell back to Abingdon. At Bristol a large amount of valuable stores were captured by the enemy, and more clerks and attaches of supply departments caught or scared into premature evacuation of "bummers'" berths than at any precedent period of the departmental history. They scudded from town with an expedition that was truly astonishing to those who had ever had business with them.

Not caring to make a fight, which I knew I must lose, and well aware that there was hard work before us, I left Abingdon at nightfall, and encamped about three miles from the town on the Saltville road. At 10 o'clock the enemy entered Abingdon, driving out a picket of thirty men I had left there and causing another stampede of the clerical detail. The brigade was at once gotten under arms in expectation of an advance upon the road where we were stationed, but the enemy moved down the railroad toward Glade Springs and by the main road in the same direction. After having ascertained their route, we moved rapidly to Saltville, reaching that place before 10 A.M. General Breckinridge had already concentrated there all of the reserves that could be collected, and Giltner's and Cosby's brigades, which had just returned from the valley. Vaughan had retreated, when he found himself cut off, toward the North Carolina line and was virtually out of the fight from that time. Our force for the defense of Saltville was not more than fifteen hundred men, for offensive operations not eight hundred.

The enemy made no demonstration against Saltville on that day, and at nightfall General Breckinridge instructed me to move with one hundred and fifty men of my brigade, through McCall's Gap, and passing to the right of Glade's Springs, where the enemy was supposed to be, enter the main stage road and move toward Wytheville. He had received information that three or four hundred of the enemy had gone in that direction and he wished me to follow and attack.

Moving as directed, I found the enemy, not at Glade Springs, as was expected, but at the point at which I wished to enter the main road. Driving in the pickets, I advanced my whole force to within a short distance of the road, and discovered convincing proof that the entire Federal force was there. I did not attack, but withdrew to a point about a mile distant, and, permitting the men to build fires, and posting pickets to watch the enemy at the cross-roads, awaited daylight. My guide had run away when the pickets fired on us, and I could only watch the movements of the enemy and let mine be dictated by circumstances.

Just at daylight, a force of ten or twelve hundred of the enemy appeared in our rear, and between us and Saltville. This force had passed through Glade Springs and far around to the rear. Fortunately the men were lying down in line and by their horses, which had not been unsaddled. They were at once formed, and sending to call in the pickets, I moved my line slowly toward the enemy, who halted. The noise of the pickets galloping up the road perhaps convinced them that reinforcements were arriving to us. Not caring to fight when directly between two superior bodies of the enemy, and but a short distance from either, I wheeled into column, as soon as the picket detail arrived, and moved toward a wood upon our right. I was satisfied that I could check pursuit when there, and that some sort of trace led thence over the mountain to Saltville.

The enemy did not pursue vigorously, and soon halted. Only one shot was fired, and that by one of my pickets, who killed his man. No one in my detachment knew the country, but a citizen guided us over an almost impracticable route to the road which enters Saltville by Lyon's gap.

Learning that the enemy had crossed at Seven Mile ford and gone on toward Wytheville, General Breckinridge determined to follow. He wished to harass him, and prevent, as well as he could with the limited force at his command, the waste and destruction, which was the object of the raid. He accordingly marched out from Saltville on the night of the 16th, with eight hundred men, leaving the reserves and the men belonging to the cavalry whose horses were unserviceable. The enemy captured Wytheville without firing a shot, as there was no one there to fire at, but defeated a detachment of Vaughan's command not far from the town, taking and destroying the artillery which was attached to that brigade. A detachment also took and did serious damage to the lead mines.

On the 17th, Colonel Wycher, who had been sent in advance of the column commanded by General Breckinridge, attacked a body of the enemy near Marion, and drove it to Mt. Airy, eight miles from Wytheville, General Breckinridge pressed on to support him, and when we reached Marion we found Wycher coming back, closely pursued by a much stronger party of the enemy. Cosby's brigade, which was in the front of our column, at once attacked, and the whole command having been deployed and moved up, the enemy were easily driven back across the creek, two miles beyond Wytheville. Giltner and Cosby halted without crossing the creek. My brigade crossed and pressed the Federals back some distance further on the right of our line of advance. Night coming on I took a position on a commanding ridge, which stretches from the creek in a southeasterly direction. My left flank rested near the ford at which we had crossed, and my line was at an obtuse angle with that of the other brigades, which had not crossed, and inclining toward the position of the enemy. During the night I kept my men in line of battle.

On the next morning, it became soon evident that Stoneman's entire force, or very nearly all of it, had arrived during the night and was confronting us. After feeling the line, commencing on our left, the enemy apparently became impressed, with the belief that the proper point to attack was upon our right, and he accordingly made heavy rushes in rapid succession upon my position. I had but two hundred and twenty men, and was reinforced at midday by Colonel Wycher with fifty of his battalion.

The line we were required to hold was at least half a mile long, and I say without hesitation, that troops never fought more resolutely and bravely than did those I commanded on that day. The men were formed in a single slim skirmish line, with intervals of five or six feet between the files, and yet the enemy could not break the line or force them away. We were forced to receive attack where the enemy chose to make it, not daring, with our limited number and the important responsibility of holding our position, to attack in turn. Had the position been taken, the ford would have fallen into the possession of the enemy, and he would have been master of the entire field. The fire which met the advancing Federals at every effort which they made was the most deadly I ever saw. Our ammunition gave out three times, but, fortunately, we were enabled to replenish it during the lulls in the fighting. The sharpshooting upon both sides, in the intervals of attack, was excellent. Charlie Taylor, the best shot in my brigade, and one of the bravest soldiers, killed a man at almost every shot. I would gladly mention the names of those who deserved distinguished honor for their conduct, but it would require me, to do so, to give the name of every officer and private in the brigade.

About three o'clock, Colonel Napier, who was commanding upon the extreme left, advanced, and, sweeping down the line, drove back a body of the enemy immediately confronting his own little battalion, and struck the flank of another moving to attack the right of the position. But coming suddenly upon a miscegenated line of white and colored troops, which rose suddenly from ambush and fired into the faces of his men, his line fell back. The combatants fought here, for a while, with clubbed guns, and the negroes, who seemed furious with fear, used theirs as they would mauls. One unusually big and black darkey seemed to be much surprised, when first stumbled upon, and exclaiming "Dar dey is!" almost let his eyes pop out of their sockets. Soon after this, the most serious charge of the day was made upon the right and center. The enemy came in two lines, each twelve or fifteen hundred strong. The front line swung first one end foremost, then the other, as it came on at the double-quick, and my line, facing to the right and left, massed alternately at the threatened points. This time the Federals came up so close to us that I believed the position lost. Their repulse was chiefly due to the exertions of Captain Lea and Colonel Wycher, so far as the efforts of officers contributed to a victory which nothing but the unflinching courage of the men could have secured.

The first line, after driving us nearly a hundred yards, and completely turning our right, finally recoiled, and the second ran as early. But they left many dead behind. Our loss was surprisingly small in this fight—the enemy fired heavy volleys, but too high.

Receiving a reinforcement of sixty men, just before sundown, I sent it to get in the enemy's rear, and attack his horse-holders, expecting great results from the movement. But the officer in command was timid and would do nothing.

The enemy made no further attack, and seemed hopeless of fencing us away.

Late that night, our ammunition having almost entirely given out, we quitted our position and fell back, through Marion. Marching then southwardly, through the gorges of the mountain, we reached Rye Valley, fifteen miles distant, by morning. The enemy did not move during the night, nor indeed until ten or eleven, A.M., next day, and certain information had reached him of our retreat.

It can safely be asserted that we were not worsted in this fight, although for lack of ammunition we quitted the field. Every attack made by the enemy upon our position was repulsed, notwithstanding our greatly inferior numbers. Our loss was slight; his was heavy. General Breckinridge declared that no troops could have fought better or more successfully than those which held the right.

From Rye Valley we moved to the main road again, striking it at Mount Airy, thirteen miles from Marion. Here General Breckinridge learned that the enemy had marched directly by to Saltville. He entertained grave fears that the place would be taken, having no confidence in the ability of the small garrison to hold it. His fears were realized. He instructed me to collect details, from all the brigades, of men who were least exhausted, and the most serviceable horses, and follow the enemy as closely as I could, relieving Saltville, if the garrison held out until I arrived. I accordingly marched with three hundred men, arriving at Seven-mile Ford at nightfall on the 19th. I halted until one o'clock at night, and then pressed on, over terrible roads, and reached the vicinity of Saltville at daylight. The night was bitterly cold, and the men were so chilled that they were scarcely able to sit on their horses.

Passing through Lyon's gap we discovered indication, scarcely to be mistaken, that Saltville had indeed fallen. Still it was necessary to make sure, and I moved in the direction of the southern defenses. Shortly afterward, the sight of the enemy and a skirmish which showed a strong force in line, convinced me that I could not enter the place. Scouts, sent to reconnoiter, returned declaring that the enemy held all the entrances. I lost one man killed. Falling back three miles I went into camp to await the time when the enemy should commence his retreat. This he did on the 22nd, and marched toward Kentucky. We immediately followed. At Hyter's Gap the forces of the enemy divided. Those under Gillem moving in the direction of Tennessee, those under Burbridge going straight toward Kentucky. We followed the latter. There is no word in the English language which adequately expresses how cold it was. Our horses, already tired down and half starved, could scarcely hobble. Those of the enemy were in worse condition, and it is scarcely an exaggeration to say that for ten miles a man could have walked on dead ones. They lay dead and stark frozen in every conceivable and revolting attitude, as death had overtaken them in their agony. Saddles, guns, accouterments of all kinds strewed the road like the debris of a rout. We picked up many stragglers. Some pieces of artillery were abandoned but burned.

When we reached Wheeler's ford, fifty-two miles from Saltville, I had left, of my three hundred, only fifty men. Here we had our last skirmish with the enemy, and gave up the pursuit. More than one hundred prisoners were taken, many of them unable to walk. The Federals lost hundreds of men, whose limbs, rotted by the cold, had to be amputated. Such suffering, to be conceived, must be witnessed. The raid had accomplished great things, but at terrible cost. Soon after this, my brigade went into winter quarters. Forage was scarcely to be had at all in the department, and I sent my horses, with a strong detail to guard and attend to them, to North Carolina. The men could scarcely be reconciled to this parting with their best friends, and feared, too, it preluded infantry service. In the winter huts built at Abingdon, they were sufficiently comfortable, but were half famished. The country was almost bare of supplies. Still they bore up, cheerful and resolute.

In March we were ordered to Lynchburg to assist in defending that place against Sheridan. He passed by, however, and struck at larger game. About this time the men who had lain so long, suffered so much, and endured so heroically in prison, began to arrive. The men who had braved every hardship, in field and camp, were now reinforced by those who were fresh from the harsh insults and galling sense of captivity. Six months earlier this addition to our numbers would have told—now it was too late.

Our gallant boys would not halt or rest until they rejoined their old comrades. Then they crowded around with many a story of their prison life, and vow of revenge—never to be accomplished. All asked for arms, and to be placed at once in the ranks. Very few, however, had been already exchanged, and all the others were placed, much against their will, in "Parole camp" at Christiansburg. In April, the enemy advanced again from East Tennessee. Stoneman raided through North Carolina—tapped the only road which connected Richmond with the Southern territory still available, at Salisbury, and then suddenly turned up in our rear, and between us and Richmond. This decided General Early, who was then commanding the department, to move eastwardly that he might get closer to General Lee. All the troops in the department were massed, and we moved as rapidly as it was possible to do. At Wytheville, Giltner met a detachment of the enemy and defeated it. At New river, we found the bridge burned by the enemy, who had anticipated us there, and we marched on toward Lynchburg, on his track. General Early having fallen ill, the command devolved upon General Echols. This officer did all that any man could have done, to preserve the morale of the troops. He was possessed of remarkable administrative capacity, and great tact, as well as energy. While firm, he was exceedingly popular in manner and address, and maintained good humor and satisfaction among the troops, while he preserved order and efficiency.

General Echols had, at this time, besides the cavalry commands of Vaughan, Cosby, Giltner and mine, some four or five thousand infantry—the division of General Wharton, and the small brigades commanded by Colonels Trigg and Preston. My brigade was doing duty as infantry—the horses having not yet returned. Marching about twenty-five miles every day, the men became more than ever disgusted with the infantry service, and their feet suffered as much as their temper. It was observed that the men just returned from prison, although least prepared for it, complained least of the hard marching.

We well knew at this time, that General Lee had been at length forced to evacuate Richmond, but we hoped that followed by the bulk of his army, he would retreat safely to some point where he could effect a junction with General Joseph Johnston, and collect, also, all of the detachments of troops which had previously operated at a distance from the large armies. The troops which General Echols commanded, were veterans, and they understood the signs which were now rife and public. But they were not altogether hopeless, and were still resolute although their old enthusiasm was utterly gone. They still received encouragement from the citizens of the section through which they marched.

It is but justice to the noble people of Virginia to declare that they did not despair of their country until after it was no more. There were individual defections among the Virginians—rare and indelibly branded—but as a people, they were worthy of their traditions and their hereditary honor. With rocking crash and ruin all around her, the grand old commonwealth, scathed by the storm and shaken by the resistless convulsion, still towered erect and proud to the last, and fell only when the entire land had given away beneath her. Two strange features characterized the temper of the Southern people in the last days of the Confederacy. Crushed and dispirited as they were, they still seemed unable to realize the fact that the cause was utterly lost. Even when their fate stared them in the face, they could not recognize it.

Again, when our final ruin came, it was consummated in the twinkling of an eye. We floated confidently to the edge of the cataract, went whirling over and lying utterly stunned at the bottom, never looked back at the path we had followed. The Southern people strained every nerve to resist, and when all efforts failed, sank powerless and unnerved.

The struggle was a hard one. Since the days of Roman conquest the earth has not seen such energy, persistency and ingenuity in arts of subjugation. Since Titus encompassed Jerusalem and the Aurelian shook the east with his fierce legions, a more stubborn, desperate and lavish resistance has not been witnessed against attack so resolute, systematic and overwhelming. The Roman eagle never presaged a wider, more thorough desolation than that of which the flag of the Union was the harbinger. For four years the struggle was maintained against this mighty power. When in the spring of 1865, one hundred and thirty-four thousand wretched, broken-down rebels stood, from Richmond to the Rio Grande, confronting one million fifteen thousand veteran soldiers, trained to all the vicissitudes, equal to all the shocks of war—is it wonderful that when this tremendous host moved all at once, resistance at length, and finally ceased. And this struggle had worn down the people as well as the soldiery. Four years of such bitter, constant, exhausting strife, racking the entire land, until the foot of the conqueror had tracked it from one end to the other, accomplished its objects in time. Even the women, whose heroism outshone any ever displayed upon the battlefield, whose devoted self-sacrificing charity and benevolence can never be justly recorded, whose courage had seemed dauntless, were at last overcome by the misery which surrounded them, and a power which seemed resistless and inexorable.

While we were marching to join General Lee, and after the news of the evacuation of Richmond had been confirmed, we heard of an event which was as ominous as it was melancholy. We learned that a man had been killed, whose name had so long been associated with the army of Northern Virginia and its victories, that it almost seemed as if his life must be identified with its existence. The officer who was the very incarnation of the chivalry, the big-souled constancy, the glorious vigor of that army—General A.P. Hill—was dead. He *was a hero,* and he died like one. When the lines around Richmond were forced—his gallant corps overpowered, he was slain in the front still facing the enemy. His record had been completed, and he gave his life away, as if it were worthless after the cause to which he had pledged it was lost.

While General Echols was still confident that he would be able to join General Lee at some point to the south west of Richmond, most probably Danville, we learned with a dismay which is indescribable, that he had surrendered. If the light of heaven had gone out, a more utter despair and consternation would not have ensued. When the news first came, it perfectly paralyzed every one. Men looked at each other as if they had just heard a sentence of death and eternal ruin passed upon all. The effect of the news upon the infantry was to cause an entire disorganization. Crowds of them threw down their arms and left, and those who remained lost all sense of discipline.

On the next day, General Echols called a council of war, announced his intention of taking all the men who would follow him to General Joseph E. Johnston, and consulted his officers regarding the temper of the men. The infantry officers declared that their men would not go, and that it was useless to attempt to make them.

General Echols then issued an order furloughing the infantry soldiers for sixty days. He believed that this method would, at the end of that time, if the war was still going on, secure many to the Confederacy, while to attempt to force them to follow him would be unavailing and would make them all bitterly hostile in the future. He issued orders to the cavalry commanders to be prepared to march at four P.M., in the direction of North Carolina.

I obtained permission from him to mount my men on mules taken from the wagons, which were necessarily abandoned. My command was about six hundred strong. All the men furloughed during the winter and spring had promptly reported, and it was increased by more than two hundred exchanged men. Of the entire number, not more than ten (some of these officers) failed to respond to the orders to continue their march to General Johnston's army. The rain was falling in torrents when we prepared to start upon a march which seemed fraught with danger. The men were drenched, and mounted upon mules without saddles, and with blind bridles or rope halters. Every thing conspired to remind them of the gloomy situation. The dreadful news was fresh in their ears. Thousands of men had disbanded around them, two Kentucky brigades had left in their sight to go home, they were told that Stoneman held the gaps in the mountains through which they would have to pass. The gloomy skies seemed to threaten disaster. But braver in the hour of despair than ever before, they never faltered or murmured. The trial found them true, I can safely say that the men of my brigade were even more prompt in rendering obedience, more careful in doing their full duty at this time, when it was entirely optional with themselves whether they should go or stay, than they had ever been in the most prosperous days of the Confederacy. To command such men was the proudest honor that an officer could obtain.

We moved off in silence, broken by a cheer when we passed Vaughan's brigade which was also going on. On the next day we were overtaken by ninety men from Giltner's brigade, who came to join us. Colonel Dimond and Captains Scott, Rogers, Barrett, and Willis, and Lieutenant Freeman, well known as among the best officers of the Kentucky Confederate troops, commanded them. These men felt as we did, that disaster gave us no right to quit the service in which we had enlisted, and that so long as the Confederate Government survived, it had a claim upon us that we could not refuse.

The reports that the gaps were occupied by the enemy proved untrue, and we entered North Carolina without seeing a Federal. At Statesville, General Echols left us to go to General Johnston's camp. Vaughan was instructed to proceed to Morgantown, south of the Catawba river, and I pushed on toward Lincolnton, where I expected to find Colonel Napier with the horses. Just after crossing the river, information was received that a part of Stoneman's force was marching from the west in the same direction. I hoped, by moving rapidly, to get to Lincolnton first. The enemy's column moved upon a road which approached closely to the one by which we were marching. Our scouts were fighting, during the afternoon, upon the by-roads which connected the main ones. When within two miles of Lincolnton, videttes came back rapidly to tell me that the enemy had occupied the town, and were coming out to meet us.

I was unwilling to fight, and knew that to countermarch would be ruinous. Fortunately an officer had, a little while before, mentioned that a small road turned off to the left two miles from Lincolnton, and led to other traces and paths, which conducted to the main road to Charlotte. The head of the column was just at a road which answered to the description he had given, and, strengthening the advance guard to hold the enemy in check, I turned the column into it. It proved to be the right one, and, pressing guides, we reached, after a march of twelve or fifteen miles, the Charlotte road, and were between that place and the enemy. At daybreak next morning we moved on slowly. The enemy reached the bridge over the Catawba after we had passed and had partially torn up the bottom. At Charlotte we found a battalion of General Ferguson's brigade of Mississippi cavalry.

On the next day, Mr. Davis and his Cabinet arrived, escorted by General Debrell's division of cavalry, in which was Williams' Kentucky brigade, commanded then by Colonel Breckinridge. In a day or two the town was filled with unattached officers, disbanded and straggling soldiers, the relics of the naval forces, fleeing officials and the small change of the Richmond bureaux.

The negotiations were then pending between Generals Johnston and Sherman. General Breckinridge, in his capacity of Secretary of War, assisted at these conferences, but he was impatiently expected by Mr. Davis. The latter, on the day of his arrival, made the speech which has been so much commented upon. It was simply a manly, courageous appeal to the people to be true to themselves. The news of the assassination of Mr. Lincoln was received, during this period, but was almost universally disbelieved. When General Breckenridge arrived, he brought the first authoritative account of the Sherman and Johnston cartel. But two days later, General Johnston telegraphed that the authorities at Washington had repudiated it; that the armistice was broken off, and that he was preparing to surrender. Then there was another stir and commotion among the refugees. The greater part chose to remain at Charlotte, and accept the terms granted General Johnston's army.

Mr. Davis, accompanied by General Breckinridge and the members of his cabinet, quitted Charlotte, to march, if possible, to Generals Taylor and Forrest, in Alabama. The five brigades of Ferguson, Debrell, Breckinridge, Vaughan, and mine, composed his escort. At Unionville I found Colonel Napier, with all the forces he had been able to save from the enemy, and seventy or eighty men. This increased the strength of the brigade to 751 effectives.

I asked and obtained promotion, well won and deserved, for several officers. Major Steele was made Colonel; Captains Logan and Messick, Lieutenant-Colonels; Sergeant Jno. Carter, Captain; Captains Davis and Gwynn, of my staff, to whom I owed gratitude for inestimable assistance, were made Majors. I wished for promotion for other officers—indeed they all deserved it—but was assured that so many commissions could not be issued at once. Even the gallant officers who had joined us with the detachment from Giltner's brigade, could not obtain commissions, which they would have valued the more highly, because they were soon to expire.

We moved through South Carolina with great deliberation—so slowly, indeed, that with the detachments constantly passing them on their way to surrender, the morale of the troops was seriously impaired. Nothing demoralizes cavalry more than dilatory movements in time of danger. They argue that it indicates irresolution on the part of their leaders.

While in South Carolina, an old lady reproached some men of my brigade very bitterly for taking forage from her barn. "You are a gang of thieving, rascally, Kentuckians," she said; "afraid to go home, while our boys are surrendering decently." "Madam," answered one of them, "you are speaking out of your turn; South Carolina had a good deal to say in getting up this war, but we Kentuckians have contracted to close it out."

At Abbeville, where we were received with the kindest hospitality, was held the last Confederate council of war. Mr. Davis desired to know, from his brigade commanders, the true spirit of the men. He presided himself. Beside Generals Breckinridge and Bragg, none others were present than the five brigade commanders. Mr. Davis was apparently untouched by any of the demoralization which prevailed—he was affable, dignified and looked the very personification of high and undaunted courage. Each officer gave in turn, a statement of the condition and feeling of his men, and, when urged to do so, declared his own views of the situation. In substance, all said the same. They and their followers despaired of successfully conducting the war, and doubted the propriety of prolonging it. The honor of the soldiery was involved in securing Mr. Davis' safe escape, and their pride induced them to put off submission to the last moment. They would risk battle in the accomplishments of these objects—but would not ask their men to struggle against a fate, which was inevitable, and forfeit all hope of a restoration to their homes and friends. Mr. Davis declared that he wished to hear no plan which had for its object, only his safety—that twenty-five hundred brave men were enough to prolong the war, until the panic had passed away, and they would then be a nucleus for thousands more. He urged us to accept his views. We were silent, for we could not agree with him, and respected him too much to reply. He then said, bitterly, that he saw all hope was gone—that all the friends of the South were prepared to consent to her degradation. When he arose to leave the room, he had lost his erect bearing, his face was pale, and he faltered so much in his step that he was compelled to lean upon General Breckinridge. It was a sad sight to men who felt toward him as we did. I will venture to say that nothing he has subsequently endured, equaled the bitterness of that moment.

At the Savannah river, next day, the men were paid, through the influence of General Breckinridge, with a portion of the gold brought from Richmond. Each man got from twenty-six to thirty-two dollars—as he was lucky. Generals Vaughan and Debrell remained at the river to surrender. At Washington, Georgia, on the same day, the 7th of May, Mr. Davis left us, with the understanding that he was to attempt to make his escape. General Breckinridge had determined to proceed, with all the men remaining, in an opposite direction, and divert if possible all pursuit from Mr. Davis. That night, General Ferguson's brigade went to Macon to surrender, Ferguson himself going to Mississippi. On the next morning, some three hundred fifty of my brigade and a portion of William's brigade, under Colonel Breckinridge, marched to Woodstock, Georgia.

Many men of my brigade, dismounted and unable to obtain horses, and many of the paroled men, hoping to be exchanged, had followed us out from Virginia, walking more than three hundred miles. When at length, unwilling to expose them to further risk and suffering, I positively prohibited their coming further, they wept like children. A great portion of the men with Colonel Breckinridge were from his own regiment, the Ninth Kentucky, and the former "Morgan men," so long separated, were united just as all was lost. The glorious old "Kentucky brigade," as the infantry brigade, first commanded by General Breckinridge, then by Hanson and Helm, was not many miles distant, and surrendered about the same time. Upon leaving Washington, General Breckinridge, accompanied by his staff and some forty-five men, personally commanded by Colonel Breckinridge had taken a different road from that upon which the brigade had marched. When I arrived at Woodstock I did not find him there as I had expected.

Hours elapsed and he did not come. They were hours of intense anxiety. In our front was a much superior force of Federal cavalry—to go forward would provoke an engagement, and it could only result in severe and bloody defeat.

Retreat, by the way we had come, was impossible. Upon the left, if we escaped the enemy, we would be stopped by the sea.

I could not determine to surrender until I had heard from General Breckinridge, who was, at once, commander of all the Confederate forces yet in the field, in this vicinity, and the sole remaining officer of the Government.

Nor, until he declared it, could I know that enough had been done to assure the escape of Mr. Davis.

The suspense was galling. At length Colonel Breckinridge arrived with a message from the General.

While proceeding leisurely along the road, upon which he had left Washington, General Breckinridge had suddenly encountered a battalion of Federal cavalry, formed his forty-five men, and prepared to charge them. They halted, sent in a flag of truce, and parlied.

General Breckinridge saw that he could no longer delay his own attempt at escape, and while the conference was proceeding; set off with a few of his personal staff.

After a sufficient time had elapsed to let him get all away, Colonel Breckinridge marched by the enemy (a flag of truce having been agreed on), and came directly to Woodstock. General Breckinridge directed him to say, that he had good reason to believe that Generals Forrest and Taylor had already surrendered. That if we succeeded in crossing the Mississippi, we would find all there prepared to surrender. He counseled an immediate surrender upon our part, urging that it was folly to think of holding out longer and criminal to risk the lives of the men when no good could possibly be accomplished. He wished them to return to Kentucky—to their homes and kindred. He forbade any effort to assist his escape. "I will not have," he said, "one of these young men to encounter one hazard more for my sake." Bidding his young countrymen return to the loved land of their birth, he went off into exile.

The men were immediately formed, and the words of the chieftain they most loved and honored, repeated to them. They declared that they had striven to do their duty and preserve their honor, and felt that they could accept, without disgrace, release from service which they had worthily discharged. Then the last organization of "Morgan men" was disbanded. Comrades, who felt for each other the esteem and affection which brave and true men cherish, parted with sad hearts and dimmed eyes. There remained of the "old command," only the recollections of an eventful career and the ties of friendship which would ever bind its members together. There was no humiliation for these men. They had done their part and served faithfully, until there was no longer a cause and a country to serve. They knew not what their fate would be, and indulged in no speculation regarding it. They had been taught fortitude by the past, and, without useless repining and unmanly fear, they faced the future.

www.ingramcontent.com/pod-product-compliance
Lightning Source LLC
Chambersburg PA
CBHW011202090426
42742CB00019B/3377
* 9 7 8 1 6 4 7 9 9 1 8 4 5 *